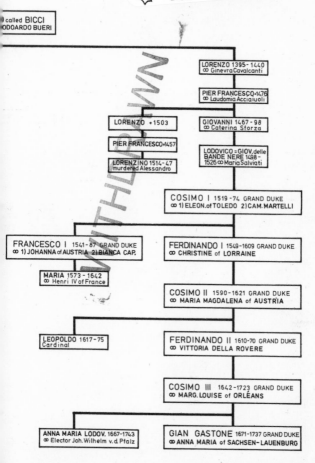

called BICCI
ODOARDO BUERI

LORENZO 1395-1440
∞ Ginevra Cavalcanti

PIER FRANCESCO +1476
∞ Laudomia Acciaiuoli

LORENZO +1503

PIER FRANCESCO +1457

LORENZINO 1514-47
murdered Alessandro

GIOVANNI 1467-98
∞ Caterina Sforza

LODOVICO = GIOV. delle
BANDE NERE 1498-
1526 ∞ Maria Salviati

COSIMO I 1519-74 GRAND DUKE
∞ 1) ELEON. of TOLEDO 2) CAM. MARTELLI

FRANCESCO I 1541-87 GRAND DUKE
∞ 1) JOHANNA of AUSTRIA 2) BIANCA CAP.

MARIA 1573-1642
∞ Henri IV of France

FERDINANDO I 1549-1609 GRAND DUKE
∞ CHRISTINE of LORRAINE

COSIMO II 1590-1621 GRAND DUKE
∞ MARIA MAGDALENA of AUSTRIA

LEOPOLDO 1617-75
Cardinal

FERDINANDO II 1610-70 GRAND DUKE
∞ VITTORIA DELLA ROVERE

COSIMO III 1642-1723 GRAND DUKE
∞ MARG. LOUISE of ORLÉANS

ANNA MARIA LODOV. 1667-1743
∞ Elector Joh. Wilhelm v. d. Pfalz

GIAN GASTONE 1671-1737 GRAND DUKE
∞ ANNA MARIA of SACHSEN-LAUENBURG

Florence

Florence

Art treasures and buildings

Georg Kauffmann

A Phaidon Guide

Translated by Edith Küstner and J. A. Underwood

Phaidon Press Limited, 5 Cromwell Place, London SW7

Published in the United States by Phaidon Publishers Inc.
and distributed by Praeger Publishers, Inc.
111 Fourth Avenue, New York, N. Y. 10003

First published 1971
Translation © 1971 by Phaidon Press Limited
ISBN 0 7148 1438 5
Library of Congress Catalog Card Number: 75–111059

Originally published as *Florenz*
© 1962 by Philipp Reclam jun. Stuttgart

Printed in Germany

CONTENTS

FOREWORD

"son' fiori – ma son' dipinti . . ."

In accordance with the declared aims of this series, the present volume deals only with the most important works of art in Florence; works of lesser importance are mentioned only cursorily. I have, however, been at great pains to treat in more detail those works which demand such treatment and those cases where the importance of a particular historical event made this unavoidable. It should, of course, be understood that, in order to keep the book to a manageable length, certain compromises have had to be made.

In this case the close correlation between art and history has necessitated placing the alphabetical section *after* a section dealing with particular topographical areas. The alphabetical section is also divided into two sections: sacred and secular buildings. Using the index, the reader will have no trouble in finding his way about the book.

Florence is such an unique city that it would be an arrogant presumption to treat a guide-book as simply a manual for the enjoyment of individual aspects of its historic past. The visitor who wishes to study the book before his visit may find his enthusiasm very much aroused, but he should bear in mind that any 'description' will pale into insignificance before the eloquence of the original. However useful this little compendium may be for reference purposes, its true purpose can only be appreciated in conjunction with the works themselves, the buildings, the magnificent sculptures, the incomparable paintings, in the splendid museums and in the twilight of the churches. This is the way it has been written and this is the way it is intended to be read. The work was compiled in Florence itself.

Florence, of course, is a city with a life of its own and is thus subject to change. In recent years in particular, many things in its churches, palaces and museums have been altered and beautified. Research is also continuing all the time and the monumental reference book by W. and E. Paatz, *Die Kirchen von Florenz* [The Churches of Florence] (1941–54), one of my principal sources, is in many respects out of date by now. The already vast literature on Florence is continually being added to. Indeed, hardly a day passes without our knowledge of the city being increased. When I learned of the limited space at my disposal, I was unable to suppress a shudder. I wish therefore to acknowledge those sources which I was able to use, if only to make clear which sources I was *not* able to use.

I would like to thank in the first place the members of the Institute of Art History in Florence and their director, Professor Dr. Ulrich Middeldorf. Dr. Sandra Galigani gave me a great deal of valuable advice, and Miss Anna Barbieri and Miss Jolanda Galigani much help over details. All questions concerning fresco painting were illuminated by the remarkable scholarship of Dr. Eve Borsook, while Drs. Klara Steinweg and Margrit Lisner gave me the benefit of their expert knowledge of early panel painting and fifteenth century sculpture respectively. Dr. Gerhard Ewald helped considerably on seventeenth century painting and Dr. Isolde Ragaller-Härth with the art of the sixteenth century. Dr. Gottfried Kiesow allowed me to peruse his as yet unpublished researches into the architectural history of the Cathedral, while Dr. Peter Meller was able to solve many problems of iconography. I was particularly delighted that Dr. Peter Anselm Riedl, a great Florence specialist, was able to draw the illustrations for the book, and I am also grateful to Miss Christa Baumgarth, who made a number of suggestions concerning language and folklore.

I remember with especial pleasure discussions with many scholars who gave me much advice concerning their respective subjects, and wish to express my particular indebtedness to the late Dr. Werner Cohn and Dr. Evelyn Sandberg-Vavalà. The rest I can only name in alphabetical order: I am grateful for advice from Herbert von Einem, Marita Horster, Hans Kauffmann, Herbert Keutner, Wolfgang Lotz, Luisa Marcucci, Millard Meiss, Richard Offner, Fritz Oswald, Ugo Procacci, Roberto Salvini, Gunther Thiem, Martin Weinberger, Rudolf Wittkower and Manfred Wundram, and I retain a particularly happy memory of some rewarding discussions with Hermann Voss.

I have also made use of published work by all of the foregoing, my own researches being confined to the sixteenth and seventeenth centuries. In addition, I am indebted to Stegmann-Geymüller's still indispensable work on Tuscany.

Lastly, I have drawn upon detailed studies by R. Abbon-
danza, W. Amelung, U. Baldini, G. Bandmann, P. Barocchi,
L. Bartoli, B. Bearzi, L. Becherucci, M. H. Bernath, L. Berti,
G. Bing, W. v. Bode, W. Braunfels, A. E. Brinckmann,
J. Burckhardt, F. Burger, E. Camesasca, G. Castelfranco,
A. Chastel, K. Clark, V. Daddi-Giovanozzi, B. Degenhart,
L. Ernst, O Fischel, E. Fraenckel, C. Frey, M. J. Friedländer,
W. Friedländer, L. Fröhlich-Bum, A. Grabar, W. Haftmann,
P. Halm, D. Heikamp, L. H. Heydenreich, G. F. Hill,
W. Holzhausen, W. Horn, E. Hubala, K. W. Jähnig, Ch.-A.
Isermeyer, H. W. Janson, R. Jaques, H. Keller, H. Kiel,
R. and T. Krautheimer, F. Kriegbaum, W. Krönig, K. Lank-
heit, J. Lauts, I. Lavin, A. Lensi, H. Mackowsky, G. Man-
suelli, G. C. Marri, E. A. Maser, C. Mauclair, A. Modi,
F. Morandini, Th. Müller, S. Müller-Christensen, R. Oertel,
G. Pacchioni, E. Panofsky, A. Parronchi, K. Piacenti,
E. Pieper, L. Planiscig, G. Poggi, J. Pope-Hennessy, Ph.
Pray-Bober, G. Previtali, G. Pudelko, G. M. Richter, F. Rin-
telen, A. J. Rusconi, H. Saalman, E. Sanchez, P. Sanpaolesi,
U. Schlegel, J. v. Schlosser, A. Schmitt, F. Schottmüller, Ch.
Seymour jun., J. Shearman, H. Siebenhüner, C. H. Smyth,
E. Steingräber, K. M. Svoboda, H. Taine, N. Tarchiani, H.
Thümmler, Ch. de Tolnay, M. Tosi, H. v. Tschudi, E. Vo-
doz, L. Wachler, A. Warburg, H. R. Weihrauch, P. M. Wolf,
H. Wölfflin, Fr. Yates. – I hope no one has been overlooked.
Needless to say I have used the works of Vasari and
Borghini as prime sources.
Finally, a word to the reader. Some nations show a tendency
to confuse literature and experience. 'Italian experts', in
particular, are fond of talking about 'experiences' which
they have in fact only read, and writing about things they
have never experienced. The Tuscans are different. They
draw a clear distinction between the real and the purely
imagined. We can come near their clarity of approach if we
use this art guide simply as what it is – a work of guidance.
For so it is intended. The tuneful Florentine refrain with
which we began may serve as a reminder.

FOREWORD TO THE SECOND GERMAN EDITION

Six years after the first publication, a second edition of this book has become necessary. Florence has changed. The flood disaster of 4 November 1966 hit the city very hard and threw it into a state of feverish agitation which still affects it today. Many works of art were destroyed or disappeared, or were so heavily damaged that they have had to be removed for restoration, and many of the works that survived are now in different places. In the circumstances, it will probably be impossible for some time to produce any totally reliable guide as to where things are.

The publishers have therefore decided to leave the second edition largely unchanged, which has meant that the fresh discoveries of recent research have also had to be left out of account. It will be appreciated that I did not find it easy simply to repeat my original text, confining myself to making a few additions here and there and correcting some mistakes which had come to my attention, but since the book has made a good many friends and can still serve as a useful basis for discussion, I was finally persuaded to set aside my reservations.

I acknowledge with gratitude the friendly suggestions of my colleagues. My thanks to Kurt Bauch and also to Harald Keller for extensive advice. The observations and remarks of Heinrich Lützeler and Theodor Müller were delightfully helpful. The late Erwin Panofsky's illuminating comments on the subject of Titian's Florentine paintings could not, I am afraid, be included, and will have to be considered on another occasion. This second edition also owes a great deal to my faithful friend Eve Borsook.

I have received a large number of letters from readers and have studied all of them carefully. I am grateful to all who wrote, and especially to Dr. Victor Freiherr von der Lippe, whose letters were of particular value.

HISTORICAL INTRODUCTION

Florence is situated at the heart of the rich belt of land which cradled the Etruscan civilization and which Vasari reckoned among the most beautiful in the world. After a long struggle, the Etruscans were finally subjugated by the Romans and in 90 B.C. the town of Faesulae (now Fiesole) on the hill and the little hamlet of Florentia in the valley below were granted Roman citizenship. Ten years later, Sulla stationed troops in both places. Here, as happened everywhere else, the growth of commerce brought prosperity to the region, prosperity that grew even greater following the construction of the Via Cassia, which led over the inhospitable highlands of the Apennines to Bologna. Public buildings, including thermae, a capitol, temples and theatres, were constructed in Florentia, and the town on the hill, sharing in this prosperity, also received its public buildings. Following the collapse of the Roman Empire, both places relapsed into obscurity.

In Tuscia (the ancient name of the region was a reminder of its Etruscan origins), the Dark Ages were really dark, and it was not until the time of the Frankish Margravine Mathilde, a confidante of Gregory VII, that Florentia (the name was first changed to Fiorenza, then to Firenze) once again became a place of some importance. For one thing, it lay near the main line of communication between Rome and the North, and for another, with the sack of Fiesole in 1125 (ten years after Mathilde's death) removing its chief rival, the town in the valley gained a new impetus from the influx of refugees.

As the population of the town increased, so did its political importance. From 1200 onwards, during the struggle for power between Emperor and Pope, Florence remained a Guelph town and was governed by four consuls. However, when Manfred of Tarent became King of Sicily, he supported the Ghibelline faction to such an extent that with the help of the traitor Farinata degli Uberti, this party managed to seize power. So ended the first ten years of the democracy which Dante and Giovanni Villani had praised so highly (Battle of Montaperti, 4 September 1260). After Manfred's death in 1266, however, the tide turned. The people began to rebel against the presumption of the Ghibelline leaders. After numerous complex disputes, the party managed to retain the upper hand and began to reorganize itself. In 1282, an executive council, the Signoria, was set up. It consisted of masters chosen from the Priori delle Arti, or guilds, comprising the Arti Maggiori (judges, lawyers, bankers and other members of the educated classes) and the Arti Minori (dyers, wool-carders, smiths, etc., and members of the labouring class). In this true democracy, merchants and simple labourers possessed virtually the same rights. Only the noble possessed no rights at all, and could only gain influence by joining a guild. The reason for this general antipathy towards the aristocracy was that the town had so often been harmed by their personal feuds. It was even taken as far as forbidding young aristocrats entry to the city's high-schools. A military system, too, was set up. The citizens were divided into twenty companies led by the Gonfalonieri, the chief of whom, elected by the Signoria, was the head of all the armed forces. The man principally responsible for this highly effective reorganization was Giano della Bella. However, since the Florentines could never suffer a powerful man at their head, they overthrew in 1295 this first real leader they had ever had and banished him from the city.

At the battle of Campaldino, Florence, now once more Guelph, beat the combined armies of Pisa and Arezzo to which the expelled Ghibellines had fled. The young Dante, whose own banishment followed shortly afterwards, took part in this battle. The defeat of Pisa threw the whole of Florence into a whirl of enthusiasm. The city at that time had 90,000 inhabitants, 110 churches and 25,000 men under arms. Yet, as Dante rightly prophesied, this triumph was illusory. Civil war loomed on the horizon and the future was to be far from peaceful.

In 1310, Pope Clement V and Emperor Henry VII of Luxembourg joined forces in order to impose some order on the confused Italian scene. Dante, the Ghibelline, greeted them as peacemakers. But Henry died prematurely, and the result was fresh confusion. A further attempt at unification was made in 1330 by King Johann of Bohemia, but this was a failure both politically and militarily, and Florence finally surrendered to the Duke of Athens, Gautier de Brienne, an unscrupulous adventurer who rapidly assumed complete control of the city. He was too cruel and tyrannical to survive for long, however, and on S. Anne's Day, 1343, the populace besieged him in the Palazzo Vecchio and drove him out with scorn and ridicule.

Meanwhile, in 1321, Dante had died in Ravenna, a lonely man. The Florentines began to feel they had dealt unjustly with their illustrious son, all the more so as the *Divina Commedia* came increasingly to be regarded as the national poem of the whole Italian people. In his place another poet was raised to a position of high honour. This was Petrarch, the son of a Florentine who, like Dante, had been exiled. Around his person, the growing feeling for unity became fanned into a roaring blaze of genuine national enthusiasm. But the political climate of the time was not conducive to the success of these idealistic hopes, as witness the extraordinary attempts which Cola di Rienzi made in Rome to found a quasi-Classical Italian republic, and in addition there were various epidemics, including the plague, to contend with. Towards the end of the fourteenth century, the politics of the region had become almost inextricably complex. Petrarch, like Dante before him, made an appeal to the Pope and the Emperor, but in vain. He died in 1374, as lonely as his predecessor.

Meanwhile Florence had once again become Ghibelline. Repeated attempts to organize the people (by the Gonfaloniere Silvestro de'Medici) met with failure, and in 1382 the Guelphs returned to power. With the assistance of Charles III of Naples, they overthrew every democratic reform. Throughout all this confusion, however, one family never ceased to keep a watchful eye on public affairs – that of Silvestro de'Medici. For some time they were banished by the Albizzi family, which ruled for a number of years, but in 1434 Cosimo de'Medici was recalled, and once the exceptional talents of this born statesman had been recognized, he was elected 'Father of the Fatherland'. Cosimo engineered Francesco Sforza's entry into the service of the town, defeated Piccinino, the Condottiere of the Visconti, near Anghiari, became banker to the Sforza family and helped to overthrow the Republic of Milan. From then on, Cosimo's efforts were concentrated on consolidating the two important princely houses of Northern Italy, the Sforza and the Medici. This alliance between the two powers was destined radically to alter the state of affairs. Under the dictatorship of these two autocrats, the century-long conflict between Guelphs and Ghibellines was brought to an end. Slowly, under the authoritative rule of the Medici dynasty, Florence found peace, a peace that was to foster the unparalleled flowering of scholarship and art that began around this time.

When Cosimo de'Medici died in 1464, he left a stable community behind him. The example of his great statesmanship and generous patronage was never forgotten. Although following his death there was an attempt to abolish restraints and restore the freedom of republican times, this was not successful. The great man's example had impressed itself too deeply. His son, Piero de'Medici, set up a five-man Gremium which elected the Gonfalonieri and the Priori. In 1469 Lorenzo and Giuliano became the heads of government. Lorenzo, who was rapidly nicknamed *the Magnificent*, was also a man of immense stature. He strengthened the political position of the city, showed himself an extremely liberal patron of the arts and interested himself in all aspects of cultural education. Only once was he in serious danger, when the rich banking family of the Pazzi attempted a coup in league with Pope Sixtus IV, the so-called Pazzi Conspiracy of 1478. Giuliano de'Medici was killed in Florence Cathedral and Lorenzo had an extremely narrow escape, taking refuge in the sacristy which was secured by heavy bronze doors. His revenge was terrible. Everyone involved in the conspiracy was put to death. Only because he was sure of his people was *Il Magnifico* able to do this. No longer tempted by the old republican freedom, they were content to be guided by the Medici. The position of the latter appeared to be more secure than ever before. But meanwhile Pope Sixtus IV was not idle, and managed to shift the balance of power in his favour. Desperately, Lorenzo attempted to withstand the pressures of his own people, of invaders from the North and of the Turks at sea. Only with a combination of extreme cunning, cold calculation and deep scepticism (everything that Machiavelli later brought together in one formula) could he hope to remain in power. But what finally robbed his efforts of the success he had hoped for was a force he had not foreseen.

Savonarola was one of that breed of men who, when surrounded by wealth and luxury, feel their inner purity is compromised. The increasing prosperity of the city was threatening to drown it in a flood of sumptuous and carefree pleasure. Uttering prophesies of doom, he preached openly for a return to a strict morality. These prophesies were destined to come true. Piero de'Medici and Ferdinand of Naples made common cause with the ambitious Lodovico il Moro, and Charles VII of France, heir of the House of Anjou in Naples, was summoned to Florence. He came and Florence submitted to him. Piero left with him and the populace took advantage of this opportunity to seize the property of the Medici. The mob ran riot, not only banishing the Medici but also bringing about one of the darkest hours in the history of art – the sack of the Medici Palace with its incredible store of art treasures of which almost all traces have since disappeared. Only inventories remain to give us an idea of the riches it once contained. However, the Dominican preacher of penitence soon assumed control of the town. Savonarola's attitude can only be understood properly when we realize that he never ceased to be a monk. The ultimate aim of his reforms was the transformation of the community into a lay monastery. He might have succeeded in this had he been able to count on the Pope's support, but the immoral Alexander VI not only paid little heed to the spiritual leader's warnings, but even tried to get rid of him. Savonarola, however, was not to be intimidated. He went so far as to deny the authority of the unworthy Pope and to call upon the divine moral law. At this the Augustinian friar Francis of Rueille suggested a divine judgement – Savonarola was to walk through fire. He accepted the challenge but insisted on taking the sacrament with him, which the Franciscans would not allow. This theological wrangle was eventually terminated by a thunderstorm. Next day, however, the disappointed populace stormed the monastery of S. Marco, took the monk prisoner outside the library and condemned him to death by fire on the Piazza della Signoria. But the spirit of Savonarola had deeply affected men's minds. Many artists, Botticelli among them, destroyed their work because they felt ashamed of using such bright colours. Michelangelo mourned the death of the glorious martyr.

The city had become poor; there was a dearth of leaders. The arrival of Louis XII of France sparked off fresh quarrels. Cesare Borgia turned his hatred against Florence, which had entered into negotiations with him through the mediation of Machiavelli. During this period the politics of Italy were dominated by the immense power of Pope Julius II, whose strong arm was felt even in Florence. In 1512, after eighteen years of exile, the Medici family returned to power. Julius II died in the following year and twenty days later Giovanni de'Medici ascended the papal throne as Leo X. So, after the gloomy years of exile, Lorenzo il Magnifico's son became master of both Florence and Rome, and the most powerful ruler in all Italy.

A new spirit was abroad in Europe. In 1515, Luther levelled his first accusations against the church. In 1519, Charles V became Emperor of Germany. The Pope became involved in far-reaching conflicts, both political and spiritual, and Florence too was caught up in the whirlpool. Things did not improve under Hadrian VI nor under his successor, Clement VII. On the contrary, under Clement VII, another Medici (Giulio, natural son of Giuliano, grandson of Piero di Cosimo), they took a turn for the worse. Meanwhile not only the emperor but also Francis I of France were in the country. In 1525, the French king was defeated at Pavia and Italy came under the dominion of the emperor. German mercenaries marched on Rome and in the 'Sacco di Roma' of 1527, perhaps the most notorious event of the century, the town was destroyed. During the subsequent series of extremely brutal battles against the foreign mercenaries Florence, with the energetic assistance of Michelangelo, began to organize its defence, but to no avail. The city avoided being sacked by paying a ransom of 80,000 thaler but had Alessandro de'Medici foisted upon it as duke by Charles V, and at the same time lost its traditional form of government. The Signoria and Gonfalonieri ceased to exist. A senate of forty was set up, and in 1530 this body vested the rule of the city in the duke during his lifetime and in his heirs in perpetuity.

It is no exaggeration to describe this man on the throne as a libertine. In 1537 he was killed by his cousin Lorenzino, and the tyrant's murderer was gratefully, even exuberantly, fêted by the town. Michelangelo's bust of Brutus reflects the

*Baptistery, detail from Andrea Pisano's bronze doors, Christ
(from the relief 'John makes known the Christ')*

Baptistery, interior wall articulation

general feeling about him. He was succeeded by Cosimo,
the son of the brave Giovanni delle Bande Nere and Maria
Salviati. Cosimo was still a young man at the time, but
possessed of an energy which most people had underrated.
It was as if this latter-day Medici united in his person all
the powerful characteristics of his predecessors. With un-
yielding severity, he forced obedience upon the rebellious
families and drove Siena, the last free town in Tuscany, to
capitulation in 1555. He successfully stabilized the internal
politics of the region. In 1569, Pope Pius V confirmed
Cosimo I as Grand Duke of Tuscany, and his marriage with
Eleonora of Toledo brought, if not good, at least neutral
relations with Spain.

Under Cosimo's sons the history of Florence became rather
less colourful, but in many respects the people were happier
than ever before. Ports were built (Livorno in particular
was developed), colonies were founded (Jews emigrated
and settled on the coast), education was improved (with the
foundation of universities, scientific research establishments,
and the Botanical Gardens of Pisa), the courses of rivers
were straightened, swamps were drained and the infertile
lands of the Maremma were brought under cultivation.
During this period, the eminent scientists Torricelli and
Galileo worked in Florence.

The end of the Medici family was rather tragic; the old line
degenerated and finally petered out. The last Grand Duke,
Giangastone, had no male heir. After his death in 1737,
Anna Maria Lodovica returned to Italy as a widow from
Germany where she had been married to Johann Wilhelm
von der Pfalz ('Jan Wellem'). As the last surviving member
of the family, she disposed of the incredibly rich inheritance
which had fallen to her in lengthy and complicated testa-
mentary provisions. It is to her eternal credit that the art
treasures of the Medici remained in Florence and were not
scattered to the four winds like those of so many other
princely houses. Our debt of gratitude to this woman
forms a fitting conclusion to this survey of the fortunes of
the city.

What happened after that is hardly worth relating. The
great powers quarrelled over the succession and Don Carlos,
the son of the Spanish king, was nominated by the emperor
as heir. Then, in 1737, as political alliances were undergoing

a reshuffle, Duke Franz Stephan of Lorraine was elected Grand Duke. As the husband of Maria Theresa he became emperor, but kept Tuscany to some extent independent of Austria. His son, Peter Leopold, allowed a greater degree of French influence. The horrors of the revolution brought Tuscany closer to the Austrian camp, until in 1799 Berthier set up a republican government in Florence. It did not last. Following a brief resumption of power by the Grand Duke, Florence, on the instructions of Napoleon, was elevated to the position of capital of the Kingdom of Etruria and was given to the son of the Duke of Parma and Piacenza. In 1808 the former Tuscany was united with France, but six years later it reverted to the Austrian crown.

The growing struggle for freedom led to an increasing self-awareness all over Italy, and the power of Austria entered a period of gradual decline, marked by various occasionally dramatic stages. In 1864 Victor Emmanuel, now master of a large part of Italy, finally chose Florence as his capital, until in 1871, having abolished the Papal State, he established himself permanently in Rome. The history of this marvellous city did not end there, of course, but it did mark the end of the period of Florence's historical greatness.

DISTRICTS

The Cathedral District

Cathedral Square – Baptistery – Campanile – Cathedral – Cathedral Museum – Archbishops' Palace – Loggia del Bigallo – Misericordia

Cathedral Square – Piazza del Duomo

The Cathedral Square is the principal sacred complex of the city of Florence. Its chief elements are the Cathedral itself, towering above the little square like a mountain of marble, the handsome Campanile and the more delicate Baptistery. A great Roman (possibly Augustan) palace once stood on this site, so there is a core of truth to the legend that the Baptistery was originally a Roman Temple of Mars. The square is enclosed on the west by the Archbishops' Palace. To the south of the Cathedral stands the headquarters of the *Misericordia*, a brotherhood founded in time of plague to assist the sick. On the east side is the **Palazzo Guadagni-Strozzi** (sixteenth and seventeenth centuries). The column (1384) to the north of the Baptistery marks the site of an elm tree said to have sprouted leaves in winter when the body of S. Zenobius († 429) was moved to the old cathedral. At the entrance to the Via Calzaioli is the Loggia del Bigallo. – The arcade running from west to east right along the north side of the Cathedral is evidence that an overall architectural design existed as early as the Middle Ages. The rest of the square was radically altered during the nineteenth century. The district around the Cathedral, which was for centuries the centre of the artistic enterprise of the Florentine bourgeoisie, constitutes one of the most important historic sites of Renaissance art.

The Baptistery – Battistero S. Giovanni

The baptismal church of S. Giovanni (there is an epigraphic invocation of the saint on the base of the right-hand column of the north portal, thirteenth century) was built on top of older cultural strata: Roman, Late Roman (smaller dwellings) and finally German, with several burials. Despite partial excavation to the west and later in 1912–15 beneath

*the church (approachable from inside by means of an
awkward staircase behind the altar), very little light has been
thrown on the early history of the site. The nature of the
earlier building first mentioned in 897 remains uncertain.
We do know that the foundation stone of the present church
was consecrated by Pope Nicholas II in 1060. In 1113 a
wall-tomb was built for Bishop Rainer inside the church, so
the walls must have been standing by that time. By 1117,
the entire lower storey appears to have been complete since
no use was found for two columns presented by the people
of Pisa. They were set up instead on the square in front of
the church as memorials – like the two columns Jachim and
Boaz which stood before Solomon's temple. They collapsed
and were smashed in a flood of the river Arno and the
figures finally found a place on the corner pillars of the east
side. The whole church appears to have been in use by 1128.
The lantern, which bears a building inscription on the stone
ring beneath the bronze globe and cross, may have been
completed by 1150. The present building represents virtually
the original design apart from one alteration: in 1202 the
semicircular apse was added and the rectangular choir chapel
built. Arnolfo di Cambio adorned the grey quarry-stone
corner pillars with green-and-white marble facing in 1296,
bringing the exterior a little more in line with the ideal of
the Cathedral, which was then in the early stages of construction. In 1339 the upper ornamental ledge of the cornice
was restored. In the nineteenth century, more cleaning took
place than restoration.*

Exterior   The best view is from the Via de'Martelli. The
beautiful symmetry of its serene proportions makes it easy
to understand why the great masters of the Renaissance,
such as Brunelleschi, Leonardo, G. da Sangallo, so often
allowed their thoughts to wander to this church. The freshness of the white marble, articulated by the dark lines of the
incrustation, had already inspired Dante to speak of *bel
San Giovanni*. It should, of course, be remembered that this
unencumbered aspect is relatively recent. At first the church
was surrounded by tombs (many of these were removed in
1296, including the two Late Classical *column sarcophagi*
which were re-erected in 1930 to the right and left of the
south portal; the one on the right is carved with marriage
scenes, the one on the left with an allegory of death; the

lids are not original), then it was fenced in behind by houses
and the Archbishops' Palace (in 1895 this was set back about
50 m, eliminating an entire street). Now there is open space
all round it.

The Baptistery, an octagonal centralized structure, was
derived from Early Christian models, although it surpasses
all other known examples in its monumental dimensions.
Despite the large number of Classical and Byzantine formal
elements contained in the church – in the ornamentation, in
the trophies with inscriptions, most of which can be seen at
eye-level on individual slabs of the marble incrustation,
and in relief panels such as the *Pressing and shipping of
wine* (on the outside of the choir chapel, south side, on the
lower part of the base) – and despite the Classical form of the
capitals inside, the building none the less has a predominantly medieval character, and is by and large typical of the
Proto-Renaissance style, a period which thoroughly explored Classical forms long before the Renaissance.

The choir chapel, jutting out on the west side, establishes a
directional axis which is emphasized by a slight extension
in length, barely perceptible to the eye, in the east-west
sense. Three portals, on the north, east and south sides, give
access to the interior. The execution of the tabernacles is
noticeably richer on these sides, and the incrustation, i.e. the
facing of inlaid marble, more decorative. Three storeys can
be distinguished: the portal zone, an intermediate storey
containing windows, and the attic storey. This is stepped
inwards slightly, with a delicate relief; the two lower
storeys have a rich and strongly outlined structure, with the
incrustation forming simple patterns of rectangles and
arches. The choir chapel is popularly known as the *scarsella*
because of its vague resemblance to a pilgrim's bag. Although it was added later, its system of ornamentation
follows that of the main building. The outer corners – and
this is typical of the Proto-Renaissance style – are adorned
with masks (very weathered) and fabulous beasts. Around
the intermediate storey of the Baptistery runs a series of
perfectly semicircular arches, starting from the corner pillars
and supported by half-octagonal pillars with dosserets. The
central arch on each of the portal sides is wider and higher
than the outer ones. There is a window in each bay. These
tabernacle windows have alternately round and pointed

gables and constitute an early medieval example in Tuscany
of an alternating order, an idea which was taken up in
a major way in the Renaissance. The attic storey, with its
wall panels separated by fluted pilasters, is closer to the
Classical tradition. There is an exquisite ornamental band
between the cornice and the roof. On top sits the lantern,
a visible expression of the building's central vertical axis,
like a point breaking through from inside. White, delicate
and richly decorated, its magnificent ornamentation (which
is properly visible from the ground only through binoculars)
is the clearest example of the local style within the Proto-
Renaissance to which the building is chiefly indebted, that
of Pisa. – Typical of Proto-Renaissance architecture as a
whole, the walls of the Baptistery represent an intermediate
stage between solidity and relaxed articulation. The compact wall with its small windows (notice the tiny slit-
windows in the attic) is articulated in depth. In this the
incrustation plays an important and architecturally signifi-
cant role; the rectangles delineated above the windows
appear to continue behind the spandrels of the arches, thus
giving the impression of a free-standing wall plane in front
of them. The attic appears to rise like a third plane out of
the lower and intermediate storeys. These various planes of
articulation have the effect of lightening what seems at
first an extremely solid building.

External Decoration   The quality of the architecture is
matched by the exquisiteness of the decoration. The fact
that the Baptistery is one of the most important monuments
of European art is due also to the work of the ornamental
masters. The decoration of the exterior is at its most intense
around the portals. Each portal contains double *bronze
doors* signed by their respective masters. The oldest of these,
on the south side, with reliefs depicting the life of John the
Baptist, was begun in 1330 by *Andrea Pisano* (*ill. facing
p. 16*). The story is told in little scenes set on stage-like bases
within quatrefoils which taper upwards slightly. Each leaf
is treated as a unit like the page of a book, to be read from
top left to bottom right. In the lower part various Christian
and worldly virtues are depicted. The charm of the individual panels lies not only in their lovingly executed detail
(birds, beetles, lizards, etc.) but also particularly in their
expressive power and sensitivity. The simple clarity of every

gesture and movement has an immediate impact, and the interplay of lines, folds and clearly delineated, rarely over-lapping contours is deeply impressive. One senses the in-fluence of the art of Giotto with its expressive strength; the delicacy of feeling may possibly have been learned from Siena. The exquisite lion-heads let into the frames reveal the influence of the goldsmith's art. Various ornamental details such as the denticulation in the frames and in the brackets below the bases show a debt to architecture. Each of these little scenes is placed within a definite setting, exe-cuted with great economy and consummate assurance. – The decoration of the frame around the portal is gloriously alive. Worked in bronze by Vittorio Ghiberti, possibly with the assistance of Pollaiuolo in 1453–61, these sprouting, bud-ding, crackling, fleshy leaves and fruits show the Renaissance style already fully developed. The two garlands are held at the base by two figures, female on the left and male on the right, representing an ideal of Classical beauty which later found its most mature expression in the work of Botticelli. – Above the portal is a trio by Vincenzo Danti, 1570, the *Beheading of John the Baptist.* Danti was a disciple of Michelangelo and this late work of his shows a tendency towards mannerism (particularly in Salome, on the left); it is highly stylized, the division between objects and ornamen-tation is sometimes unclear, and the head-dress is extremely artificial. The tabernacle above the central figure is probab-ly also by Danti.

The *bronze doors on the north side* correspond to Andrea Pisano's in elevation but are more richly decorated. The reliefs are set within square quatrefoils, the panels are surrounded with garlands, and instead of the lion-heads there are human faces, one of which is that of *Lorenzo Ghi-berti* who, with assistants, carried out the work in 1403–24 (left-hand leaf, centre of the fifth row down). The scenes are taken from the New Testament and lower panels contain Evangelists and the Early Fathers. In this case, unlike the south doors, the scenes are intended to be read from bottom to top, in pairs (the traditional pattern of early stained-glass windows, e.g. the apse windows in the Upper Church at Assisi). This somewhat complicated succession corresponds with a particular style of relief sculpture which was con-cerned not so much with immediate comprehension as with achieving a new kind of aesthetic intensity and dramatic impact, a style which the Florentines adopted quite deliberately. These doors were the result of a competition held in 1402 in which six famous masters participated. They were asked to produce a model on the theme of *the sacrifice of Isaac* (so originally an Old Testament programme was planned). The models entered by Brunelleschi and Ghiberti have survived (they are in the Bargello), and show the difference between the one style, which consisted of arranging a number of pictorial elements on a flat plane, and the other which immediately captured the sense of a picture, producing an instantly appreciable atmosphere. It was obviously on these qualities that Ghiberti won the competition. The novelty of his style is most clearly seen in the *Storm at Sea* (right-hand leaf). Using a rich variety of artistic resources, in terms of composition, use of light and of deep, cavernous shadows, skilful gradations of relief and technically refined chisel-work, he achieved new heights in the pictorial treatment of bronze (the perfect craftsmanship of these doors matches the great tradition of the marble pulpits of the Pisani). Given such an extended working period (twenty-one years), it is only natural that certain stylistic changes can be observed. The older scenes (chiefly in the top and bottom rows, e.g. *The Resurrection*) are succeeded by scenes which have a delicate flavour of French Gothic (e.g. *Christ before Pilate*) and by others of a more Classical equilibrium (e.g. *The Flagellation*). On the inside of the leaves are twenty-eight lion-heads of most expressive physiognomy; they are well worth looking at. – The bronze surround is earlier (1423) than those of the other two portals. The bunches of delicately leaved flowers represented here were a feature of earlier, medieval altar surrounds. The bands of relief on the inner faces of the door pillars are particularly interesting, being the first example of the treatment of ornamental forms – in this case a strip of moulding – in foreshortened perspective, according to the recently discovered laws of optics. The same treatment appears in a more developed form on the east and south portals. – Above the doors is a superbly cast bronze group, *The Baptist teaching the Pharisee and the Levite*, 1506–11, by Francesco Rustici, possibly with the collaboration of Leonardo, which replaced an older (Gothic) group with the same theme. Above the round arches of the central window can be seen the *bronze eagles* of the merchants' guild (Calimala), which was responsible for the upkeep of the Baptistery. – Both the north and south doors have been moved from their original positions. Andrea Pisano's doors were originally intended for the east side (facing the Cathedral). They were moved from there to make way for a more 'advanced' pair, which in turn were moved to the north entrance as soon as Ghiberti had completed his contract for a further set of doors; begun in 1425, these were erected in 1452.

The present *east doors* were regarded as a truly miraculous piece of work (inside the master's signature on the right-hand leaf is written 'mira arte fabricatum') and were therefore granted the place of honour. Brilliantly gilded down to the smallest detail, they far outshine the other two portals. Michelangelo considered them worthy of the Gates of Paradise themselves (hence their name, *Porta del Paradiso*). The relationship between the articulation of the surround (statuette niches and medallion heads, including again that of Ghiberti himself, on the left-hand leaf, third along the bottom, and one of that *Aristotelian* type which remained one of the favourite subjects of portraitists right up until the High Renaissance) and the mighty, dish-like panels is highly ingenious. These ten relief panels, comprising an almost inexhaustible pictorial universe, are constantly besieged by a crowd of visitors. The themes are taken from the Old Testament. Each panel contains several scenes and represents in itself a series of stories around a single character. Here and there inscriptions elucidate the situation of the scene and the identity of the characters.

Themes of the reliefs, from top left to bottom right: 1. Creation of Adam and Eve. 2. Adam and Eve at work, Cain and Abel performing a sacrifice, Abel watching the cattle, Cain working in the fields, Cain murdering Abel, God asking Cain where Abel is. 3. Noah leaving the Ark, performing a sacrifice, planting vines, being ridiculed. 4. Abraham and the three angels, Abraham sacrificing Isaac. 5. Jacob and Esau (the hunt and the blessing). 6. Joseph being sold into slavery and given to Pharaoh, explaining Pharaoh's dream, being given land, recognizing his brothers and Benjamin, the return of the brothers. 7. Moses receiving the tablets of the law, the Israelites at the foot of Mount

Sinai. 8. Joshua before Jericho, the camp of the Israelites, the miracle of the trumpets. 9. David killing Goliath, the defeat of the Philistines, David's dance and return. 10. The Queen of Sheba visiting Solomon.

At top and bottom of the vertical mouldings of the surround are two pairs of reclining figures: Adam and Eve, Noah and Puarphera. The statuettes in the niches of the surround represent various Prophets and Sibyls (not all identifiable with certainty). The outer bronze surround, dating from the mid-century, is by a number of artists from Ghiberti's workshop and was mounted at the same time as the door.

Ever since men began to write the history of Renaissance art, Ghiberti's Paradise Doors have been valued as a prime example of the 'language of the new century' (Burckhardt). His achievement in freeing the relief from its natural limitations and making of it a true picture is of a very high order. The reliefs towards the top gradually recede into the surround, while those at the bottom jut out beyond it. They are three-dimensional creations, offering to the eye not only various objects lying one behind another and overlapping, but also fully rounded figures. This gives rise to that critical problem – shared by all perspective constructions – of the angle of vision. The reliefs assume that the spectator is standing directly in front of them, and not beneath them as, of course, the visitor is obliged to do. So some optical distortion is bound to occur. Various attempts were made in the individual panels to overcome this. Each panel represented a separate experiment, for which the artist had no precedents to draw on. – Above the portal is a marble group depicting the *Baptism of Christ*. The figures of Christ and John are by Andrea Sansovino; though completed in 1505, they were not erected until 1569. The adoring angel by Spinazzi, 1792, replaced a similar (clay) figure by Vincenzo Danti. The pillared tabernacle above the principal figure is also by Sansovino. This is the oldest of the large sculptured groups, and was originally intended for the south portal.

Interior   When the visitor steps inside the church, he finds the solemn majesty of its architecture all the more striking for the great contrast which exists between the general impression of dark mystery and the stereometric clarity of the exterior. Indeed, considerable differences exist between interior and exterior in such important matters as the height

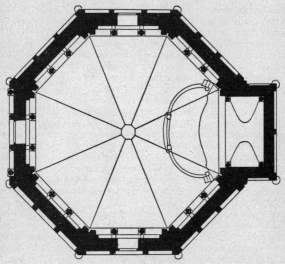

Baptistery of S. Giovanni, ground plan

of the storeys. The pattern of the walls is also different. And there is nothing outside to suggest the enormous, octagonal, pointed *dome* (diameter 25.6 m). This consists of a double shell; Brunelleschi made a rewarding study of its construction before undertaking the dome of the Cathedral. There are, however, strong constructional links between the interior and the exterior of the church. Two orders can be distinguished in the interior, the lower consisting of Corinthian columns of oriental granite with gilded capitals, and the upper consisting of a pilaster order with three pairs of arches on each side opening into a passageway (*ill.* facing p. 17). Between the storeys is a massive entablature. The outer windows open off the passageway. The whole system is hinged on the corner pillars. These extend right through from the inner to the outer walls and support the dome. The walls themselves and the orders fill the intervening space. The volume of the wall mass is accounted for by the

(invisible) abutments which lead down from between the
two shells of the dome through the intermediate storey to
the pairs of columns on the ground floor. This 'self-
supporting' construction, which, once recognized, can also
be detected outside, is derived from the architecture of the
Late Classical period. It was worked out so rigorously by
the architect that with a little effort one can visualize the
pure skeleton of the building. Between the ground-floor
entablature and the inside of the outer wall is a series of
abutment vaults. On the south-west side, the underside of
the entablature is decorated with a simple (probably Classical) pattern. Otherwise the use of Classical remains is limited
to columns and capitals. All fourteen of the ground-floor
column shafts are Classical (to the right of the east portal is
a fluted one), as well as the four capitals of the north and
south wall columns, and several of the small columns between the double openings of the intermediate storey, with
three of their Ionic capitals (north-west wall). The rest of
the capitals in this medieval building are faithful copies of
these originals. – The interior incrustation is livelier and
freer than the exterior. The rich variety of stars and rosettes
above the arches shows the influence of S. Vitale, Ravenna.
Above and to the right and left of the triumphal arch leading into the choir chapel can be seen two beautiful incrusted
vases. – The floor is a particularly fine example of medieval
Tuscan inlaid work. The simple, carpet-like patterns date
from the twelfth century; the more complicated motifs are
of rather later derivation, some from as late as the fourteenth century (ill. facing p. 32). Because of constant wear
the floor has had to be restored frequently. In the south-
east part a zodiac can be seen, together with a few, dimly
recognizable figurative motifs, probably from the early
thirteenth century.

Interior Decoration   The main decorative effect is in the
dome mosaic, the second most remarkable of its kind after
S. Mark's, Venice. It covers the interior of the dome with a
soft warmth, like a kind of furry moss, breaking up the
incoming light with sparkling brilliance (artificial lighting
is available). Christ the Judge of the World is the central
subject, a gigantic figure (more than 8 m high) pointing
towards the choir chapel. He is enthroned on a rainbow,
with the resurrected ones rising at his feet. Angels bring

instruments of torture, the blessed and the damned (right) are there, and all around are the enthroned Apostles, headed by Mary (left) and John (right). The whole composition is divided into five sections. At the top, around the lantern opening, are series of richly decorative motifs (creepers, stylized dolphins and angels). The individual pictorial bands portray the story of the Creation, the story of Joseph, the lives of Mary and Christ and the life of John the Baptist (*ill.* facing p. 33, the same iconographic arrangement as Andrea Pisano used on the south doors). The whole decorative programme thus regards the story of John the Baptist as an integral part of the story of Redemption, itself conceived as the story of mankind. The presence of numerous patriarchs and Early Fathers is a reminder that the story of mankind continues within the protecting arms of *Ecclesia* or Holy Church. It is this dome mosaic that gives the Baptistery its theological legitimization as a Christian site. There is considerable doubt as to the date of the mosaic and the artists responsible for the different sections. We know it was begun during the twenties of the thirteenth century and that by 1300 the work was well advanced, but it was still not complete in the fifteenth century. The ornamental wreath and series of angels around the lantern opening may be regarded as the earliest section. – The present overall impression of the mosaic must still be very close to that of the original, despite numerous restorations and even the complete renewal of some pictures (the three panels of the story of Noah on the south side are stucco copies of 1906). A close study of the best preserved sections reveals great poetic imagination on the part of the artist (e. g. the 'fairytale' forest in the *Creation of Man*). In the coffers between dome and galleries are mosaic half-figures of Early Fathers, bishops and deacons with the names inscribed. On the sills are patriarchs and prophets. Mosaics are also to be found inside the galleries and beneath the door lintels on the ground floor, and on the architrave is a frieze of winged angels' heads. – The best-preserved mosaic is the one in the choir chapel. It was begun by Jacobus, a Franciscan (inscription). On the inner face of the main arch, to the right and left of a beautiful medallion of the Madonna, are prophets, and on the front, set among ornamental creepers, is a half-figure of Christ. On the frontal arch of the apse

vault are the twelve Apostles and the four Evangelists, and
in the centre a half-figure of John the Baptist. In the groin
vault, the Apocalyptic Lamb supported by four figures
kneeling on the capitals, and more prophets and patriarchs
among vases with animals and angels. The enthroned
Madonna in the right spandrel is especially noteworthy.
Opposite is John the Baptist.

The principal items of the furniture of the Baptistery are
two masterpieces by *Donatello*. On the north-west side is
the *tomb of John XXIII*, the deposed Antipope Baldassare
Coscia, *c.* 1425, on which Michelozzo collaborated. In the
niches of the base are *Faith*, *Hope* and *Charity*. The imposing bronze figure of the deceased reclines on a beautifully
patterned cloth which was originally coloured. In the lunette
above the tomb is a half-figure of the *Madonna and Child*.
The tomb stands in the same plane as the two columns of
the Baptistery near it to right and left, thus making possible
the emergence of a style of relief which turned away from
a composition in greater depth, even to the extent of flatten-
ing out the statue niches. This is the earliest Renaissance
example of a tomb with a baldacchino. Opposite, against
the south-west wall, is Donatello's *S. Magdalen*, dating
probably from slightly before 1455 (the halo does not belong to it). The sunken eyes, bitter mouth and ragged clothes
appear all the more frightening since the finely shaped legs
and the nobility of the whole figure testify to the saint's
former beauty. – To right and left are two Roman sarcophagi, altered for re-use in the thirteenth century. – The
Sarcophagus of Bishop Rainer on the north-west wall is a
remarkable early example of marble incrustation, dated
1113. On the south-east side (it has been moved several
times) is a possibly *Venetian font* of 1371 with reliefs depicting scenes of baptism from the Bible and from legend.
Above the font is *The Baptism of Christ* by Alessandro
Allori, 1591. The oldest parts of the incrusted high altar
are early thirteenth century. Near the steps on the right are
angels with candlesticks, reliefs of the school of Arnolfo di
Cambio (dated 1320). Behind the altar is a marble statue of
John the Baptist by Piamontini, 1688. The bronze candlesticks in front are seventeenth century.

The overall impression of the interior, the severe spirituality
of its architecture, the splendour of its decoration, so much

a part of the artistic world of the Mediterranean, all breathe the spirit of Tuscany. For all Florentines, the Baptistery represents the focus of their home. It is the life-giving house of God. Hence, too, the constant alterations to the interior. Two early fourteenth century pulpits have completely disappeared. In 1577, Buontalenti destroyed the great and precious octagonal baptismal font (the place it occupied in the middle of the Baptistery is still marked with broad bands; individual panels are preserved in the Cathedral museum). Vasari attempted to impart a fashionable aspect to the interior; costly organs filled the church with music (an organ-screen is also in the Cathedral museum). Leaving aside the Baroque altars which have justly passed into oblivion, we will mention only the silver antependium, begun in 1366 and completed after 120 years of work, one of the greatest treasures of the Florentine goldsmiths' art. Until quite recently it still graced the high altar, but it is now so fragile that it too has had to take refuge in the Cathedral museum (see p. 48).

The Campanile

The history of the construction of the Campanile is closely connected with that of the Cathedral. When Giotto became architect-in-chief of the Cathedral in 1334, he concentrated his efforts during the short period left to him (he died in 1337) on this project: to give his city this Campanile towering above it. He was able to finish only the lower part of the first double storey. Andrea Pisano completed the upper part and the next double storey with its statue niches. It is not known exactly when his successor, Francesco Talenti, took over. He built the three upper storeys (finishing in 1359). The spire originally intended to cap the tower was never erected. All the visitor can see are the incomplete foundations on the topmost platform.

Exterior   The building is 82 m high and is built on a square ground plan with projecting corner supports. It soars up like some beautiful plant, glittering in the sun, its architecture and decoration in marvellous harmony. At the bottom is a firmly contoured base with a wide green band. The double storey above is articulated with tall, rectangular wall panels. The reliefs on the lower part are hexagonal (the entrance portal is in the east wall), and on the upper part rhomboid. The rhythm of the next double storey is different: two powerful pilaster-strips separate the side panels from a larger central panel, the central axis of which

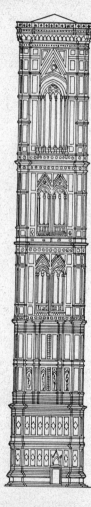

is stressed by tall slit-windows closed with perforated panels. The next three storeys are airier, the top storey being of considerable height, with splendid triple openings on each side. The two storeys beneath it each have double openings surmounted by crocket gables. All the openings contain tracery (most abundant in the top storey) with small, skilfully turned columns on either side. The top storey is terminated by vigorously articulated bracket cornice.

Exterior Decoration Possibly the most beautiful campanile in Italy, it is decorated with coloured stone in such a way as to show it to be the work of minds as sensitive to painting as to architecture. The whole building in fact may be enjoyed like a picture. The figurative apparatus appears as something added, and indeed it was possible to remove the sixteen statues from the niches of the second double storey and place them in the museum to rescue hem from disintegration. Unfortunately, however, this has disturbed the overall programme. The decoration of the Campanile followed a plan which may even have come from Giotto himself: to place before a wide public the story of the world and its redemption in a cycle of pictures both historical and symbolic, the former to illustrate the story of the Creation and of man's struggle for earthly and spiritual sustenance, the latter to be a reminder of ethical powers, the christian virtues and the holy sacraments. In scope this picture cycle matches the decorative world of the French cathedrals. In other respects, it corresponds to the iconogra-

Cathedral campanile

Baptistery, detail of the floor

Baptistery, 'The Visitation' (from the dome mosaic)

phy of the Cathedral (viz. the position of the Virgin Mary among the row of prophets). In Italy, the groundwork had been prepared in the rich decoration of pulpits and fountains by the Pisani.

Of the hexagonal reliefs in the bottom row, most are probably by Andrea Pisano and his school, *c.* 1340. The five panels at the west end of the north side are by Luca della Robbia, 1437–9. Beginning on the west side, they represent: 1. Creation of Adam. 2. Creation of Eve. 3. Adam and Eve at work after the Expulsion. 4. Jabal, the first cattle-breeder. 5. Jubal, inventor of flutes and violins. 6. Tubalcain, the first smith. 7. Noah, the first wine-grower. 8. (south side) Gionitus, the first astronomer. 9. House-building. 10. Medicine. 11. Hunting (*ill.* facing p. 48). 12. Weaving. 13. Phoroneus, the first judge. 14. Daedalus, the first artisan. 15. (east side) Shipping. 16. Hercules with the conquered giants. 17. Agriculture. 18. A chariot race. 19. (beyond the portal) The architect. 20. (north side) The sculptor. 21. The painter. 22. A school of grammar. 23. A dispute between logic and dialectics. 24. Poetry, in the person of Orpheus. 25. Euclid and Pythagoras, masters of geometry and arithmetic. 26. Music in the person of the smith Tubalcain, already portrayed on the west side (the melodious beating of hammers being regarded as the first form of human music-making!). – The rhomboid reliefs above, depicting the seven planets, the seven virtues, the seven liberal arts and the seven sacraments, are probably by followers of Andrea Pisano. Those on the north side are stylistically rather different. In detail: 1. (west) The moon. 2. Mercury. 3. Venus. 4. The sun. 5. Mars. 6. Jupiter (as a monk). 7. Saturn. 8. (south) Faith. 9. Charity. 10. Hope. 11. Prudence. 12. Justice. 13. Temperance. 14. Fortitude. 15. (east) Astronomy. 16. Music. 17. Geometry. 18. Grammar. 19. Rhetoric. 20. Logic. 21. Arithmetic. 22. (north) Baptism. 23. Absolution. 24. Marriage. 25. Ordination. 26. Confirmation. 27. The Eucharist. 28. Extreme Unction. All the originals are now in the Cathedral museum.

Within the arch of the small door beneath the fourth relief on the north side is a half-figure of the Virgin (after Andrea Pisano). The figure of Christ on top of the gable above the entrance portal on the east side (the portal itself, *c.* 1430, may be constructed of older parts) possibly dates from

around 1400. Moses and the unknown figure on the pinnacles
on either side are both *c.* 1410. The lamb in the arch is the
symbol of the woolweavers' guild which has been responsible
from the beginning for the upkeep of the Campanile.

Interior   Two separate staircases lead up inside the
double-shelled bell-tower to the platform of the top storey,
and a single staircase continues from there to the top. One
of the two lower staircases begins at street-level from the
east side entrance, and the other from the higher portal on
the north side, facing the Cathedral. This was once connected with the Cathedral by a passage. The core of the building, around which both staircases wind, consists of three
rib-vaulted chambers of different heights. – From the top of
the tower, the visitor has a magnificent view, particularly
of the dome of the Cathedral.

The Cathedral – S. Maria del Fiore

*Work on the Cathedral began shortly before 1296 under
Arnolfo di Cambio, on the site of the old twelfth century
cathedral of S. Reparata. It was then that the Cathedral
was named S. Maria del Fiore, after the contemporary
name of the town – Fiorenza. The earliest mention of a
previous building dates from 987. Before the new building
was erected, the Baptistery seems occasionally to have taken
over the functions of the cathedral. The idea of building a
new cathedral was probably inspired not only by the de-
crepit state of the old one, but also by the competition
provided by the larger monastic churches such as S. Maria
Novella, S. Trinita and S. Croce. Work began with the
facade and continued with the side-walls (ills. facing pp. 49
and 64). It was proceeding apace when it was interrupted
by Arnolfo's death, but a fresh impetus was given by the
discovery of the bones of S. Zenobius in 1330. Giotto became cathedral architect in 1334, but concerned himself
chiefly with the Campanile. His death in 1337 brought a
new interruption. Work was resumed in 1355 on an extended design under Francesco Talenti until 1365, and under
Giovanni di Lapo Ghini until 1367. Arnolfo's site was still
taken as the starting-point, but there were various projects
to give the building greater splendour. Work at this stage
was concentrated on the nave and chancel. In 1366 a commission of architects, goldsmiths and painters submitted a*

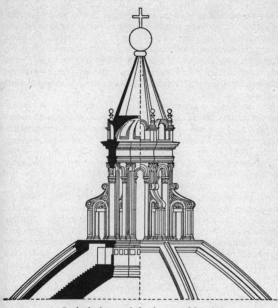

Cathedral, top of the dome and lantern

model which in 1368 was declared to be 'final', and which every subsequent architect had to pledge himself on oath to abide by. After that, the main stages of construction were the laying of the chancel foundations (1379–86), the erection of the crossing pillars and arches (1397–8) and of the drum of the dome (1412–13), and the commencement of the dome vault (c. 1420). Meanwhile work proceeded slowly on the façade, bringing it up to the height of the gable above the main portal. From 1420 onwards, all efforts were concentrated on the dome. After lengthy debates, Brunelleschi and Ghiberti were elected architects of the dome. The dome was complete in 1436 and work began on the lantern. It proceeded very slowly, however, and when Brunelleschi died in 1446 only the foundations had been completed. Miche-

*lozzo continued the work, following a model which he had
inherited but altering details. He got as far as the entablature
of the lantern, and completed one of the voluted abutment
piers. He died in 1451 and was succeeded until 1460 by
Manetti, who completed the remaining supports. He was
succeeded in turn by Bernardo Rossellino and then by Tommaso Succhielli, who finished the lantern. The consecration
took place in 1467.*

*After an epoch of various small undertakings by several
famous artists, the façade of the Cathedral was pulled down
in 1587 to make way for a more modern and homogeneous
piece of work. Various wooden models were made, among
which those of Buontalenti, Cigoli, Giovanni da Bologna
and Don Giovanni Medici are preserved in the Cathedral
museum. Nothing, however, was executed. – Work on the
interior had meanwhile progressed so far that by the beginning of the sixteenth century, the marble floor could be
laid down. At the same time a gallery was begun around the
outside of the drum, but this found little approval (Michelangelo referred to it scornfully as a 'cricket cage') and was
left unfinished. The bare frontal wall of the Cathedral was
decorated for feast days with ornaments of perishable
material. Some of the stucco figures made for such occasions
were set up in the exedra through which the visitor gains
access to the dome. In 1688, this frontal wall was covered
with a smooth wall which was then painted with a simulated
architecture. There exist old photographs of this decoration.
The present façade was built in 1875–87 by the architect de
Fabris. – Repairs to the cathedral are in hand almost continually. The lantern, damaged by lightning several times,
has frequently been renovated.*

*Research into the architectural history of the Cathedral is
still going on, and all attempts so far made at reconstruct-
ing earlier plans must be regarded with some scepticism.
For example, it has only recently been discovered that more
of Arnolfo's work has survived than had previously been
suspected, and that in fact virtually the whole of the lower
part of the nave dates back to him.*

Exterior   The new façade put the finishing touch to a
building of which the dome is one of the most important
products of Renaissance architecture but which is otherwise
Gothic in construction, even retaining certain Romanesque

elements, as for example the characteristic colourfulness of
the marble – white, green ('verde di Prato') and red ('rosso
di Maremma'). The view along the *side-walls* shows the
very full decoration. The first panels along the right (south)
side are among the oldest parts still visible. The first window
panel has a somewhat different incrustation from the others,
being more Classical in form, and may date from Arnolfo
di Cambio's time, as does the whole of the lower part of the
north and south sides up as far as the chancel. The section
comprising the first four windows provided the basic pattern (later varied) for the whole of the exterior of the building. Here the windows with their pointed arches are particularly richly decorated. They are crowned by stilted
tabernacles (containing rosettes) with shallow niches which
appear to push up the entablature of the side aisle wall in
a curious way. It should be noted that nothing in this whole
order corresponds to the (more recent) articulation of the
interior. The windows are blind; this is purely a show-wall
without any architectural depth. The whole of the attic
storey was added later when the side aisles were extended in
height (under Talenti). – In the sections nearer the *chancel*,
this system is developed in the freer High Gothic style.
Here each interior bay has a corresponding window outside,
in the middle of a wall-section. The windows are taller and
wider and the projections are developed to form a system
of buttresses. The chancel constitutes a triconchal structure,
with each arm (*Tribuna*) representing five-eighths of an
octagon. Here there are definite traces of the influence of
the Baptistery, particularly in the positioning of the arches
(*ill.* facing p. 49). Each tribune comprises two storeys: a
lower storey with a ring of chapels and an upper storey, set
back and supported by a triangular buttress at each corner.
In the four angles are projecting structures rising above (to
the west) the corner abutments and (to the east) the two
sacristies. These support some of the thrust of the dome, as
do also Brunelleschi's *exedrae* which are built above them,
leaning against the oblique faces of the drum. These powerfully articulated exedrae are extremely original and highly
individual pieces of architecture. Each one contains four
niches let into the walls and surmounted by delicately
moulded scallops with many groins. The pairs of columns
between the niches support on their capitals rather unusual

reduced dosserets and an entablature. Above is a semi-
conical roof. The massiveness of these exedrae is typical of
Brunelleschi's late style. – The best view of the chancel area
is from the Via del Proconsolo. The integrity of the whole
complex, tightly knit by means of rigid vertical strips within the incrusted ornamentation, shows how close it is in
essence to a centralized structure.

The *drum* was incrusted by Manetti in 1451–60, but the
upper part remains virtually in its raw state. The unfinished
gallery along the south-east side (above a marble frieze with
garlands between huge lion-heads), built in 1508–15 by
(probably) Baccio d'Agnolo with the collaboration of Giuliano da Sangallo and Cronaca, appears frivolous in such
monumental surroundings. Over the outer shell of the 107 m
high dome eight ribs of white marble, strongly profiled in
the Classical manner, lead up to the ring on which rests the
lantern. The function of the pillars of the lantern is two-
fold: on the one hand they form a natural continuation of
the ribs, and on the other they constitute an integral part
(derived from the goldsmith's art) of the lantern itself. They
link the dome and lantern in such a matter-of-fact way that
the visitor does not immediately appreciate the complete
originality of this solution, which was to be of such importance for the Renaissance and also for the Baroque style. At
the same time they create the illusion that the lantern is
reaching down with long arms to gather up the majestic
soaring strength of the dome, leading it to a serene conclusion. Round-arched openings beneath the supporting
pillars create a passage around the lantern. – The aesthetic
perfection of the dome leaves no hint as to the immense
difficulties which had to be overcome in dealing with such
an enormous mass. Careful studies of the construction of
older domes led to the solution of the double-shelled dome,
which may already have been envisaged by Arnolfo. This
was achieved without centring through the additional
strength provided by abutment ribs between the two shells
(they can be seen on the way up to the lantern). The remarkably steep pitch of the dome helped too, and at the
same time created that incomparable impression of soaring
tension that informs the whole structure. Brunelleschi's freedom was somewhat limited by the fact that he took over
after the drum and some parts of the vault had already been

built. We can only admire all the more the assurance
with which he realized his idea and left on it the stamp
of his personality, although the planning was done together with Ghiberti (who left the project in 1433 in
order to concentrate on the second set of doors for the Baptistery).

Exterior Decoration The sculptural decoration is concentrated around the portals, the chancel area and the
façade. At one time it offered a rich compendium of styles
stretching over three generations. Florence Cathedral became the birthplace of Renaissance monumental sculpture.
– *South wall:* Near the façade end is a beautifully carved
inscription referring to the building of the Cathedral. Nearby, a relief depicting the Annunciation, dated 1310. Higher
up is the door (now walled in) of the passage which formerly led from the Cathedral to the Campanile. Next, the
shallow *Porta del Campanile*, with its beautiful polychrome
marblework. In the gabled tabernacles on either side are the
angel Gabriel, on the left, and Mary on the right (forming
an Annunciation group). In a medallion in the gable, *Christ
giving a Blessing*. In the lunette, a *Madonna with Child*
(mid-fourteenth century). The next portal (before the
tribune), known as the *Canons' Door*, was begun by Lorenzo
di Giovanni d'Ambrogio (late fourteenth century) and continued by Piero di Giovanni Tedesco. In the lunette, a
Madonna with Child by Lorenzo di Giovanni d'Ambrogio
(1402) and two angels, the one on the left by Niccolò Lamberti. There is further decoration inside and on top of the
gable. – Walking around the chancel part to the *north wall*
the visitor comes to the famous *Porta della Mandorla*, the
most recent and most beautiful of all the portals. In composition it resembles the 'Canons' Door'. We know for certain
that many famous artists contributed to it (Giovanni
d'Ambrogio, his son Lorenzo, Piero di Giovanni Tedesco,
Niccolò Lamberti, Jacopo di Piero Guidi and Nanni di
Banco among others) but no agreement has been reached as
to each master's contribution. The portal was completed in
three sections: 1. The jambs (1391–7); foliage interspersed
with small figures, very obviously in the Classical manner,
and hexagons containing half-figures of angels. In the
middle of the lintel, which is supported by two brackets in
the form of angels playing musical instruments, is a half-

figure of Christ; the two prophets in tabernacles to the right
and left above the entablature also belong with it, and are
by Lorenzo di Giovanni d'Ambrogio. 2. The intrados
around the tympanum (1404–9); foliage with figures,
similar to those on the jambs (the three half-figures of angels
on the right and the *Man of Sorrows* on the keystone are
copies; the originals are now in the Cathedral museum). The
two prophets on the pinnacles on either side of the gable
also belong to this phase. The one on the left is probably by
Ciuffagni, the one on the right is by *Donatello* and is the
earliest tangible evidence of the development of his style.
There is still a touch of Gothic in the gentle sweep of the
robe. 3. The relief panel in the gable is Nanni di Banco's
masterpiece, the *Donation of the girdle to S. Thomas* (*ill.*
facing p. 65). This important piece of early Renaissance
sculpture stands out with detached corporeality against a
plain background which is still Gothic in style. The frame is
decorated with incrusted motifs (candlesticks and crowns).
The prophet on top of the gable must date from *c.* 1400
though it was not placed here until 1423. The two heads in
profile (prophet and sibyl?) by Donatello in the corner beneath the onset of the gable also belong to this last phase.
– The Annunciation mosaic in the lunette is by Domenico
and Davide Ghirlandaio and is dated 1490. – The next
portal to the west formed part of Arnolfo's plan but was
not completed until towards the end of the fourteenth
century. The jambs are flanked by two freestanding turned
columns resting on lions. They are richly incrusted, with a
late fourteenth century *Madonna and Child* in the lunette,
and two standing angels. The relief of Christ in the gable
medallion and the other figures on the pinnacles, pilasters
and gable-top belong to the same period. The authorship
of most of the figures in the niches on this side of the
Cathedral (they are from the fourteenth or fifteenth centuries) is unknown. Waterspouts, dating from the same
period, jut out below the cornice all round the building. –
We know what Arnolfo's old *façade* (continued by Talenti)
looked like from a drawing in the Cathedral museum (*ill.*
facing p. 64). It was pulled down in 1587 and the statues,
some of which had been there since 1420, were distributed
among various gardens and palaces. The present façade, by
de Fabris, was built in 1875–87. It was modelled on forms

taken from the Campanile and the aisles of the Cathedral. The theme of its lavish decoration is *The greatness of Christianity*, with popes, bishops, and also busts of important Florentine citizens. The mosaics above the portals were made from cartoons by Nicola Barabino (1887). The façade disturbed the overall decorative scheme of the Cathedral, which had previously been devoted entirely to the Virgin.

Interior Basilican in plan, the interior measures 153 m in length and 38 m (*c.* 90 m in the transept) in width, and has the form of a Latin cross. Four bays, rhythmically divided by powerful pointed arcades, lead eastwards to the centralized structure around the dome. At the level of the groin vaults is a passage which begins inside the façade-

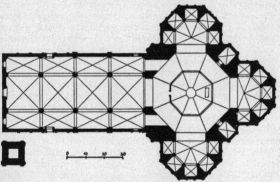

Cathedral, ground plan

wall and runs along the nave and round the domed crossing. Iron tic-bars link the tops of the pillars. The height and width of the arches give a feeling of immense spaciousness to the Gothic aisles. The pillars, with their high bases and rich foliate capitals, were inspired by those of Or San Michele. The space below the dome, slightly wider than the nave and side aisles together, opens out into three identical arms which are surrounded by square chapels with pointed rib vaults. Portals beneath the organ galleries lead to the two sacristies. A visit to the dome is highly recommended; a door in the left side aisle gives access to a staircase which

rises between the two shells of the dome to the lantern.
Here something of the interior structure of the dome can be
seen, among other things a ring-shaped wooden anchor and
skilfully indented brick abutments.

Interior Decoration   The dominant note is provided by
the earthy tints of the colouring. The simple austerity of
the interior is original and deeply moving. The furniture,
however, has been extensively altered, particularly during
the thorough restoration of 1842, which was also responsible
for the present regularity of arrangement. Decorative
material for the Cathedral was produced in an uninterrupted stream. Works were continually being completed or
moved about or changed, and many artists involved in
collaborations have remained anonymous. Many of these
works were only intended to be temporary; even the finest
artists did not hesitate to create perishable works, such as,
for example, Francavilla and Caccini, whose monumental
stucco figures for the decoration of a marriage ceremony in
1589 can still be seen, on the way up to the dome, in one of
Brunelleschi's exedrae, where they are now kept. Just as,
outside, the decoration of the façade was in a constant state
of flux from the end of the sixteenth century onwards, that
of the interior was equally constantly changing, and it is
hard for us today to picture the candlesticks, lamps, carpets
and oil-paintings which so splendidly beautified the Cathedral right into the nineteenth century.

Something of the old joy in decoration still remains, however, in the famous *clock* on the inside of the façade-wall
and in the three important *stained-glass windows*. The fifteenth century clock has heads of prophets painted by
Uccello in the four corners (1443) and originally indicated
all twenty-four hours (the present face with twelve divisions
dates from 1669). The three round windows were executed
by the German glass-painter Niccolò di Piero to designs by
Ghiberti. From left to right they represent S. Stephen (enthroned), the Assumption and S. Lawrence (enthroned). –
In the lunette above the main entrance, a fine mosaic *Coronation of the Virgin* (c. 1300), accompanied on either side
by angel frescoes on gold backgrounds in the blind arches
added by Santi di Tito in the late sixteenth century. This
mosaic constitutes the oldest extant part of the decoration
of the Cathedral, and it may have come from S. Reparata.

The nave and side aisles have always been a place for burials. Entering the main portal, the visitor finds on his left, still in its original position, the *tomb of Bishop Antonio d'Orso* by Tino da Camaino, completed in 1321. This bracketed wall-tomb (the only known fourteenth century tomb where the body is enshrined in a sitting position) is in an incomplete state of preservation (nor can it be reconstructed with any certainty). The great sculptor's courtly style here shows something of the influence of Giotto; the allegory on death on the spandrels of the two arches supporting the sarcophagus is full of poetic symbolism. – Most of the busts which line the walls of the side aisles are both tombs and memorials. The first on the left is a round medallion of Brunelleschi by his pupil and confidant Cavalcanti, known as Buggiani (1447). A statue of Isaiah by Nanni di Banco follows (1408) and then Giotto is similarly represented as a mosaic artist by Benedetto da Maiano. The inscription below is by Poliziano. Under the last of the two beautiful stained-glass windows in the third and fourth bays (designed, like the corresponding ones in the left side aisle, by Agnolo Gaddi) the bust of Marsilio Ficino gazes out of a tabernacle niche; the inspired founder of Renaissance Platonism is holding a large book like a lyre in his hands (by Ferrucci, 1521). In the second bay of the left aisle, a medallion bust of the organist Squarcialupi (by Benedetto da Maiano), and nearer the façade-wall two modern ones (nineteenth century), based on the others and resembling Arnolfo di Cambio and de Fabris, the architect of the Cathedral and the architect of the façade.

The enormous *equestrian painting* by Uccello in the third bay of the left side aisle constitutes both a culmination and a turning point in the history of warrior's memorials. John Hawkwood was the idolized English commander of the Florentine mercenary army in the fourteenth century, who in Italy went by the name of Giovanni Acuto. The 'terra verde' sarcophagus, seen from below in shortened perspective, and the carved and painted frame, contrast strangely with the horse and rider, which are in strict profile. This may be due to a change in plan, for when the artist began work in 1436 he was obliged to alter or destroy or remodel sections which had already been completed. This was the first great equestrian monument of the Renaissance which was purely pictorial, and its importance lies not least in the way in which it was created. The whole design, including the colours, was established in a detailed sketch (Uffizi) and then transferred to the wall to the required scale by means of a squared grid. Although the artist may have been inspired by the sculptured tomb of Pietro Farnese (originally above the door to the Campanile but now removed; the sarcophagus is in the Cathedral museum), that mule with its rider (lost) surely bore no comparison with Uccello's magnificent horse, which is equalled only by the bronze horses of S. Mark's, Venice. The fascination of the simulated marble tomb effect of this fresco (transposed on to canvas in 1842) can be seen in the painted *equestrian memorial to Niccolò Manuzi da Tolentino*, also transferred to canvas, to the left of it, though this in turn bears little comparison with its model. It was executed by Castagno in 1456 as a pendant. – The two frescoed tombs of Luigi Marsili and Cardinal Pietro Corsini by Bicci di Lorenzo have also been transferred to canvas. After many changes of position, they are now back in their old place in the right side aisle. As fresco simulations of marble tombs they were important precedents for Uccello's equestrian one.

If the Hawkwood memorial evinces that desire to glorify the great which was so powerful a part of the Renaissance, its place in the Cathedral shows how Florence took to herself the fame of her subjects. A beautiful example of this is the picture which hangs in the fourth bay of the left side aisle (to the left of the door), depicting Dante (buried at Ravenna) with the *Divina Commedia* in his hand, pointing towards heaven and hell, with Florence spread out beside him, its walls shimmering golden in the radiance of its illustrious son. The design, by Baldovinetti, was executed in 1465 by Domenico di Michelino.

The decoration of the *dome area*, centred entirely on the cult of Christianity, is quite different. Eight marble niches all around it contain Apostles. *James*, on the left-hand nave pier, is an important work by Jacopo Sansovino, the earliest piece definitely attributable to him, with still a touch of Gothic in the gathering of the drapery (1511–18). Also noteworthy is the colossal *Matthew* by Vincenzo de' Rossi in the opposite niche and Baccio Bandinelli's *Peter* (1515–17) on the left wall before the central tribune, which

in its posture and its ascetic lines reveals the influence of
the *Peter* of Or San Michele. Most of the figures were put
up after 1565, for the wedding of the Grand Duke Don
Francesco to Johanna of Austria. It was for this occasion,
too, that Ammannati erected the marble tabernacles. Before
that date the fate of this vast centralized area had been
uncertain. In 1503 Michelangelo had accepted an amazing
commission to deliver twelve more than life-sized Apostles
in an incredibly short time, but he only began one, *Matthew*
(now in the Academy, incomplete). Meanwhile the Florentines contented themselves with Apostle frescoes which the statues had been intended to replace. The last were put up in 1580.
In the centre of the dome area is a low octagonal enclosure
consisting of plain marble panels alternating with reliefs.
Bandinelli and Baccio d'Agnolo delivered the first designs
in 1547 and the work was executed by Bandinelli (most of
his pieces, some of them signed and dated, are around the
eastern sides) and his pupil Giovanni Bandini, known as
dell'Opera. Originally the whole structure was more complex, with columns and an entablature. The area around
the high altar was then decorated with marble statues. Today a remarkable wooden crucifix rises behind the altar. It
is a late work by Benedetto da Maiano, *c.* 1490, painted by
Lorenzo di Credi in 1510. The whole of the figurative
decoration followed a programme which included Adam
and Eve (by Bandinelli, now in the courtyard of the National Museum, the Bargello) and was focused on Christ and
the Virgin, as can be seen from the glass in the round windows of the drum, which formed part of the original scheme.
The *Coronation of the Virgin* above the central tribune was
designed by Donatello, the *Resurrection* above the left
sacristy and the *Nativity* above the left side aisle by Uccello,
the *Pietà* above the left tribune by Castagno, and the others
by Ghiberti (the work was always carried out by specialists).
Crowning the whole arrangement was originally envisaged
for this. The present *Last Judgement* was begun (at the
crown) by Vasari in 1572–4, after a programme by V. Borghini, and completed by Zuccari and his school. The models
for this dome fresco ranged from the Baptistery mosaic (the
architecturally conceived figures of the upper ring) to Michelangelo (hell).

The decoration of the two oblique walls flanking the east
tribune is today unworthy of the magnificent architecture.
The organ screens were once much richer; the choir galleries
by Donatello and Luca della Robbia which used to run in
front of them have now gone (they have been reconstructed in the Cathedral museum). Of the two bronze doors
orignally planned by Donatello the one on the right dates
from the nineteenth century. The more interesting of the
two sacristies is probably the left or northern one (the
Sagrestia Vecchia). The inscriptions commemorate the consecration of the Cathedral in 1436 by Pope Eugenius IV (on
the right) and the Florentine Council of 1439. The *bronze
door*, through which Lorenzo the Magnificent made his
escape at the time of the notorious Pazzi Conspiracy, is by
Michelozzo and Luca della Robbia, the latter being responsible for most of the reliefs. They are the only bronze works
by this master, and may have been chased by another
hand. The twin leaves with their ten square panels include
a *Madonna with Child* (top left), *John the Baptist* (top
right), and for the rest Evangelists and Early Fathers
accompanied by angels. The heads in the corners of the
panels, placed not quite satisfactorily in quatrefoils which
are cut into by the surround, mirror motifs from Ghiberti's
Baptistery doors. There is an important terracotta relief by
Luca della Robbia, 1442–5, in the lunette. This *Resurrection
of Christ* is the earliest documented example of a terracotta
technique which was to become extremely popular. Immediately on the left, inside the sacristy, is a *lavabo* by Cavalcanti, possibly derived from designs by Brunelleschi. The
wooden cupboards with their marvellous intarsie were
greatly admired when, after thirty years' work, they were
completed in 1468. Much of Giuliano da Maiano's fame
stemmed from them, although other masters participated in
the work – Baldovinetti, for example, and Maso di Finiguerra, whose inlaid *Annunciation* and *S. Zenobius with
Two Deacons* (the latter is now in the Cathedral museum;
it was once where the curator's lodge is now placed) are the
only extant works definitely attributable to this legendary
inventor of the art of copper engraving. – Notice also the
life-sized putti with their finely carved robes and their
wooden garlands. – The right or southern **Sagrestia Nuova**
is rather less uniform in decoration. Two inscribed plaques

by the portal commemorate the transfer here of the body of S. Zenobius and the laying of the foundation stone of the Cathedral in 1298; the texts are by Poliziano. Above the door, *The Ascension of Christ* by Luca della Robbia (1446); the posture, with Christ standing with outspread arms, is unusual. Inside, a font similar to that in the north sacristy (also by Cavalcanti); on the right, *Tobias with the Angel and Donor*, a painting by the school of Botticelli, and on the window side two terracotta candlestick angels in an arrangement which is not original, with their wooden wings (added later) framing an early sixteenth century crucifix. According to Vasari the *Archangel Michael* on the left wall is by Lorenzo di Credi. The Early Fathers and Evangelists in octofoils are by Matteo di Nardo and Lorenzo di Bicci.

As well as those in the dome area, Ammannati also erected marble tabernacles in the side aisles (the last two before the façade-wall are wooden imitations). The figures now inside them came from the exterior and follow no particular plan. On the right in the first bay is Nanni di Banco's *Isaiah* and a relief by Ciuffagni also depicting Isaiah, and on the left, still in the first bay, a figure wrongly thought to be that of the humanist *Poggio Bracciolini*, which is an interesting 'pasticcio'; it was begun by Ciuffagni, possibly continued by Donatello (look at the head) and finished by Nanni di Bartolo, known as 'Il Rosso'. Finally on the left in the third bay, Ciuffagni's realistic figure of *David*.

The principal decoration of the **tribunes** consists of a fresco cycle of holy figures by Bicci di Lorenzo running right round them (heavily restored *c.* 1440; special mention should be made of the Thomas group in the east chapel of the right tribune because of its formal relationship to Verrocchio's bronze group at Or San Michele) and the windows, most of which were designed by Ghiberti. In the second chapel of the central tribune is a miraculous image of the *Madonna and Child* (*c.* 1360; it is sometimes covered), an old fresco which was probably taken down from the inside of the façade-wall. – A particular gem is housed beneath the altar of the Chapel of the Sacrament (the middle one, set off by its more splendid decoration and delightful rose-leaf capitals). This is the embossed bronze shrine (originally gilded) of S. Zenobius, a masterpiece by Lorenzo Ghiberti which the artist himself describes at length in his memoirs.

From a distance these large relief scenes are reminiscent of the old traditional painted chests ('cassoni'); here the same stylistic problems can be seen as preoccupied the master on the Paradise Doors, only in this case the story is more concentrated. It was completed in 1442 (*ill.* facing p. 80). – The first chapel on the east side of the left tribune contains one of the most impressive pieces in the whole Cathedral, the *Pietà*, a late work by Michelangelo. The group (*c.* 1550; it is incomplete) was originally intended for the master's own tomb, but he destroyed it himself. Calcagni fitted the broken pieces together and added a few pieces to make it complete; the great sculptor's original signature can still be seen on Christ's body. The head of the meditating Joseph of Arimathaea is deeply moving. Beside this great work of art the rest of the decoration of the tribune loses something of its effect, but mention must be made of Michelozzo's *marble altar* in the central chapel, with its showcase for relics.

Like so many of the great churches of Italy, Florence Cathedral also provided space for scientific research. A round brass plaque (with moulding) in the left tribune marks the spot where the astronomer Ximenes carried out his experiments to measure the height of the sun. (There is an inscription referring to this in the passage to the left side aisle.)

The Cathedral Museum – Museo dell'Opera del Duomo

The Opera del Duomo *is mentioned for the first time in 1390 as being the seat of the Cathedral building commission. It was then on the south side of the square, in what are now nos. 17–19. From time to time it was located in one of the present sacristies, and it was probably Brunelleschi who moved it to its present position on the eastern side of the square behind the Cathedral chancel. Today the museum forms part of a considerably more extensive site, the headquarters of all artistic activity connected with the Cathedral. A large repository for works of art existed there from the earliest times. – In 1822 many monuments were moved from there to the Uffizi and then to the National Museum (Bargello). The fragments of the two singing galleries were the first items to return to the present locality. They form the core of the present collection, which was opened to the public in 1891.*

Above the portal of this venerable building, which is near Donatello's workshop (inscribed plaque), is a bust of Cosimo I by Giovanni dell'Opera, placed there in 1572 to signify the fact that the Grand Dukes had assumed the highest lay patronage of the Cathedral. Columns from

Campanile, 'Hunting' (workshop of Andrea Pisano)

Cathedral, exterior, detail of the chancel

Bandinelli's marble enclosure under the dome stand in the passage. The visitor first enters a **courtyard** containing various fragments (Baroque figures from the Baptistery, coats of arms, lion-heads from the drum) before coming to the vestibule. The two handsome *terracotta lunettes* by Luca della Robbia (1489) formed part of the original decoration ordered by the Cathedral building commission; the remarkable profile portrait of Baccio Bandinelli (1556) was curiously enough situated beneath the statue of *God the Father* which once dominated the high altar and now stands in the first cloister of S. Croce.

The most important pieces in the first room are on the wall opposite the entrance. On the right are the fragments from the *Porta della Mandorla*; to the left of them are some very fine individual slabs from the Baptistery *font*, and finally a remarkable, round, hollow *cast* depicting an eagle, which may have been used for casting series of stucco reliefs. On a smaller slab below is an Early Christian inscription. There is a particularly handsome and expressive *head of the school of Camaino* (c. 1350) below the second vault bracket from the right.

Walking on, the visitor comes to the main **hall of sculptures**. Most of the pieces are from the Cathedral façade. The large-scale *drawing* (*ill.* facing p. 64) to the right of the entrance shows the façade as it was before it was pulled down in 1587. With the help of this most of the pieces can be assigned to their original positions. The four monumental seated figures against the left-hand wall flanked the entrance portal in pairs. The blocks of marble, all of the same light honey colour, were quarried together. They are all considerably taller and wider than they are deep, and must have posed special problems for the artists. Nanni di Banco's *Luke* lacks real depth because of the shortness of his thighs. He is spread out in a commanding posture of spiritual authority. Donatello's hunched-up *John*, with the huge head and flashing eyes beneath knotted brows, is quite different. The boring out of the pupils, which gives the eyes that accentuated look, was probably of a later period. Here it is the torso that lacks depth; it has no back and is not fully rounded. This left more room for the thighs, which are turned out to the right, so that despite the shape of the block this figure is more true to life. Completed before 1415, it is one of the most important of the master's youthful works. – Ciuffagni's *Matthew* is a very fine example of this master's art of realistic characterization. The tall, lean figure contrasts strongly with Niccolò di Piero Lamberti's *Mark* (the fourth figure beyond the side room), whose full robe swirls around him, making an indistinct piece of character portrayal even less clear.

At the narrow end of the room a *seated figure* in pale marble

catches the eye. According to the inscription, it is Boniface VIII,
but since the inscription was only added in the seventeenth century
(based on the inscription on the first panel of the outside wall on
the south side of the Cathedral), this is far from certain. It is
more likely to be the Early Father, Pope Gregory the Great. Its
original position is not known for certain; it may never have
been moved. The Gothic style dates it at around 1310. The letters
'A.P.F.' at the end of the stole have not yet been explained. The
picturesque *arch* above the figure is sixteenth century; it once
formed the entrance to Bandinelli's octagonal altar enclosure. –
The *Madonna and Child* against the right-hand wall merits
particular mention, with its shining eyes and glassy stare. Neither
the author nor the intended destination of this votive image are
at all clear. Stylistically it belongs to the school of Arnolfo di
Cambio. It was taken down from the façade in 1587, but whether
it had originally been intended for that position remains questionable in view of the unusual depth of the block. We do know of a
statue for the adoration of the Madonna inside the Cathedral at
one stage, and it is not difficult to imagine this sensitive piece
serving as an object of devotion. – Above the figure is a delightfully fresh piece of delicate inlaid work, showing that this kind
of ornamentation was not confined to Rome. – In the middle of
the hall stands a Classical *sarcophagus*. During the Middle Ages
three of the sides were very skilfully worked to prepare it for
re-use as the tomb of the Farnese family. The equestrian figure
with which it was originally crowned is now lost. The lions
(waterspouts) on which the tomb stands today do not belong to
it. – The *aspersorium*, with a figure that has been several times
restored, is from the Cathedral, where it formed the upper portion
of the beautiful Gothic font (there is a copy there today).

Climbing up three steps, passing on the way two pairs of very
weatherbeaten Early Fathers whose heads have been altered to
poets (laureati), the visitor enters a room which houses part of the
Cathedral treasure. The late sixteenth century *lectern* in the
middle stood in the chancel of the Cathedral. The *antiphonaries*
in the glass cases are decorated with beautiful miniatures. Several
examples of the goldsmith's art are worth particular attention:
first of all, the *silver reliquary* in the form of a burial shrine in
the far left of the middle case on the right. It is by Vittorio
Ghiberti (the son of Lorenzo, known from his work on the
surrounds of the Baptistery doors), the only independent piece
of work definitely attributable to this master, and is remarkable
particularly as a very early example (1476) of 'pietra-dura'
coating. The jewels adorning the sloping roof and the side walls
were left unset. A case on the left contains, among other things,
a *processional cross* (c. 1480, possibly by Antonio di Salvi) with
figures on blue enamel by a different hand (Luca della Robbia?).
– A door at the rear of the room leads to the octagonal chapel.

The first case on the right contains a beautiful *S. Anthony reliquary*, dating from the 1470's, and the next case a *S. Jerome ostensory*, both by Antonio di Salvi (the gilded wooden base is Baroque). The jaw and an arm of the saint are contained in the central lantern and in the superstructure. The lower part of the piece is still Gothic but the angels (with the Saint's attributes) and the delicately chiselled architectural forms are in the style of the Early Renaissance. The influence of Antonio del Pollaiuolo is noticeable in the cast statuette on top.

Climbing the stairs, where there are some relief-panels from the Abruzzi region and some heads of varying quality, the first room the visitor comes to on the upper floors is the **hall of the singing galleries**. High up on the wall in a corner opposite the entrance is *Donatello's* masterpiece, reconstructed from single pieces. The purpose of the gallery, which was made in 1433–9, is not clear, since it does not contain enough room for a choir. Probably it was to conceal the organ console. Behind columns which rise from powerful corbels appears a frieze of dancing angels against a mosaic ground. There is a certain sketchiness about the execution of these relief plates which gives rise to great complexity and depth of vision as the different planes recede from the columns. The sculptural skill behind this manipulation of optics is of a very high order indeed. The frieze of angels was not created all of a piece. The left half (similar in detail to the putti of the pulpit at Prato) is stiffer and more forced than the continuous stream of figures of the right half. The side reliefs are rather weaker in execution (help from pupils). Below, in the outer panels between the brackets pairs of highly polished putti (without wings) in a different style stand out against a dense, coarse-grained mosaic ground. They are based on Classical prototypes, as are the bronze heads on the round panels. It is not certain whether these belong together (both are from the National Museum and one may be Classical and the other a Renaissance copy). Rising gaily above the heavy, old-fashioned base, the frieze of dancing and singing putti represents jubilation in honour of the Blessed Virgin, patroness of the Cathedral. The upper terminating band has not been properly restored. Above the pairs of columns were originally dolphins facing shells, a Classical motif like the pairs of putti below. Donatello's ornamental inventions are considered to be of great historical importance. The brackets appear to consist of heavy balls of rope. The heads in the wreath of foliage (on the entablature) had a powerful influence on the sixteenth century, and were taken up by Michelangelo among others. The dolphins and shells of the upper cornice represent the very first use of this motif in the Renaissance. This magnificent work of art is in many respects of seminal importance.

Luca della Robbia's singing gallery on the opposite wall is rather different, though it is the same size, served the same purpose, and also features jubilant angels. Its place was above the north sacristy (Donatello's above the south). Little has been preserved of the Classical architecture of this gallery (finished slightly earlier than Donatello's, in 1438), although the reconstruction is relatively accurate. The lovely relief panels with angels playing musical instruments remained intact and the originals have now been placed at eye-level below the gallery where they can be seen better. Luca della Robbia was one of the founding fathers of the Renaissance style and this is one of the great sculptor's most important marble works. It uses formal elements already known in the fourteenth century, and the strict division of its panels gives it a traditional appearance when compared with Donatello's solution. Its great artistic importance lies in the reliefs. The illustrations are based on texts from the 150th psalm, engraved in large Roman script on both cornices and on the lower moulding so that each panel is accompanied by the appropriate text. The angels are playing the instruments mentioned in the psalm; in the upper left panel below the trumpeters, 'LAUDATE EUM IN SONO TUBAE'; below the central panels depicting harpists and lutists, 'LAUDATE EUM IN PSALTERIO ET CYTHARA'; below the kettle-drummers on the right, 'LAUDATE EUM IN TIMPANO'. The choristers, string-players, organists and cymbal-players of the lower row of panels are accompanied by the words, 'ET CHORO . . . IN CORDIS ET ORGANO . . . IN CIMBALIS', not forgetting the soloists, 'LAUDATE EUM SONATIBUS'.

Besides the galleries this room also contains a number of statues from the Cathedral and the Campanile, among them some important pieces by Donatello. The *Zuccone* (Big-head) received its name from the strange shape of its head. It is not clear which Saint it represents (Job, perhaps). He is dressed in a toga-like cloak and was carved in 1423–5. The pronounced and very Florentine physiognomy of this ascetic figure put Vasari in mind of a portrait likeness, but it should be understood rather as an ideal representation of the penitent. To the right of it is *Jeremiah*, the last of the original Cathedral statues, by a fifteenth century Florentine sculptor (completed 1435). On the narrow wall opposite, *The Sacrifice of Isaac* (1421); it was designed by Donatello, who also carved Abraham's head, and was completed by his pupil Nanni di Bartolo, 'Il Rosso'. The group, with its half-turned bodies and powerful movement, appears as one piece, and one has to visualize it, and the other figures, in niches. In form it betrays the influence of Late Classical sarcophagi reliefs. The *Beardless Prophet* belongs to Donatello's early period (1416–18).

In the next room (entrance on the 'Zuccone' side) hang the original hexagonal reliefs from the lower storey of the Campanile. The pieces previously exhibited here were moved to the ground-floor room next to the entrance, but after the flood disaster of 4 November 1966 they were removed from exhibition until further notice. The collection includes a much treasured relic, the *death mask of Brunelleschi*. There is also a delicately carved *organ gallery* from the Baptistery. The wooden *models for the Cathedral façade* are of particular interest. They include a white-tinted design by the Accademia del Disegno which uses incrustation in the same way as it appears on the sides of the Cathedral. Further models are by Buontalenti, Don Giovanni de'Medici, Giovan-antonio Dosio, Cigoli and Giovanni Bologna. The series of models of the dome dates from after the completion of the building. The collection also includes various schemes for the decoration of the drum, the stylized maze floor from the first bay of the Cathedral nave and a modern model of the dome.

Returning to the singing gallery and passing through a tiny ante-room containing seal-stamps and measures (principally for the masts of the Grand Dukes' galleys, after 1600), the visitor enters a larger hall in which, apart from some very fine *embroidered vestments* depicting scenes from the life of John the Baptist after designs by Antonio del Pollaiuolo (completed 1480), the chief piece is the *silver altar* from the Baptistery. This unique testament to the art of the Florentine goldsmiths is in five parts: a central niche with a pointed arch (containing Michelozzo's statue of John the Baptist), two groups of relief panels to either side of it and two panels on each end. The whole is held together by an enamel-work frame, articulated with richly inlaid pilasters and terminated at the top by a frieze containing niches with figures. The altar is 115 cm high, 263 cm wide and 53 cm deep. In the lower left-hand part of the base an enamelled inscription in Gothic lettering gives the date of the commencement of the work as 1366. The original design had been only for a 'dossale' or altar-frontal. The end panels were the last to be added, at the end of the sixteenth century. The detailed chronology is as follows: 1366 onwards, manufacture of the eight relief panels of the front; 1452, 60 cm (2 ft) high statuette of John the Baptist by Michelozzo; 1477–80 Cennini's *Visitatio* and below it the *Birth of John the Baptist* by Antonio del Pollaiuolo on the left-hand end, and on the right-hand end *Herod's Banquet* by Antonio di Salvi and Francesco Giovanni, and Andrea del Verrocchio's *Beheading*. The magnificent *altar-cross* on the sixteenth century wooden top of the silver altar is by Antonio del Pollaiuolo (1457–9). It contains a highly venerated relic of the Cross from Constantinople. Almost 1 m high and only slightly altered, it is one of the most glorious pieces of its period. The delicacy of the silverwork is particularly noticeable on the base (unfortunately all the enamel covering has been lost). The figures set within round forms show the influence of Florentine medallion art.

The Archbishops' Palace – Palazzo Arcivescovile

Begun in 1582 by Giovanni Antonio Dosio for Cardinal Alessan-

dro Medici, later Pope Leo XI (hence the papal coat of arms on the north corner; the matching one on the south corner is modern), the building was left unfinished in 1605 until Ciurini completed it in 1737. With its numerous elements of medieval architecture, the building was a picturesque sight until in 1895 it was pulled down because of a rearrangement of streets and re-erected 50 m further back. During this operation, the façade was extended southwards from eight bays to eleven. Both side-walls and the rear are modern.

The building once looked very different. Since all the bays were treated identically, and the entrances were in the loggia openings (the present two portals are new), its appearance was rather dry. The façade, with its square windows between the floors, is stretched between powerful corner pilasters. Windows with pointed gables, all furnished identically with the builder's inscription, alternate with round-arched windows. – The **courtyard**, by Ciurini, is a rare High Baroque example of Late Renaissance imitation. On the left is the entrance to **S. Salvatore nell'Arcivescovado**, a church first mentioned in 1032. It has an incrusted façade facing on to the Piazza dell'Olio. The interior decoration dates from after 1737. Domenico Ferretti and Vincenzo Meucci had a hand in the remarkable architectural paintings.

Loggia del Bigallo

This decorative, mid-fourteenth century building, initially the home of the 'Misericordia' (see below), was from 1425 onwards the headquarters of the Compagnia di Santa Maria del Bigallo, an order devoted to the relief of the sick, whose founder, S. Peter Martyr, is represented by a statue under the left canopy on the north side. The open loggia is reputed to have been used for the display of orphans for adoption.

The extremely ornate style is the work of Alberto Arnoldi, who modelled himself on the founder of this kind of rich decoration, Andrea Orcagna. It is an interesting mixture of sacred and secular architecture. Although blocked up in the seventeenth century, the building has been well and almost completely restored. The *fresco* on the outside is only partially ancient. Inside the loggia is a venerated statue of the *Madonna with Child* with two angels (1359–64) in an early sixteenth century tabernacle. This is best seen in the evening when it is illuminated. The stained glass in the round north window is of the nineteenth century, as is the window itself.

The Sala del Consiglio contains some important works of art but is closed at the moment.

The Misericordia – Arciconfraternità della Misericordia
This oldest and most famous of Florentine charitable institut-ions, under the pressure of a series of devastating pestilences, has since the thirteenth century united citizens of all classes in the care of the sick. Even today, the voluntary helpers wear distinctive black hooded cloaks (formerly red, now white, in summer). The present building, to the south of the Cathedral, was begun by Alfonso Parigi and has been occupied by the brotherhood since 1567. It has been altered and extended many times since then. The visitor can enter the **chapel** from the street by a door on the left. Behind the altar is some fine blue-and-white terracotta work (*Madonna and SS. Cosmas and Damian*, the patron saints of doctors) in the style of Andrea della Robbia, *c.* 1480–90. Ask per-mission to visit the **main building** for it contains two sculptures that should not be missed: a *Madonna with Child* and a Michelangelo-like *S. Sebastian* (*ill.* facing p. 81), both unfinished. They are the last works of Benedetto da Maiano (*c.* 1497).

The Santa Croce District

The Square – The Church – The Pazzi Chapel

The visitor finds himself in a particularly spacious **square**, which is all the more unusual in that the building of most interest is medieval, and medieval piazze of this size are not to be found anywhere else in Florence, with the ex-ception of the Piazza della Signoria, but that had a public function. Over the centuries the square has been encroach-ed upon to some extent. The **fountain** at the west end dates from the seventeenth century but was completely restored in the nineteenth century (according to Borghini the re-mains of a Classical amphitheatre were uncovered here at the time of the first digging of foundations in 1572). The large **Dante monument** in the middle dates from 1865. The palazzi around the square mostly date from the sixteenth century, but buildings of a similarly demonstrative nature existed here throughout the Middle Ages. As to the purpose of such an extensive site, one can only see it in terms of an informal meeting-place for the populace. Some famous Franciscan sermons were preached here, and here too the noble families produced splendid plays and gave great pageants.

Two of the palazzi merit special attention: no. 1., the **Palazzo Serristori**, attributed to Baccio d'Agnolo, with its corbelled projection, and no. 21, the **Palazzo dell'Antella** by Giulio Parigi, also with corbels (1619), and decorated with murals that were completed in only twenty days by various artists under Giovanni da San Giovanni. They include among other things a copy of Caravaggio's *Sleeping Putto* (now in the Palazzo Pitti) which must therefore already have been in Florence at that time. On the façade is a bust of Cosimo II; below it, a round plaque bearing the date 10 February 1565 and marking the centre-line of a kind of ceremonial football game (*Calcio in Costume*) that was played here quite frequently.

S. Croce

At the east end of the piazza, the monumental façade of the church of S. Croce immediately catches the eye. This is the largest of all known Franciscan churches and one of the most beautiful buildings in Italy. A number of masterpieces of the first order make it a veritable treasury of art. Latterly, particularly during the nineteenth century, S. Croce became a sort of pantheon of the Italian spirit, housing both tombs and cenotaphs.

The first Franciscan establishment in Florence is thought to have been founded by S. Francis himself. It was on a different site, nearer the northern edge of the city. The first Franciscan building on the present site may have been erected as early as 1228. By about 1252 it had already been enlarged, but it must still have been on a pretty modest scale. It was probably a hall-like church, situated more or less where the transept now stands, i.e. in a more easterly position than the present church.

This goes back to an expansive design which began to take shape in the eighties of the thirteenth century. The ex-

tremely imposing character of the design ran rather contrary to Franciscan principles, and the explanation may lie
in the rapidly growing influence which the Franciscans were
beginning to enjoy in Florence, particularly among aristo-
cratic families. However, it was not entirely without opposi-
tion that the design was adopted and begun. The architect,
according to Vasari, was Arnolfo di Cambio.

The foundation stone was laid in 1295. Following the usual
practice of the time, the walls were erected while the smaller, original church was still being used. About 1300, the
transept was near completion; the nave, which while still
incomplete already housed a number of tombs, was finished
somewhat later. The old church was pulled down shortly
afterwards, and part of the new building then used.
Except for the façade, which remained in its rough state
until the nineteenth century, the church was completed
shortly before 1385. Curious loggias were added on to the
sides to north and south. These appear nowhere else in
Florence and may have originated in North Italy (Bologna).

On the whole, subsequent periods produced little fresh
initiative. From the fifteenth century onwards, repeated
attempts were made to complete the façade – in 1450, for
example, an incrustation was begun – but most of these
attempts got no further than the drawing-board. Among
others, Cronaca has been mentioned in this connection. –
The most important changes to be made to the fabric were
undoubtedly Vasari's systematizations, begun in 1566. He
superimposed upon the irregular medieval decor of the
interior a row of stone altar tabernacles in the side aisles
and (probably his most decisive interference) removed
the high monks' choir which had stood in the centre of
the nave; adopting Brunelleschi's solution for S. Lorenzo,
he installed choir stalls in the chancel chapel. – The Niccolini chapel in the north-west corner of the transept was
built by G. A. Dosio in 1584–1608 (the cupola was not
added until 1652–64). A number of other alterations were
carried out during the Baroque period. – The original belfry
on the roof of the chancel collapsed in the sixteenth century,
and Francesco da Sangallo began to erect a separate bell-
tower beside the façade (in the first bay of the north loggia).
Never finished, it was demolished in 1854, after the present

*bell-tower behind the south transept had been completed in
1842 (the architect, Gaetano Baccani, modelled it on that
of the Badia). – The present façade also dates from the
nineteenth century. It was completed in 1863 by Nicola
Matas, who based it on a gothicized drawing from the
seventeenth century (in the Opera di S. Croce), and was
consecrated in the presence of Pope Pius IX.*

*Extensive restorations during the nineteenth century un-
covered numerous fragments of fourteenth-century frescoes
which had been overlaid with whitewash. All attempts to
restore the church to its original medieval state, however,
were doomed to failure by the insurmountable obstacle of
Vasari's alterations.*

*Of the extensive monastic buildings attached to the church
the most important examples date from the Renaissance.
These are Brunelleschi's Pazzi Chapel, a noviciate by
Michelozzo and a beautiful cloister.*

We begin on the **left side** of the church with the *loggia*
added after 1350: an arcade of pointed arches with keystones painted black and white and a gable above each bay.
The third bay is slightly higher than the others, and once
contained a portal leading into the church. At the east end
of the arcade is a *marble tomb* by a disciple of Tino da
Camaino (*c.* 1330). On the west side of the transept arm is
the entrance to the *crypt*, now a war memorial. Architecturally speaking, this constitutes a kind of lower church;
the central room is typically Arnolfian. – The **façade** (by
Nicola Matas) was based on a seventeenth-century gothicized sketch. The marble technique was copied from the
Cathedral. The central wooden door was brought here from
the Cathedral in 1903.

The **interior** measures over 115 m in length and the transept
is more than 73 m wide. Its lofty spaciousness and simple
grandeur are reminiscent of certain of the Early Christian
basilicas in Rome. The building has three aisles (it is 6 m
wider than Amiens Cathedral) and an open timber roof
(*ill.* facing p. 96) with richly painted rafters (last restored
1958–9). A passageway runs along the central longitudinal
axis. On first impression, the church is like one of the
'preaching-barns' of the mendicant friars. The octagonal
pillars stand on bases; the treatment of the stonework is
delicately differentiated. There is a gallery along the clere-

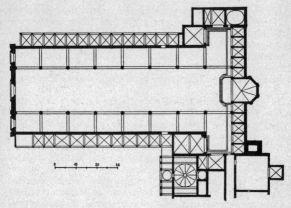

S. Croce, ground plan

story. The nave extends without interruption to the wall at
the extreme east end of the church, in the main chancel
chapel. The transept arms meet the nave in pointed arches
of the same width as those of the nave arcades, emphasiz-
ing the continuity of the central space. The clerestory passage
rises before the transept, giving the impression that the
interior increases in height towards the east end. Warm
greyish-brown stone predominates in the interior. At one
time everything was painted with frescoes and ornamental
surrounds, and traces of the original decoration have been
preserved in the last chapel but one of the left transept arm
and on the entrance arch of the right transept arm. The
whole colossal structure goes back to a homogeneous plan
which reveals connections with the somewhat earlier Badia
(in part of façade) and S. Trinita (in the treatment of the
pillars).

The most outstanding feature of the **decoration** of the
interior is a series of paintings on glass, probably the most
important in Florence from the period between 1320 and
1450. Second place is taken by the 276 tombstones let into
the floor of the church. Those of the dal Pozzo family are
particularly noteworthy; they are situated to the left of the

first pillar, pointing towards the aspersorium depicting S. Francis (seventeenth century). Also there are two reclining figures in front of the central portal on the axis of the church, one of which is the tomb-slab of Agostino Santucci wearing his scholar's gown and lying on a rich Baroque pall (possibly by Domenico Rosselli). And thirdly there are many examples of good early nineteenth-century sculpture.

The façade is embellished with a magnificent *circular window* depicting the Deposition, after a design by Giovanni dal Ponte. The relief containing the monogram of Christ after the manner of S. Bernard of Siena (1437) was still on the exterior of the façade until the nineteenth century. – On the right, near the pillar, is an aspersorium of 1418, donated by a Franciscan whose tombstone lies at the foot of the font. – On the third pillar on the right can be seen the famous *pulpit* by the young Benedetto da Maiano (1472–6). It is warm ivory in colour, a masterpiece of architectural elevation which furnished the example for the decorative taste of a whole generation. The pulpit is firmly fixed to the pillar, which, since it is perforated to give access to the pulpit, has been somewhat strengthened at this point. The entrance door (round the back of the pillar) contains beautiful inlaid work from the sculptor's workshop. The pulpit is covered with figures and ornaments; the use of enamel is reminiscent of medieval custom (as on the pulpits of the Pisani). Five important marble reliefs depict scenes from the legend of S. Francis: (from the left) Confirmation of the Rule of the Order, Trial by Fire before the Sultan, Stigmatization, the Saint's Death, and the Martyrdom of the first Franciscans in Africa. Three clay models for these reliefs have been preserved in London, and a further one in Berlin represents a scene which was obviously rejected. Between the six supporting brackets can be seen the beautiful figures of Faith, Hope, Charity, Fortitude and Justice. – Against the last pillar on the left of the nave stands a nineteenth century memorial statue to L. B. Alberti (Bartolini, 1840–5).

In the side aisles is a cycle of pictures on the subject of Christ's Passion. Chronologically they begin in the far corner of the right side aisle. The visitor thus finds himself moving in the opposite direction to the sequence of events, and starting with Santi di Tito's *Crucifixion* (1568). – Turning from there to the first nave pillar, we see an aspersorium in the shape of a ship and above it a relief of an *enthroned Madonna* before a marble curtain gathered in knots. This gentle piece by Antonio Rossellino, originally painted and gilded, marks the tomb (below) of Francesco Nori who died in the Cathedral during the Pazzi Conspiracy. – Next, on the outer wall, is the *tomb of Michelangelo*. The body of the great artist was brought to Florence on 10 March 1564 where, on the instigation of Grand Duke Cosimo I, it was accorded the veneration normally reserved for a holy relic. The feast which was given by the Guilds to mark the occasion went down in history. The representatives of 'Great' art (Vasari, Borghini) were obliged to defend themselves against colleagues who veered more towards craftsmanship. The main differences hinged on the question as to whether sculpture or painting was to be considered first of the arts, and how the decoration should consequently be arranged and in what order the participating masters should be seated. Compared with the pomp displayed on that occasion, the tomb itself, designed by Vasari, seems rather modest. On top of the sarcophagus sit three figures: on the right, *Architecture* by Giovanni dell'Opera; in the centre, *Sculpture* (here therefore regarded as the 'first' art) by Valerio Cioli; and on the left, *Painting* by Battista Lorenzi. This last figure holds in her hand a statuette which, it is claimed, is a replica of a figure of a slave (now lost) belonging to the tomb of Julius II. It is not surprising to find such a statuette in an allegory on painting because, as we know from engravings of Bandinelli's school of drawing, such small figures were used by artists as models. The implication here is that painting drew exemplary inspiration from Michelangelo's sculpture. In fact a whole school of Manneristic painting grew up in Florence which was derived from Michelangelo's sculptural style. Painting equipment can be seen to the right of the statue. All the figures date from between 1568 and 1573. The bust of Michelangelo was executed by Battista Lorenzi after a bronze model by Daniele da Volterra. – A late work (*c.* 1572) by Vasari, *Christ carrying the Cross*, adorns the next altar. – The vast cenotaph to Dante (by Stefano Ricci, 1829), Florence's memorial to the greatest of her sons who died in 1321, an exile in Ravenna where he is buried, follows. The two allegorical female figures represent Italy and the mourning muse of poetry. The inscription reads: 'This memorial, which our forebears decreed in vain three times, was erected in 1829.' The first impulse for the monument came from a patriotic manifesto of 18 July 1819. Leopardi's second canzone, which is dedicated to the memorial, was composed in 1818. – The next panel picture is Jacopo Coppi del Meglio's *Ecce Homo* of 1577. – The monument to Vittorio Alfieri by Canova, a fine product of the Neo-Classical style in Florence, was completed in 1810. – The next panel, *The Flagellation* by Alessandro Fei, is dated 1575. – The *monument to Machiavelli* (1787) is by Innocenzo Spinazzi; on top of the sarcophagus sits the figure of Diplomacy. – Andrea del Minga's *Agony in the Garden* is supposedly based on a design by Giovanni da Bologna; the Flemish artist Giovanni Ponsi painted the scenery *c.* 1575. Behind this picture, as behind most of the altars, are remains of the fourteenth century frescoes. Important sections by Orcagna including *The Triumph of Death* (*c.* 1350) have been taken down and are now in the Opera di S. Croce. – The next altar tabernacle is one of Donatello's major works. He carved this *Annunciation c.* 1435 for the Cavalcanti family. The greenish stone is highlighted with gold paint (restored in 1884). An architectural frame surrounds the inner area where Mary and the angel appear in relief, with only their heads carved in the round. Perspective is used to increase the depth of the room in which they move; for example, the seat is set back from the plane of the relief. The beautifully expressive and delicately attuned movements by which the group is made to 'rhyme' may have been inspired by Ghiberti's melting style (the font at Siena). The tabernacle ornamentation, however, is inspired by Classical forms, principally Roman; the expressions of the masks on the pilaster capitals are quite demoniac. Red clay figures for the acroteria had already been suggested by Alberti; the putti with garlands above the entablature belong to the Annunciation scene. Whether the round form in the niche-like lower entablature once contained an inscription plaque is not known. – Beyond the door to the first cloister is the *tomb of Chancellor Leonardo Bruni* (1369–1444) by Bernardo Rossellino, another seminal work of the Florentine Renaissance. The man who is buried here came from a simple family, rose to the position of secretary to Pope John XXIII, became Chancellor of Florence and ended life as a world-famous scholar. On his chest lies the folio volume of the history of Florence, his chief work. His body was laid out in this manner at his funeral, so that he should be 'honoured in the tradition of the ancients'. The two eagles of Zeus seem about to carry the bier off to Olympus (traditionally their place was taken by lions). The sarcophagus is tall and powerful. On the front, two winged angels bear an inscription, the text of which was composed by Bruni's successor, Chancellor Marsuppini, and speaks in Classical fashion of the mourning of the muses and of the Greeks and Romans at the passing of so highly respected a man. The chisel-work of this niche tomb of 1444–5 is incredibly fine, like sculptural chamber music, as it were, showing the delicacy of which Renaissance sculptors were capable. The entire work was originally richly painted. – The next monument, to Gioacchino Rossini, is by Cassioli and dates from 1900. – The altar-piece, *Christ's Entry into Jerusalem*, is the first of the Passion sequence which extends down to the entrance-wall and then continues in the left side aisle. This picture was begun by Ludovico Cigoli, who completed the heads but left the rest for Biliverti to finish. – At this point there are some particularly beautiful tomb-plates let into the floor. On the left, that of Ugo Foscolo (by Antonio Berti, 1939). On the pillar are the oldest decorative frescoes in the church. Let into the wall is an inscription referring to the laying of the foundation stone, giving the date as 3 May 1295. – On the corner into the transept is the heavily worn tomb-slab of the knight Lodovico degli Albizzi, after a design by Ghiberti, 1427.

Turning into the right transept (tomb of Count Neri Corsini de'Fantacchiotti, 1860; above it a fourteenth-century ornamental moulding), the visitor comes to the **Castellani chapel**. Added in 1383, it consists of two bays roofed with rib-vaults. In the corner immediately to the right can be seen the stairs up to the nave gallery. The whole chapel was frescoed by Agnolo Gaddi and a number of collaborators including – according to Vasari – Starnina. The *frescoes* tell the stories of S. Nicholas (right, first bay), John the Baptist (right, second bay), S. John the Evangelist (left, first bay) and S. Anthony Abbot (left, beside the altar, and continued

on left wall of second bay). The S. Anthony frescoes are
attributed to Starnina. In the seventeenth century all the
frescoes (except the vaults with their Early Fathers and
Evangelists) were painted over with whitewash and were
not seen again until 1870, when they were found to be in a
good state of preservation. They were restored in 1920–2.
Apart from the frescoes, the chapel contains some beautiful
early nineteenth century tombs, including that of the coun-
tess Stolberg-Albany, which was designed by Percier though
executed by Italians (structure and ornament by Luigi
Giovanozzi, putti and reliefs of Faith, Hope and Charity
by Santarelli). It is an interesting return to the style of the
Renaissance. – Two glazed terracottas of the school of della
Robbia: on the right S. Francis and on the left S. Bernard
of Siena (both c. 1500). – The niche tomb on the left wall
of the second bay is early sixteenth century. – The modest
'pietra dura' altar must date from c. 1600. Above it and
below the windows is a painted crucifix by Niccolò di
Pietro Gerini, dated 1380. – On the outer wall, two Prophets, and in the arches, Apostles, S. Louis of Toulouse and
S. Giovanni Gualberto.
Next to it, also comprising two bays, is the **Baroncelli**
chapel, added in 1328. The interesting tomb immediately to
the right of the entrance is that of the family. Dated 1327,
it represents Florentine sculpture at the period when, though
still noticeably under the influence of Pisa, it was just beginning to develop a style of its own. The tomb is attributed
to Giovanni di Balduccio, a Pisan colleague of Tino da
Camaino. In its architectural elevation, elements of the
tabernacle mingle with those of the sarcophagus. Developed
on both sides, it is designed to be viewed either from outside
or from within the chapel. The aperture is closed by a
grating, an idea which Verrocchio took up in the Old Sacristy of S. Lorenzo. To the right and left are small twisted
columns. The entablature on top of these columns is surmounted by a delicate bracketed cornice which bends at
right angles, linking the columns organically with the rear
wall. In the *lunette*, a half-figure of the Madonna by
Taddeo Gaddi (c. 1328). On the lid of the sarcophagus is
an inscribed plaque borne by angels. Originally the tomb
was resplendent with blue and gold. It is important as a
forerunner of the Florentine niche tomb. – The frescoes in

Cathedral, the old façade (drawing in the Museo dell'Opera del Duomo)

*Cathedral, Porta della Mandorla, head of S. Thomas
(Nanni di Banco)*

this chapel are the principal work of Taddeo Gaddi, probably the most faithful of Giotto's pupils; they represent scenes from the life of the Virgin. Painted in 1332–7, they are remarkable both stylistically (being a mixture of Giotto and the Sienese style) and iconographically (containing novel elements taken from Christian literature). Around the inner face of the entrance arch are ten medallions with Saints. On the vault-heads of the first bay, four medallions in grisaille depicting Virtues. On the transverse arch of the second bay, octofoils with Christ, four Evangelists and four Early Fathers. On the vault-heads of the second bay, another four medallions in grisaille depicting Virtues. – On the left-hand end-wall, on the base, are two panels with arrangements of objects comprising the incunabula of still-life painting. Above are powerful frescoes in two rows and in the arch. Small painted columns and an entablature separate the individual paintings.

In the arch, Joachim being chased out of the temple; on the right, the annunciation to Joachim. Below, left, the meeting at the Golden Gate; right, the birth of Mary. Bottom left, Mary going to the temple. Part of the stairs and the figure of Mary were renovations (they have now been removed); it is possible to reconstruct the original from a drawing in the Louvre. On the right, the marriage of Mary. – Turning to the window-wall, around the window are fifteen medallions with allegorical illustrations; in the left arch panel, the *Annunciation to the Shepherds*, on the right the *Adoration of the Shepherds*. Bottom left, the *Star appearing to the Magi*, and right, the *Adoration of the Magi*. – On the pillar before the next bay: above, Joseph; below, David with the head of Goliath. – The right end-wall was moved forwards slightly during the fifteenth century when Brunelleschi's Pazzi chapel was added on behind it. Traces of this operation can be seen in the shortened vault ribs. The fresco is therefore also of a later date: it shows the *Assumption of the Virgin* and the *Donation of the Girdle to S. Thomas*, painted in 1480 by Sebastiano Mainardi after a design by Ghirlandaio. In front of this wall stands a large statue of the Madonna by Vincenzo Danti (*c.* 1568). The totally unmanneristic style of this phase of his work can be seen very clearly in the rather summary treatment of detail (notice too the flat fingers, worked as if in relief) and the generally restrained impression. – The fine *stained-glass windows* probably go back to designs by Gaddi.

Leaving the chapel, the visitor sees on the outer wall on the right (above the Baroncelli tomb) a painting of the *Guardians of the Sepulchre*, and in the spandrels of the entrance arch four prophets. Further to the left is the twelve-year-old Jesus in the Temple, partly destroyed by Michelozzo's beautiful *portal* (*ill.* facing p. 97). This portal, erected *c.* 1445, is one of the master's most influential pieces of work. The handsome but slightly damaged doors with their intarsie are by Giovanni di Michele. The portal leads to a corridor with stone benches to right and left and windows which are still basically Gothic in form. The lunette on this side of the portal depicts a *Madonna with Saints*; at the crown of the arch, a *S. Francis* attributed to Raffaellino del Garbo, as are the fresco remains (*c.* 1500) to the right of the portal, with fragments of an angel. The corridor leads to Michelozzo's **Novitiates' chapel**, built after 1434 under the sponsorship of Cosimo Pater Patriae. This contains some more recent tombs, including those of the sculptor Bartolini and in the far right that of the art collector Lombardi; in style (pseudo-Donatello), this is typical of the nineteenth century's leaning towards imitation (until quite recently the relief was regarded as being fifteenth century). Above the altar, a *Coronation of the Virgin* by the school of della Robbia.

Passing through a door, the visitor finds himself in an interesting Florentine leather-workers' workshop. A second portal leads to an ante-room in which modern completions of *frescoes by Giotto* were once exhibited (they have since been removed). They were remarkable for the extraordinary degree of empathy with their subject which the nineteenth century restorers achieved. – Beyond this is the **sacristy**.

This is a large, self-contained room almost like another church, with an open-frame roof and a separate, rib-vaulted chancel, known as the Rinuccini chapel, one of the most perfect examples of a fourteenth century chancel in existence. It is separated from the main room by a magnificent wrought-iron *screen* (1371). An inscription at the top of the screen states that the chapel is dedicated to the Birth of the Virgin and to S. Mary Magdalen. The *frescoes* constitute the principal work of Giovanni da Milano, together with assistants (c. 1366); stylistically they derive from Taddeo Gaddi (Baroncelli chapel) but introduce new elements stemming from a specifically Tuscan tradition. The story of S. Mary Magdalen is represented on the right, that of the other patron, the Virgin, on the left; Prophets are depicted on the ceiling and on the inner faces of the arches. — An interesting feature of the main body of the sacristy are the beautiful fifteenth and sixteenth century cupboards. They were decorated partly with small pictorial panels now in the Museo dell'Accademia. The chests on the south wall contain *miniatures* (c. 1400), vestments and articles of gold. There is also a fifteenth century lavabo by Pagno Portigiani and a small cupboard with inlaid doors. — The glazed terracotta bust of Christ is by Giovanni della Robbia. — The polyptych of the *Madonna with Child and Ten Saints* is by Lorenzo di Niccolò Gerini (early fifteenth century). — The triptych, *Madonna with S. Gregory the Great and Job*, is by Nardo di Cione (1375); the predella, depicting scenes from the story of Job, in collaboration with Jacopo di Cione. — Here too there is an interesting series of frescoes: *The Way to Calvary* by a pupil of Spinello Aretino, c. 1400, *The Crucifixion* by a disciple of Gaddi, c. 1340–55, *The Resurrection* by Niccolò di Pietro Gerini, c. 1400, and *The Ascension* by a pupil of the latter, c. 1400.

Returning to the church, the visitor finds a series of **ten transept chapels** (not including the chancel), containing a number of priceless masterpieces. The first is the *Velluti chapel* or chapel of S. Michael, with frescoes by an immediate follower of Cavallini or Cimabue. On the right is the *Victory of Michael the Archangel*; on the left a bull marks the site of the chapel of S. Michael in Gargano. The pictures, in the Byzantine style, are badly damaged. By the window are two saints. The lower part has been restored. A work by Giotto that belonged in fact to the Baroncelli chapel now stands on the altar; it displays the beginning of his late style. A polyptych, painted for the Baroncelli, it depicts the coronation of the Virgin in the centre with saints and angels playing musical instruments on the side panels, and is entitled *Opus magistri Jocti* and dates from c. 1330. The signature with the frame may have been renewed in the fifteenth century. — The next chapel is the *Calderini* or *Riccardi* *chapel.* The exceptionally beautiful decoration was executed by Gherardo Silvani *c.* 1620; the ceiling recalls the decorative style of Giovanni da San Giovanni. On the right, a *S. Francis* by Matteo Rosselli; on the left, *S. Lawrence distributing gifts to the Poor* (Passignano). On the altar, Biliverti's *Discovery of the Cross by S. Helen.* – The next chapel is called the *Bonaparte chapel* because members of the emperor's family are buried there. The window is modern.

In the next chapel, the *Peruzzi chapel*, the visitor finds some important frescoes by Giotto; they are among his most mature works (after 1320). They were painted over with whitewash in 1714 and uncovered and much restored between 1841 and 1863. A modern restoration, begun in 1960 with the intention of exposing remains of the original, led to the result that most of the painting was done *a secco.* In detail: in the archivolts are eight busts of Prophets and on the ceiling symbols of the Evangelists (that of Matthew appears to be an addition); on the right wall, the story of S. John the Evangelist: from the top, *S. John on Patmos*, the *Raising of Drusiana* (some expressive figures among the crowd here; the cupolas in the background are reminiscent of Padua) and the *Assumption of S. John.* On the window-wall are four not easily identifiable saints. The left wall depicts scenes from the life of John the Baptist. On the top, Zacharias, with the angel announcing that soon a son will be born to him, then the birth, the naming, and finally Herod and the scene with Salome. – The influence of Giotto's style upon the art of the period was like that of a new gospel. The principles of composition which the master introduced were as simple as they were novel, isolating individual actions and confining each picture to one particular moment in time. Into these simplified physical events he breathed a totally new power and immediacy. Every movement of his figures is entirely natural and meaningful. On a horizontal plane, which recedes back into the picture, he placed these figures in such a way as to make them appear firmly rooted to the ground. Through this, the master absorbed himself in some of the problems of Classical sculpture, which he overcame in his later stylistic period, introducing a further degree of calm and relaxed solemnity.

The same applies to the decoration of the adjoining *Bardi chapel*, which Giotto apparently executed before the Peruzzi chapel. Here scenes from the legend of S. Francis are depicted. The *Stigmatization* high up on the outer wall is particularly beautiful and well-preserved (with two medallions bearing the heads of Adam and Eve). Inside the chapel on the left wall, the changing of the Saint's clothes before Bishop Guido and Father Bernardo, and the Saint's appearance to the brothers at Arles. Michelangelo particularly admired the death scene, with the sceptical Girolamo who doubts the stigmata. – Right wall: the founding of the Order, the ordeal by fire before the Sultan (*ill.* facing p. 112) and the visions of Brother Augustine and Bishop Guido of Assisi. – In the archivolts, eight busts of Saints; in the vault, the three virtues of S. Francis – *Poverty* (in rags, with a little dog barking at her), *Obedience* (holding the Rule of the Order and with her forefinger to her lips) and *Chastity* (guarded by angels in a tower). The fourth figure, that of S. Francis, is modern. – On the window-wall, S. Louis (the matching figure was a forgery and has been removed) and below, SS. Elizabeth and Clare. – The Bardi chapel frescoes were restored in 1958–9 and now contain large holes which distract from the continuity. But if one can no longer admire the series in its entirety, one can at least enjoy the unspoilt purity of the detail, the bright colouring and the wonderfully confident brushwork. The figure of the Sultan in the scene of the ordeal by fire is virtually incomparable. – On the chapel altar is a panel depicting S. Francis with twenty scenes from his life, late thirteenth century, school of Lucchesi (Berlinghieri), a typical Romanesque altar-piece terminated at the top by a gable. The strongly silhouetted figure of the Saint in the middle is most impressive. The band around and between the pictures is decorated with foliage and contains small busts of Franciscan monks stretching out their hands towards the founder of the order.

On the altar of the **chancel** is a polyptych with a Madonna and Saints (by Niccolò Gerini) and four Early Fathers (by Giovanni del Biondo). The ornaments and the predella are by other masters, including Mariotto di Nardo. The arrangement has been assembled from fragments of other altars. The central part of Lorenzo Monaco's predella (Death following a young hunter) is particularly beautiful, though

rather awkward to study. – The walls and ceiling of the
Alberti chapel were frescoed by Agnolo Gaddi. The theme is
the legend of the Cross. Painted shortly after 1374, these well-
preserved frescoes are a good example of the Florentine art
of the last quarter of the fourteenth century, when picture
and frame were regarded as being of equal decorative
importance. The story begins in the right arch panel, with
two scenes one above the other. In the top one the Archangel Michael appears to Seth as he kneels on the mountain;
below, Seth plants the sprig he has received from the Tree
of Knowledge on Adam's grave. Lower down, the tree
which grew from the sprig has been turned into a bridge,
and the Queen of Sheba kneels before it. The wood is then
collected and buried. Later the Israelites pull the wood
from a fountain and make out of it the Cross of Christ. In
the last scene on this wall, S. Helen finds the Cross which
has been buried again after Christ's Ascension. The story
continues on the left wall: S. Helen carries the Cross
triumphantly to Jerusalem, and Chosroes, the Persian king,
has it taken out and mocked. In a dream the Byzantine
emperor Heraclius is commanded to join battle with Chosroes. The emperor is victorious (the battle is on the right),
has the Persian king beheaded, returns to Jerusalem and,
having divested himself of the emblems of his authority,
enters the city with the Cross. According to Vasari the
figure at the bottom right with the beard and the red ker-
chief is a self-portrait of the artist. – On the window-wall
are Saints, and in the windows some beautiful *stained glass*.
On the side pillars, Saints in tabernacles. On the inner face
of the entrance arch, twelve busts of Saints. In the sex-
partite vault, S. Francis, John the Baptist and the four
Evangelists. – The great painted triumphal cross (hanging
up) is attributed to the master of the *Fogg Pietà*.
The first of the five **transept chapels** north of the chancel
is the *Tosinghi chapel*, renovated during the nineteenth
century. On the outer wall, an *Assumption of the Virgin*
by the school of Giotto; on the altar, a polyptych by Giovanni del Biondo (1372; predella by Neri di Bicci). – The
two following chapels have also been completely renovated.
– The fourth is the *Pulci chapel*, decorated with early frescoes by Bernardo Daddi and his assistants. These are the
only monumental paintings (*c.* 1330) by this master to have

been preserved. They are painted over an older layer of simulated marble incrustation which can still be seen in the lunette. Looking at these paintings, the Martyrdoms of SS. Lawrence (right) and Stephen (left), one must bear in mind that the parts which were applied 'al secco' have to-day completely disappeared. – On the altar is a rather un-pleasantly coloured terracotta by Giovanni della Robbia, a *Madonna with Saints*, the hair and flesh picked out with oil paint (c. 1525).

Last of the row is the *Bardi di Vernio chapel*. Powerful frescoes by Maso di Banco, a pupil of Giotto, depict scenes from the life of S. Sylvester. Left, Constantine's dream, with the vision of Peter and Paul. Right, Constantine listens to the forebodings of S. Sylvester and allows himself to be baptized; the Saint raises a bull; he closes the mouth of a dragon and raises two Magi who had been killed by the monster (an interesting landscape of ruins, intended either to illustrate the dragon's misdeeds or to symbolize Classical Rome). – The heavily damaged lunette on the left represents Constantine's reluctance to bathe in the blood of Christian children, as he had been advised to do to cure his leprosy. – On the left wall of the chapel are two *tombs*; in the niche of the larger one, surrounded by a handsome Gothic frame, is a fresco of the *Last Judgement* by Maso di Banco, including the adoring figure of Bettino de'Bardi rising from the dead. The historical importance of the tomb lies in the fact that it accords to a lay person the pomp and splendour normally reserved for the ecclesiastical class. Although a papal decree of 1221 had allowed laymen to be buried inside churches, this was usually done in a very simple manner, tombs of the more elaborate 'avelli' type being confined to the exterior. The resurrected figure is ingeniously painted in such a way that it appears to be floating out of the carved tomb; two Saints facing each other to right and left act as his intercessors. The paintings have been touched up since 1830 and it has become difficult to say what is original and what is not. In the niche of the smaller tomb to the right is an *Entombment of Christ* with a modest lady donor (attributed to Taddeo Gaddi).

In the north-east corner of the transept arm, a beautiful portal flanked by Corinthian columns leads to Dosio's **Niccolini chapel** (if closed, contact the sacristan) which is

richly decorated in marble. Begun in 1584, it was not finished until 1650. The frescoes in the cupola are by Volterrano, the statues by Francavilla. Clay models of Aaron,
Moses and Humilitas (after 1585), possibly from the hand
of Giovanni da Bologna, are preserved in the Bargello. The
pictures (*Assumption* and *Coronation of the Virgin, c.* 1590)
are by Allori. – On the altar of the adjoining chapel is
Donatello's well-known *wooden crucifix*. This early work
came in for some severe criticism from Brunelleschi, who
objected to this manner of portraying Christ as a 'peasant',
not a point of view from which one might be expected to
arrive at an accurate assessment. Today this very sensitive
piece is regarded neither as 'crude' nor even as 'realistic'.
The highly stylized features seem to go back to the Middle
Ages. The arms of the sculpture are hinged so that they can
be folded together when, at Easter, the figure is lowered
into a Holy Grave. Doubts have been raised occasionally
as to whether this really is the early crucifix by Donatello
that sparked off Brunelleschi's criticism, or whether in fact
it was the one from S. Francesco al Bosco (now in the
repository of the Bargello), but as yet nothing has been
proved. – To the left of the entrance is the *tomb of the
Bardi*, an example of the fourteenth century Pisan style. It
is the counterpart of the Baroncelli tomb in the corresponding position in the south transept arm, and in form is related
to the tomb in the Bardi di Vernio chapel. – On the south
side of the transept arm is the *Salviati chapel*, redecorated
in 1661 by Gherardo Silvani. On the left wall is the tomb
of Princess Sofia Zamoyska Czartoryska (by Bartolini) which
in Italy has always been highly regarded for its fine realism.
On the altar, a *Martyrdom of S. Lawrence* by Jacopo
Ligozzi.
Towards the corner of the nave is the monument erected
in 1869 to the composer Luigi Cherubini, who was born in
Florence in 1760 and died in Paris in 1842, and on the
corner, to the right, the tomb of Raffael Morghen, the
famous copper engraver who tirelessly reproduced the
masterpieces of Raphael and other artists of his period (both
monuments are by Odoardo Fantacchiotti). – The altar-
piece, Vasari's *Pentecost* of 1568, is the last of the Passion
cycle. – Among the memorial tablets is that of Amerigo
Vespucci. – Next to an inscribed plaque commemorating

Vespasiano da Bisticci is the *tomb of Carlo Marsuppini*, one of the chief works of Desiderio da Settignano (1455–66). Modelled on B. Rossellino's Bruni tomb in the south aisle opposite, it is one of the most beautiful examples of this Renaissance type. The ornamental detail is developed richly and abundantly. The angel on the right of the Madonna in the lunette may possibly be by the young Verrocchio. Set into the floor in front of the tomb is the heavily damaged tombstone of Gregorio Marsuppini (also by Desiderio). – Above the side door is the huge organ designed by Vasari and built by Noferi da Cortona in 1579. Its famous and richly sonorous works had to be renovated in 1931. – To the left is a frescoed *Assumption of the Virgin* by Agnolo Gaddi, and below it another tomb by Bartolini, that of Vittorio Fossombroni, statesman and hydraulic engineer. – Notice, too, the *Ascension of Christ* by Stradanus, 1569, and the hallowed spot on the floor which marks the last resting place of Lorenzo and Vittorio Ghiberti. On the wall, Bronzino's *Pietà*, *c.* 1560. – Vasari's *Doubting Thomas* (*c.* 1570) adorns the fourth altar.

The overall impression of the aisles of S. Croce, so strange and yet so characteristic, is the result of the mixture of fourteenth-century paintings, important Florentine altarpieces of the sixteenth century and nineteenth-century tombs. The end of the left side aisle is very much an example of this, with Santi di Tito's *Supper at Emmaus* (one of his most important works, dated 1574) and on the next altar the same master's *Ascension of Christ* (the pleasant clarity of both works typifies the fundamental differences between him and the school of Vasari) standing in immediate juxtaposition to Niccolò di Pietro Gerini's fresco fragments *(Noli me Tangere)* and the monument to Galileo Galilei. The bust of *Astronomy* on the Galileo monument is by Foggini, that of *Geometry* by Girolamo Ticciati (1737). – An *Entombment of Christ* by Battista Naldini adorns the last altar; on the wall, Saints in the manner of Uccello (possibly), *c.* 1450.

Leaving the church by the west end and turning south, the visitor finds on his left the entrance to the cloisters of the convent (there is an entrance fee). The buildings on the right or south side of the first cloister date from the Gothic period; on the left is the arcade of the loggia of the

church and straight ahead the vestibule of Brunelleschi's
Pazzi chapel. Originally this court was formed of two small
fourteenth century cloisters, but these were gradually
merged to form the present cloister, which is somewhat
irregular in plan. On the wall between the church and the
Pazzi chapel, to the left, is the tomb of the Patriarch of
Aquileia, Gastone della Torre († 1317), attributed to Tino
da Camaino and originally situated inside the church. At
the time of writing it has been removed for restoration
work but it will probably be re-erected in the same place.
The tomb is incomplete. Some of the details are in the Opera
di S. Croce. One has to picture an additional Gothic arcade
of small turned columns. (Compare the Petroni tomb in
Siena Cathedral.)

The **Pazzi chapel** is one of the earliest and best-known
examples of Renaissance architecture. It served both as the
monks' chapter-house and as the funeral chapel of the Pazzi
family. Brunelleschi began it in 1430 for Andrea de'Pazzi.
Certain sections, e.g. the upper storey of the front, remain
incomplete. Six tall Corinthian columns support an attic
of which the centre is stressed by a triumphal arch. The
balustrade between the two left-hand columns, a modern
reconstitution from remains which have been discovered,
originally ran between all the columns. There are interesting
similarities with the architecture of the Baptistery; lateral
pilasters cut into the main arch, winged cherub-heads adorn
the entablature, and the transverse arches of the tunnel vault
have an ornamental band (in the Baptistery this occurs on
the underside of a horizontal entablature supported by
columns). In the centre of the tunnel vault is a cupola (not
detectable from outside), decorated with beautiful glazed
terracotta *rosettes* by Luca della Robbia (*ill.* facing p. 113),
who was also responsible for the relief of S. Andrew (*c.* 1445)
above Giuliano da Sangallo's *wooden doors* (1470–8).

The extraordinary influence which this little chapel was to
have on the stylistic development of European architecture
calls for some explanation. It is impossible to grasp the
building as a whole either from the outside or from within,
but only by entering it and proceeding through each of its
individual parts. The vestibule is very wide, resembling a
rounded beam. The centre is accentuated by the relatively
small cupola which can be understood as a sort of three-

Pazzi chapel (S. Croce), longitudinal section

dimensional correlative of the large entrance arch. The principal room is different. Its gay interior, also with a lateral stress, is crowned by a very much more powerful dome in twelve segments. The relative effect of this dome is greater than that of the vestibule, and this progression reaches its climax in the chancel, where the whole ceiling is one dome. This part of the building is completely centralized, gathered together under the dome which dominates and at the same time protects it. In order to understand the extent of the development of Brunelleschi's style from the Old Sacristy of S. Lorenzo, one must appreciate the progression inherent in the layout of these three rooms (from vestibule

to main room to chancel). Here for the first time (and this
was later to be the basic problem at S. Spirito), the master
treated a building with a combination of directional and
centralized spatial units. This first example of a 'scenic'
building treated in succeeding elements, an idea which was
seldom taken up again, is not without a certain psychological
drama which should not be overlooked. – The return to a
Classical style is shown by the use of details from the Baptistery (which Brunelleschi must have regarded as being
Classical). The clarity and rationality of his architecture is
seen at its best in the geometrical purity of the articulation
of the interior. In each corner, two pilasters come together
forming an axial point which is the point of intersection
of two wall planes. The floor, with its axial division, is
very similar to that of S. Spirito. Brunelleschi may have
intended the interior to be painted throughout, as is
suggested by the four terracotta tondi in the pendentives.
These depict seated Evangelists and are probably by Luca
della Robbia (some authorities name Brunelleschi as the de-
signer). The twelve tondi depicting Apostles in the wall
panels can be attributed to Luca della Robbia on stronger
evidence. The colourful frieze of cherubim with the Apocalyptic Lamb on the altar with the seven seals was inspired
by the decorated capitals of S. Lorenzo. – The signs of the
Zodiac painted in the dome above the altar have not yet
been attributed beyond doubt to a particular master. The
very remarkable paintings on glass were designed by Baldovinetti.

Leaving the chapel, the visitor sees on his right Vasari's portal
leading to the church, and beside it the recently uncovered
remains of an old fourteenth century entrance with black
and white voussoirs and a painting of S. Francis in the
lunette. – On the left, on the lawn, stands Bandinelli's *God
the Father* (1549), a powerful monument originally designed
for the high altar of the Cathedral. Jupiter-like features give
the figure an expansive power. In the corner a handsome
portal, probably by Benedetto da Maiano, leads to the
second cloister. This was designed by Brunelleschi but not
built until after his death, with the possible assistance of
Bernardo Rossellino. Its simple, large and (in the inter-
columniation) generous proportions radiate such a feeling
of calm contentment that many people consider this

cloister, once richly painted, to be one of the most beautiful that the Renaissance produced.

A corridor leads down the south side of the Pazzi chapel to a war memorial, and from this small courtyard the visitor has a view of the east side of the chapel. An interesting old waterspout in the corner near the church shows that Brunelleschi incorporated part of a fourteenth century wall.

The first part of the south side of the first cloister is taken up by the **Canigiani chapel**, at present being restored, which houses among other things a large altar-piece by the school of della Robbia. Further on down the same side is the **Museo dell'Opera di S. Croce**, once the refectory. The vast representation of the *Last Supper* on the end wall, the oldest preserved example in Florence, was painted by Taddeo Gaddi and his assistants in 1330–40. Vasari thought it was by Giotto himself. It was the first time the theme of the Last Supper of Our Lord had been used to decorate a refectory. The figures of Christ and the Apostles are almost larger than life-size, and they overlap the ornamental bands that separate the main picture from the other scenes in such a way that they appear to sit in front of these. The large picture above depicts *S. Bonaventura's Vision* of the Crucified Lord as the Tree of Life. Bonaventura (in the mitre) is seated before the trunk of the Cross writing down what has been revealed to him. S. Francis, kneeling, embraces the Cross. On the right stand S. Louis of Toulouse, S. Dominic and another Franciscan bishop. The small female figure kneeling on the left probably represents a benefactress. On the extreme left is a group of mourners including Mary and John. On the twelve branches of the Tree of Life are scrolls inscribed with references to the life of Christ. Four side pictures depict (above) the miracles of SS. Francis and Benedict and (below) the deeds of SS. Louis and Mary Magdalen. The frescowork has been restored several times and the socle is modern. Originally there were benches here so that the monks sat immediately beneath the Apostles' feet. – On the south wall is Donatello's gilded statue of *S. Louis* in a copy of its former niche in Or San Michele, from which it was removed as early as 1463. The figure is completely draped; technically it consists principally of monumental folds moulded together and mounted around a framework; this drapery is among the most splendid produced during the Renaissance. In style

it formed the basis for Donatello's figures for the Campanile. The features of the royal saint are shown in the
purity of youth; otherwise every single part of the body is
covered, even the hands (gloves). The figure, cast after
1420, is holding in his hand a crozier which is interesting
from the stylistic point of view. A small round temple rises
on brackets above a Corinthian capital. Naked, winged
shield-bearers stand guard before its scalloped niches. Probably one should picture a curved top to the end of the
pommel. – *Cimabue's crucifix* is a work of tremendous inner
power. For a long time its place was inside the façade-wall
of the church. It was then moved to the Uffizi but was
damaged in the floods of 1966. – Notice too the frescoes
which have been taken down (Orcagna's *Triumph of Death*)
and the fragments of the della Torre tomb by Tino da
Camaino. – And the visit would not be complete without
a look at a picture which was for a long time a neighbour
of Donatello's *Annunciation* in the Cavalcanti chapel – *John
the Baptist and S. Francis.* This famous fresco, painted after
1455 by Domenico Veneziano, was long thought to be by
Castagno, to whose work it bears a strong stylistic resemblance (compare his *Jerome* in SS. Annunziata, *ill.* facing
p. 144). Both figures are seen from below, standing inside an
arch before a landscaped background. Important from the
technical point of view are the dotted lines (pouncing),
showing an early use of cartoon. It is not known where the
picture was placed originally. It once bore an inscription
commemorating Benedetto Cavalcanti. The saint's expressions are devout: John ecstatically acknowledging his inner
voice, Francis listening to the voice of faith. It is important
to note that the above description relates to the pre-flood
(1966) situation. At the time of writing, restoration is
imcomplete.

The Santissima Annunziata and San Marco District

*SS. Annunziata: the square and the church – Archeological
Museum – Palazzo Grifoni – Ospedale degli Innocenti –
Accademia – S. Marco and the Fra Angelico Museum –
Casino Mediceo*

If the Cathedral area constitutes the religious centre of Florentine life and the Signoria area the secular centre, the two neighbouring squares in the northern part of the city, those of SS. Annunziata and S. Marco, constitute the spiritual and intellectual centre. The Medici once had a large garden here which was decorated with Classical sculpture and of which Donatello and Bertoldo were appointed curators. Here the sculptors of the Early Renaissance were able to absorb the influence of Classical style. Such diverse spirits as Savonarola and Fra Angelico, as well as the subtle theologian Antonino, even today one of the most highly respected figures in the history of the city, were associated with S. Marco. In the *Rotonda* of SS. Annunziata, Alberti developed his intellectual ideas. With, in addition, two important museums, to say nothing of the University, this is still very much the 'intellectual quarter' of present-day Florence.

SS. Annunziata: the square and the church

The Piazza Santissima Annunziata can with justice be described as one of the most harmonious architectural creations of the whole of Florence. It is enclosed on three sides by arcades which, while belonging to various different periods, are all stylistically related. Approaching by the Via dei Servi, the visitor finds himself opposite the portico of SS. Annunziata. Beyond it on the left, the upper portions of five Gothic windows belonging to the old Servite monastery can still be seen. Down the right-hand side of the square runs the colonnade of the Ospedale degli Innocenti, a pioneer building by Brunelleschi, and opposite this, on the left, the matching (it is a copy) Loggia by Antonio da Sangallo the Younger (together with Baccio d'Agnolo, 1516–25). The former Palazzo Grifoni (now Riccardi-Mannelli) juts out on the left, in the south-west corner of the square. This is one of the principal works of Bartolommeo Ammannati. – In the northeast corner of this extensive complex is the Archeological Museum.

A monument and two fountains subtly articulate the broad expanse of the square. The equestrian statue of Grand Duke Ferdinando I was designed by Giovanni da Bologna but not completed until 1608 by Tacca. Approached in this direction, from the Cathedral, it constitutes the focal point of the square. It is simple in style, with the horse smooth and plain. An inscription on the underneath of the girth tells that the metal used in the casting came from booty captured from the Turks. The rear side of the socle, which was decorated in 1640, bears Ferdinando's seal: a swarm of bees clustered round the queen, with the motto, 'Majestate tantum'.

The **church**, lying on an almost north-south axis on the north side of the square, is famous throughout the Roman Catholic world for its venerated *Annunciation* fresco.

In 1250 the Servite Order of Monte Senario (to the north of the city), which at that time had only been in existence for a few years, established a settlement on this site. Its church was later to become the principal church of the Order, but to begin with only a small chapel was built. Then, according to legend, a fresco inside the church, which a monk named Bartholomew started painting in 1252, was miraculously completed by an angel. Following this the church began to receive so many pilgrims that it had to be enlarged.

In 1254 a considerable extension was planned and this was completed by 1262, but it was not long before further extensions were being undertaken, financed partly by private persons (including the cloth merchant Chiarissimo de'Falconieri). By the fourteenth century the convent had reached approximately its present size (with two large cloisters). The architect is thought to have been Neri di Fioravante, assisted by the carpenter Antonio Pucci (who also worked on the Loggia dei Lanzi). Pucci made a wooden model for a further extension of the church which was undertaken in 1350. There were no radical alterations until the fifteenth century. Prompted by the general upheaval of artistic ideas which was taking place, the Medici formulated a plan for reorganizing the entire site and put Michelozzo in charge of its execution. The Renaissance was considerably to alter the overall appearance of the building.

The fourteenth-century basilica, of which the octagonal pillars were retained (and are still partly visible today), was taken as the basis. The side aisles were converted into rows of chapels and the nave was made higher. Instead of the normal medieval chancel, a powerful dome structure was erected. These were the principal alterations, but the new

Cathedral, detail of the shrine of S. Zenobius (Lorenzo Ghiberti)

Misericordia,
'S. Sebastian'
(Benedetto da Maiano)

design also extended to the forecourt and the sacristy. Classical influence is everywhere in evidence. Borghini himself referred to the forecourt as an 'atrium'. The transformation of the basilican church into a hall with rows of chapels represents a decisive turning-away from the Gothic tradition. The 'Rotonda' (as the centralized chancel structure is called) is modelled on the Classical temple of Minerva Medica in Rome. It was with the laying of the foundation stone of the Rotonda in 1444 that rebuilding began.

Soon afterwards the foundations of the sacristy and the nave chapels were being laid. The left-hand row of chapels was finished in 1450, and by 1453 the whole nave was complete, including the roof. The forecourt, too, was complete by then, as well as the baldacchino-like arch over the entrance, which was to form the core of the colonnade erected at a later date (1601–4).

Meanwhile, however, no progress had been made with the rotonda. Work did not really get under way until 1453, under the patronage of the Marchese Gianfrancesco Gonzaga, only to be held up again shortly afterwards, possibly because of technical difficulties. The next phase in the history of this important building took the form of a series of theoretical architectural discussions, with Brunelleschi's voice being raised in criticism. It was Alberti, however, who won the day. Supported by the Duke of Mantua, he stuck to the old plan and in 1471 linked the rotonda with the transept, thereby eliminating the old side chancels. By making the two semicircular niches on either side of the opening smaller than the others, he was able to make the opening wider and thus relate the rotonda strongly to the rest of the church. By 1477 the building was vaulted and complete.

The effects of the miraculous Annunciation fresco continued to be as beneficial as ever. The Baroque period brought a fresh wave of beautification and the whole of the interior was renovated. The richly carved flat ceiling was donated in 1669. Further embellishments in stucco, gilding and coloured marbles continued right up into the eighteenth century. This decoration required great care and restoration work was consequently continuously in progress. A particular problem were the votive images of wax and papier-mâché

*which once hung in their thousands from the rafters. They
were larger than any that have been recorded elsewhere
and their weight constituted a considerable static hazard.
We know of at least six hundred life-sized effigies, including kings and even generals on horseback, and more than
forty times that number of smaller images.*

The *arcade* along the front of the church was developed by
Caccini out of the original 'baldacchino' of the central arch,
and he designed it to match Brunelleschi's Ospedale degli
Innocenti on the east side of the square. Above this central
arch, erected by Manetti in 1453, can be seen the figures of
Caritas and *Fides* by the young Pontormo (1514), beside
the marble coat of arms of Leo X. Above the portal is a
mosaic *Annunciation* by Davide Ghirlandaio, *c.* 1510. –
Passing through, the visitor enters the **cloister** of the forecourt (roofed with glass in 1833) which lies across the front
of the church. With its characteristic capitals (*ill.* facing
p. 128) it is an excellent example of Michelozzo's style. It is
painted; above on the left, a monk holding a book is looking out of a simulated window, and to the right of him is a
vase with white lilies. The most important paintings, however, are on the walls inside the cloister. They give the visitor
his first great impression of the art of Andrea del Sarto
(whose bust, by Caccini, 1606, is in a niche on the left-hand
side) and his school. Those on the right depict scenes from the
life of the Virgin, those on the left the miracles of S. Filippo
Benizzi, patron saint of the Servite Order.

The first panel on the right just beside the entrance is an
Assumption by the young Rosso (*c.* 1515), his first important painting and a work of solemn majesty and vigorous
compactness. There is something at once simple and monumental about the balance the artist achieved between the
Apostles and the ascending Virgin (not unlike Titian's
Assunta in this respect). The comparative lack of differentiation in the colouring is a pointer towards the future. –
Beside it is Pontormo's *Visitation*, also the work of a young
man on the threshold of great deeds (1516). The figures
appear larger than is customary in Andrea del Sarto's own
work. There is an almost architectural mastery in their undulating flow; painted steps seem to lead from the spectator
up into the apse, creating a strong formal framework and
at the same time increasing the illusion of space, so that thi

powerful work has the eloquence of a historical image. – Next, on the right-hand wall of the cloister, is the *Betrothal of the Virgin* by Franciabigio, painted shortly before 1515. The painter himself destroyed the Virgin's head and refused to repaint it because the monks had exhibited his work before it was finished. Later a head was added but this has now been removed, leaving the damage visible. – The *relief of the Madonna* next to it is by Michelozzo (moved here in 1922; the frame is modern). Its severe, compact style is slightly reminiscent of Mantegna. – The next work, the *Birth of the Virgin* by Andrea del Sarto, dated 1514, signed and monogrammed, is an example of the master's mature Classical style. The tectonic severity of his early work (seen in the S. Filippo Benizzi murals around the opposite corner; the visitor is virtually walking backwards through Andrea's stylistic development!) has given way to a freer, more rhythmic style. The standing women give firm support to the magnificent curve of the figure composition. Wölfflin draws attention to their air of nonchalance. The problems presented by filling up the space with ornamental architecture are here solved; the fireplace no longer looks as 'lost' as it appeared in earlier pictures. The woman who is glancing behind her is thought to be the artist's later wife, Lucrezia del Fede. The group of angels on the baldacchino may have been executed by Pontormo. – On the façade of the church the visitor finds Andrea's *Procession of the Three Magi*, painted in 1511. We know from Vasari that the three men grouped together on the right are portraits of Jacopo Sansovino, the musician Aiolle and the artist himself (sketches have been preserved). Notice how the figures are composed in a sort of garland; the lightness of the colouring shows this to be a work of the artist's early period. – On the other side of the door of the church the visitor will find one of the most beautiful landscapes produced by the new art, Alesso Baldovinetti's *Nativity* (between 1460 and 1462). Its original matutinal colouring is now somewhat changed. – The S. Filippo Benizzi scenes begin on the left wall with the *Vision and Investiture of the Saint* (there is a view of Florence in the background), and above it the *Triumph of Chastity*, by Cosimo Rosselli, c. 1475. – All the remaining murals were painted in 1510 by Andrea del Sarto. In the first, the Saint clothes a beggar. Beyond the tabernacle of coloured marble containing Caccini's bust of Andrea, lightning strikes down some bandits who have ridiculed the Saint. Next, the Saint heals people possessed by demons (notice the beautiful landscape backgrounds in these two pictures), and on the entrance-wall, the Saint's death and the healing of a child who had touched the Saint's clothing. The old man on the right of the latter picture, wearing a red robe and kneeling on one knee, supporting himself with his stick, is reputed to be a portrait of Andrea della Robbia. The whole series still shows clearly the master's stylistic influences: Leonardo, Fra Bartolommeo and the young Raphael.

On the east side of the cloister is a door (usually locked) to the **chapel of the Pucci family** (there is a second entrance from the square). This was built in 1606–7 by Caccini and his pupil Gherardo Silvani, replacing an earlier, fifteenth-century chapel. The decoration consists of frescoes by Poccetti and a number of late sixteenth and seventeenth century tombs.

It is not easy for the visitor, entering the **church** of SS. Annunziata for the first time, to absorb this important architectural monument correctly. It is very different, for example, from a building by Brunelleschi, which is lucid, rational, and immediately impressive. Here one is confronted with a wide, freely developed space which is articulated in a way that is difficult to grasp as a whole and which, aesthetically, lacks the enthralling, almost moral severity imparted by Brunelleschi's architecture. However, the historical importance of this building should not be underrated; it represents the first manifestation of a type of architecture that was to be developed further by Alberti in Mantua and by Vignola in Il Gesù, Rome, an architecture which is more 'confessional' than 'intellectual' in character. Yet there are certain similarities here with Brunelleschi's style, for example in the debt it owes to Gothic. While, however, in the case of S. Lorenzo, one senses the Gothic influence initially in the ground plan, in Michelozzo's church Gothic elements have influenced the actual substance of the building; the high architrave, for example, was determined by the old Gothic transept arms. The later Baroque additions naturally mitigate this impression.

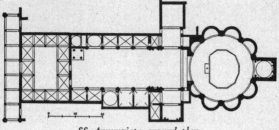

SS. Annunziata, ground plan

The splendid **decoration** dates for the most part from the late seventeenth century, but the individual chapels were completed at different periods. The handsome ceiling was designed by Volterrano, who also painted the *Assumption* at its centre. The clerestory is uniformly decorated with stucco (apparently after designs by Pier Francesco Silvani); a series of pictures represents the miracles wrought by the venerated *Annunciation* fresco, as do the (later) medallions above each side chapel.

The miraculous fresco itself is now situated inside a *tabernacle* which was designed in 1448 by Michelozzo and executed by Pagno di Lapo Portigiani (from Fiesole). It was donated by Piero di Cosimo de'Medici. The ornamentation on top of the entablature does not belong to it; it was designed by Volterrano and executed in 1674. The floor (renovated) is by Bernardo Rossellino, 1462. This tabernacle enjoyed a certain influence in Tuscany, for example in Impruneta. The *venerated image*, usually concealed behind a curtain and a metal blind, is on the south or façade-wall. The Medici had many copies made in order to present them to friends and a number of these have survived (there is one in Cologne Cathedral). The oldest of these copies is on the façade-wall inside Ognissanti. The fresco, a warmly introspective *Annunciation*, was painted in 1252 but was obviously heavily restored in the fourteenth century so that it looks in effect like a fourteenth-century work. – Parts of the decoration of the tabernacle are worth particular attention – the beautiful grating of interlinked ropes of bronze, reminiscent of Verrocchio, the remarkable silver relief on

the altar (the son of Ferdinando I praying for recovery
before the miraculous image, after a design by Matteo
Nigetti, c. 1600), the rich silver frame around the fresco
itself, designed by Giulio Parigi (1624), and the many lamps
(most of them quite recent) which cast a subdued light.
To the right of the tabernacle a small *chapel* extends westwards. The fine, richly ornamented marble facing *(ill.
facing p. 129)* of 1461–2 is unique. The lower part of the
wall was incrusted with 'pietra dura' work in 1670. On the
wall is a silver tabernacle, donated in 1617, and inside is a
half-length portrait of Christ by Andrea del Sarto (1515).
Leaving this holy place, which is always thronged with the
faithful, and crossing the nave, the visitor comes to the first
side chapel on the right. The wall-tomb on the left is fourteenth century; the frescoes were painted in 1627 by Matteo
Rosselli. The altar-piece *(Madonna with Saints)* is regarded
as the last work by Jacopo da Empoli. On entering the
chapel and turning, the visitor can see the remains of the
octagonal Gothic nave pillars with their foliate capitals on
either side of the front wall. – The next chapel is similarly
decorated, with an altar-piece by Empoli (c. 1590) and an
old tomb-slab in the floor. – The third chapel is one of the
principal works of Matteo Nigetti. The abundant, rather
florid style of 1643 divided the walls into Michelangelo-
like blocks. The vault, now so dark as to appear virtually
black, was painted by Volterrano. In the niches on either
side are powerful sarcophagi with small kneeling figures by
Francesco Mocchi in their coats of arms. The next chapel
but one, i.e. the fifth chapel, was frescoed in 1677 by Ulivelli; these scenes, depicting Servite martyrs and painted
partly in grisaille, are now in rather bad condition. The
lunette-monument on the left was carved for Orlando
Medici in 1455 by Bernardo Rossellino, on the model of the
tomb of the Strozzi family in S. Trinita. The garland of
oak leaves surrounding the arch is particularly beautiful.
The last resting-place of Admiral Tommaso Medici (c. 1590)
opposite is a more economical example of the same genre. –
The whole of the decoration around the organ was designed
in 1521; both the designs and execution of these sculptured
members suggest the authorship of Benedetto da Rovezzano.
The *Resurrection* over the altar is attributed to Maso da
San Friano (mid sixteenth century). The two fluted balusters

which support the table belonged originally to the altar
of the miraculous fresco (*c.* 1450).

Turning into the **right transept**, the visitor will find, inside
the entrance arch of the *first chapel* on the right, and immediately to his left, an oval niche containing a bust of the
painter Stradanus (born in Bruges) which was erected by
his son Scipio. Lower down on the right, farther into the
chapel, is an interesting tomb-plate, that of the Lübeck
goldsmith Heinrich Brunick (known as Arrigo Fiammingo)
who was responsible for the silver dossale on the high altar.
The lively sgraffito was probably based on a design by
Foggini. – The chapel at the end of the transept is decorated
in the 'Roman' style by Ferdinando Fuga. The chapel on the
north side contains a large *Pietà* in which Christ's body is
supported by a Nicodemus whose features are those of Baccio
Bandinelli. Bandinelli signed and dated the work in 1559;
according to Vasari, it was completed by his son Clemente.
Baccio had intended the tomb for the bones of his father,
but after transporting them here himself, he caught a disease
which killed him a week later, so that he was buried here
as well (together with his wife). The cross-shaped sword
– from Jerusalem – is the Bandinelli coat of arms.

It requires a measure of abstraction to visualize the **tribune**
in its present form as an epoch-making building. This
monumental structure completely rejects the traditional
medieval treatment of space, not least in the way in which
it is related to the church. The idea for a circular domed
building with nine semicircular apses came from the temple
of Minerva Medica in Rome, but the execution departed
from the complete symmetry of the model, e.g. in the two
apses which Alberti reduced in size so as to improve the
connection with the church and in the extension of the
north apse into a rectangular chapel which was carried out
by Giovanni da Bologna. One can only guess at the original
articulation of the walls here. Basically, of course, it goes
back to the fifteenth century (round-arched openings with
flat pilasters, the cornices above the arcade), but the present articulation dates from Foggini's Baroque renovation
of 1685–1703. – In front of the powerful opening to the
nave are two tombs: on the left, Francesco da Sangallo's
tomb of Bishop Angelo Marzi-Medici, signed and dated
1546, and on the right that of Bishop Donato da Antella

by Foggini (1702), which attempts in a curious way to match the left pendant for aesthetic reasons. Beneath the triumphal arch are two further tombs: the design and figures of both are by Caccini, the architecture by Gherardo Silvani (the one on the right is dated 1609). The figures represent SS. Peter and Paul. Turning to the high altar, the visitor cannot help but admire the splendid silver dossale, designed by Foggini and executed by Heinrich Brunick of Lübeck (1680–3), and the silver tabernacle dated 1655. The Neo-classical marble tabernacle of 1822 on the altar table itself has an embossed silver door which was made after a design by Bertel Thorwaldsen. – Walking past the northward-facing chapel to the left of the opening (simulated architecture by Cosimo Ulivelli, altar by Volterrano, both 1671), the visitor comes to a small door which leads out of the rotonda.

Volterrano's great painting of the *Assumption and Coronation of the Virgin* (1681–3) dominates the dome. One's view of it is somewhat impeded by the high wall of the monks' choir. This was designed by Gherardo Silvani and executed by Alessandro Malavista in 1667 (the doors beside the high altar were added later, in 1705). Figures from various periods adorn the corners of the polygon; those worth particular attention are Francavilla's stucco *Caritas* (*c.* 1600) above the door on the north side, a *S. Gaudenzio* by Montorsoli, and some figures by Casali; the authorship of the latter figures is attested but they are not easy to decipher in detail. The choir-stalls are nineteenth century copies of Giovanni d'Unghero's originals (1528–39). From the north side one can occasionally catch a glimpse of the interior of the monks' choir, where there are two brass lecterns in the form of eagles. The smaller one is the better; it bears an inscription (almost worn away by cleaning) which identifies the donor as Bardi and also a – very rare – workshop mark in the form of an A. Both lecterns may have been cast in England, shortly after 1500.

Starting from the high altar and moving round in an anticlockwise direction, the *second chapel* the visitor reaches contains an altar-piece of the *Betrothal of S. Catherine* by Biliverti (1642), a pupil of Cigoli; Vignali painted the fresco on the ceiling and also the two side pictures. The polygonal decorative architecture was carried out by

Gherardo Silvani; the bands of incrustation behind the columns are reminiscent of Tuscan Proto-Renaissance. – The architectural decoration of the *third chapel* represents a rare venture into this field by Passignano (1604–5), who usually worked as a painter; the altar-piece, in fact, is from his brush (*Jesus healing the man born blind*, the same subject as the picture on the right by Empoli, 1605). – In the next chapel (eighteenth century), which is very similar in pattern, the altar-piece is by Vignali. – The *central chapel* at the north end was decorated by Giovanni da Bologna and houses his tomb. Poccetti's cupola fresco of *Paradise* has darkened. The *Resurrection* (right, by Passignano) and *Lamentation* (rear wall, by Ligozzi) strike a note of solemnity. The chapel also contains a number of stucco figures, friendly round-faced angels and Apostles (?). The artist's sarcophagus, with two putti carved by himself, is on the wall behind the altar; the fourteenth century panel (restored) of the *Madonna* came from his own collection. The two candelabra beside the altar date from 1749. The stucco figures were made by Tacca, Giovanni da Bologna's powerful bronze crucifix was executed with the assistance of Francavilla, and the six bronze reliefs below the figures were likewise made by pupils after the master's originals, which are in the University chapel in Genoa and are slightly different in detail. They give a good though rather too smooth impression of Giovanni's relief style in the period 1575–9.

In the following *chapel*, decorated in the Baroque style in 1741, a wooden sculpture of *S. Roch* (on the right) by Veit Stoss immediately catches the eye. This sculpture was recently stripped of a coat of white paint which had been applied to make it look more like the marble figure on the left, and it became evident immediately that it was a work of high quality. This nordic figure contrasts rather strangely with its Italian surroundings, not least because Roch is represented as a frail old man; the Italians tended to depict their saints as youths or men in the prime of life. The theory, recently revived by de Salas, that this work is in fact by the Spaniard Juan de Juni who died in 1577 in Valladolid, is a somewhat improbable one. The altar panel of the *Resurrection* is by Bronzino (after 1548). – The next *two chapels*, featuring respectively an altar-piece by the school of

Perugino and late seventeenth-century decoration, can be passed over quickly. The *ninth* and last *chapel* of the rotonda deserves more careful attention. Its decorative architecture, probably the earliest of all the chapels, was designed c. 1600 by Alessandro Allori. The altar-piece was painted by the same master; the composition of the details reveals draughtsmanship of a very high order. This work, dated 1602, has a somewhat luxuriant air; the high angle of vision brings out each element very clearly. Painted during the last phase of Allori's life, it shows a characteristic tendency towards the picturesque. The name *Bronzinus* in the signature refers to Allori's foster-father and teacher. The chapel also contains four scenes from the life of S. Manetto d'Antella: top right, Clement IV conferring privileges upon the Servite Order (Ligozzi, 1602); below, the Saint healing a lame man (Cristofano Allori, a youthful work, signed on the crutch which is lying on the floor); top left, the Saint setting out for Monte Senario (Alessandro Allori); below, election of the Saint as General of the Order (Passignano, 1602).

Turning right on the way back to the nave, the visitor comes to the *sacristy*. This still has the form Michelozzo gave it in 1444 – a rectangular hall with two domical vaults and a semicircular apse. The capitals are beautiful; as was always the case with Michelozzo's capitals. The richly decorated door is by Ambrogio da Fiesole (c. 1459). Parts of the decoration are seventeenth and eighteenth century (the painted architectural simulation!). Terracotta statues on the cupboards (by Ticciati, 1766) depict various Servite saints. – The passage leading to the rotonda was once a chapel, as can still be recognized from the ornamentation. The terracotta bust on the right wall is of S. Filippo Benizzi, and comes from the house where the saint was born. – The small *chapel* at the end of the corridor which branches off was built in 1622 by Passignano, who is buried there. Its name *(delle Reliquie)* derives from the holy relics which are preserved on the left of the entrance.

In the chapel at the end of the **left transept** is an important clay *statue of John the Baptist* by Michelozzo (1444–50). In posture, expression and physique it is not unlike the statuette in the silver altar from the Baptistery (now in the Cathedral museum). The simulated architecture was painted by the Frenchman Chamant in 1746. – The portal in the

south wall of the transept, with its small, gilded, Gothic
foliate tympanum, leads to the first cloister. The chapel
beside it was decorated by Cavaliere Radi after 1643.
More remains of the old Gothic nave pillars can be seen in
some of the chapels of what used to be the **left side aisle.**
Certain of the decorative pieces here deserve mention. In
the *second chapel* is an interesting altar-piece of the *Assumption*; the composition is familiar from the work of Perugino
but the execution is such that the piece must surely be attributed to the master's school. The *Crucifixion* in the *third
chapel* is by Stradanus, probably painted in 1569 (this is not
entirely clear because the last number is partially covered by
the frame). The two frescoed saints on the window-wall to
right and left are by the same master. Alessandro Allori's *Last
Judgement* on the left wall, painted in 1560, is particularly
interesting as a variant of the type created by Michelangelo.
The following chapel was decorated throughout by Allori,
although it appears that Vasari drew up a design before him.
The frescoes – left, the twelve-year-old Jesus in the temple
with the Pharisees; right, Jesus chasing the money-changers
out of the temple – were also inspired by the work of Michelangelo, particularly in the Sistine Chapel. Allori's *Last
Judgement* in the previous chapel originally belonged here;
the whole decoration seems to have been painted as a sort of
homage to Michelangelo. The 'Last Judgement' was moved
for a particular reason; beneath it was the now uncovered
masterpiece by Andrea del Castagno, depicting S. Jerome
(flanked by two adoring female saints) praying to the
Trinity, which can be dated *c.* 1454–5 (*ill.* facing p. 144). The
fifth and last *chapel* is resplendent with rich Baroque decoration after designs by Foggini, 1690–3. Among the numerous
artists who cooperated in this project was Soldani. Though
from a Roman school (he studied with Cirro Ferri and Ercole
Ferrata) he was nevertheless associated with the Florentine
school of Mannerism (by marriage as well; he married one
of Susterman's daughters). His bronzes are supreme works:
Abbondanza is seated on the sarcophagus on the right, with
the ship on her shield, on the left a portrait head in relief,
and on the altar, gilded bronze furnishings, a cross and
candlesticks. Above the altar is a fragment of an earlier
fresco (the upper part, depicting S. Julian, with Christ
above) by Andrea del Castagno, painted *c.* 1455.

The visitor can enter the **first cloister** either from within
the church (left transept arm) or from the colonnade outside. On the left in the passage leading from the colonnade
is the (closed) *Sacristy of the Madonna* (after 1635); on the
arch of the passage, a half-figure of Christ between *Misericordia* and *Justitia*, by Poccetti. – Passing through into the
cloister and turning round, the visitor can still see above the
south wing the remains (windows) of the **monastery building** of the years following 1364. – The cloisters are decorated
with paintings in the lunettes. Above the door in the north
wing that leads into the church is the *Madonna del Sacco*, a
masterpiece by Andrea del Sarto dated 1525. The remaining
frescoes, depicting the history of the Servite Order, are
masterpieces of the early seventeenth-century Tuscan school
(Poccetti, Giovanni da San Giovanni, Rosselli, Salimbeni and
others).

The principal feature of the first cloister, however, is the
famous **Painters' Chapel** in the north wing, designed by
Vasari (visitors should apply to the curator). Originally
the chapter-house of the monastery, this was given in 1552
to the Compagnia di San Luca and then subsequently to the
Accademia del Disegno (founded by the sculptor and Servite monk Montorsoli) as a meeting and burial place
(Cellini, Pontormo and Franciabigio are buried here). The
decoration was completed in 1575 (the ceiling being added
later). The visitor enters by way of a vestibule which contains
a number of beautiful pictures, including *The Martyrdom of
the Ten Thousand* by an artist who was close in style to the
late Bacchiacca; also the cast of a *Madonna* relief by Agostino
di Duccio, now in the Bargello. The ceiling of the chapel
itself depicts *S. Bernard's Vision of the Virgin*, and was
painted *c.* 1650 by Luca Giordano. Everything else dates
back to the original decoration: the emblems of the arts in
the floor (on the cover of the burial vault) by Montorsoli,
the handsome statues in their niches (twelve were planned,
but only ten executed), and the pictures, which cannot all
be attributed accurately. Four statues on the right wall
represent *Abraham* (Stoldo Lorenzi), *Moses*, *Paul* and *Peter*
(Giovanni dell'Opera). The grisailles refer to the figures
below them. The *Trinity* in the centre bears a date on the
left-hand side – 1571 and the letters 'IA. PU'; they cannot
refer to Pontormo, however, since he died in 1557. The true

signature is on the right-hand side, with the letters AN.BR.; the commission was given to Angelo Bronzino and his pupil and foster-son Alessandro Allori in 1567. The picture is slightly patched on the sides and on top. – The statue of Cosimo I on the rear wall is by Giovanni da Bologna, the fresco beside it depicting the *Madonna with S. Luke* is by Vasari, the altar predella is by Alessandro Allori. The second statue on this wall, Melchizedek, is by Camilliani; it originally stood against the entrance-wall beneath the painting depicting the same character. All the figures are of stucco. – On the left is a *S. Luke* by Vincenzo Danti. The fresco, *Madonna with Saints*, a typical example of the young Jacopo Pontormo's work, was painted *c.* 1513; it was moved here from the church of S. Ruffilo. The painted curtain is modern; the upper terminating semicircle has been destroyed. – On the entrance wall is *The Building of Solomon's Temple*, an allegory on architecture by Santi di Tito, who managed to include in the work (completed in 1571) a number of portraits, including those of Vasari, Sansovino, Michelangelo and himself. The whole painting was exactly prepared in sketches, and is meticulous, cool and severely stylized; the light colouring exemplifies the artist's move towards the High Renaissance style. There have been many changes since the flood of 1966.

There are other rooms containing works of art but they are not open. The second cloister (Baroque on a Gothic basis) to the north of the first is also closed to the public.

Archeological Museum (Piazza SS. Annunziata, 9b)

(After the flood of 4 November 1966, the museum was closed until further notice. The following description relates to the old collection.)

This is the most important museum of its kind in Northern Italy and it has been here since 1880. The core consists of the Egyptian collection brought back by Ippolito Rossellini's expedition, organized by Grand Duke Leopold II in 1828. It was a similar undertaking to those which the Frenchman Champollion performed with such success. The booty was first placed in the Uffizi, where it was immediately subjected to scientific investigations, some of the results of which were published. An Egyptian museum was founded as early as 1831 and was housed in various places. After 1870 it was augmented by the Etruscan collection as well as by the Graeco-Roman items from the treasures of the Medici family, including the 'Chimaera', the 'Idolino' and the François vase. The Egyptian collection itself was also increased after 1880, as a result of the expedition led by Ernesto Schiaparelli, making it the second largest collection in Italy after Turin. – The Etruscan collection, which was begun in the early sixteenth century, provides the most comprehensive survey of Etruscan culture that exists today. This is due to the efforts of L. A. Milani, who established a separate museum dealing with Etruria. The gallery of Etruscan painting (established in 1928 by A. Minto) was also a proposal by Milani.

Such is the wealth of material on show in the museum that it is only possible to provide here a rather cursory guided tour. – The visitor first enters the **hall of the Muses of Ferento**, with statues and architectural fragments from the Theatre of Ferento, excavated in 1902. Among these are the Muses, originally part of a group which was influenced by the work of Scopas. – The next room contains Greek, Roman and Etruscan sculptures.

Next come the rooms devoted to the **Museo Topografico dell' Etruria**. Objects are grouped according to where they were found. This gives an idea of the extent of Etruscan culture, which roughly covered the part of Italy west of the Apennines between Florence and Rome.

Rome, Veio, Cere (Capenates, Veientani, Caerites): Early graves with characteristic bronze fibulae. Painted geometrical vases. Well burials. Plaster-cast of the so-called *Throne of Claudius* from the Lateran with figuration from Tarquinia, Vulci and Vetulonia.

Agro Falisco (Naharces-Falisci): Various types of individual graves. Most of the items excavated from this rich necropolis are in the Villa Giulia, Rome.

Tarquinia (Tarquinienses): Assembled here are the principal findings from the three burials of the Villanova period in the Tarquinia necropolis, as well as other objects dating from the fourth century B.C.

Tuscania: Sarcophagi with pictures of the deceased lying on top of them in groups.

Bisenzio (Capodimonte): Various grave objects, including a helmet and an Italian vase in imitation Dipylon style. In the middle case, bronzes from Capodimonte and objects from the Palazzetta necropolis.

Orvieto (Volsinienses): Grave objects. In the cases in the window, a bronze amphora, a Greek crater with black figures, and the alabaster feet of a deathbed. In the following cases, fifth century Greek vases with black figures, as well as some Etruscan imitations. Some beautiful cinerary caskets. Above the doors, decorative terracottas from an Etruscan temple near Poggerello in the neighbourhood of Bolsena; the group with Minerva is particularly remarkable.

Vulci (Volcetani): Etruscan composite capital with the heads of Juno, Venus and the Dioscuri. Sarcophagi and fragments of sarcophagi, grave ornaments.

Poggio Buco, Sovana, Pitigliano (Statonenses, Suanenses): Grave objects.

Marsiliana d'Albegna (Caletrani): Fragments of graves; the remains of a war chariot are remarkable. In the middle case, some particularly fine oriental-style gold and ivory pieces; below them, a gold fibula (the *fibula Corsini*, named after the finder and donor) and a female statuette in ivory with traces of gilding. Of particular scientific interest is a small ivory writing-tablet with the oldest extant example of the Western version of the Graeco-Chaldean alphabet.

Saturnia, Heba, Cosa (Saturnini, Hebani, Cosani): Grave objects. Also the famous lead tablet by Magliano with a double spiral inscription giving the names of the gods and descriptions of votive rites.

Talamone (Telamon): Grave objects. On the exit side is the north gable of the temple with remains of terracotta figures depicting the fall of Adrastos and Anfiaraos.

Roselle: Grave fragments from this as yet largely unexplored centre of Etruscan culture.

Next come four rooms containing objects from *Vetulonia* (Vetulaniensis): Unusually shaped cinerary urns. A sacred bronze ship of the Sardinian type, symbol of the voyage to the life beyond. Gold bracelets. The grave stele of Aule Feluske, with one of the oldest extant inscriptions and incised drawings depicting a helmeted warrior with a spear and a two-headed axe. A bundle of lictors with a two-headed axe, as used later by the Romans. A tripod fragments of a chariot, jewellery, a deathbed, some fragments of sculptures which are among the oldest found in Etruria, helmets.

Populonia (Populonienses): This port was trading with Greece and the Near East as early as the seventh century B.C., reaching its peak in the fifth and fourth centuries. Three rooms are devoted to finds from this site. Gold, ivory, alabaster and bronze objects. A statuette of Ajax killing himself (Greek, fifth century B.C.). A bronze fibula with a statuette of Venus. Fragments of the two oldest chariots to have been discovered (partially restored).

Volterra (Volterrani): Cinerary urn in the form of an Etruscan temple. Stele of the warrior Larth Atharnie. Alabaster urns with various figurations (including Circe with the comrades of Ulysses).

Pisa: Inscriptions.

Valdelsa: Large terracotta candelabrum. Primitive Apollo (bronze). Front portion of a biga.

Florence and Fiesole: Fragments of graves. Primitive bronzes. Stele with the goddess of death; at the top is an Ionic palmette. A warrior stele from Fiesole. In the adjoining courtyard, fragments of the capitoline thermae and of the temple of Isis (which stood on the site now occupied by S. Firenze), as well as of a Roman amphitheatre from the Borgo dei Greci. Forum columns.

Chiusi (Clusini): This room shows the development of Etruscan portraiture. Further rooms contain burial urns, pieces of furniture made partly of bronze, ceramics, some very varied grave decorations, and sculptures.

Arezzo and Cortona (Arretini, Cortonenses): Ceramics. Tombs, some of which formed part of an architectural complex.

Perugia: Bronzes, javelins, a bronze mirror with the murder of Itys engraved on it. In the middle case, large Italic craters.

Luni: Gable terracottas of the second century B.C., the time of the Roman colonization, representing among others Artemis, Apollo, Jupiter, Juno, Neptune and the Niobides. Cameos, glass and cut stones.

The garden, too, forms part of the exhibition. This is of particular interest since here a number of tombs have been faithfully reconstructed from original material. Some of them can be visited inside. The visitor is recommended to use the museum guidebook.

One of the most important sections of the museum is the **Egyptian department**. It begins at the bottom of the stairs and comprises eight rooms on the first floor. Space is available here only for the mention of some of the most outstanding exhibits. Various statues of priests crouching include the priest Amenemehet on a stepped platform with sacrificial bowls before him. The polychrome woman grinding corn is very realistic. Note too the particularly fine painted mummy-cases, the relief depicting a crowd of busy scribes, the head of Rameses II, several steles with many illustrations of everyday life, the painted funerary chest, the busts of Pharaohs and the carved and painted portraits.

The following fourteen rooms contain **Etruscan, Greek and Roman antiquities**. These continue on the floor above, which also houses the collection of vases. Numerous Etruscan sculptures, most of them relating to the cult of death, are followed by a collection of bronzes. The most notable piece is the well-known figure of Idolino, which may have served as a lamp-standard. It is an original Greek work of the fifth century B.C. Attico-Peloponnesian school and one of a very few examples of its type. The nobility of the posture and the graceful beauty of the body have evoked profound admiration ever since the work was found (in 1530, in the ruins of a Roman villa near Pesaro). The base was renewed during the Renaissance. – No less well-known in Tuscany at least is the *Chimaera*, crouching as if ready to spring. The lion-like body is surmounted by a ram's head; the tail, in the form of a snake turning round to face forward, is of later derivation (sixteenth century). On the right front leg is the inscription *tinscuil*. Discovered in Arezzo in 1555, the work was brought to the Palazzo Vecchio through the agency of Vasari. – The *Standing Orator*, also famous, is probably a monumental burial sculpture of the third century B.C. It represents Aulus Metellus at the climax of a speech. A full

S. Croce, ceiling of the nave

S. Croce, portal of the passage leading to the sacristy (Michelozzo

inscription is engraved on the hem of his robe. The statue was found at Sanguineto in 1566. – Next comes a marvellous **collection of coins and a collection of cameos, glass, and gold and silver work.** – In the particularly fine vase collection the visitor must not miss the legendary *François vase*, an extremely elaborate crater – probably a wedding present – painted in the workshop of the Greek Ergotimos in the sixth century B.C. This priceless piece was found by Alexandre François in 1845 near Chiusi. In 1900, as a result of an unlucky accident, the vase was broken and had to be restored. The painting is in six bands. From top to bottom: the hunt of Meleager and the feast of Theseus and Ariadne (after the death of the minotaur); the funeral games of Patroclus and the fight between the lapiths and centaurs; the marriage of Peleus and Thetis; Troilus being wounded by Achilles and Vulcan recalled to Olympus; more animals, battle-scenes of pygmies, Diana and Ajax with the body of Achilles.

A visit to the museum would not be complete without a glance at the **Etruscan plaster collection** and the **Etruscan picture gallery**, particularly the latter; its fourteen rooms include copies of the most important grave paintings as well as panel paintings and painted sarcophagi, among which the first prize certainly goes to that of Lathia Seianti, discovered near Chiusi and dating – according to coins found on the site – from between 217 and 147 B.C.

Palazzo Grifoni (now **Riccardi-Mannelli,** on the corner of the Via dei Servi)

This remarkable palace dominates in an unforgettable way the south side of the Piazza SS. Annunziata. The site, which until then had been wasteland, was purchased in 1465 by a member of the Pucci family, who built on it a modest house with loggias. In 1515 the building became the property of Roberto de'Ricci, who enlarged it. S. Caterina de'Ricci was born there in 1522. The present palace was built for Ugolino Grifoni, a wealthy administrator under Grand Duke Cosimo I. Grifoni had bought the previous building in 1549. The architect was Bartolommeo Ammannati; he began the palace in 1557 and completed it in 1575. Certain alterations (particularly extensive inside) were made . 1890.

This handsome, reddish, shimmering palace is one of the most ostentatiously representative in the whole city. Ammannati wanted to erect a façade that would be worthy of the square. A problem was presented by the fact that the existing building had its façade on the side (the entrance is towards the street). Traces of the old house can still be seen on the side facing the square, e.g. the old portal, the eccentric position of which meant that the rusticated articulation had to be grouped around a window in order to give it a central axis. There are indications that Ammannati originally planned a somewhat lower building – two storeys with mezzanine windows and a double-portal structure in the middle. Some authorities believe that Buontalenti also participated in the palace as it now stands but this is doubtful. Alterations were certainly made, as witness the undulating inscription plaque on the left-hand corner pilaster and the fact that the coat of arms, which was probably situated on the central axis originally, has been moved to the extreme right. – Ammannati's mastery can clearly be seen in the extremely fine workmanship and the variety of the individual elements, e.g. the supporting brackets of the lower windows and in particular the interesting portal on the Via dei Servi. The fact that the ram – the *impresa* of Cosimo I – appears above the lintel and not the Grifoni coat of arms constituted a not unusual gesture of respect to the ruling house. The rams' heads in the passage are particularly beautiful. The courtyard suffered most from the alterations.

Ospedale degli Innocenti

The hospital is named after the massacred children of Bethlehem, who are regarded as the patrons of the many orphans who, over the centuries, found here a model home. The foundation was established by the silk-weavers' guild, which decided as early as 1419 to build an orphanage on this site. The task of erecting the necessary buildings was entrusted to Brunelleschi. The result was one of the first pieces of architecture in the Renaissance style.
Brunelleschi designed the whole complex, i.e. the loggia, the church and the buildings around the court. The work of building proceeded slowly. The first column of the loggia was erected in 1422. By 1424 the loggia was finished in its initial state, with the exception of the upper storey. Francesco della Luna took over the direction of the buildings around the court, of which the principal parts were probably finished by 1430. The upper storey above the loggia was completed in 1439. In 1444 the dressing of the columns of the central court was begun, together with the erection of the vaulting above the ambulatories. The first child was admitted on 5 February 1445. – The central court, however, was not completely in service until 1447–9; the church was consecrated in 1451.

The **loggia** is important from the historical point of view as the earliest example of the use of a colonnade supporting arches in conjunction with a large order of framing pilasters. Two aims had to be fulfilled – to do justice to the requirements of the orphanage, and to enhance the beauty of the Piazza SS. Annunziata. There are considerable differences between the façade facing the square and the parts behind it. The width of the loggia arches was determined by the width of the street (Via della Colonna) which had to be incorporated into the building. The units of measurement of the hospital behind, however, were derived from the arch-openings of the central court. The stepped platform and nine arches of the loggia, as well as the adjoining rooms to right and left, were designed by Brunelleschi himself. Francesco della Luna made many alterations, adding the building at the south end, which disturbs the proportions, and the frieze – criticized as being too high – above the loggia arches. The fact that the architrave turns at right angles at the end of the building which was added on and descends to the base was also strongly criticized. But there were precedents for this in a number of the buildings of the Proto-Renaissance (e.g. the façade of S. Miniato) which furnished abundant material for the styles of Brunelleschi and of his pupils. – The adjacent building to the left was not added until 1819. The arch on the right should be visualized as being open, like the corresponding street arch on the left. This arch, above the Via della Colonna, was built in 1600; the corner projections framing it were altered in 1845. It should be remembered that only the middle nine arches are Brunelleschi's own creation. The greater part of the pillared loggia on the roof is nineteenth-century; of its nineteen arches the four northern ones – like the corresponding part of the façade below – date from 1600. In the spandrels of the loggia arcade are the ten famous terracotta *medallions* depicting infants. Early works by Andrea della Robbia were not added until after Brunelleschi's death, *c.* 1463. In the arcades are four copies dating from 1845. The frescoes in the middle vault heads of the loggia are by Poccetti, 1610–11; above the doors are busts of Grand Dukes. – During the eighteenth century the **church** was altered and extended towards the east. – On the right of the **court** is a small picture gallery containing some interesting works, mostly sixteenth century.

Accademia (Via Ricasoli, 52)

The loggia of the deconsecrated church of **S. Matteo** opens

on to the street. Reconstructed in 1934–5, it is one of the
most important Florentine hospital loggias to have been
preserved, and an interesting forerunner to Brunelleschi's
loggia for the Ospedale degli Innocenti. – The supports carry
an arcade of arches. Above the central portal is a glazed
terracotta relief, *Madonna and Child with Saints*, by Andrea della Robbia, 1480–90. Beyond is a seventeenth-century **cloister** in the style of Buontalenti's school. The buildings are now used for lessons by the Accademia di Belle
Arti. – The entrance to the museum is in the next house
on the right.

In 1784 Grand Duke Leopold united here into one academy al
the drawing schools scattered about the city, and for the purpose
of study this academy received a picture collection. The 'Accade-
mia' has been housed since its inception in the spacious interior
of the old hospital of S. Matteo as well as in some vacant rooms
of the deserted convent of S. Niccolò, which until 1855 it shared
with the neighbouring Opificio delle Pietre Dure. In 1873 Michel-
angelo's 'David', which was threatening to become seriously
weathered, was moved here from its position in front of the
Palazzo Vecchio. The tribune (architect, de Fabris) was built in
1882 especially for this enormous sculpture. Later the collection
was considerably reorganized. A number of pictures were moved
to the Palazzo Pitti and the Uffizi, and some older paintings
were transferred from these two galleries to the Academy museum.
Today this excellent museum offers the visitor a chance to study
in greater depth those areas of the history of art of which the
Uffizi and the Palazzo Pitti hold the most exemplary pieces.

Since the collection is now again being reorganized, a detailed
description will be given only of those pieces which have been
definitively placed. The rest will be mentioned only briefly.

In the vestibule are a number of Classical Roman sculptures. Then
the visitor comes to a long room in which rows of Michelangelo's
colossal figures lead down either side towards the *David*. His
Matthew (before 1506) was to have been the first of a series of
twelve Apostles which Michelangelo planned for the Cathedral,
but not even this one was finished. Michelangelo's method was
to work from the front inwards, as if making a three-dimensional
drawing. Thus the nearer the front a particular part is, the more
perfectly it is finished. At the back the block is still untouched,
surrounding the figure like an aura; this is the core of the marble,
out of which Michelangelo never ceased to draw the lineaments
of life. Rather than developing freely in the manner of a Classical
sculpture, this figure takes form only within the limits of the
material, revealing the medieval legacy which lay behind the
genius of its creator. – The figures of *slaves* were carved c. 1519

or the tomb of Julius II, principally by assistants working from Michelangelo's models. In their complicated movements they appear to be wrestling with the stone from which, despite their burgeoning, incoherent strength, they are unable to free themselves. Cosimo I had them built into the corners of Buontalenti's grotto in the Boboli Gardens (today they have been replaced by plaster copies); in 1909 they were cleaned and transferred to the Academy. On the back of the second figure on the left is a small portrait (Michelangelo himself?), carved in the bark-like shell of the marble block. – The powerful *Pietà* (far right), a late work which was carved from a Classical block (viz. the remains of an architrave on the top rear edge), was in Palestrina, a small town in the Roman Campagna until 1939 when it was purchased by the nation and brought here. The figure of Christ is slumped like a paralysed giant. Some polishing and repairing has probably slightly altered the original finish. – The figure of *David* is justly the centre of attention. Michelangelo began it when he was 26 and took three years to complete it (1501–4), working from a block that had already been rejected as spoilt. This symbol of youth and strength once stood as a guardian of republican freedom in front of the Palazzo della Signoria. In the riots of 1527, during which the Medici were expelled, the left arm was broken in three pieces. These valuable pieces were saved for posterity through the efforts of Cecchino Salviati and Giorgio Vasari, who were still boys at the time, and the figure was reassembled in 1543 on the instructions of Cosimo I. Over the centuries the stone became considerably eroded by the weather; the top of the head and the back had suffered to such an extent that it became imperative to move the statue to the shelter of the museum. The naked body is Classical in its freedom. The expression on the youthful face is unforgettable as David steels himself for the imminent fight. This head dominates the magnificent body, giving it that sideways balance which transforms a solid statue into the image of a moment. It is as if the hero were also searching for some support, or for cover. The vibrant chiselling of the back surpasses anything known either before or since.

The *River God* on the right resembles a model for the Medici chapel; Michelangelo's nephew sold it to Cosimo I from whom it passed to Ammannati who in turn left in to the Academy. – The *portrait* of the master in bronze is by Daniele da Volterra; it is thought to be one of the most faithful portraits of Michelangelo (based on a mask which was made shortly after the master's death). – On the left are two plaster models by Giovanni da Bologna, the *Rape of the Sabines* and the group *Virtue conquering Vice* (the marbles are in the Loggia dei Lanzi and the Bargello respectively). – Tapestries on the walls include seven pieces of a Brussels series depicting Adam and Eve, which were acquired by Cosimo I in 1552, and a number of pieces woven in Florence between 1569

and 1573; the latter were designed for the quartiere of Leo X
in the Palazzo Vecchio and immortalize events in the lives o
important members of the Medici family (executed by Benedett
di Michele Squilli after designs by Stradanus).

Some of the other works contained in this gallery are: a *Magdale*
with eight scenes from her life (8466) by the so-called 'Master o
the Magdalen' (named after this work) who also painted the
two panels depicting the story of S. John (121 and 122); tw
beautiful crosses from S. Pier Scheraggio (436 by a pupil of th
Master of S. Cecilia, 442 by a worthy disciple of Bernard
Daddi); a *Misericordia-Madonna* in the style of Agnolo Gadd
(8562); a *Coronation of the Virgin* by Niccolò di Tommas
(8580); a superb but rather badly preserved lunette of the *Virgi*
with Child by Taddeo Gaddi (448); a fine *Crucifixion* from th
workshop of Daddi (8563); three panels by the school of Agnol
Gaddi depicting the *Nativity*, *Conversion of S. Paul* and *Stigma*
tization of S. Francis (8565); a *Man of Sorrows* by Giovanni d
Milano (signed and dated 1365), an artist who had immigrate
from Lombardy and whose influence on a Tuscan contemporary
is shown in a delightful triptych (8465); a signed polyptych b
Pacino di Buonaguida (8568), *Crucifixion with Saints*, which ha
made possible a more accurate assessment of this master's ar
(whether the date is to be read as 1315 remains an open question)
a richly figured *Coronation of the Virgin* by the school of Dadd
which once graced the high altar of S. Maria Novella (3449)
three panels with saints (8571–3) by Jacopo del Casentino whic
originally formed part of a large altar-piece; a Giottesqu
Annunciation of the late fourteenth century (3146); a *Crucifixio*
in the style of Niccolò Gerini (4670); an *Annunciation* by the
school of Agnolo Gaddi (455) with the predella by a lesse
successor; four panels of a dismantled polyptych by Pacino d
Buonaguida (the 'Virgin' was discovered beneath a nineteentl
century painting); a large cross, another of the same master'
principal works, painted with the skill of a miniaturist (8459)
a *Doubting Thomas* by the so-called 'Griggs' master (457), a
artist who was close in style to Rossello di Jacopo Franchi; tw
Coronations of the Virgin by Neri di Bicci (8618 and 8613) anc
two *Annunciations* by the same master (8622 and 480); a signec
Donation of the Girdle to S. Thomas by Andrea di Giusto
an eclectic who also worked as Masaccio's assistant (3263); a
S. Bernard with Angels (3452) and a *Tobias and the Archange*
(8624) attributed to Domenico di Michelino (best known for his
picture of Dante in the Cathedral); and a *Virgin with Saints* by
his school (3440).

In the small side room to the left of the tribune are two half-
lunettes, *Annunciation* and *Assumption*, and mounted below then
twenty-six small panels of walnut and poplar wood depicting
scenes from the lives of Christ and S. Francis. They are by Taddec

Gaddi and came from the old sacristy of S. Croce where they adorned a reliquary cupboard (on the east side) containing highly venerated relics of the Crown of Thorns and a piece of the Cross.

Among the pieces not yet definitively placed are some famous painted wedding chests. The marvellous one for the wedding of Boccaccio Adimari and Lisa Ricasoli (8457) is worth particular attention. The costumes are interesting in that they represent the fashions of 1440–50, showing that this piece was painted at least twenty years after the wedding, which took place in 1420. The view of the Baptistery is important topographically. Lorenzo Monaco, the greatest of the Florentine Late Gothic artists, is represented by some important works: *Mount of Olives* (438), *Man of Sorrows* of 1404 (467), *Crucifixion* (3153), a small *Crucifixion* (2141), *Mary* (2140), *John* (2169), and finally the most important, the *Annunciation* in the central panel of the triptych (8458) and the predella depicting scenes from the lives of SS. Onofrius and Nicholas (8615 and 8617). – Other works are by the 'Griggs' master, the so-called 'Master of Karlsruhe' (Thebais), Botticini, Lorenzo di Credi, Fra Bartolommeo, Jacopo del Sellaio, Cosimo Rosselli, Baldovinetti, Filippino Lippi, Botticelli, and there are some important works from the middle and late sixteenth century. Everything is clearly labelled.

S. Marco and the Fra Angelico Museum (Piazza S. Marco)

The church and convent were founded in 1299 by the Silvestrines on a site previously occupied by a Vallombrosan monastery. In 1436, when the Silvestrines had moved out, Pope Eugenius IV made over the property to the Dominicans of Fiesole, and Cosimo the Elder, 'Pater Patriae', generously took upon himself the renovation of the derelict buildings, appointing Michelozzo as architect (1437–52).

Work began immediately on the monastery buildings, the church, the cloisters and the library, and soon the spiritual life of the community began to blossom. Archbishop Antonino, canonized in 1526 and still today one of the most respected figures in Florence's history, was a Dominican from S. Marco. When he died, an elaborate tomb was planned. Clement VII himself took charge of the project. Possibly it was intended to modernize the whole church at that time; at any rate, Antonio da Sangallo the Younger drew up some designs which can be seen in the Uffizi. It fell to Giovanni da Bologna, however, on the instructions of the brothers Averardo and Antonio Salviati, to erect a dignified funeral chapel, in which the bones of the saint were placed in 1589 (on the occasion of the wedding of Ferdinando I).

There was no longer any question of rebuilding the entire church. Giovanni da Bologna had also designed new altar tabernacles for the nave, and in 1594 the Serragli family added a chapel on the left of the chancel (the architect is thought to have been Cigoli).

In 1679 the church was further altered by the erection of a new
main chancel chapel by Pier Francesco Silvani, who was also
responsible for the handsome flat ceiling in the nave. – In 1869 a
museum of Florentine antiquities was opened in the monastery.
Thorough restorations were undertaken in 1900, and in 1919 the
present Fra Angelico Museum was opened to the public.

The façade, with its two enormous statues of saints and its
extended relief in the upper part, is a late work by Gioacchino Pronti, 1777–8. – There is a human, domestic feeling
about the clear lines of the interior, with the old substance
of the building, still Gothic in its overall proportions,
appearing beneath the new dressing. Above Silvani's wooden
ceiling (1679; with a *Glorification of the Virgin* by G. A.
Pucci, *c.* 1725), the earlier handsomely painted open roof
framework is still there. At one time all the walls were
covered with frescoes. The chancel end has changed most
over the centuries, but Michelozzo's old polygonal termination (the function of the two capitals half-hidden in the
south wall has never been explained) is still there behind
Silvani's chancel, and the visitor is permitted on request to
see these remains of Cosimo the Elder's undertaking (notice
the Medici spheres – 'palle' – used for the decoration; their
freedom of form is unusual for such an early date).

Vasari drew upon the huge *Crucifix* on the inside of
the façade-wall to make one of his comparisons between
Giotto and Cimabue, but today it is thought to be the work
of only a remote follower of Giotto. – The *Annunciation*
fresco on the wall above the first altar inside the portal is
a copy of the famous miraculous fresco of SS. Annunziata.
The only thing that distinguishes it from the original is the
one supplementary figure – a donor or possibly a supplicant.
– Also on the aisle wall is a painted *Man of Sorrows* from
Cartapesta, *c.* 1600 (a mixture of canvas, plaster and card-
board). – The next altar has one of Santi di Tito's most
outstanding works; it depicts S. Thomas Aquinas who, in his
meditation, receives the impression that the figures of a
painted Crucifixion are stepping out of the picture as if
they were alive (this interpretation seems more apt than the
usual one, which sees S. Thomas dedicating his works to the
Crucified Lord). The picture is signed and dated 1593. –
Fra Bartolommeo's famous *Madonna del Baldacchino* dates
from 1509; it marked the beginning of a series of similar

Sacre Conversazioni', with the pathos of deliberate representation in a new, more formal ecclesiastical sense. – The next altar has an early eighth-century (706) *Roman mosaic*, a fragment of an oratory in Old S. Peter's, pulled down in 1608. The picture, which is cut in two parts, was placed here through the agency of Bishop Ricci of Arezzo (other fragments are said to exist in Rome). Mary is represented in the costume of a Byzantine empress; the imitation mosaic saints and angels beside here are fresco additions of 1609, when the mosaic was mounted. – Above the fourth altar is a large arch, modelled on the corresponding one on the opposite side which leads to the Antonino chapel. These arches give a kind of lateral axis to the hall-like building. The figure of S. Zenobius on the crown of the arch was executed by Francavilla after a model by Giovanni da Bologna (stucco).
A particularly beautiful door to the right of the main chancel chapel gives access to the rooms of the *sacristy*. On the left is a *Christ* by Antonio Novelli, dated 1640 (the flanking bronze reliefs are eighteenth century). The next room is a memorial to Savonarola (with a modern statue and a picture of his execution, 1498). Then comes the sacristy itself, built by Michelozzo in 1437–43; it makes use of Brunelleschi's system but is more medieval in approach, the individual forms are heavier and it is roofed with a domical vault. The reclining bronze figure (in the chancel) represents S. Antonino; designed by Giovanni da Bologna and cast by Domenico Portigiani, it originally lay beneath the high altar of the Antonino chapel. The large picture of the Virgin on clouds, with a picture of S. Dominic in her hands and accompanied by saints, was painted in 1589 by Simone Ferri. In a case on the wall is a Greek pallium, presented in 1439 during the Florentine Council.
Returning to the church, the visitor comes to the main *chancel chapel*, decorated in 1679 by Pier Francesco Silvani; the cupola fresco was added in 1717 by Gherardini. The *Adoration of the Magi* on the right wall was painted in 1712 by the much-travelled Frenchman, Ignaz-Jacques Parrocel (signed). – A door on the left of the chancel (if it is closed the visitor should apply to the sacristan) leads to the very lovely *sacrament chapel* of the Serragli, built by Cigoli, c. 1594. The well-preserved paintings on the ceiling are the work of Poccetti, as is the decoration of the walls, to which

has been added a series of paintings on canvas depicting symbolic scenes relating to the Holy Sacrament. The inscriptions above each work do not always tally with the scenes depicted below, so the pictures have presumably been shifted. Starting at the rear right: *Christ at Emmaus* (Corradi), *The Sacrifice of Isaac* (Empoli), *The Last Supper* (Santi di Tito), *The Gathering of the Manna* (Passignano), and *The Feeding of the Ten Thousand* (Corradi). The four niche statues are by Salvetti and Pieratti.

Returning to the church and turning right, the visitor reaches the elaborate *Antonino chapel*, one of the principal structures of Giovanni da Bologna (1578–89), who displays here the influence of Giovanantonio Dosio. (The beautiful marble figure of S. Antonino above the entrance arch outside is thought to have been designed by Giovanni da Bologna and executed by Francavilla.) The chapel consists of two spaces. The *ante-room* with its carved ceiling dates from 1588. The grotesques beside the windows of the upper story are interesting from the stylistic point of view. The strange, cool frescoes on the wall are by Passignano; they are his best-known works, with strong, well-drawn nudes in the foreground, and they were painted for the Salviati family. On the right, Bishop Ugolino Martelli delivers the oration at S. Antonino's lying-in-state (in the right foreground, turning to face the people, are the two donors, Averardo and Antonio Salviati, wearing ruffs); on the left wall the saint's body is transferred to the new chapel in S. Marco, with Grand Duke Ferdinando I walking before the coffin (in the extreme foreground on the left, below the two donors who are depicted here as well, is a self-portrait of the artist). – The *main space* of the chapel was frescoed by Alessandro Allori. Of the three important panel-paintings that on the right, representing the *Vocation of Matthew*, is by Giovanni Battista Naldini; with its firm composition and the assured formation of the figures, it is regarded as his best work. Alessandro Allori's *Christ's Descent into Limbo* (with Mary interceding) on the high altar shows his characteristically fine figure-drawing and cool colours. The *Healing of the Leper* on the left is a typical example of the many-figured style of Francesco Morandini, known as 'Il Poppi' compared to Allori's work, his nudes appear slightly crude his composition confused. – As important as the paintings

– which represent some of the best work by Florentine artists of the late sixteenth century – are the sculptures. These give a very good impression of the work of the school of S. Antonino. The marbles were executed by Francavilla, the bronzes by the Dominican brother, Portigiani. Altogether six life-sized marble statues and six bronze reliefs adorn the chapel. Another artist, Susini, may also have had a hand in the latter. They depict scenes from the life of S. Antonino. The fully-rounded archangel standing on one leg above the main portal (between bronze putti) was modelled by Susini (possibly with the assistance of the German, Hans Reichle). The bronze candelabra and the antependium were designed by Giovanni da Bologna. – A frescoed burial vault lies beneath this main room; it is reached through the door on the left in the anteroom.

On the first altar in the *left side aisle* is a painting by Cigoli of *Heraclius carrying the Cross to Jerusalem*; the fresco remains beside it show that the same illustration existed there as early as 1390. – On the partition wall before the next altar are the tombstones of Pico della Mirandola and Poliziano. The next picture is a copy of Fra Bartolommeo's *Betrothal of S. Catherine*. The third altar-piece, *S. Vincent healing the sick*, was painted by Passignano.

On the way out of the church the visitor should pause before the last resting-place of the founder of Renaissance architecture, Filippo Brunelleschi. His tomb-plate is on the right in front of Fra Bartolommeo's *Madonna del Baldacchino*.

Then, leaving the church and turning eastwards, the visitor comes to the **Silvestrine Convent** itself, which was modestly and harmoniously renewed and enlarged by Michelozzo in 1437–52. In this venerable place Fra Angelico lived and worked for ten years (1435–45), painting his immortal works. Here, too, Savonarola preached against luxury and the easy life, and from here was led out to be burned at the stake. Fra Bartolommeo, one of the greatest masters of the period of Raphael, also worked here. – A passage containing Baroque tombs leads to the **Cloister of S. Antonino**. On the left is the side wall of the church, which dates in substance from the fourteenth century, and further back the belfry with the Medici spheres worked in the style of Michelozzo on the upper frieze. This impressive cloister is an example of the Gothic transitional style of architecture.

Modern tombs and late sixteenth century frescoes depicting scenes from the life of S. Antonino have somewhat
altered the original appearance. Fra Angelico's frescoes belong, of course, to the original decoration; above the door
to the passage leading off to the right is a fresco depicting
Jesus as a pilgrim being accorded a friendly reception by
two Dominicans – a beautiful way of denoting that this
long room was the pilgrims' hostel.

Today it houses a small **museum** of works by Fra Angelico
and his school. Of these the most outstanding is the altar
which was painted for the linen drapers (the Tabernacolo
dei Linaiuoli) in 1433. This splendid piece marked the end
of the first creative phase of the artist's life. Here for the
first time his style appeared in its full maturity. In the
middle is the enthroned *Madonna with Child* and grouped
around her are twelve angels playing musical instruments.
On the wings, inside and outside, are four powerful figures
of saints; on the predella, the *Adoration of the Magi* between (on the right) the *Martyrdom of S. Mark* and (on the
left) the *Sermon of S. Peter*. The marble frame was designed
by Ghiberti. The many formative influences that nourished
Fra Angelico's work are here welded into a pictorial style
that surpasses them all. The elegance of Lorenzo Monaco,
the sweet colourfulness of Gentile da Fabriano, the delicacy
of Masolino and the strength of Masaccio are all brought to
fruition in this masterpiece. Present too is the influence of
the statuary of the Cathedral (in the saints on the wings)
and that of the type of architectural sculpture of the niches
of Or San Michele (in Ghiberti's surrounding tabernacle).
The stylized rocky ground beneath the feet of the saints
reaches back into the Gothic past, while the relationship of
these standing figures to the enthroned Madonna seems to
look forward to the new type of Sacra Conversazione. –
The paintwork has been skilfully restored in a few places,
e.g. the dress of the Madonna and some of the heads in the
Sermon of S. Peter on the predella; we can still obtain an
impression of the (slightly different) original appearance
of the piece from old photographs or from a copy of Fra
Angelico's school. – Among the other works exhibited here,
the visitor's attention is drawn to the following: thirty-five
scenes from the lives of Christ and the Madonna, originally
tabernacle doors for the great crucifix of SS. Annunziata,

some by Alesso Baldovinetti, the remainder by pupils of
Fra Angelico; an *Entombment with Saints* (school); a *Last
Judgement* (school); and another *Entombment* (school; the
small panels on top by Lorenzo Monaco).

Returning to the cloister and following the east side to the
end, the visitor reaches a door above which is an *Ecce Homo*
by Fra Angelico. Immediately on the left, inside, is a large
altar-piece, *Madonna with S. Anne and other Saints*, by Fra
Bartolommeo, designed for the council chamber of the
Palazzo Vecchio but never completed. The panel is fully
primed and the design set out in brown, but the colours are
missing. This gives us an unusual insight into the painting
technique of the period around 1510–12 – Adjoining is the
great refectory. An elaborate signed and dated fresco by
G. A. Sogliani (1536) depicts the Crucified Christ above,
with SS. Anthony and Catherine beside him, and below,
angels bringing bread to S. Dominic and his brothers who
are sitting round a bare table. – On the wall opposite the
windows is a fresco with a rounded top which was originally in the Villa Dami. It is by the young Franciabigio (1510),
who was still under the influence of Albertinelli at the
time, and depicts the *Adoration of the Shepherds* above and
the *Man of Sorrows* below. – Nearer the entrance wall is a
well-known *Last Judgement* fresco (basic design by Fra
Bartolommeo, execution by Albertinelli, restored by Matteo
Rosselli in 1618 and transferred to canvas in 1871) which
was painted *c.* 1500 and comes from S. Maria Nuova.
Raphael was inspired by the upper group of figures in the
composition of his *Disputa* in the Vatican.

In the north wing of the cloister stands a finely modelled
bell known as 'La Piagnona'. When Savonarola was burnt
this bell, which had summoned people to his sermons, was
banished from the city and taken to S. Francesco al
Monte. – The **chapter-room** (on the right of the outside
wall is a fresco by Matteo Rosselli, the *Death of S. Antonino*)
is dominated by a powerful *Crucifixion* by Fra Angelico,
with biblical figures and the patron saints of the Medici
on the left and ecclesiastical figures on the right. The effect
of the reddening sky, appearing as if it were reflecting
flames, is highly dramatic; this is, however, no more than
the colour base which was left after the blue, applied 'al
secco', had disintegrated. The clarity of composition, the

incredibly assured treatment of the figures and the depiction
of suffering are immediately effective. Below, S. Dominic
holds a branch from which spring sixteen medallions with
half-figures of saints and beatified members of his Order.
At the crown of the arch-surround can be seen the Christian
symbol of the pelican; to right and left, busts of Prophets. –
Back in the cloister, in the north-west corner (under glass) is
another fresco by Fra Angelico, *S. Dominic at the foot of the
Cross*; the figures of Mary and John and the putti were
painted by Cecco Bravo. On the west side, above the door
leading to the church, is a pointed-arch lunette with *S. Peter
Martyr*, also by Fra Angelico; *Faith* and *Hope* are by Francesco Vanni (1562).

Turning back, the visitor reaches a corridor. The large
wooden Crucifix on the wall is an early work by Baccio da
Montelupo, authentically dated 1496, which is still related
stylistically to the realism of the fifteenth century. The
second cloister can be seen beyond but this cannot be visited. – Passing through the door leading to the staircase and
turning immediately left, the visitor enters the **small
refectory** containing Domenico Ghirlandaio's famous *Last
Supper* (1480–90), a variant of that in Ognissanti. This
fresco too incorporates the actual room in the painted one,
and in this the sculptured console plays an important part
as intermediary. The room contains a number of other works
of art. – The **staircase** – which with its single flight is still
fundamentally Gothic in form – is the earliest monumental
Renaissance structure of its kind. It was built by Michelozzo
in 1437–43. The tunnel vault above gives way to groin
vaults over the middle and upper landings, creating the
effect of a canopy above the points of rest. The logic of this
pioneering master's architectural thinking is expressed
everywhere. Notice, for example, the interruption of the
band on the wall; it accompanies only the rise of the stairs
and not the horizontal landings.

At the top the visitor comes to the dormitory. This consists of a corridor with numerous small tunnel-vaulted **cells**
running off it to left and right, the whole spanned by the
open framework of the enormous ceiling. Each cell and
also parts of the corridors are decorated with *frescoes* by Fra
Angelico and his school (1439–45). Those worth particular
attention are (in the cells) the *Adoration of the Magi* and

Coronation of the Virgin and (in the corridors) the *Crucifixion with S. Dominic*, the *Madonna Enthroned* and, immediately opposite the stairs, the *Annunciation*. Taken together, these frescoes form an absolutely unique religious cycle. Their style is marvellous in its simplicity; particularly eloquent examples of this are the *Noli Me Tangere* (first cell on the left), the *Annunciation* (next cell but one) and the *Transfiguration* (sixth cell on the left, *ill.* facing p. 145). – At the end of the passage are the **Prior's quarters**, where Savonarola lived. The vestibule was originally a chapel; on the right is a portrait of the great preacher by his fellow brother, Fra Bartolommeo, and a *S. Peter Martyr* with Savonarola's face, painted by the same master after the prior's death. There are further pictures of his execution and some (restored) frescoes by Fra Bartolommeo. – On the right is the small study. On the writing desk (a modern copy) are two Latin Bibles with handwritten annotations and a volume of sermon notes. Against the entrance wall, Savonarola's chair and a small sixteenth-century cupboard containing some of the modest requirements of his daily life. – On the wall of the adjacent room is the banner depicting the Crucified Christ (painted by Fra Angelico) which the monk used to carry with him when he went out to preach in the city. Returning to the stairs and proceeding along the corridor on the left side, the visitor finds on his immediate left S. Antonino's cell, containing a death-mask, manuscripts and relics. – The double cell next door but one is thought to have been that of Fra Angelico. – In the one after is the *Mount of Olives* and following this the *Communion of the Apostles*, both frescoes by his hand. The double cell at the end on the right was used by Cosimo the Elder when – as he very often did during his later years – he went into retreat at S. Marco. An unusual feature here is the hole which has been made in the ceiling to illuminate the fresco.

The **library** (*ill.* facing p. 160) was built by Michelozzo. This delicate, airy three-aisled hall became a model for other Renaissance libraries. The room off to the rear served as a store room for Greek manuscripts. Savonarola was taken prisoner in the vestibule.

Casino Mediceo (Via Cavour, opposite S. Marco)
Built in 1574 by Bernardo Buontalenti on the site of the former

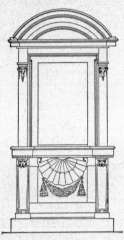

Casino Mediceo,
ground-floor window

*Medici Gardens, this large palace represents as it were the new
princely generation's more expansive counterpart to the old town
palace in the Via Larga. The building was thoroughly restored in
1805. Today it houses a Court of Appeal.*

The exterior, with its fantastic window decoration, its
extremely impressive door (the stone of the surround
appears to be folded in pleats) and the balcony above with
its characteristic balusters, may be regarded as a typical
example of Buontalenti's mature and pronouncedly Manneristic style. The large wooden leaves of the door are original.
In the court is a fountain sculpture by the school of Giovanni da Bologna; in some of the rooms at the back are
stucco decorations and murals.

S. Croce, Bardi chapel, detail of the 'Ordeal by fire before the Sultan' (Giotto)

*Pazzi chapel (S. Croce), dome of the vestibule
(Brunelleschi and Luca della Robbia)*

The S. Lorenzo District

Rather less than 100 m from S. Lorenzo, on the corner of the Via Cavour and the Via Gori, stands the palace of the Medici. The ruling family were thus parishioners of the church, which explains why they buried their dead there and why they took such an interest in the embellishment of and architectural alterations to the entire complex. And since they were also concerned to give Florence as many splendid buildings as possible, to inspire the rich talents of its inhabitants to ever newer artistic achievements, and in short to set a supremely impressive example of generous patronage, it is natural that the very best masters were called upon for designs and for advice. Brunelleschi, Donatello and Michelangelo all owed decisive phases of their development to the study of the problems of S. Lorenzo, not only as regards the church buildings themselves but also in the construction of tombs for the Medici family. Earlier members of the family were laid to rest in Brunelleschi's **Old Sacristy**, their successors in Michelangelo's **New Sacristy**, and the princely members of the dynasty in the vast domed structure which was erected at the west end of the church. This – as has been the case with so many elements in S. Lorenzo – remained incomplete, and only received some definitive form in the eighteenth and nineteenth centuries. The relationship between the Medici and S. Lorenzo in fact became extremely close. In the sixteenth century they donated their priceless library to the canonry and – a remarkable sign of community spirit – stipulated that the collection be opened to the public, which resulted in Michelangelo's library building, the Biblioteca Laurenziana. It will thus be abundantly clear that S. Lorenzo is not simply a church but a whole complex of artistic endeavour, the study of which will furnish excellent examples of every turning-point in the development of style from the beginnings of the Early Renaissance through Michelangelo's freer constellations of forms derived from the high Classical period right up to the threshold of Baroque. – In what follows the individual parts of the complex will be described in the following order:
Church – Old Sacristy – New Sacristy – Cappella dei Principi – Biblioteca Laurenziana

The Church

The basilica of S. Lorenzo is among the oldest monumental churches in Florence. It was first founded by the Roman widow Juliana in 380 (her tombstone is preserved in Michelangelo's house) and in 393 it was solemnly consecrated by S. Ambrose. A new building was begun in 1058 and this remained virtually without alteration until the fifteenth century.

In 1418 a plan for a new church was decided upon (the 'Dolfini Plan'). Still very Gothic in character, this plan initially envisaged the construction of an elaborate transept with nine chancel chapels, of the type of S. Croce. When that was completed the nave was to be pulled down and replaced by a more advanced building. Work had already begun on the main chancel when Brunelleschi entered the scene. This great master of Renaissance architecture immediately threw a new light on the whole project. At first the Medici only assigned to him the modest task of erecting a new sacristy. However, his model differed to such an extent from the tradition of the period that Giovanni di Averardo de'Medici decided to let this as yet little known master draw up a plan for the whole church. That must have been in the winter of 1420–1. By the autumn of the following year, the foundation stone had been laid and the construction of the first church of post-medieval architecture was under way.

Despite the rapidity with which this complete change of style had been decided upon, the actual construction of the church proceeded very slowly and Brunelleschi never saw it completed. As early as 1425 work was interrupted by war. The sacristy and the adjoining chapel were completed in 1428. It was again due to a Medici, Cosimo the Elder, that work on the other parts of the building was again resumed in 1442. At the same time, the original plan was extended to include a row of chapels in each side aisle. When Brunelleschi died a few years later (1446), the transept and the chancel chapels were certainly almost complete. The dome was still missing and the nave only just begun.

Manetti, who also inherited his master's job at S. Spirito, then took over and began the first two bays of the nave adjoining the transept. He roofed the transept and added a dome of his own design. About 1457 work on the *sides of the nave as well as parts of the adjacent monastery buildings was undertaken. One must, of course, realize that at that time the medieval church (which must have been smaller than the present church by two nave bays) was still standing quite untouched and continuing to fulfil its function. It was removed only in 1461, as the new church was extended westwards. In 1465 the chapels of the south aisle were completed and the northern row followed shortly afterwards; work was terminated by 1469.*

This completion date, however, refers only to the interior of the church. The exterior and the façade were still in a rough state. Around 1500 – if a drawing by Leonardo has been correctly interpreted – an order of blind arcades was applied to the exterior of the church. Shortly afterwards Michelangelo built the 'New Sacristy' and furnished it with some immortal works, and in 1532 he designed the simple north portal of the church and built a gallery inside the façade-wall for the exhibition of the relics presented to S. Lorenzo by the Medici pope, Clement VII. – The bell-tower was added in 1740–1 by Ferdinando Ruggieri (slightly to one side of the foundations of the old campanile).

The impact of Brunelleschi's architectural style began to have its effect as soon as the first parts of the building had been completed. Many smaller communities came to S. Lorenzo to study the measurements of columns and bases for their own new buildings.

Exterior The wide, lively market street that runs along the north side of the church expands at the eastern end to form a square, the **Piazza di S. Lorenzo**. In the north-east corner of the square, on a diagonally positioned base the size of a small house, stands the (incomplete) **monument to Giovanni delle Bande Nere**, father of Cosimo I and founder of the grand-ducal dynasty. It was originally designed as a tomb for the end chapel of the right transept. In 1543 the base was set up in its present position and used as a market-place fountain. Inspired by Sansovino's Santa Casa at Loreto, it was designed by Bandinelli. The statue – also by Bandinelli – was kept in the Palazzo Vecchio until 1851 when it was transferred to this present setting. In composition the monument was influenced by Michelangelo (the seated statues of the 'capitani' in the New Sacristy combined with the house-like base of one of the models for the tomb

of Julius II). This seated figure, with its firm posture and
leathery vigour, is typical of Bandinelli's 'courtly' style, of
which it marks the beginning. The beautiful relief of the
base (*Tribute to Giovanni delle Bande Nere*; the condottiere
is seated on the right) may date from slightly earlier. – A
large inscription plaque above the fountain commemorates
the restoration of 1850.

Turning towards the **church** the visitor sees, instead of a
façade, only rough masonry. When in 1515 Leo X visited
his home town for the first time, he formed the project of
crowning the work of his ancestors with a monumental
façade. Rejecting the numerous designs submitted by Giuliano da Sangallo and Jacopo Sansovino, he entrusted the
work to Michelangelo together with Baccio d'Agnolo. Michelangelo, dismissing Baccio d'Agnolo's model as 'child's play',
came up with a superior, stylistically adventurous design
(which cannot now be reconstructed with certainty). He was
not unaffected by the work of his predecessors in so far as
he adhered from the beginning to a non-basilican scheme, i.e.
a façade with upper and lower storeys of the same width.
Giuliano da Sangallo had got as far as this. Michelangelo
first made a small clay model, and then in 1517 a larger
wooden one with twenty-four wax figures. He then super-
vised the laying of the foundations and left for Carrara,
remaining there until 1519 controlling the quarrying of
the marble blocks. Few reverses in his lifetime affected
the master as severely as the relinquishing by the pope of
the plan for the projected façade for lack of money and
the withdrawal of the commission. Art historians speak of
the 'tragedy of the façade' as they speak of the 'tragedy of
the tomb of Julius II'. – The only pieces of decoration on
the front wall of S. Lorenzo are the doors, carved inside
and out, which date from the time of Cosimo I.

If the visitor walks along the *north side* he will find that
this richly graduated complex of structures offers a satisfy-
ing view. Each storey is terminated by an entablature
supported on brackets, built according to Brunelleschi's
model. The wavy relief pattern of the upper frieze has its
prototype on the Pazzi chapel. The lower storey was dressed
c. 1500 with a rather poor blind arcade. The door near the
transept is one of Michelangelo's simplest architectural con-
ceits (1530–4). In the corner between the transept and the

New Sacristy two doors (*c.* 1600) lead to the large crypt and to a storage room respectively.

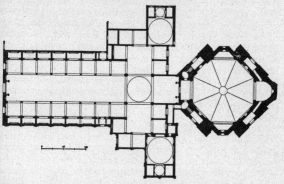

S. Lorenzo, ground plan

Interior   The visitor is recommended to enter the building through Michelangelo's north door since the key-point of the interior is the transept and the beautifully graduated and composed west end, largely completed during Brunelleschi's lifetime. The interior – a columnar basilica with flat ceiling (*ill.* facing p. 161), square transepts, main chancel and side chancels – follows a medieval scheme. The plan which Brunelleschi found when he arrived (the 'Dolfini Plan') may not have differed greatly from the present ground plan. The chapels in the end-walls of the transept arms, the graduated nave chapels leading to the transept, the rows of chapels in the side aisles – all these features were characteristic of medieval architecture and are present in S. Maria Novella, S. Croce and S. Trinita. The new features were the symmetrical articulation, the abundance of light, and the incredible way in which each detail fits logically into the whole, as if one law penetrated to every part of the building. The basis of Brunelleschi's architectural invention and the measure of his intellectual accomplishment was the almost abstract geometrical schema which was his point of departure. He thus built up his church almost like a process of cell formation, and the fact that he did it with such suitable and successful forms indicates a creative achievement of a very high order. The conception of the crossing as the point from which everything radiates thus gains in importance. The effect is somewhat diminished by Manetti's dome, which is too dark and too squat, but it is there all the same and Brunelleschi's novel solution of situating the monks' choir in the main chancel beyond the dome rather than centrally below it serves further to underline the self-sufficient, imperturbable character of the interior. (Vasari admired this solution greatly and copied it in his reorganizations of medieval churches.) The crossing is central in other respects as well: from it and the main chancel the rest of the building is developed. The articulation of the walls of the aisles was derived from the chancel articulation. Brunelleschi applied Corinthian pilasters to the ends of the walls between the chancel chapels, and placed above them an entablature that runs round the chapels themselves. He applied a second entablature above the arches of the nave chapel. This gave an intermediate storey which determined the height of the side aisles and of the chapels, and an upper storey (corresponding to the pendentive zone under the dome) which determined the height of the nave clerestory. Thus not only is the ground plan based on the square system but also the elevation, and both take their measurements from the crossing and the chancel area. The church was then decorated – and this shows clearly how close Brunelleschi was to the Proto-Renaissance (compare SS. Apostoli) – with motifs derived from the Classical period, not only in the ornamentation but also in the columns, the capitals, and in the profile of the arches.

The nave has eight bays and the same number of chapels down each side. The chapels are three steps higher than the nave floor. The bays of the side aisles are each vaulted with a domical vault and the articulation of the walls is derived from that of the transept, as already mentioned. The interior of S. Lorenzo is the earliest example of that completely homogeneous articulation of spatial units which subsequently became a first principle of Renaissance architecture. The dosserets on top of the columns are decorated with Seraphim and the symbol of the Apocalyptic Lamb on the altar with the Seven Seals. On the inside of the façade-wall, Michelangelo's *gallery for relics* with its three small portals (1530–2) catches the eye. – A number of additions from later periods should be mentioned: the decorated surrounds on the rear-wall of each chapel (nineteenth century), the new floor, and the colouring of the coffered ceiling with its slightly too 'Baroque' effect (eighteenth century). The whole rear-wall of the main chancel is also new. It was erected in 1860 (the façade-wall was altered at the same time); before that the Cappella dei Principi which lies beyond the chancel used to open grandly into the church.

Interior Decoration   The following brief tour of the church will introduce the visitor to the most important works to be seen within it. Resplendent on the altar of the second chapel in the right side aisle is one of the masterpieces of Rosso Fiorentino, the *Marriage of the Virgin*, the last work of his Florentine period and also his last dated work (1523). Its rich arrangement and the varied colourfulness of the costumes show it to be the work of a branch of the school of Andrea del Sarto; the refinement of the costumes and the graduated composition involving a flight of stairs and hinging around the two seated figures to right and left combine to make the work one of the most glorious products of Florentine Mannerism. A particularly delicate feature of Rosso's style are his rosy flesh tints. The marble tombstone (with full-length figure) of the famous organist Francesco Landini († 1397) which is let into the left wall of the chapel was until recently almost completely concealed by a confessional. It lay originally in the middle of the old church. – In the fourth chapel of the right side aisle is a tombstone engraved like a woodcut in the style of Vasari (after 1592); on the altar, an *Assumption of the Virgin* by the school of Ghirlandaio. – The *Adoration of the Magi* on the altar of the sixth and last chapel, painted *c.* 1565 by Girolamo Macchietti, was the artist's first work for public exhibition. The simple, natural, clear draughtsmanship and rich, almost glazed colouring reveal Macchietti's training in the workshop of Michele Ghirlandaio.

The *altar tabernacle* before the corner to the right transept is one of the principal works of Desiderio da Settignano, completed in 1461. It had already been moved several times before (by accident) it reached this particular spot. At that time the original elevation was altered. The small door towards which the angels bow and which may have born a *Man of Sorrows* is lost; the antependium of the altar with its *Pietà* received a new surround. The figure of Christ on top was used for some time in a Christmas crib (hence the damage to the raised hand); then its place here was taken by a copy by Baccio da Montelupo. The original arrangement of the candlestick angels is impossible to reconstruct. These problems aside, however, the work is one of the most delightful creations of the Renaissance. The delicate beauty of the angels, the lovely refinement of the ornaments, the extraordinary perfection of the workmanship and finally the roguish charm of the Christ-child on top (copies of which were distributed far and wide at the turn of the century) all combined to make this work so famous that it is still one of the most admired pieces in Florence. Notice the richness of the ornamental invention and the perspective construction of the space within the tabernacle.

The fresco in the dome of the crossing, a Baroque *Apotheosis of Florentine Saints* (with four Early Fathers in the pendentives), was painted by Francesco Meucci in 1742. The round memorial slab of coloured marble for Cosimo the Elder in the floor below is an early work by Verrocchio; it is supported by a tall sarcophagus which stands on a base in the crypt and which also contains the bones of his brother Lorenzo di Giovanni and of Donatello. – On the altar of the first chapel in the right transept is an *Adoration of the Child*, a Florentine work of *c.* 1500 in the style of Botticini; also here is the tomb of the missionary to Denmark, Nicola Stenon (Classical sarcophagus). – The powerful porphyry sarcophagus in the side room of the chapel at the end of the right transept was erected in 1832 for Caroline of Saxony, wife of Leopold II. – High up on the right wall of this chapel is a small but good crucifix in the style of Corradi, *c.* 1607. It is rather difficult to see.

The splendid 'pietra dura' altar in the *main chancel* comes from the Cappella dei Principi, as does the crucifix which stands upon it. Of the excellent inlaid work (in the centre, *The Sacrifice of Isaac*, after a design by Cigoli, 1607), that on the sides was begun as early as the sixteenth century. The whole construction received its present form only in the eighteenth century. – In the next chancel chapel to the left stands a venerated miraculous image, the harsh wooden statue of the *Madonna la Bentornata*, which dates from the mid-fourteenth century (recently painted). – The altar-piece of the next chapel is by the school of Ghirlandaio (*c.* 1500). – Proceeding past the entrance to the Old Sacristy and entering the chapel at the end of the left transept, the visitor will see in the opening, which is pierced through into the sacristy, the sarcophagus of the Medici by Verrocchio (this piece is discussed in detail on p. 127 in the section on the Old Sacristy) and above it the accompanying coat of arms. The large wall-cupboards once housed the collection of relics rescued from the Turks at Constantinople in 1452. They are now kept in the Cappella dei Principi. Outside the chapel above the doors are, on the right, SS. Cosmas and Damian, the patron saints of the Medici, and on the left Bonaventura and Carlo Borromeo, painted by Poccetti and dated 1611. – In the first chapel on the east side of this transept arm, on the right wall, is a cenotaph to Donatello, a typical example of the imitative style of *c.* 1896 which was compiled from a wide variety of fifteenth century elements. The particularly beautiful altar-piece is among the finest works of Fra Filippo Lippi. The connection between this *Annunciation* and its predella, which was added in 1447 and depicts scenes from the life of S. Nicholas of Bari (*The Rescue of the Youths before Execution, Gift of the Golden Apples, Awakening of the Youths*), lies in the identity of the donor, Niccolò Martelli (note the coat of arms!), whose marble sarcophagus in the shape of a rush-basket can be seen on the left wall. This curious burial container, which also served Martelli's wife and parents and was originally crowned with the golden figure of a knight, was made *c.* 1440 by the school of Donatello.

Turning into the left side aisle, the visitor will notice immediately an enormous fresco by Bronzino depicting the *Martyrdom of S. Lawrence*, 1565–9. It is difficult at first to analyse this gigantic piece accurately, but soon the characteristic traits of the artist emerge – the harsh colouring, the strangely interrupted rhythm of the contours and the loose, free composition. One is reminded that at times Bronzino was very close to Bandinelli. – The beautiful *singing gallery* above the door leading to the cloister is by the school of

Donatello and was based on the master's gallery for the Cathedral. – The altar-piece in the next chapel was painted by Jacopo da Empoli, c. 1580–90.

Having looked at the decoration up to this point, let us turn to those two pieces that are rightly counted among the most precious possessions of this church – the two *pulpits* by Donatello. Today they stand to right and left of the last bay of the nave. Their original position was against the pillars of the crossing arch (probably on wooden supports; the present marble substructures with their Mannerist columns may be by Francesco da Sangallo's circle) where they stressed (in the Renaissance sense) a certain independence of the chancel area in relation to the nave. The two rectangular, box-shaped pulpits are reminiscent of sarcophagi; they stand in an iconographical tradition of sculptured decoration depicting the sufferings and glorification of Christ that had in fact been prefigured on fourteenth century tombs. The composition is framed by a decorative frieze of putti accompanied by horse-tamers, centaurs and vases. The sides are decorated with relief panels which on the left pulpit are framed by pilasters and on the right by buttressing pillars in foreshortened perspective. The relationship between figures and architectural forms is extremely well handled; quite often the figures overlap the frames at top and bottom, appearing to develop the scenes beyond the frames. Donatello himself was not able to complete these extraordinary works of art. Bertoldo and Bellano took part in the execution c. 1460–70; the pulpits were completed by the school of Giovanni da Bologna.

On the front of the left pulpit are depicted *Crucifixion*, *Deposition* and *Lamentation*. The deep feeling conveyed by the figures gives these bronze panels the awesome power of an emotional record. On the narrow left-hand end is *Christ before Caiaphas and Pilate*, set in a splendid double hall; the scene is given a deeply moving human quality by the unusual presence of the governor's wife, in whom the emotional tension is powerfully reflected. The two-headed Janus figure near Pilate may be intended to symbolize the struggle going on in the Roman's heart. On the right-hand end is the *Entombment* and on the rear the *Mount of Olives*; the wooden reliefs of *John the Evangelist* in the centre and the *Flagellation* on the left, based on Ghiberti's north

Baptistery doors, are by a pupil of Bologna. – The *Descent into Hell*, the *Resurrection* and the *Ascension* on the front of the right pulpit were executed by Donatello himself (signature in the frieze above the *Ascension*, on the panel between the centaurs). In the *Descent into Hell*, which in its symmetrical grouping is somewhat Byzantine, the figure of Christ is set like a giant among the imploring throng; the sense of violent emotion, of penitence and a longing for salvation, creates a most powerful impact. – In the *Resurrection*, Christ climbs painfully like a dead man (Lazarus), still swathed in his shroud, up on to the rim of the tomb. – On the left-hand end, the *Maries at the Sepulchre*; 'the many strong walls surrounding it make the Lord's disappearance even more miraculous'. – The *Pentecost* on the right-hand end transforms the descent of the Holy Ghost into a phenomenon of light before which all attributes fall to the ground. – The *Martyrdom of S. Lawrence* on the rear was probably executed by Bertoldo; it bears the date 16 June 1465 in the left gable (not visible from below) and was thus completed during Donatello's lifetime. The *Luke the Evangelist* and the *Mocking of Christ* are wooden reliefs of the school of Bologna, *c.* 1619–35.

Both pulpits radiate a sense of eternal life. The bronze was chiselled everywhere after casting, giving it a delightful grainy surface down to the smallest detail. The panels appear in fact as if they were still in the process of being created; they demonstrate strongly the primary purpose and potential of sculpture.

Even if, in the altars and frescoes (among which should be included some late works by Pontormo in the chancel, which have now disappeared), posterity has removed from the overall impression of S. Lorenzo a great deal of Brunelleschi's original vision, Donatello's pulpits, standing near the tomb of their creator, still recall the never-to-be-surpassed grandeur of Florence. In S. Lorenzo, a very great architect and a very great sculptor created a permanent monument to an epoch.

The Old Sacristy

With this, his first building (1419–28), Brunelleschi not only created the first centralized structure of the Renaissance but also reached such a peak of artistic achievement that the Old

Sacristy, in construction and detail, remains a model building even today.

The Old Sacristy, which is entered from within the church, in the south-west corner of the left transept, consists of a square domed **main space** and a smaller adjacent chancel (flanked by two side rooms with bronze doors). The conception of the sacristy was derived from the Gothic chapter-house. The execution, however (following the same artistic principles as were applied to the church), is based on Classical models and the proportions obey the laws of geometry. Not one irregularity, not one accident is tolerated. The Gothic tradition is here purified by a new systematization. – The proportions are simple. The space between the ring of the dome and the floor is firmly divided into two halves by an impressive bracketed entablature supported by pilasters, leaving space in the upper section for a fully semicircular arch with pendentives leading up to the dome. The *dome* itself (*ill.* facing p. 176) is an original and curiously-shaped invention with no real precedents at all; the segments of the so-called 'umbrella' vault are separated by twelve deep ribs; at the top is a narrow drum, and all round the base of the dome *oculi* throw concentrated direct light.

The **chancel** is given similar treatment to the main space with the exception of the dome, which is a single, un-articulated shell. All the walls of the chancel, however, bulge out in large niches, giving the impression that the space has been inflated. This was the first appearance of the concept of the centrifugal dynamic which was to characterize S. Spirito with its rows of chapels. The walls of the main space too seem to give way in the door niches, allowing the thorough plastic articulation of the doors, each of which becomes a Classically-styled tabernacle.

The **rich decoration** (see *ill.* facing p. 177) creates a feeling of warmth; reliefs enliven the walls and the use of different techniques (terracotta, stucco, bronze, marble, paint) gives an impression of animation which must have been even greater when the rich colours were still there. The master in charge of the decoration, which was executed in 1435, a few years after the building had been completed, was Donatello.

The *decoration* is informed by the spirit of Cosimo the

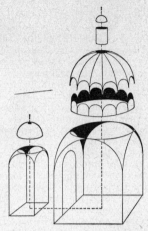

S. Lorenzo, *schema of the Old Sacristy*

Elder. His small wax portrait (relief) above the entrance door conjures up the shades of the first ruling generation of the Medici. The Old Sacristy is dedicated to S. John the Evangelist, in memory of Cosimo's father Giovanni d'Averardo, under whose patronage the building was erected. Hence the four medallions (heavily damaged in parts) in the pendentives with scenes from the Saint's life (*Raising of Drusiana, Vision on Patmos, Martyrdom* and *Assumption*). Stucco reliefs in the same technique depicting the four Evangelist decorate the blind arches. Here too S. John has the place of honour above the chancel. Above the doors to the two rooms on either side of the chancel, within the blind arches with their ornamentation of foliage, are two further stucco reliefs, depicting (against blue backgrounds) the life-sized figures of SS. Cosmas and Damian, on the right, and SS. Stephen and Lawrence on the left. They were also patron saints of members of the Medici family, so that the figurative decoration of the Old Sacristy reads rather like a sort of family tree. The combination of doors and supraportal reliefs is unusual; it has its roots in the Romanesque style,

and may have stemmed from the initiative of Dona
tello himself. The master was also responsible for th
extremely powerful portals, the oldest Classical tabernacl
portals of the Italian Renaissance. Brunelleschi, apparently
did not approve of them in this particular place, and it is i
fact true that they do not fit very smoothly into the linear
diagrammatic elevation of the wall. But the overall effec
is admirable none the less. There is tremendous charm i
this encounter between the 'delicate' and the 'forceful', an
what the modern visitor is aware of, over and above th
difference between two artistic temperaments, is a commo
drive towards a renewal of art.

The *bronze leaves of the doors* are among Donatello's mos
important works. Each portal contains two leaves, and eac
leaf has five relief panels, with disputing martyrs on the lef
and Apostles and Early Fathers on the right. SS. Peter an
John on the right door (top row) were the patrons o
Cosimo's sons, Piero and Giovanni. – All the panels consis
of the same motif – a pair of figures – varied in ever differ
ent combinations. Notice the part the frame plays in eac
scene: as well as defining the limits of the action it give
effective psychological support to the figures containe
within it. This definition of space was a new feature, stem
ming essentially from the postures and movements of th
individual figures. – It may be suggested that these disputin
saints were intended to reflect the splendour of the Floren
tine Council of 1439.

In the centre of the room stands a large marble table, whic
was probably used for laying out vestments (?). It cover
the *marble sarcophagus* of Cosimo the Elder's parents
Giovanni d'Averardo Medici and his wife Piccarda (b
Buggiano, *c*. 1433; on each side of the lid are two flyin
putti bearing a plaque). The beautiful *inlaid cupboards* als
formed part of the original decoration (1440–60). The inter
esting *aspersorium* by the entrance, which is in the shape o
a Classical vase, is said to have been designed by Donatello
An important feature of the decoration is a rather curiou
re-use of Early Christian forms. The fine marble altar-rail
in the chancel are somewhat reminiscent of works i
Ravenna; the *chancel altar* (probably the oldest item o
decoration, with the date inscribed as 1432, and possibl
designed by Brunelleschi) was inspired by the altar of th

Baptistery. (The frieze of angels' heads on the entablature may possibly originate from there also.) The central panel once bore Brunelleschi's first relief design for the present north door of the Baptistery, the *Sacrifice of Isaac*. This precursor of the sacrificial death of Christ is linked – a typically medieval train of thought – with the crucifix above the altar (wood, second half of the fifteenth century). The altar decoration features the prophets Daniel and Jeremiah on the front and Ezekiel and Isaiah on the back. – The *chancel dome* is painted blue, like the sky; its rim is in the form of a curtain tied up with cords, seeming just drawn aside. On closer inspection the shell of the dome reveals a painted constellation of stars which may have appeared in 1440–50 (its meaning is not entirely clear).

In the **tunnel-vaulted room** to the left of the chancel (the one on the right is closed), in the right-hand corner, the visitor can see a deep well, and on the wall above it a fantastically decorated *lavabo* (c. 1465, probably by Verrocchio) bearing the devices of Piero de'Medici, the griffon, the diamond ring, and the motto 'SEMPER'. – Returning to the main room, the visitor will find near the entrance the tomb of this Piero and of his brother Giovanni (both sons of Cosimo the Elder) in the opening in the wall which goes through to the adjacent chapel. It is one of the chief products of Verrocchio's first creative phase (1469–72). This type of tomb, set in a wall-aperture and designed to be viewed from both sides, originated in the fourteenth century (compare the Bardi tomb in S. Croce; for its further development into a lunette tomb, see the Strozzi tomb in the sacristy of S. Trinita). An inscription let into the green marble roundel on the front gives the names of the deceased (a corresponding inscription on the other side gives the date of completion, 1472). In the inscription on the socle (on both sides) Lorenzo the Magnificent and his brother Giuliano are named as the donors. The frame is a simple round arch (possibly by Francesco di Simone Ferrucci), the sloping inner face of which is decorated with a wreath of flowers and fruit growing out of vases on either side. The sarcophagus stands on a marble slab supported by tortoises. The body of the sarcophagus, of bronze and porphyry, reflects the style of Desiderio da Settignano, whose pupil Verrocchio may have been. However, it is much more powerfully

constructed than the Marsuppini tomb in S. Croce. There
is tremendous energy in the voluptuous leaves and writhing
foliage. The wreath around the inscription plaque reveals the master's extensive training: he was also a very
good goldsmith. The lid is crowned with a diamond over an
acanthus bud which stands up in the middle and from which
cornucopias pour forth their plenty over the sarcophagus.
The marvellous contrast between stone and metal is resolved
in a grating of woven strands of bronze by which the work
is held firmly yet elastically in its aperture. This tomb is
one of the triumphs of those artistic talents which were
awakened and sponsored by the Medici.

Before leaving the Old Sacristy through the inlaid wooden
doors (Verrocchio?), the visitor should not miss the clay bust
of the young *Cardinal of Portugal* (by Desiderio da Settignano, 1462) which is kept under glass on one of the cupboards on the entrance wall. This strong yet delicate piece
is not unlike some of Donatello's work.

The New Sacristy

After the projected façade had not materialized, Leo X
succeeded in pacifying a very angry Michelangelo with a
new plan – the erection of a funeral chapel for Lorenzo the
Magnificent and his brother Giuliano, as well as for two
younger members of the Medici family who had risen to the
position of dukes. Work on the New Sacristy, which was
located to the north of S. Lorenzo in the corresponding
position to that of the Old Sacristy on the south side, had
begun on 4 November 1519, and the walls were probably
already standing when Michelangelo took over the project
in 1521. The dome was hardly vaulted when in 1523 work
had to be interrupted for financial reasons. Pilasters of
dressed stone were envisaged for the interior, matching the
corner articulation of Brunelleschi's Old Sacristy. In this
and in other respects, the work of his great predecessor
provided Michelangelo's point of departure. He took over
the already existing north and west walls; the east and south
walls were altered if not completely rebuilt. When Cle-
ment VII became pope, the financial problems were re-
solved, and by December 1523 the dome and lantern could
be completed and the architectural marble and the first part
of the tomb decoration delivered.

SS. Annunziata, capital in the forecourt (Michelozzo)

SS. Annunziata, chapel by the tabernacle

S. Lorenzo, wall articulation of the New Sacristy

This is the earliest building still standing on which Michelangelo worked as architect. The plan to use the uncompleted

fifteenth-century building as a funeral chapel must have
originated with Cardinal Giulio di Giuliano (later Clement VII). He was a son of the Don Giuliano who was to
be buried here together with Lorenzo the Magnificent
(father of Leo X). Thus Michelangelo's first designs would
have been submitted to him. Originally a freestanding tomb
was planned, but the interior was found to be too small for
this. Opinions differ as to what subsequently happened, but
it is known for certain that at one time the idea of erecting
monuments to the two Medici popes was broached. As already mentioned, it had been decided from the very beginning that Giuliano, Duke of Nemours, and Lorenzo,
Duke of Urbino, were to be buried in the sacristy.

In 1532 Giovanni da Udine began work on the stuccoing
of the dome. In 1534, Michelangelo left Florence for Rome.
The statues of the dukes had been erected by that time, but
the entrance wall was unfinished and little concern was
expressed regarding the future of the building. Vasari
complained in a letter about the statues being blackened
with fire and the fact that water was percolating everywhere. The recipient of this letter, Cosimo I, remembering
this legacy of his forefathers, restored the building (with
the help of Vasari, who laid down the floor, plastered the
entrance wall and had the allegorical figures mounted on
the sarcophagus) and in 1559 brought here the bones of
Lorenzo the Magnificent and Lorenzo's brother Giuliano
and buried them near Michelangelo's 'Medici Madonna' and
the figures of SS. Cosmas and Damian on the entrance
wall.

Exterior   The building juts out powerfully to the north
and west. The door on the east side leads to a room beneath
the sacristy. The blind arcade of the side of the church is
extended round the east and north sides of the sacristy. This
contains window surrounds, some of which – and this is our
criterion for the state of the walls before Michelangelo's
intervention – were left blind and without openings into
the interior. Consequently the interior windows on these
two sides are blind. The wall articulation breaks off at the
north-west corner, for houses originally stood here which
were only pulled down in 1938–9. The bend in the west
wall is also due to previously existing buildings. The lower
part of the drum sits on a square base of dressed stone with

indows in its sides, only a few of which correspond to
penings in the interior (through a shaft leading downwards
: an angle). Above the semicircular cupola rises Michelangelo's twelve-sided lantern. At each corner of the lantern
a freestanding column; the transition to the concave
onical roof of the lantern is effected by smooth, unarticu-
ted volutes.

terior   The visitor enters the New Sacristy from the
iazza Madonna, passing first the **Cappella dei Principi**
ee p. 134; entrance fee). Michelangelo's sacristy is not only
ller than Brunelleschi's, but is made to appear so. It has
n intermediate storey (the pendentives, instead of begin-
ing above the first entablature, begin above the second)
nd the windows narrow towards the top, creating a per-
ective effect of greater height. The articulation of the
ancel wall of Brunelleschi's sacristy was taken as the
asis for that of the New Sacristy, and applied to all four
alls. Architectural forms in marble, some incomplete, are
tted into the skeleton of darker stone. Only the lower
orey (except on the entrance wall) was finished. The
terior would have given a very much richer impression
ad it been completed as planned. The lunettes were to
ave contained paintings, and Giovanni da Udine had be-
un to apply gilded stucco decoration to the coffers of the
ome. There were to have been more figures, and super-
ructures had been planned to complete the architecture
f the central panels. The present impression of coolness is
us not authentic, and it is therefore difficult to visualize
e rich decorative programme that was intended to trans-
orm this room into a cosmic symbol.

he key to this original intention is to be found in the
mbs. Five men were laid to rest in the New Sacristy: on
e entrance wall, Lorenzo the Magnificent († 1492) and
is brother Giuliano (murdered during the Pazzi Conspi-
acy, 1478); on the right wall, Giuliano, Duke of Nemours
1516), and on the left wall Lorenzo, Duke of Urbino
† 1519), and Duke Alessandro (murdered 1537). The theme
f the sculptural decoration is the mourning of the universe
nd the conquest of temporality by eternity. A fresco of the
esurrection on the entrance wall was to be a reminder of
e comforting doctrines of the Church. The tomb walls are
ominated by seated figures (ideal portraits) in niches.

Below them, on the sarcophagi, are the mourning figures of
Day and *Night* (on the right) and *Dawn* and *Dusk* (on the
left). Beneath the sarcophagi, reclining river-gods had been
planned, symbolizing the four rivers of the world. For these
water allegories (representing the entire globe), Michelangelo
designed two sets of models (for Lorenzo's tomb) in 1524 and
in 1525–6, but only one, in clay, has been preserved (in the
Accademia; it belonged to Ammannati). *Day* and *Night*
were originally designed for the tombs on the entrance wall.
Figures of *Heaven* and *Earth* (these according to a written
note of Michelangelo's), *Fire*, *Water* and possibly further
mountain allegories are said to have been planned (*Morning*
is leaning against a rock and has consequently been interpreted as being a mountain goddess) but there is insufficient
evidence. According to Giovanni da Udine, Michelangelo
also envisaged having the entire chapel frescoed. Were these
frescoes to have depicted battles, the story of Judith, the
brazen serpent? Opinions differ.

Giuliano, Generalissimo of the Church of Rome (hence the
rod of the commander), is absent-mindedly holding a
number of coins in his left hand (a reference to his having
been born under the auspicious sign of Jupiter), and has
his head turned towards the left. He is seated on his throne
in a stiff, erect, attentive posture. This must be the figure
that was begun in 1526, somewhat later than that of the
'first' duke. *Night*, beneath him, is unmistakable with her
half-moon and the star in her hair, and the poppy, owl and
mask. Both *Night* and the corresponding figure of *Day*
appear to be struggling against the instability of the sloping
lid. Curve (of the sarcophagus) and countercurve (of the
bodies) are in perfect harmony. Both figures are leaning on
one side, their generous bodies fully rounded, their relationship to the base necessitating this posture of support
through a sort of inner tension. Beyond the man's powerful
shoulders, his unfathomable gaze rises like a heavenly body
above the horizon. The woman's gaze is heavy and lowered.
She is the essence of motherhood; the melancholy gravity
of her emotional introspection gives the stone from which
she is carved its poetic meaning – a fact equally expressed
by Michelangelo in a poem.

Enthroned in a niche opposite, lost in thought, is *Il Pensieroso*,
the saturnine Duke Lorenzo who died insane. On his head

s a grotesque helmet which conceivably could be the
product of his brooding. Below him are *Dawn* and *Dusk*.
Both figures appear more open than their counterparts on
the tomb opposite. The completely naked and daringly
human figure of the woman is seen rising as if from sleep.
Beside her, the man's glance is sinking, heavy with dreams.
– All the reclining figures are set in beds of unpolished
marble from which they appear to be peeling themselves,
like skin coming away from fruit.

Michelangelo worked for a long time on the *Madonna* of
the entrance wall. This was the first sculpture in the chapel
and was begun as early as 1521. It, too, remained incomplete. The master may have had in mind his earlier
Bruges Madonna (with the child standing between the
mother's legs) when he began, but he seems then to have
changed his mind and, orienting himself on a small Classical
statue in the Medici collection, aimed towards a 'Penelope'
type. The work is extremely attractive; the smooth, virginal
and yet sibylline face is irresistibly charming. The figures of
SS. Cosmas (left) and Damian (right) were executed by
Raffaele da Montelupo after models by Michelangelo which
were in Vasari's possession for a long time. – Both dukes
glance out from their niches towards the Madonna and the
Child. The altar is positioned in such a way that the priest
celebrating from behind it) also has the holy image in his
field of vision. The group thus constitutes the terminal point
of the connections which run longitudinally and diagonally
through the room.

Michelangelo's *altar with two candlesticks* (the one on the
right was faithfully renovated in the eighteenth century)
also merits particular attention, above all for its characteristic ornamentation. Apart from that, the visitor should
quietly allow himself to be affected by the curious atmosphere of the whole room, which emanates from the articulation of the walls with their massive supra-portal niches
pressing down on the doors, from the tension which informs
every detail of the architecture (*ill.* facing p. 192), and from
the friezes of demoniac masks. The attic storey was to have
been animated with figures (only the *Crouching Boy* has
survived; it is now in Leningrad) and ornamental arrangements of weapons (two of which now stand in the passage
to the Cappella dei Principi). No inscriptions are left. These

unrealized ideas still live on amid the heavy, silent, surging life of the chapel. The unresolved enigmas of the allegories pervade the room. Before leaving, the visitor should lift his gaze from them towards the spot where the statues of the dukes, turned to face the Madonna, appear to be tearing themselves out of the eternal cycle of creation and dissolution.

Cappella dei Principi

Cosimo I, to whose patronage we owe the pious decoration of the New Sacristy or Medici Chapel, was also the instigator of this burial place for the ducal line, so that it is in many respects a parallel undertaking to Michelangelo's building. The first model was prepared by Vasari in 1561–8. It was to be of the same dimensions as the Old and New Sacristies and dressed with 'pietra dura'. The collection of precious stones from all over the world for the decoration began shortly afterwards, but the foundation stone was not laid until 1605. With virtually every well-known architect in Florence engaged on the project, it grew to such colossal proportions that it began to be rumoured that this unprecedented lavishness was a prelude to the capture of the Holy Sepulchre in Jerusalem by a pirate fleet for subsequent re-erection in the middle of this splendid building. – The final design was supplied by Don Giovanni Medici; the execution was taken over by Matteo Nigetti whose contribution was probably rather more independent than has been thought hitherto. The extent of Buontalenti's contribution cannot be accurately ascertained, in spite of the numerous designs preserved in the Uffizi. Among his collaborators the name of Remigio Cantagallina, who was later to achieve such success as an engraver, occurs for the first time. What is known is that Buontalenti (like Vasari) started from a small cross-shaped building which was designed to contain only the tombs of Cosimo I and his closest relations. – In 1613 the ground floor was so far advanced that, under cover of a temporary wooden roof, the application of the 'pietra dura' decoration could begin.

It proved impossible to finish the Cappella dei Principi during the reign of the Medici dynasty, in spite of heroic efforts on the part of the last surviving member, Anna Maria Lodovica. The present bell-tower of S. Lorenzo was built in her time (architect, Ferdinando Ruggieri) and the walls of the main chancel were rebuilt. – The dome was only closed in the nineteenth century and – Anton Raphael Mengs having spent several months in Florence in 1772 designing the pictorial decoration for it – was finally painted by Pietro Benvenuti.

The effect of the building was intended to be overwhelming. Part of the original plan was to take out the rear wall of the main chancel of the church so that this huge centralized hall could be viewed from the nave. This would have made the Cappella the culmination of the whole building, and reduced the Renaissance church to the status of a sort of vestibule. But already by Nigetti's time, the Cappella was being regarded as a separate structure, and when in 1787 the wall to the church was taken down, it was only for a short period. In 1860 the aperture was closed once more; the individual character of the newer building was found to be too obtrusive, and at the same time the spirit of Brunelleschi proved strong enough to preserve the individual character of his building.

The visitor re-enters the Cappella dei Principi through a narrow passage from the New Sacristy (passing the two recently rediscovered arrangements of weapons intended for the cornice zone of the latter). The dark colour of the wall decoration imparts a kind of incense-laden atmosphere to the wide, echoing space. In the three receding corners are polygonal apses. In each wall of the two lateral apses is a colossal wall-tomb (cenotaph) with a statue tabernacle. They are for six Medici rulers: beginning on the right, Ferdinando II († 1670), Cosimo II († 1621), Ferdinando I († 1609), Cosimo I († 1574), Francesco I († 1587) and Cosimo III († 1723). Not all the statues were completed. Only the second and third sarcophagi have powerful portraits in gilded bronze above them. It was originally planned that Giovanni da Bologna should design marble statues, followed by some designs for porphyry portraits by Buontalenti, but the present portraits were finally made by Pietro Tacca (the figure of Ferdinando I was apparently completed by Ferdinando Tacca). The sarcophagi themselves bear impressive witness to craftsmanship of a very high order indeed. Each one consists of more than two hundred parts which seem to be fitted together without

seams. The one which is most nearly complete is that of
Ferdinando I; the capitals of the pilasters that frame the
panels are gilded, and superstructures dominate the volutes
of the sarcophagus (their purpose is unclear; they may have
been for figures), a feature which is not possessed by the
others. Of the enormous Medici coats of arms above, only
a few are made of stone; the rest are wood-and-cardboard
dummies. Crowns, richly decorated with precious stones, lie
on cushions on each sarcophagus. The sixteen *coats of arms*
of Tuscan towns (below), with their inlaid mother-of-pearl,
lapis-lazuli, etc, are among the most valuable works in the
chapel. – The dome fresco, with scenes from the *Creation*
to the *Last Judgement* (with four Patriarchs and four
Evangelists), does not entirely harmonize with the rest of
the decoration. Originally the dome should have been inlaid
with precious stones, which would have given a similar
effect to that of the tribune dome in the Uffizi. – The floor
was not completed until this century, continuing the design
of the already existing parts. – The splendour of the high
altar was to have equalled the rest. A ciborium was planned
for it, possibly similar to that of S. Spirito. Designs for it
occupied Buontalenti for some years, but without result.
The only completed works were individual 'pietra dura'
panels which were very splendid nevertheless, including the
Supper at Emmaus on the front. For the rest, wooden and
painted imitations were provided. One can observe the very
high quality of these substitute pieces on the sides and the
back, where a piece of stone carving, an exquisitely worked
double wreath (laurel and olive), is let into an otherwise
entirely wooden panel.

On either side of the chancel apse, tunnel-like passages lead
to two small rooms like sacristies where the legendary
collection of **treasured relics**, once kept in the cupboards of
the end chapel of the south transept, is now housed. Here,
set out in well-lit glass cases, it can be studied at leisure.
– Proceeding first to the left-hand room, the visitor will
find in the middle of the bottom shelf of the case opposite
the window wall the relic of the Crown of Thorns in a
vessel of mountain crystal (fifteenth century) richly set
with jewels and enamel-work and supported by two
(Baroque) angels. On the same shelf, second from the left,
is a relic of S. Bartholomew in a hemispherical vessel,

namelled on the base and on the handles, which are in the
orm of small dragons (*c.* 1500). On the top row, extreme
eft, is a relic of S. Cosmas; again handles are in the
orm of dragons and the piece is richly set with gold and
namel (same period). Fifth from the left on the top row is
 flask of (perforated) mountain crystal decorated with
nimals and what appear to be Arabic letters. The enamel-
vork and the handles (dragon and lizard) date from the
ifteenth century and were restored during the sixteenth
entury. It is usually called the *S. Catherine Reliquary* – an
bvious misnomer. – Some of the reliquaries bear the name
f Lorenzo the Magnificent, e.g. the sixth from the right on
he top shelf. – The cases in the right-hand room contain
nainly Baroque pieces, including some excellent ebony
abernacles.

Returning to the main space of the chapel, the visitor will
ind a *plan of the building* hanging on the partition wall to
he church to the left of the postcard stand. In section
looking south-west), it differs slightly from the present
tate of the building. The lantern was modelled on that of
he Cathedral (there is another model in one of the side-
ooms of Michelangelo's New Sacristy, but the room is not
pen).

A flight of stairs takes the visitor down to the crypt-like
asement. On the way there is an *Annunciation* relief (the
eads only), and below it a (metal) plaque commemorating
he laying of the foundation stone. The lower steps bulge
ut strangely in imitation of Michelangelo's stairs in the
estibule of the Laurentian Library. Slabs let into the
asement floor mark the places where the sarcophagi of
he members of the family rested until the eighteenth
entury. After they had all been plundered, they were
emoved to the equally large crypt on the floor below.
At the same time the wall on to the Piazza Madonna was
ierced with a door, giving the former burial chamber its
resent character of a passage room; it is occasionally used
or services.

`rom the **outside,** the Cappella dei Principi represents an
ctagon with massively buttressed corners. The complexity
f the outside walls stands in strange contrast to the
elatively little articulated interior. The upper windows
arrow towards the top like those in Michelangelo's New

Sacristy. Their volutes owe a debt to Buontalenti's styl
There is an important element of colour contrast betwee
brown and white: the upper brown panels have whit
surrounds, the panels below are white with brown sur
rounds. This contrasting design was also derived fror
Michelangelo – from his 'Manneristic' style, as exemplifie
by the vestibule of the Laurentian Library. – There is
building inscription on the keystone of the window nex
to the entrance.

The Cappella dei Principi belongs on the whole to
specifically Florentine architectural style, a kind of secon
blossoming of the Renaissance that occurred nowhere els
not even in Rome. There is a certain anachronism about
which is seen most clearly in the dome. In the context of th
city as a whole, this rather slack and ponderous structur
bears no comparison with Brunelleschi's marvellous creatio
for the Cathedral.

Biblioteca Laurenziana

To the south of the nave of S. Lorenzo, against a back
ground of medieval canons' quarters, lies one of the mos
beautiful two-storeyed **cloisters** in Florence. It was built b
Manetti after 1457. From the impressive calm of th
setting, the visitor has a marvellous view of the Cathedr:
dome (the view is best from the north-west corner). Th
cloister contains a number of tombs. The *seated figure c
Paolo Giovio* (by Francesco da Sangallo, signed and date
1560), which is on the west side of the cloister near the sid
door of the church, deserves particular mention. It wa
placed here in 1574 to commemorate the instigator of th
portrait gallery in Como which had such an influence o
its period, and was responsible, for example, for giving Vasa:
a great deal of inspiration for his *Lives of the Painters*, etc.

However, the most remarkable feature of the cloister
the **Biblioteca Laurenziana**, the library of the Medici, whic
was founded by Cosimo the Elder. In 1508 it was trans
ferred to Rome for a period but it was later restored to i
home town by Clement VII. Here, in Michelangelo
memorable architectural monument, it found its perma
nent home, and was opened to the public.

*The master began to plan this addition to the west win
of the canons' residence in 1524. At first only two room*

were envisaged – one for the Greek and one for the Latin
books. The plan then went through several stages which we
can follow in Michelangelo's letters. All difficulties stemmed
from one central problem, the static problem of erecting a
new, tall building on relatively weak thirteenth century
foundations. Michelangelo thus began by building a sub-
structure. This, the pope insisted, should not inconvenience
the canons in any way and must be completely fireproof.
Work proceeded very slowly and was further impeded by
changes of plan which we will not detail here. Matters
developed a little faster merely after 1533. Michelangelo
was by that time in Rome and had to instruct others (including Tribolo and Vasari) in the completion of his work.
For the staircase, he finally sent a clay model in 1557 which
was executed by Ammannati before 1560. The new building
was finally opened to the public in 1617 (see the inscription
above the entrance door to the large reading-room). – The
library, however, was not complete at that time. It was not
until this century that the vestibule was endowed with its
present aspect.

The best view of the façade, with its long row of windows
lighting the reading room, is from the upper storey of the
east wing of the cloisters. According to the original plan,
the vestibule was to have shared a single roof with the
main building (one can see on the right corner the old
dressed-stone edge which rises to the height of the roof
cornice of the main building). Later Michelangelo conceived the idea of drawing the vestibule up higher than
the library itself. A start was made on this plan, but it was
not executed in detail until 1902–3, when the upper window storey was rather arbitrarily interpreted.

The façade is more interesting than may at first sight
appear. The question arises as to whether the rectangular
panels around the windows should be considered as let
into the flat wall surface, or whether the outer wall is
to be regarded as a superstructure, with the window panels
as the primary wall. The ambiguity of this situation is
heightened by the absence of any articulating elements,
such as, for example, bases or capitals (which might have
defined the strips of wall between the windows as pilasters
and thus as a definite 'front'). The function of the 'order'
within an architectural composition is just as determinative

here – where it is missing – as anywhere else. This is a
characteristic feature of the Mannerist style, and this ex
ample of Michelangelo's work has been quoted to illustrate
the concept of 'permutation' or the interchange of archi
tectural elements which became possible in Mannerism.
Entering the **vestibule**, the visitor is confronted with one
of the climactic moments of European architecture. The
'ambiguous impression' and 'indifference to structural con
siderations' into which the visitor is here coerced have in
spired art historians to ever new interpretations. For, once
through the entrance, where do we find ourselves? On the
main floor or in a kind of basement, and is it an 'interior'
or an 'exterior'? A very curious flight of stairs leads up to
a magnificent portal which is modelled rather like an
exterior portal, and adds decisively to the impression that
this is an ante-room. In the panels of the wall are tabernacle-
like structures which are neither windows nor niches (they
are too shallow for that; in spite of the slabs, which look
like stands, the tabernacles cannot have been intended to
contain figurative decoration). Their form is equally
strange: the pilasters at the sides taper downwards (which
makes them diverge from the vertical sides of the inside
frame), they are fluted, but only as far as the centre, and
they support elements which resemble capitals but which are
narrower, and at the same time appear like fragments of an
entablature. The canons of architecture seem to be everywhere reversed. This applies particularly to the volutes of
the lower storey; they merely support themselves and merge
together in the corners in a purely decorative fashion. But
the climax of 'permutation' is reached in the pairs of
columns which, instead of standing in front of the wall, are
placed so far inside the wall that they are behind the plane
of its surface. Here the reversal of the laws of architecture
is at its most extreme.
These 'captive' columns in particular have provided the
stimulus for interpretations of this room. They have been
regarded as 'an incredible aberration of the great master'
and 'the columns' impotent straining against the wall' has
been compared to the slaves of the tomb of Julius II. It
should, however, be remembered that Alberti already regarded the column as being part of the wall, that columns
had been recessed in the wall as early as 1450 in Venice

façade of the Arco Foscari, Scuola della Misericordia), hat this arrangement appears in a drawing by Leonardo, hat the Romans used it in the 'Casa dei Crescenzi', and that apart from anything else Michelangelo's building does not tand on the ground but on top of an older building; the oundations are no stronger than the walls themselves, and f the columns had been placed in front of the walls, nothing could have been placed on top of them. The solution of putting these colossal monolithic shafts inside the wall on he one hand strengthened the wall, and on the other hand rovided the necessary support for the roof with its very wide span. Statically, too, the columns are the strongest element in the whole structure. We have here in fact the curious and highly creative process of a technical, engineering solution becoming, through sheer mastery of form, an artistic motif. This kind of columnar composition was to fascinate architects, particularly in Florence, for a long time to come, and was to be applied even in cases where, statically speaking, it was not absolutely necessary (e.g. the façades of Ognissanti and S. Giovannino).

If one is inclined to forget the actual purpose of these columns because of their form, the same holds even more true with regard to the *staircase* which dominates the room like some curious piece of furniture (and which, appropriately, Michelangelo first planned in wood). The broad, curved central flight flows down from the portal like a stream of molten lava. Climbing the side flights, which have no banisters, one experiences a feeling of insecurity as if one were treading on some living creature. (Traces of Tribolo's stairs can be seen on the walls behind the side flights.) The central flight was for the Grand Duke only, the side flights for his subordinates.

Mathematical calculations stand in surprising juxtaposition to quite irrational effects. Studying the interplay of light and dark shapes on the walls, the visitor will notice, above the tabernacles and providing as it were a dream-like echo of them, 'complementary forms' made up of the simplest mouldings and a section of carved entablature, the formal value of which one feels one understands at first sight, though one would be hard put to it to explain their origin.

The **reading-room** extends longitudinally from the

entrance portal. The inside gable of the portal makes use of
one of Leonardo's ideas, combining round and triangular
shapes. The raftered wooden ceiling (the first time in
Florence that a coffered ceiling was not used), with its
transverse beams dividing it into separate, broad panels,
accords with the pilaster order of the side walls. The delicate, almost Rococo elements of the decoration are among
the finest of Michelangelo's smaller forms (sculpture executed by Marco del Tasso and Antonio Caroto). The
master also designed the desks, to which the codices were
originally chained (some particularly valuable ones are on
display); they were made by Battista del Cinque and
Ciapino. The floor of terracotta slabs is by Santi Buglioni
after designs by Tribolo; it matches the ceiling.
On the right is the entrance to the *Rotonda* of 1841, which
is available as a reading-room. A permanent exhibition of
smaller works from the library's collection is on display in
the three rooms beyond the end-wall of the library itself.

The Signoria District

*Piazza della Signoria – Loggia dei Lanzi – Palazzo Vecchio
– Uffizi*

Piazza della Signoria
During the thirteenth and fourteenth centuries entire rows
of houses were demolished to make room for this, the most
important and representative of all the squares in Florence.
An immensely wide, rectangular site was planned, though it
appears to be more regular than is in fact the case.
In the same way as the Cathedral area represents the
religious centre of the city, so the Piazza della Signoria
represents the secular centre. Both were founded on Roman
sites, for here, too, remains of Classical buildings were
excavated (to the east these extend beneath a part of the
Palazzo Vecchio). Even today the square remains the centre
of the city's political life. Among the many historical events
associated with it we may mention the burning of Savonarola in 1498, which is commemorated by an inscription let

ito the pavement about ten metres in front of the large
ountain in the middle of the square. Unlike the Cathedral
irea, which developed more or less according to natural
iws of organic growth, the Piazza della Signoria represents
 deliberately ordered arrangement – a conscious work of
irt, as it were. The decisive steps were taken in the sixteenth
:entury, with the Uffizi providing an axis and the extended
ow of statues in front of the Palazzo Vecchio not only
iving the latter a splendid and imposing quasi-façade, but
ilso optically dividing the eastern part from the main body
f the square and giving it a character of its own.

he present appearance of the square is rather spoilt by
ineteenth century additions, particularly a Renaissance-
:yle insurance building of 1871 which stands directly
ipposite the Palazzo Vecchio. In the course of the exten-
ive renovations undertaken at the beginning of this cen-
ury, the old **commercial court** of 1359 (No. 10, on the
iast side) was very considerably treated and retains more
ir less its original appearance. On the façade, a **relief of
Christ** and twenty-two coats of arms of the guilds. Near-
iy, on the north side, stands the **Palazzo Uguccioni** (No. 7,
. 1550); it introduces a foreign, Roman note into this
itherwise so typically Florentine square. The architect is
iaid to have been Mariotto di Zanobi Folfi. The contrast
ietween the rusticated storey and the extended upper
toreys is typical of the Mannerist style.

he **statues** that decorate the square merit close inspection.
f we deal with them in order of celebrity, Michelangelo's
David undoubtedly takes pride of place. He stands on a
iocle slightly to the left in front of the palace portal, on a
ipot chosen by the master himself. (The fact that the present
itatue is a copy made in 1905 – the original had to be taken
o the Academy museum in 1873 because the marble was
iecoming weathered – does not detract from the appearance
if the square. A more detailed study of the statue is given
n the section dealing with the Accademia, p. 101.) The pale
tone contrasts with the dark, uniform masonry of the
ialace. The figure, like some monumental memorial, stands
juite detached from any kind of architectural relationship,
:xcept possibly that it senses with its back the nearness of
he massive wall. The stylistic novelty of this arrangement
ippealed strongly to the Florentines when the young giant

was unveiled on 18 May 1504. – Donatello's bronze group
Judith and Holofernes, to the left of the *David*, is very
different. Its present arrangement, on a tall baluster pedestal
which has been treated as a work of art in itself, is hardly
compelling. Constructed originally as a fountain (notice the
water-holes in the corners of the cushion) shortly before
1460, it was later moved to the courtyard of the Palazzo
Medici (Via Cavour), where it first drew attention. In 1495,
after the expulsion of the ruling family, it was set up before
the Palazzo Vecchio as an 'exemplum publicae salutis'; the
inscription runs round the top of the pedestal. Then, to
make room for Michelangelo's *David*, it was moved into the
courtyard of the Palazzo Vecchio, then shortly afterward
to the Loggia dei Lanzi, and finally in 1919 it reached its
present position. Though skilfully constructed, using mould,
taken from a live model, and daringly cast, Donatello's
masterpiece does not really make its mark here, surrounded
as it is by more gigantic figures. The compelling beauty of
this once gilded bronze group only really becomes apparent
on closer inspection. – To the left of it stands a somewhat
simplified copy of the *Marzocco* lion (1418–20; the name
is derived from the fact that it originally stood at the foot
of a column of Mars). Donatello's sandstone original is now
in the National Museum. This powerful animal, with its
expressive heraldic features, is the emblem of the city of
Florence. – The story behind the large fountain is a remarkable one. It was by far the greatest structure of its kind in
the whole of Florence. Hastily erected, partly of wood and
stucco, for the wedding of Francesco, son of Cosimo I, to
Johanna of Austria in 1565, it was not completed until
much later. The figure of Neptune in his horse-drawn water
chariot (with signs of the zodiac on the wheels representing
spring and autumn) is a very ancient symbol of authority.
In him is mirrored the pride of the Medici family at seeing,
for the first time, one of their number married to a child of
the imperial blood. With him, too, the Palazzo Vecchio,
which was the young couple's home, was to receive an
effective symbol of power and authority, for did not
Cosimo I owe his regal title of Grand Duke to this marriage?
The principal figure, Neptune himself, who looks like a
'kindly old marble dodderer' compared with the rest of this
series of monumental works, is not one of Ammannati's best

SS. Annunziata. 'S. Jerome adoring the Trinity' (Castagno)

S. Marco, monastery, 'The Transfiguration' (Fra Angelico)

pieces. Despite the experience he had gained in Rome, his style inclined more towards the delicacy of his Venetian schooling; he was unable to inform this enormous body with any real feeling of strength. The bronze figures around the curved Baroque rim of the fountain are mainly by Ammannati's school and only in part by himself. The figure on the left, on the corner of the palace, is modern. Florentine fountains differed from those of Rome in their economical use of water. But here, too, water was precious and had to be brought from a long way away. Some of the figures involved do not seem consistent with this fact. Their terrified gestures, as if expecting great torrents of water, are slightly inappropriate to the harmless, gurgling trickle presented. – The next statue, the *equestrian monument to Cosimo I*, the pious gift of his son Ferdinando I, bears the date 1594 on the horse's rein. It is a late work by that pioneer of style, Giovanni da Bologna, Flemish by birth and Florentine by adoption, and has often been compared to the Roman statue of Marcus Aurelius on the Capitoline Hill in Rome. Detailed, true to life and strong with northern massiveness, it stands on a narrow pedestal with three relief panels: *The Tuscan Senate bestows on Cosimo I the title of Grand Duke, Pius V gives him the insignia of his new position, Cosimo I triumphs over Siena*. These reliefs, in which the emphasis is on drawing and in which the figures peel themselves away from the background in a curious way, were particularly influential stylistically. – Finally, at the Uffizi end of the Palazzo Vecchio, stands Bandinelli's colossal marble group, *Hercules and Cacus*. The block from which this muscle-flexing victor was to emerge had already been worked by Michelangelo. Bandinelli arrived at the final composition only after a number of preliminary studies, including a model which is now in Berlin, and probably through orienting himself on Michelangelo's *David*. The base is a typical example of the master's decorative style.

Loggia dei Lanzi (*ill. facing p. 193*)

This building was erected in 1374–81 by Benci di Cione and Simone Talenti for the public ceremonial of the reigning parliament and 'for the honour and esteem of the community'. In the context of the historical process of the secular power's emergence into independence, the Loggia assumes a place of commanding importance as a symbol of the whole square. While it was under

construction the square itself was extended and became more
regular in shape, and the adjacent tangle of streets was resolved.
The second part of its name, 'dei Lanzi', only became current in
the time of Cosimo I when the bodyguard of mercenaries (with
their horses) was housed here. During festivals, e.g. that of 'San
Giovanni' on 24 June, this noble building is still decorated with
splendid tapestries and decked with garlands.

This grandiose and artistically inspiring Loggia opens on to
the piazza in three powerful semicircular arches, the daring
construction of which was long an object of admiration.
Stylistically it represents the same transitional stage towards
modern times as does, for example, Or San Michele. The
Feldherrnhalle in Munich is in some ways a copy. The
Virtues, on blue enamelled backgrounds, were carved in
1384-9 after designs by Agnolo Gaddi. Some traces of
previous painting and gilding have survived. From the
right: *Strength* by Giovanni di Francesco Fetti, *Temperance*
by Jacopo di Piero Guidi, *Justice* and *Prudence*, both by
Giovanni d'Ambrogio; on the side, *Hope*, *Faith* and *Charity*
by Jacopo di Piero Guidi. *Charity*, which is treated as a
freestanding sculpture, above the cornice, was the last
figure to be completed; her marble tabernacle is probably
a modern addition.

Inside the Loggia, a number of excellent statues have been
assembled to form a small museum. Of the two *lions* flanking the staircase, that on the right is a Greek original and
that on the left a copy (by Flaminio Vacca). Beneath the
right arch Giovanni da Bologna's famous group of three
figures can be seen writhing upwards (1583), a masterly
study of movement which seems to have been carved simply
in order to solve a figurative problem and which – this was
something quite new – presents an interesting view from all
sides. It was subsequently entitled the *Rape of the Sabines*,
the somewhat later relief on the socle also deals with the
same subject. In the corresponding position beneath the left
arch is Cellini's masterpiece, *Perseus*, holding up the Medusa's head in triumph (1545-54, *ill.* facing p. 208). The hero's
cruelty has been caught with the same flair for the sensa-
tional as is evident in the bizarre and very precisely
executed marble socle. The work, which Cellini discusses in
his memoirs, took him almost ten years; all that remain
from this long working period are two small model
(now in the Bargello) and a drawing. The socle can be

regarded as a typical example of Mannerist art. It is resplendent with curious detail, and includes four bronze statuettes n niches (*Jupiter, Minerva, Mercury, Danaë with the infant Perseus*) which relate to the hero Perseus; its great delicacy and charm, almost like a piece of chamber music or a precious piece of furniture, would be more suited to an interior. The relief on the front wall of the Loggia depicts the *Liberation of Andromeda*. Notice the richly graded modelling and the astonishingly large intervals in size between the figures. This is a rather indifferent copy of the original in the Bargello. – In the middle of the Loggia, on the right, is *Hercules fighting the Centaur Nessus* (Giovanni da Bologna, 1599). This group is based on Classical models (compare the piece in the Uffizi) and offers interesting perspectives from all angles. For many years it stood as a monument in one of the squares of the city. The composition s admirably gathered on its narrow socle. – To the left of t is *Menelaus with the body of Patroclus*, a copy of a fourth century Greek original. – Next comes the *Rape of Polyxena* by Pio Fedi (1866). – Of the six Classical female statues on the rear wall, particular mention should be made of the so-called *Thusnelda*, third from the left, with her deeply-felt expression of sorrow.

On the **roof** of the Loggia dei Lanzi, there was once a small pleasure garden with a little fountain by Giovanni da Bologna. The basin of the fountain is still there. Access to the roof is from inside the Uffizi.

Palazzo Vecchio

The enormous main block was designed – so legend has it – in 1298–1314 by Arnolfo di Cambio († 1301). Some time after 1343, the Duke of Athens extended it towards the south. In 1495, Cronaca extended it in depth, and in 1511 considerable extensions were made towards the north (on the piazza) and towards the east. The whole complex was extensively reorganized under Vasari's direction, after Batista del Tasso had made a further large addition to the rear of the building in 1549–55. Finally, smaller additions were made by Buontalenti in 1588–92.

The following brief history of the palace falls into four phases:

The original name was 'Palazzo dei Priori', because it was

the first regular seat of the guild masters ('Priori') and the
Gonfalonieri. It was also the seat of the chief magistrate of
the Republic and the first permanent seat of the secular
government. Since the Priori and Gonfalonieri together
were known as the Signoria, the palace (and with it the
square before it) was named 'della Signoria', and then
– since the old Florentine regime was a democracy – it was
changed to 'Palazzo del Popolo'. The original appearance
of the palace was much as it is today, except that it did not
extend nearly so far in depth. The building consists of three
storeys of irregular, 'cyclopean', rusticated masonry with
elegant double windows, crowned by a gallery which is
supported on brackets and decorated on the crenellations
with some human and animal heads (little is left of these,
the best view is from the Dogana court). Rising above this
is the daringly slender, solid tower (height 94 m) extending
to the outer edge of the gallery, with a small bell-chamber
on top opening out between four powerful round pillars
decorated with foliate capitals. The entire foundation of
the tower, from the gallery downwards, is completely solid
except for a small shaft hardly the width of a man which,
according to Vasari, was left as protection against the
possibility of damage by earthquakes. Hence all the windows vertically below the tower are blind. The ancient
emblems of Florence, the lily and the lion, can be seen on
the weather-vane. Up until the end of the fifteenth century
the Priori and Gonfalonieri, guarded by a hundred soldiers,
lived and slept in a communal room on the second floor of
the building, so that they should be protected from outside
political influences. Dante himself, who occasionally assumed the office of a Prior, spent some time here. Meetings of
the 'Council of the One Hundred' took place on the first
floor, while the Citizens' Council, comprising three hundred
members, probably met in the 'Camera dell'Arme' on the
ground floor, where the Council silver was kept. – Four
stone lions on the corners of the upper gallery (outside,
symbolize sovereignty; the Signoria also kept a pair of live
lions, on the corner where the Uffizi now stands (the street
running along the rear of the Palazzo Vecchio still bears the
name 'Via dei Leoni'). – Very little remains of the interior
decoration of that period. There are some rare and therefore
extremely precious fourteenth-century wooden ceilings, and

he old bell of 1322 can still be heard. Everything else has
disappeared, including a once famous fresco by Giotto,
1326. – The first alterations began when Walter of Brienne,
Duke of Athens and Count of Lecce', left the monastery
of S. Croce in 1342 to become master of the city. Under
his tyrant, the palace was built out into a sort of fortress.
The foreign regime was shortlived, however, and in 1343
he 'duke' was expelled and most of his vassals murdered.
The city celebrated the event with a festival. Shortly after
hat the 'Ringhiera' was constructed. This was a fairly high
platform running along the front of the palace, and was the
forerunner of the later Loggia dei Lanzi, serving as a place
or speeches and for the solemn ceremonial of the Signoria.
This first popular monument to the republican spirit was
unfortunately destroyed in the early nineteenth century. In
1353 the city graced its palace with a clock which struck the
hours, and increased the number of bells in the tower.
n the fifteenth century, a second phase began during which
he building lost its warlike appearance. Donatello's youthful marble 'David' (now on show in the Bargello) was
brought to the palace from the Cathedral in 1416, and this
characteristic 'translatio' sparked off a fresh wave of deco-
ation. In 1446 a committee was formed to supervise the
reorganization. The inspiration evidently came from Miche-
ozzo, to whom we owe the alteration and restoration of the
dilapidated court; he added some handsome Renaissance
windows (previously there had been very few openings)
and had the walls painted with sgraffiti and gold lilies. He
created new accommodation within for the Priori, regulated
he exterior cornices with a sharpened awareness of proportions, built a container for water under the roof and
made the staircases more convenient. It is, of course, no
onger possible to reconstruct the full extent of this great
architect's contribution, just as it is impossible to identify
Brunelleschi's part. Much has been lost from this period:
Botticelli worked for the palace, Verrocchio supplied some
bronze candlesticks, Michelangelo painted his cartoon of the
Bathing Soldiers' in the large hall beside Leonardo's 'Cavalry Battle' – all this has disappeared. It is as if the build-
ng, once robbed of its original purpose, no longer had the
strength to house and maintain the art treasures entrusted
o it. For from the time of Cosimo the Elder, 'Pater

Patriae', onwards the Republic was mainly governed from
the Palazzo Medici (in what is now the Via Cavour).

There were changes again in the third phase, that of the
Principate. Although under the first duke, Alessandro, who
took over from the old republican regime, the seat of
government was still the Palazzo Medici, the mock parliament which was under his control sat in the old city palace.
It so happened that the duke's first act was to melt down
the great bell in order to relieve an acute shortage of money.
But when Cosimo I assumed power in 1537, he left the
family palace and moved into the palace that had traditionally housed the Florentine government. The Palazzo della
Signoria thus became the Palazzo Ducale. As well as a new
name the palace received a new decor, the principal elements of which have survived to this day. Since this constitutes the main subject of the description which follows,
suffice it to say here that the masters chiefly responsible for
this decor were Bandinelli, Battista del Tasso and, above
all, Vasari. Vast mythological and historical frescoes give
each room a character of its own; series of rich tapestries
adorn the walls. It was from here that Cosimo I established
his factories (weaving, furniture). The arts and crafts designed by the circle around Vasari spread all over Europe
setting new styles.

The fourth phase began when the Grand Duke moved into
the Palazzo Pitti in 1565. The erection of a corridor between
the two palaces (it leads over the Ponte Vecchio to the more
freely situated garden palace) was the beginning of the end.
From then on, the city palace was known as the Palazzo
Vecchio. A part of the art treasures were removed, and
absorbed into the Uffizi at that time. Guests were still
received there (e.g. Montaigne) and it was used for festivals,
plays and marriage feasts, but the old building no longer
represented the backbone of power in Florence. The last
ruler to live there was Ferdinando I, son of Cosimo I.
Although in 1848, after the Risorgimento, a new government
moved in, it was no longer the government of Florence but
of the whole of Italy.

Exterior Standing in front of the main façade of the
palace, the visitor should bear in mind that this was
thoroughly renovated in the first half of the present century
(by A. Lensi). The bronze plaque to the left of the portal

commemorates the union of
Tuscany and the rest of Italy
which took place in 1860.
Above the entrance, between
two lions (1528), is the monogram of Christ with
Savonarola's motto, 'Rex
Regum et Dominus Dominan-
tium', which replaced an
earlier inscription in 1851.
The stone platform, on which
the line of monumental figures stands, corresponds
roughly to the old Ringhiera.
The two marble 'termini'
(boundary stones) with their
chains to the right and left
of the entrance (by Baccio
Bandinelli and V. de'Rossi)
indicate as it were in a

Palazzo Vecchio, window

humanistic way the territorial limits of the ducal seat. –
On the right side wall (Via della Ninna) one can distinguish
clearly between the original palace and the Duke of Athens'
additions. The place where the usurper's coat of arms was
chiselled out after his expulsion can still be seen above the
portal (to the Dogana court). The small iron door immediately on the left inside the passage marks the exit of the
duke's secret staircase which descends from the top storey.
Above is Vasari's passage to the Uffizi, which is the first
part of the corridor to the Palazzo Pitti. The beautiful
windows in the second storey were walled up for some
time; they were only opened again in 1921. Towards the
southern end (by Battista del Tasso) of the rear of the
building (Via dei Leoni) are the remains of medieval private
houses and of a loggia. The same architect was responsible
for the powerful portal with its inscription (1550) and a
coat of arms let into a diamond ring (a device of the
Medici). The rusticated wall dates from the end of the sixteenth century (Buontalenti). – On the north side, the three
distinct parts of the building are recognizable. In the central
portion – the end of the *Hall of the Five Hundred* – are the
remains of an arcade by Baccio d'Agnolo and Bandinelli.

Entering the palace from the Piazza della Signoria, the
visitor immediately reaches the **court** which was remodelled
by Michelozzo in the Renaissance style in 1453; because it
is built so high, the light is rather poor. Two storeys with
pairs of windows rise above an arcade. In 1565, for the
wedding of Granprincipe Ferdinando to Johanna of
Austria, the walls were decorated with frescoes and the
columns stuccoed – probably after a plan by Vasari. A
number of artists participated in this work; their names are
given in a (new) memorial inscription to the left of the
passage to the second court. Francesco del Tadda made the
delightful *porphyry fountain-basin* for the same occasion. It
is an early example of the technique of working very hard
stone, which was taken up again in the second half of the
sixteenth century. The little figure, a putto clad in a toga-
like garment and holding a fish, is by Verrocchio (1476) and
was brought here from the Medici villa at Careggi, where
it had been mounted on another, larger marble fountain
(the lower portion of this fountain may still be admired
before the entrance of the picture gallery in the Palazzo
Pitti). The figure should be understood as a 'Socratic Eros',
a leitmotive to which the revival of Classical antiquity owed
an essential part of its enchanting gaiety. (Careggi was the
seat of the 'Academy' sponsored by the Medici.) Even
though Verrocchio's little fountain figure has been taken
out of its original context so that its meaning may not be
entirely clear at first sight, nevertheless here, too, it is completely integrated with its classically inspired surroundings.
On the walls are arch lunettes with emblems and devices
painted in their oval panels. This theme is extended to the
grotesques that decorate the vault segments. On the upper
part of the walls are eighteen large *pictures of towns*,
strongholds of the House of Habsburg, which were painted
as a gesture of respect to the Austrian bride. It appears
that, in Italy, landscape painting grew out of Classical
wall-decoration (Pompeii) – i.e. not from direct observation
of nature but from humanistic roots. Proof of this is the
fact that the 'townscapes' of this court are completely
wedded to a decorative scheme of the Classical type.
Pictures of towns existed already in the Vatican. Landscapes
combined with grotesques, however, made their first appearance in the Odeon Cornaro, Padua. The stuccoed decoration

f the columns (*ill.* facing p. 209) has a strangely nordic
flavour. Vasari's inspiration came from printed graphic
design. The columns depict Bacchic motifs, putti, vine-
leaves and personifications of the seasons from the north,
mixed up with various poetic, mythological and astrological
figurations (signs of the zodiac). It is interesting that
Christian symbols too are dotted about (the two vaults to
the north-west) as well as Medici family emblems, the
decoration having been designed for the wedding feast. –
The *Sala dell'Arme* is closed but the visitor can obtain an
impression of it through a barred window. It is the only
hall in the palace to have preserved its fourteenth-century
style in its entirety. – The projecting structure on the entrance side of the court originally gave on to a flight of
stairs leading to the upper storeys. The coat of arms to the
right of the passage to the second court commemorates with
. verse by Dante the destruction of the houses of rebellious
families which took place when the palace was erected. In
the niche to the right of that is Pierino da Vinci's marble
group, *Samson and the Philistine* (the position is not original). – Standing in the centre of the court, the visitor
can see some faded paintings of trophies in the arch spandrels of the high walls (on the north-west corner a piece of
Michelozzo's old sgraffito decoration has been uncovered).
Beyond the passage, the visitor comes abruptly to the foot
of the main **staircase** which rises in two flights to right and
left. The construction of these flights underlines once more
the Classical character of Vasari's rearrangement of the
succession of spatial units. The old staircase in this court
rose in a straight line along the inside of the façade wall.
Vasari achieved what was an extremely difficult task in
erecting a new staircase of two flights beyond the court (it
impinges in fact upon the second, Dogana court). This had
the effect of demoting this first court (the core of the old
palace) to the position of an ante-room or 'atrium', or more
exactly a 'cavum' (Vitruvius' expression for such a forecourt with a fountain; it was Vasari who had the *porphyry
basin* with Verrocchio's putto installed here). Then came the
new staircase and after it the second court. In this way, the
old city fortress was forced into a new type of domestic
mould, that of the 'Casa degli antichi Romani' as Vitruvius
called it; Palladio illustrated the type in Barbaro's work

and designed a number of variants on it himself, e.g. the
Palazzo Porto Festa. With the relatively few adjustment
involved in making this new staircase, Vasari gave the old
building not only an entirely new emphasis in depth but
also an iconographically conceived ground-plan which was
Classical in origin but modern in its pattern – a performance
of Berninesque dexterity. One now regards the real entrance
of the palace as being the dignified porphyry portal in the
rear wall of the court before the staircase (1560–3). This is
stressed by the fact that the decorative scheme followed by
all the rest of the vaults is missing above this portal; several
segments are drawn together at this point into a model
tunnel, in the sail-like decoration of which amoretti play
with the Medici spheres (palle) as if the royal family were
here welcoming the visitor.

Interior Rooms   At the top of the stairs is the **Hall of
the Five Hundred** (Salone dei Cinquecento). This huge
room (length 53 m, width 22 m, height over 18 m) was
built *c.* 1495 by a number of assistants working under the
direction of Cronaca. It was the meeting place of the permanent council of representatives of the people which was
set up in 1494. At the first session, Savonarola gave a speech
that was later to become famous. After the dissolution of
this body in 1530, the hall was used for banquets. Today it
is the city's concert-hall. – Had a tragic fate not robbed
posterity of their glory, Michelangelo's *Bathing Soldiers* and
Leonardo's *Cavalry Battle* would decorate these walls.
None the less, through the many copies which were made of
their cartoons for this hall, these murals had an influence on
European art which it would be impossible to overestimate
– Otherwise the memory of that period has completely disappeared. Vasari (at Michelangelo's suggestion) had the
ceiling raised by more than 7 m and decorated with splendid carvings, paintings and other ornamentation. It is
divided into thirty-nine compartments and recounts the
story of Florence and the Medici family (1563–5). The
arrangement is strictly symmetrical. The panels of the two
narrow ends show personifications of Florence, its districts
and provinces. On the entrance side in seven panels is the
war against Pisa, and on the opposite side the war against
Siena. The central row is given over to the history of
Florence, culminating at the centre with the coronation

of Cosimo I. – The following is a more detailed description, beginning at the window wall right of the entrance. In the round panel the districts of S. Spirito and
S. Croce. The four pictures to the left of it, Arezzo, Cortona
and Montepulciano, Borgo S. Sepolcro, and S. Giovanni.
To the right of the round panel, respectively Volterra,
S. Gimignano and Colle, Chianti, and Certaldo. Against the
opposite window wall, taking them in the same order, the
districts of S. Giovanni and S. Maria Novella (round panel);
on the left the provinces of Pistoia, Prato, Pescia and Val-
darno; on the right Fiesole, Castrocaro, Casentino, Scarpe-
ria. – Along the entrance wall (the war against Pisa): the
Battle of Cascina, the Signoria decides to wage war on
Pisa, the conquest of Vico Pisano, the triumph of the
Florentines, the victory over the French, the victory over
the Venetians, Florentine galleys board corn-ships from
Pisa. Opposite (the war against Siena): the conquest of
Monistero, Cosimo plans the campaign, the conquest of
Casole, the triumphal entry of the Marchese of Marignano,
the conquest of Montereggioni, the battle near Marciano in
the Chiana valley. Central row (starting from the podium
end): the victory over Radagasio, king of the Goths, the
founding of Florence, Clement VII arms the leaders of the
Guelf party, the coronation of Cosimo I, Pope Eugenius IV
escapes from Rome to Livorno, Arnolfo di Cambio submits
his plan for enlarging the city, the union of Florence and
Fiesole.
Vasari's vast *murals* in their ornamental frames present an
impressive sight. They occupy an important place in the
history of the realistic depiction of battle scenes. On the
entrance wall (from left to right): the victory of the
Florentines near Torre S. Vincenzo, Maximilian abandons
the siege of Livorno, the conquest of Pisa. The opposite wall
glorifies the war against Siena with (from right to left) the
victory of the Florentines near Marciano, the conquest of
Porto Ercole, and the conquest of Siena. Stylistically these
pictures represent a curious synthesis of Tuscan clarity of
draughtsmanship and a Venetian disposition of masses. In
fact, there is about the whole room an element of competition with the colossal assembly hall of the Doge's Palace.
As regards the rest of the decoration, the two end walls are
most interesting. The podium end (the so-called *Udienza* or

reception-room, the official audience-room of the grand
ducal family) has a chequered history. The structure itself
constitutes one of the first architectural undertakings of
Grand Duke Cosimo I; it was built by Bandinelli and
Giuliano di Baccio d'Agnolo. Pilasters, columns, arches and
niches, together with an entablature which bends at right
angles at the sides, are arranged to form a triumphal decor
which is like a stage. The free-standing columns at the sides
have fine Corinthian-style capitals; similar capitals appear
in the Mercato Vecchio. The figured capitals on the pilasters
of the window wall are different; they continue an older
Florentine tradition (compare the capitals in the sacristy of
S. Spirito). The original design of the *Udienza* was never
completed. The stucco figures above the entablature (de'
Rossi) were added later; Romolo Ferrucci's base (handsome
lions' heads) for the seated statue of Leo X in the main
niche in the centre was not added until 1591. The *statues*
in the niches represent (from the left): Cosimo I and Giovanni delle bande nere, characteristic pieces by Bandinelli,
who also began the next figure, Leo X, although it was
completed by his pupil de'Rossi. In the niche is a stuccoed
yoke bearing the mild pope's motto, 'enim suave'. The
following figure, Alessandro Medici, is equally by Bandinelli, as is the figure of the pope in the next group, *Coronation of Charles V by Clement VII.* The kneeling emperor
and the following figure, Francesco I, are the work of
Caccini. It was on the occasion of Francesco's marriage that
the hall, with its new decoration, was inaugurated. – The
visitor should bear in mind that the present, somewhat ill-
proportioned appearance of the *Udienza* is due to Vasari's
having subsequently raised the ceiling of the hall.

The two pictures high up on the wall to either side are by
Jacopo Ligozzi (left, *Boniface VIII receives the Florentine
embassy*; right, *Coronation of Cosimo I as Grand Duke by
Pius V*). The corresponding pair at the opposite end are by
Passignano, one of the finest colourists of the late sixteenth
century (*Cosimo founds the Order of S. Stephen*, 1596),
and Cigoli, one of the best draughtsman of the century. His
picture, *The senate elects Cosimo Duke of Tuscany*, 1600,
does not really reveal all this versatile master's fine qualities.
For the rest, the architectural articulation of the end wall
opposite the *Udienza* is modern (Emilio de Fabris). For

ime there was a fountain in the place of the central niche – a large structure by Ammanati (not set up), the figures from which are now in the Bargello or distributed about the Boboli Gardens, and later a smaller one. Michelangelo's *Victory* was only placed here comparatively recently. It may have been one of the designs for the tomb of Julius II (the oak leaves in his hair recall the Rovere family device). 'Victory' is crushing a bearded old man with his knee. The group, which was probably carved in 1526 and has been subsequently touched up, is very personal in its expression and full of tremendous tension. The young hero's glance, appearing to look right through his surroundings into the future, has that velvety melancholy so characteristic of the work of Michelangelo's middle period. The statue has never left Florence. Cosimo I brought it straight to this hall from the house of its creator; it was first placed in the *Udienza*.

Two rows of sculptured groups representing the deeds of Hercules (by Vincenzo de'Rozzi) cover the side walls. A closer inspection of these pieces, which are all of high quality, will reveal some unusual details. – The tapestries (Florentine, sixteenth century) echo Andrea del Sarto's and Franciabigio's frescoes in the Scalzo court. – The four figures in the niches on the side of the 'Victory' are Classical pieces; their arrangement is random.

The visitor passes through a door in this end wall into one of the most interesting interiors of the Florentine Late Renaissance. This oblong, windowless, tunnel-vaulted chamber, decorated throughout with paintings and sculptures, is known as the **Studiolo of Francesco I** (*ill.* facing p. 224). The dismantling of this room began as early as the end of the sixteenth century and only the upper cornice and the niches of 'marmo mistio' survived. In 1910, the pictures and statues were returned to their original places; the wooden fittings of the lower part of the room were only reconstructed in 1954. Vasari was in charge of the decoration of this little 'jewel casket'. The painting on the ceiling is the clue to the understanding of the room as a whole. By Morandini (known as *Il Poppi*), it depicts Nature handing a piece of quartz to Prometheus. Grouped around the figures are the four elements and small boys playing with objects associated with the elements. The overall programme of the

very elegant decoration (devised by Vincenzo Borghini) wa
thus to represent clearly the secret connection between ar
and nature and to depict the field of operation of the geniu
of humanity between these two poles. The choice of them
was typical of the spirit of Francesco I, who was well verse
in the study of philosophy and alchemy.

Work on the study began in 1570 with the painting of th
ceiling. The two round portraits (probably by Bronzino
of Cosimo I and his wife Eleonora of Toledo, who is wear
ing magnificent pearls, were then let into the two lunette
at the ends of the tunnel vault. They are framed by painte
signs of the zodiac (like Classical sarcophagi of the Seasons)
Beneath the marble cornice the wall surface was divide
into two zones, with the lower zone reserved for wall cup
boards for books and valuables, the upper for a row o
fourteen pictures, terminating at either end of each wal
with a beautiful stucco-framed marble niche containing
bronze figure. The paintings and the bronzes continue th
theme of the four elements, treating it in allegories an
through the gods of mythology and scenes from human life
water and fire are depicted on the side walls, earth and ai
on the end walls. The statuettes, starting from left of th
entrance, are: *Opi* (Andrea Calamech), *Galatea* (Stold
Lorenzi), *Venus* (Ammannati), *Juno* (Giovanni dell'Opera)
Zephyr (Elia Candido), *Apollo* (Giovanni da Bologna)
Vulcan (Vincenzo de'Rossi) and *Pluto* (Domenic
Poggini).

The wall cupboards below have splendidly ornamente
doors set with oval paintings depicting scenes from the realn
of the gods whose bronze figures grace the niches above
The upper and lower rows of pictures (starting from lef
of the entrance): *Perseus rescuing Andromeda* (G. Vasari)
Alexander giving Campaspe to Apelles ('Il Poppi'), *Th
Passage through the Red Sea* (Santi di Tito), *Neptune an
Thetis* (artist unknown), *Collecting grey ambergris* (Battist
Naldini), *Sacrifice of Lavinia* (Mirabello Cavalori,
variant of a scene from Albrecht Dürer's 'Life of the Virgin'
Phaeton's sisters turned into poplars (Santi di Tito), *Circ
bewitching the comrades of Ulysses* (Giovanni Stradanus)
Linen weavers (Mirabello Cavalori), *Dreams* (Battista Nal
dini), *Pearl fishing* and *Cleopatra's feast* (both by Alessan
dro Allori), *Venus takes Juno's girdle to show herself to Pari*

Francesco Coscia). – Rear wall: *Aeneas landing in Italy* (Giovanni Butteri), *Diamond mining* and *Fall of Icarus* (both by Maso da San Friano). – Right-hand wall: *Daniel before Balthasar* (Giovanni Fedini), *Thermae of Pozzuoli* and *Jason and Medea* (both by Girolamo Macchietti), *Invention of Gunpowder* (Jacopo Coppi), *Hercules slaying the dragon of the Hesperides* (Lorenzo della Sciorina), *Glassmaker's shop* (Giovanni Butteri), *Hercules and Iole* (Santi di Tito), *Goldsmith's shop* (Alessandro Fei), *Sack* (Niccolò Betti), *Alchemist's shop* (Giovanni Stradanus), *Foundry* (Domenico Buti), *Canon Foundry* ('Il Poppi'), *The family of Darius before Alexander* (Jacopo Coppi), *Vulcan's forge* (Vittorio Casini). – Entrance wall: *Danaë* (Bartolommeo Traballesi), *Gold mining* (artist unknown), *Deucalion and Pyrrha* (Andrea del Minga), *Atlanta's race* (Sebastiano Marsili).

Apart from the programmatic importance of this mysterious little room, it constitutes probably the most complete collection of the work of the artists working in Florence around 1570. – A secret staircase leads to the **Tesoretto**, a similar sort of study with a ceiling painted by the school of Vasari.

Returning to the *Hall of the Five Hundred* and continuing through the passage on the other side (the ascending decoration is left over from a staircase which was once here), the visitor comes to the **Hall of Leo X**, the only one of a complex of rooms dedicated to great members of the Medici family which is open to the public. The remarkable pope is celebrated in the fresco decoration. The mural on the right is important from topographical point of view, showing as it does among other things the original position of Donatello's *Judith* beneath the Loggia dei Lanzi, Bandinelli's *Hercules*, which was made especially for this place (probably of clay, now lost) and the *Ringhiera* running along the front of the Palazzo Vecchio (see also the grisaille below the fresco). A number of portraits are particularly worth the visitor's attention: in the fresco depicting the pope's procession in the Piazza della Signoria are, among others, Ariosto, Pietro Bembo and Aretino, and in the fresco opposite *(Leo X creates thirty cardinals in the Consistory)*, a number of artists including Michelangelo and Leonardo. Between the windows are Cosimo I and Alessandro,

together with their wives Eleonora of Toledo and Margaret
of Austria. In the niches above the door are busts of Leo X
and Clement VII, as well as of Giuliano, Duke of Nemours
and Lorenzo, Duke of Urbino, the two members of the
Medici family whom Michelangelo immortalized in ideal
form in the New Sacristy of S. Lorenzo, but whose plain
faces, as depicted here, are soon forgotten (Antonio Lorenzi).
Also noteworthy are Ammannati's monumental fireplace and
the ancient floor of fired tiles bearing the emblems of the
Medici. – Through a door, the visitor can look into Vasari's
richly decorated **chapel**, completed in 1558; the masterly
animation of these paintings, gilt frames, grotesques and
small holy pictures creates a successful ensemble. On the
altar is a copy of a Raphael *Madonna*, possibly by Giulio
Romano, and to right and left two very beautiful panels by
Giorgio Vasari depicting Cosimo the Elder and Cosimo I as
SS. Cosmas and Damian.

A steep staircase leads up to the **Quartiere degli Elementi**,
and one of Vasari's earliest decorative works in Florence.
The whole of the decoration is by Vasari and his assistant
Cristoforo Gherardi. This apartment, which consists of five
halls and two loggias, received its name from the *Hall of the
Elements*, which is the first room the visitor enters. – The
importance of this room, which had a great influence on
decorative style in Italy, lies partly in the fact that it turned
away from the hitherto dominant Raphael tradition towards
the style of the school of Fontainebleau (with which Vasari
was very familiar from engravings), and also in the new
relationship which it established between pictorial and architectural details. Apart from the fireplace and the doors, all
the architectural articulation is painted, and the way in which
this blends with large-scale ornaments (cartouches) and
monumental frescoes that create an illusion of free space
gives rise to that strange, unreal, fairy-tale charm so typical
of the Mannerist style. The ceiling decoration is devoted to
the element *Air*. A strange feature of the architecture of the
ceiling, and one which recurs in the other rooms, are the
marked gradations in height. Roman motifs play a part in
the ornamentation, which also contains reminiscences to
Giulio Romano (e.g. in the panel with the *chariot of the sun*,
a variant of the theme in the Palazzo del Te, Mantua). The
murals of *Water*, *Fire* and *Earth* reveal the influence of

S. Marco, monastery, the library (Michelozzo)

S. Lorenzo, interior of the nave

Primaticcio. The entire programme is based on Classical cosmogony. The absence of the stained glass which once decorated the windows (now lost) detracts from the impression of this hall. The beautiful fireplace has an inscription commemorating Cosimo I. – The **Loggia of Saturn** next door, situated as it is on the corner above the Piazza del Grano, offers a marvellous view. The paintings on the ceiling (by Vasari) were damaged in a fire at the end of the seventeenth century, but *Saturn* in the central panel is still recognizable, as are the twelve *Hours* around him. The small bronze grotesque in the corner is by Giovanni da Bologna. – A short corridor leads to the **Hercules Room**. The mythical hero's deeds are depicted on the ceiling; on the wall is a tapestry, *Victory over the Centaur Nessus*, after a design by Stradanus. – A small ante-room decorated with grotesques gives access to the **Loggia of Juno**, now closed. Its decoration has suffered somewhat from the weather but the principal piece, a monumental niche, is well preserved. – The painting in the centre of the ceiling of the **Hall of Jupiter** which follows (showing Jupiter being reared on goats' milk and honey) is again modelled on an invention of Giulio Romano's. The tapestries (designed by Stradanus) on the walls were originally made for the Villa Poggio a Caiano. – In the following **Hall of Opi**, the goddess is shown in the centre of the ceiling, riding in a chariot drawn by lions. She is surrounded by the *Seasons*, and the twelve *Months* are grouped around the frieze. – The last hall, **Hall of Ceres**, has the most regular ground plan of all the rooms. It, too, contains, among other things, tapestries designed by Stradanus. – A small writing-room completes the apartment. The decoration of this, as of all the rooms, was designed by Vasari; on the ceiling, *Calliope with two putti* (earthly and heavenly love). A choice collection of medallions and small bronzes was once kept here.

Leaving the apartment through the same door by which he entered and crossing one of the galleries of the 'Hall of the Five Hundred' (on the left is a small, very early copy of Leonardo's Cavalry Battle or *Battle of Anghiari*), the visitor comes to the older part of the palace, and first to the **apartment of Eleonora of Toledo**. These gloomy rooms were the young duchess's first home, though she never saw them finished: she died in 1562 at Pisa. There are six rooms

of various sizes (and a chapel); they were designed by
Vasari, working together with Stradanus, and represent a
later phase of his creative activity. – The **Green Room**
(so-called from the colour of the walls) contains grotesques
by Ridolfo Ghirlandaio; the architectural scheme of this, as
of the other rooms in the apartment, is by Vasari himself.
The beautiful round picture of the *Madonna* is by the school
of Botticelli. Through the window on to the court can be
seen the powerful complex of the original building as well
as the more relaxed sixteenth century additions. – On the
visitor's left as he enters the room is a charming little **study**;
the extremely delicate ceiling decoration is by Salviati. A
door on the right leads to a private **chapel**, painted throughout by Bronzino in 1540. The paintings, which are in an
excellent state of preservation, illustrate all this remarkable
artist's finest qualities: balanced composition, quiet movement and confident, coolly modelled corporeality. On the
ceiling, surrounded by a wreath, the symbol of the Trinity
floats in a heaven of blue. Grouped around it, in brilliant
colours, are SS. Michael, Jerome, Francis and John the Evangelist. The walls depict scenes from the story of Moses
(*Passage of the Red Sea, The Brazen Serpent, The people
are given water in the desert* and the *Gathering of Manna*).
Probably no other Florentine fresco of the mid-century
combines such confident draughtsmanship with such an
unfailing instinct for the perfect decorative effect. The same
applies to the altar-piece, also by Bronzino. The two side
panels, depicting the *Annunciation*, have become even better
know than the central *pietà*. The extremely aristocratic-
looking Mary is said to have the features of Maria Medici
a daughter of Eleonora of Toledo who died young. Work or
this chapel extended over about twenty years, the artis
receiving the final payment in 1564. – The **Hall of the Sabines** is named after the central picture of the ceiling; like al
the ceiling pictures in Eleonora's apartment, this depicts a
triumph of the female sex. It represents the Sabines' suc
cessful settlement of the quarrel between their compatriot
and the Romans. On the walls of this room, which wa
originally set aside for the ladies of the court, are a *Madonna*
tondo by Lorenzo di Credi, a number of youthful portraits o
members of the Medici family painted in the style of Suster
mans, and a seventeenth-century Florentine tapestry. – Th

dining-room which follows is known as the **Hall of Esther** (again from the painting on the ceiling). Notice the remarkable fifteenth century marble water niche and the excellent head of *Apollo*, a Hellenistic copy of an original attributed to Phidias. In the frieze below the ceiling, putti play between capital letters which together form the name and title of the duchess. – Next comes the **Hall of Penelope** (on the corner overlooking the Loggia dei Lanzi; there is a fine view from the window), with an interesting frieze depicting the deeds of Ulysses, and after that the **Hall of Gualdrada** with a frieze of *vedute* of old Florence. The central panel of the ceiling depicts the beautiful woman who refused to welcome the emperor Otto IV with a kiss, arguing that this favour should be granted only to her husband.

Leaving the apartment of Eleonora and entering the short corridor that leads past the wall of the tower, the visitor will find a case containing a cast of Dante's mask and will pass beneath some of the oldest wooden ceilings in the entire city (fourteenth century). The first room after this is the much-restored Council **chapel**, with frescoes by Ridolfo Ghirlandaio. On the ceiling, the *Holy Trinity with Evangelists*, and in the lunette opposite the altar, the *Annunciation* (heavily renovated in 1841). The altar-piece by Mariano da Pescia, 1514, is a very conservative piece of work. A pupil of Ridolfo Ghirlandaio, Mariano maintained the fifteenth century tradition longer than any other artist.

The visitor then enters the extremely spacious **Sala dell'Udinza**, the first of the old staterooms of the republic. The richly carved ceiling is very fine indeed; many artists worked on it, notably Giuliano da Maiano. His brother, Benedetto, was responsible for the architectural decoration, which consists principally of two portals. Above the portal from the chapel is an inscription concerning Christ (1529); the other portal, of white marble and porphyry, contains an important though unfortunately slightly damaged *Justitia* in the pediment (the mutilated hand should grasp a golden pear). The whole thing, with its wonderful ornamentation and its pair of inlaid doors (full figures of Dante and Petrarch), represents one of the finest achievements (1476–8) of the two brothers from Maiano, a little village near Fiesole. The carpenter Francione helped with the intarsie. Francesco Salviati's highly decorative and stylized frescoes are among

the finest and purest illustrations of the principles of Mannerism that this artist ever produced. They recount the story
of Furius Camillus. On the chapel end (from the right): the
surrender of the unworthy schoolmaster of Falerii to his
pupils, and the expulsion of the Gauls. Continuing on the
side wall: Camillus liberates the Romans from tribute to the
Gauls, and the triumph of Camillus (the painter added his
own self-portrait among the soldiers taking part). Distributed over the remaining walls are allegorical figures. This
independently-minded artist had the opportunity of gaining
some experience of Rome together with Vasari before his
return to take up residence in Florence once more, and this
experience shows in the frescoes. One feels, too, the influence
of the school of Raphael, although the tradition embodied
in the 'Hall of Constantine' in the Vatican appears to have
been expanded here into something very personal and
somewhat hypertrophied by crowding the painted surface
to such an extent as to leave very little free space. However, this may also be understood as the heritage of a native
Florentine (compare Filippino Lippi). – Originally the 'Hall
of the Udienza' and the **Hall of the Lilies** together formed
one larger hall. Their partition gave Benedetto da Maiano
special problems (Vasari describes this in detail) because
the ceiling of the hall on the floor below was not strong
enough to bear a dividing wall of any weight. The result
was this 'self-supporting' construction, in which Benedetto'
door is situated. The door is also richly carved on the side
towards the 'Hall of the Lilies'; here the visitor will notice
above the doorway, the slim figure of John the Baptist with
groups of putti and candelabra. The harmoniously proportioned framing pilasters have particularly handsome figure
capitals. The *fresco decoration* is by Domenico Ghirlandaio
(1482–5). In a setting of fictive architecture, the visitor will
distinguish the figures of Brutus, Mucius Scaevola, Camillus
S. Zenobius between SS. Lawrence and Stephen, Decius Mus
Scipio and Cicero. – Straight ahead is a small room belonging
to the old **chancellery**. The arrangement, which is modern
includes a beautiful bust of Machiavelli and a portrait o
Machiavelli attributed to Santi di Tito. In the middle i
Vecchio's original fountain putto, a copy of which is i
part of the palace. Turning back, the visitor will se
the beautiful windows of the old palace, onl

recently uncovered (the central support has been renovated). – The room next door is the **Guardaroba**. The
carved wall-cupboards and the ceiling are the work of Dio-
nigio Nigetti. However, the most remarkable feature of this
room are the *maps* which cover all the cupboards, comprising fifty-three painted reproductions of cartographical sur-
veys. They were made by two famous mathematicians and
geometers, Ignazio Danti and his pupil Stefano Buonsignori,
and are of the greatest scientific importance on account of
their accuracy (note, for example, the astonishing detail
in the map of Germany on the left). The large globe in the
middle does not belong here. Originally the room contained
only documents and the core of the Medici archive collection. – A small staircase leads to the so-called **Terrace of
Eleonora**, a moving attempt to create an idyll of nature in
this massive world of stone. The adjacent study has an excellently preserved grotesque ceiling (by Tomaso di Battista del Verrocchio; a small hatch allowed whoever was
sitting in the room to look straight into the large 'Hall of
the Five Hundred'). – Turning back, the visitor finds to the
left of the staircase to the 'Guardaroba' another staircase
leading down to the mezzanine and a whole series of rooms
which contain among other things a part of Charles Loeser's
art collection, which was given to the city of Florence.
Among the many excellent pieces in the collection, particular mention must be made of Tino da Camaino's candlestick angels, Giovanni Francesco Rustici's terracotta groups
of fighting warriors, and a cavalry battle painted on a tile
by Vasari, a preliminary study for the *Battle of San Vincenzo* in the 'Hall of the Five Hundred'. Also of interest are
a portrait of Bacchiacca and a female double-portrait by the
school of Fontainebleau. – The entire mezzanine floor forms
part of Michelozzo's extension. Maria Salviati, the mother of
Cosimo I, lived here for some time. Here too, there are some
extremely interesting fourteenth-century ceilings, some of
them in a very good state of preservation. Michelozzo con-
trived these rooms by lowering the height of the rooms
below. The ceilings of the mezzanine floor were then the ceilings of the ground floor, where Michelozzo made new ceilings.
The visitor can pass fairly quickly through the rest of the
palace. After returning to the 'Hall of the Lilies', he comes
first to one of those characteristic rooms which are half

corridor and half living-room; this one houses that famous
fourteenth century fresco which shows S. Anne driving the
Duke of Athens from the throne he had usurped and handing over the flags of freedom to the Florentine militia. In
the background is the oldest preserved portrayal of the
Palazzo Vecchio. – A staircase and then a passage lead up
to the crenellated battlements (and to the tower, from which
the view is marvellous). Immediately inside the tower staircase, the visitor can see the tiny prison where old Cosimo
'Pater Patriae' and Savonarola languished (it is known as
the 'Alberghinetto'). It is well worth spending some time
up here on the top of the palace.

Before leaving this venerable old building, the visitor is
recommended to glance into the **Dogana court**, with its
enormous pillars erected by Cronaca to support the 'Hall
of the Five Hundred'. Looking at the parts that have been
added on to the building, one is reminded once more of
the way in which each generation altered and completed
what it had inherited with very little respect for its predecessors. The visitor should remember that only some of
the rooms of the palace are open to the public; from the
others, the administration of Florence is still carried on
just as it was in the past. For this reason, one has to accept
the fact that, to most visitors, the enormous complex of
the Palazzo Vecchio appears like some strange maze.

The Uffizi

In 1560, on a site that included besides the Loggia dei Lanzi
the old custom house (Zecca), and the small Romanesque
church of S. Pier Scheraggio, Cosimo I began a building to
house thirteen of the principal magistracies of the Tuscan
state. It was designed by Vasari, who was also placed in
charge of its execution. The construction of these 'uffizi'
(in English, simply 'offices') continued until 1580, the date
when the new complex was linked up with the Loggia dei
Lanzi. The work had to be financed entirely by the
magistracies themselves. The custom house and the church
of S. Pier Scheraggio were incorporated in the new building.
After Vasari's death (in 1574, the same year as Cosimo I),
work was directed by Buontalenti and Parigi.

first rooms were adapted for use as early as 1565,
under continual pressure from the grand duke

to accelerate work, and took marginally under five months to complete the long corridor which runs from the Palazzo Vecchio through the Uffizi and across the Ponte Vecchio to the Palazzo Pitti. By 1568 the building itself had got as far as the loggia overlooking the Arno; there the Medici coat of arms was set up, as well as the two reclining figures by Vincenzo Danti ('Severity' and 'Justice') between which was subsequently placed a statue of Cosimo I by the same artist. This statue, however, was replaced as early as 1585 by the work which now occupies this prominent position – a much more 'earnest' monument to the same ruler by Giovanni da Bologna (Danti's figure is now in the courtyard of the Bargello). Buontalenti's highly original 'Door of the the Petitions' on the right beneath the arch to the Via Lambertesca dates from c. 1580, i.e. from the last phase of the building.

Even after the completion of the building, however, work still continued. Cosimo's son, Francesco I, began to alter the upper storey, which had been designed from the beginning to house the Medici family's magnificent art collection. Also in this top storey, he installed flats for artists and workshops where slaves laboriously worked the precious stones ('pietre dure') to which the Medici were so partial. A great part of the valuable facing on the walls of the Cappella dei Principi in S. Lorenzo was cut in the Uffizi. Finally, rooms devoted to science and alchemy and an elaborate armoury were installed here.

The Medici had many other interests apart from the government of the state, and every one of these found its place in the Uffizi. In 1585–6, for example, they added the world-famous theatre which was to stage the first opera in history and was to have such a remarkable influence on the development of public musical performances. It was situated where the gallery of drawings is now to be found, but this part of the building has been altered beyond recognition.

Apart from a number of administrative offices, the Uffizi palace houses the archives of the city of Florence (established by Cosimo I but not brought here until 1852) and the largest art gallery in Italy.

The Building

The elongated site, resembling a luxurious avenue, is

terminated at the Arno end by a portico opening out
in an arch. The elevation comprises three storeys, with
mezzanine openings between the colonnade and the first
storey giving it an upward thrust (the first mezzanine panel
has no openings, and from then on all the central rectangles
are blind; on the old custom house they are all arranged as
windows). This alteration of the Classical type is characteristic of Mannerist architecture, as is also the fact that the
mezzanine openings do not go through to a separate storey
(except on the custom house) but to the vaults of the loggias
behind the colonnade. The inspiration for this free and
uncanonical disposition of architectural motifs may have
been derived from Vasari's Roman experience, and the work
of Peruzzi who was the first architect who attempted this
type of construction. The tunnel-vaulted loggias have always
been a traditional place for market stalls, and at carnival
time they were the scene of lively processions. – The straight
line of the entablature above the columns came in for
criticism while it was still being built. There exist designs
by Ammannati which projected an arch in the centre of each
wall panel. Vasari insisted on his version, however, giving
the building this marvellous tense line and unilateral directional stress which stand in such contrast to the centralized
architecture of the Renaissance. Here another characteristic
of Mannerist architecture became transformed into an impressive experience. Lastly, a further novel stylistic element
is the very sparing use of ornament. The charm of this
building derives from the interplay of lines, planes and proportions, whereas Renaissance architects loved to apply
ornamental details wherever possible. It is no accident, then,
that the columns of the Uffizi are without decoration. The
capitals are distinguished only by means of rings; the shafts
seem to extend right up to the abacus. This order is the
'Doric'; it was requested by Cosimo I himself, possibly in
parallel to Serlio, who was the first to give secular connota-
tions to the orders (which were dedicated to certain gods)
and who assigned the Doric to rulers. The straight entablature, too, has its own particular significance. Alberti wanted
~sed for persons of prominence, as Vasari knew very well.
~ti also discusses the problem of breaking a straight
~ure in the case of a widely spaced arcade, a question
~ari takes up at the beginning of his 'Lives',

explaining his own solution for the Uffizi entablature, which included buttressing structures. The resultant sequence is characteristic of Mannerism: we see the idea of the entablature developing in conjunction with the idea of a building for the ruler, we observe the technical realization of it in connection with a problem discussed by Alberti, and finally we find the result returned to the realm of theory in Vasari's own writings. – In the early stages, however, there appears to have been more enthusiasm for decoration, and the Palazzo Vecchio end (the first part to be built) has more ornamentation than the rest of the building (except the loggia overlooking the Arno). – The many wooden doors are interesting; the majority of them still retain the old magistrates' titles on the lintel. – The sculptural decoration is added. These statues of famous Tuscans were erected in the twenty-eight niches in 1835–6, consecrating, as it were, this essentially dry and solemn building with the breath of Romanticism. Vasari intended the niches to be empty.

Three aspects of the Uffizi complex are of particular importance:

1) **Town Planning:** The Uffizi, part open hall, part piazza and part street, is laid out along an axis one pole of which is firmly anchored by Bandinelli's *Hercules and Cacus* group. Vasari could only achieve this by slightly altering the axis of the street which had been driven through to the Arno in 1546, with the result that the end of the Loggia dei Lanzi, which had been on the line of the old street, was no longer parallel to the axis of the new building. There was no way of avoiding a distinct bend between the last section of the old custom house (behind the Loggia dei Lanzi) and the rest of the right side of the Uffizi. Furthermore, the other end of Vasari's complex did not meet the Arno at right angles as the street had done, but at a much more acute angle, thus destroying the frontal unity of the houses along the river bank with its projecting western corner, which today constitutes a considerable hindrance to traffic. This fact necessitated rebuilding the bank itself; Vasari's new foundations are easily recognizable from the other side of the river. – However, this alteration of the axis did ensure that the Uffizi enjoyed a much closer and more organic relationship to the whole of the Piazza della Signoria than had been the case with the old street. Even if this relation-

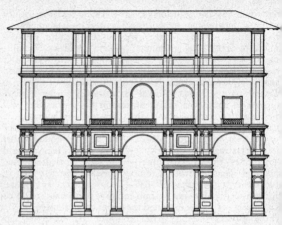

Uffizi, Arno façade

ship is only clearly evident when the Uffizi is viewed from
the north side of the square, it must be admitted that the
palace does form an essential part of the whole Piazza della
Signoria complex. In town planning terms, it represents a
three-winged building in complete dependence upon the
piazza. If we look for the historical basis of this conception
we find it in the Classical period. Since Vitruvius the forum
had been considered, for the purposes of town planning, a
representing the centre of a town. Beneath the portico of
the Uffizi there are benches. No Florentine loggia or vestibule since the fourteenth century had had benches, but
benches were demanded by Vitruvius in the forum and in
the palaestra. Furthermore, an early design has been preserved that bears a close relationship to the forum illustrated
in Caporali's 1533 edition of Vitruvius. The visitor will
find that the building does not in fact confront him from
the outside but rather from inside, when it seems as if he
were standing in the court of a basilica turning at right
angles off the main square, a disposition not unlike that of
the forum at Pompeii. And if the visitor then looks out
between the columns, he will find that the central court

lies several steps lower like a shallow basin; this again corresponds to Vitruvius, who sometimes demanded that a peristyle should be raised two steps.

2) **Style:** Apart from the Mannerist features we have already mentioned, the Uffizi has the added peculiarity that it is really only a façade, a homogeneous front super-imposed on buildings which are mainly fourteenth century. The much admired regularity of the exterior bears little relation to the interior. One would not suspect, for example, that the corner by the Palazzo Vecchio incorporates the remains of the Romanesque church of **S. Pier Scheraggio** in which Dante and Boccaccio once lectured. There are some interesting brick trefoil pillars left on the exterior (north side) and also in the entrance hall, where they still bear the remains of paintings. Skilfully moulded bricks form the capitals. The apse of the church has been preserved, and can be seen in the leather shop in the Via della Ninna. There are further fresco remains in the rooms now occupied by the administration. – The fact that it has only a front and no rear gives the Uffizi as a whole a kind of theatrical air; it resembles a stage set.

3) **Construction:** The architectural structure, like the con-ception of the building as a whole, is conceived in two separate stages. Lacking adequate possibilities of support in places, Vasari was obliged for reasons of statics to resort to auxiliary structural methods, concealed within the walls. However cement was used this time on the Uffizi. In addi-tion, the building is secured by a whole network of iron anchors, the majority of which are of an extremely daring construction. Although such 'reinforced' buildings had been erected in Italy before, during the Romanesque period and during the Renaissance, this was the first time iron anchors had been used so extensively throughout an entire building. Vasari treated the masonry in a similar way. He knew from experience that there is a limit to the load-bearing capacity of stone entablatures, and that the straight slabs above the columns of the ground floor could hardly be expected to support the architecture above for any length of time with-out serious deterioration. He therefore devised a very original system for making his straight entablature virtually self-supporting by a skilful distribution of load and thrust which took some of the pressure off the columns. This

continuous straight entablature is feigned. It consists only
of a thin strip concealing a buttressing system of round
brick arches. Ultimately this too may be regarded as a
peculiarity of Mannerist architecture, in that the architectural members no longer fulfil the functions to which they
pretend. As compared to Classical art, this represents a
considerable revolution in conception. Vasari himself regarded the process as an exemplary one, and he described
and justified the construction of the Uffizi entablature in
an introductory chapter on architecture in his famous
'Lives'.

The Gallery

*In 1581 Bernardo Buontalenti began adapting the upper
storey to serve as a gallery for sculpture, and he and his
assistants painted the first grotesque decorations on the
ceiling. Initially the collection was centred on the small
centralized 'Tribuna' in the east wing which Bernardo Poccetti decorated, and from there it spread to the other rooms.
The collection was considerably enlarged in the time of
Ferdinando I when additional pieces belonging to the
family were brought from Rome. Ferdinando II contributed
further to the growth of the collection when his wife inherited a collection of art treasures from Urbino, including
some of the best-known masterpieces of Raphael and Titian.
It was already a rich collection, when it was again augmented by the legacy of Cardinal Leopoldo, who had personally
gathered the assembly of sketches and the series of self-
portraits of artists, as well as a large collection of jewellery,
most of which is now on show in the Argenteria of the
Palazzo Pitti.
The gallery had reached its present extent by about 1658,
when the last of the ceilings was painted. We owe the fact
that we can still enjoy today the original collection in all its
wealth to the last of the Medici, Anna Maria Lodovica, who
on her return to Florence after the death of her husband,
the popular Jan Wellem of Düsseldorf, bequeathed the
artistic legacy of her forefathers to her native city. This
unique collection was thus spared the fate which robbed so
many Italian towns (e.g. Mantua) of their artistic riches. –
The stock of the gallery is still increasing today; in fact it
has never really stopped growing since the time of the*

Medici. Proof of this is the large Classicistic hall in the west wing (architect G. M. Paoletti, stuccoes by Grato Albertolli). This was constructed in 1780 to house the 'Niobides' group which was discovered in 1583 near the Lateran, passed into the possession of Cardinal Ferdinando, and was finally brought to Florence from Rome in 1775.

In the course of time, the Uffizi has thus come to house a varied collection of sculptures, tapestries, drawings, jewellery, weapons and objects of scientific and archeological interest, including among the latter some important Etruscan findings. A further classification of this vast amount of material was undertaken in the early nineteenth century and much was moved to other places. The principal removals were that of the modern sculpture to the Bargello, with the foundation of the National Museum, and the transfer of many antiquities to the Archeological Museum, which was founded for this purpose. The drawings, the most famous of which were once on show in the corridors, have been taken down and put in protective folders. One can easily imagine the incredible wealth of works of art which the gallery once contained. The setting up of large repositories in which many works can be stored has made possible a much clearer arrangement of the collection in the last few decades. Of course, in the process, our impression of the fantastic patronage of the Medici, who not only sought out works of Tuscan and Roman art but also treasures from Venice, the Netherlands and Germany, has become less striking than it must have been formerly. The Uffizi is the oldest example of a comprehensive collection embracing all branches of art.

The Collection

On show in the entrance are twelve busts of Medici princes and dukes as well as a number of tapestries woven from designs by Cristofano Allori. In the passage hangs a portrait of the generous donor, Anna Maria Lodovica, who bequeathed the family's collection to the city. The columns which can be seen in the walls are those of the old church of S. Pier Scheraggio.

From here, there is a lift to the upper rooms of the gallery, but the visitor is recommended to use the splendid **staircase**. With regard to the Classical antiquities exhibited on either side of it, one should bear in mind that probably all the Classical statues in the Uffizi include completions by Renaissance masters. In Rome, there was hardly space enough in gardens and squares for the

mass of material which was excavated, but Florence had fewe.
masterpieces and each piece was treasured as an individual work
of art, with the result that many broken pieces were completee
by experts to give them their full effect. These renovations shoulc
not be judged unfairly; they should be understood as testifying
to a conscientious concern for each individual piece expressec
in terms of active appreciation. If one adds to this the fact that
Florence was peculiarly a sculptor's city, one will readily understand why such completions should have been made so extensively
(recent research has shown that approximately 'one head in three
of the Uffizi antiquities is the work of a sixteenth century
master') and why most of the pieces are characterized by a mixture
of Classical and Renaissance styles, and even come to treasure
this as something peculiarly Florentine.

At the second turn of the staircase, the visitor suddenly finds
himself before one of the entrances of the old Medici theatre
(now the Drawing Collection), of which this is the only part to
have survived. The powerful door, carved in strong relief, bears
the emblems of the Medici coat of arms. On the left is a Classical *Venus Genetrix* (a copy of a Greek original, probably by
Alcamenes), and on the right a draped female figure (possibly a
'Muse') with the head and left hand restored; it is assumed to
date from the second century A. D. On the last turn of the staircase are two bronze figures; the one on the right is *Mars* (1559),
an example of Ammannati's heroic-pathetic style, and opposite is
a sixteenth century copy of the Vatican's *Silenus and Bacchus*. The
beautiful tapestries at the top of the stairs were made to designs
by Alessandro Allori. – The **first room of the gallery** proper
(beyond the ticket desk) also contains antiquities. The two
Molossian hounds of Pentelic marble are unusual in that they
have survived in perfect condition; only the tips of the ears have
been repaired. They were probably tomb statues (from separate
tombs). The Vatican has two which are almost identical. Originally it was thought that these extremely lifelike animal sculptures
were the work of Lysippus, but they are now attributed to the
late Pergamenian period. – The two pillars – also very well preserved – were acquired from Rome; studies were made of them
by a number of Renaissance artists. They are quite unique, possibly originating from a larger architectural complex (a portico).
They are decorated throughout with a kind of still-life composition of various weapons of attack and defence executed with
great precision (more than eight hundred types can be distinguished), and belong to the Flavian style. The best-preserved
sides are those towards the front. – The niches contain four
statues.

The view down the long **east corridor** with its painted ceilings,
its rows of statues and its valuable tapestries, strikes that note
of majesty and nobility that dominates the collection. Turning

first to the *Hercules with the Centaurs* on the right, the visitor will notice immediately the kinship between this group and Giovanni da Bologna's group of the same name in the Loggia dei Lanzi. This does not mean that the Renaissance master took this Classical group as his model, but is due rather to the fact that the figures of Hercules, as well as the head and left arm of the horseman, are by a pupil of Giovanni da Bologna's, Giovanni Caccini (1595; the restoration was suggested by the master himself in 1579, and can probably be regarded as accurate). – The small adjacent **Hermaphrodite Room** on the right is usually closed. Apart from some remarkable antiquities, it also contains a relief depicting a sacrifice which provided the inspiration for the detail in one of Raphael's tapestries (*S. Paul in Lystra*).

The principal items in the **first room of paintings** are undoubtedly the three great *Madonna* panels. *Cimabue's* work (on the right) is thought to date from 1275. It is from the high altar of S. Trinita. In this solemn and austere panel in the antique style, the Madonna is seen seated on an architecturally treated throne above half-figures of prophets and surrounded by angels. In its earthy colourfulness, it is reminiscent of the master's works at Assisi, despite the latter's poor state of preservation. – Almost as large is *Duccio's* picture (on the left), which dates from slightly later. It differs from Cimabue's marvellously aloof work in its more delicate, more animated style, and also in its basic colouring. A certain Gothic influence can be felt, though both works are principally indebted to a common Byzantine inheritance. Between them, and directly in front of the visitor as he enters the room, is the *Madonna* by *Giotto* which came to the Uffizi from the church of Ognissanti, via the Academy. This work, painted in tempera, is extremely valuable as it is the only altar-piece that can with certainty be attributed to Giotto. The subtlety of the modelling and the freshness of the colours stand in a certain contrast to the conservative and rather clumsy format. It is an early work, painted certainly before 1315 (Simone Martini's *Maestà* in Siena, which dates from that year, uses various motifs from Giotto's picture). One cannot help but admire the fascinating composition, the moving simplicity of the gestures, and the splendour of the ornamental decoration surrounding the enthroned Mother of God like some precious frame. – Apart from these three pictures, the room also contains a number of interesting works by various (mostly anonymous) masters from Tuscany, Pisa and Lucca. Particularly noteworthy are some panels by Bonaventura Berlinghieri, thirteenth century works from Lucca.

In the next, small room are two pictures from Siena which merit close attention. *Simone Martini*, and *Pietro and Ambrogio Lorenzetti* were roughly contemporary artists (born after 1280). Simone's *Annunciation* speaks a lyrical language of the greatest

and purest delicacy. A highly developed linear treatment is combined with a supreme sense of colour. Signed and dated 1333,
this dramatic picture unites all the qualities of the mature master.
The figures at the sides (SS. Ansanus and Massimo) are by Lippo
Memmi, his principal pupil. – Ambrogio Lorenzetti, the younger
of the two brothers, painted his *Presentation in the Temple*
(signed and dated 1342) during the last years of his life. His soft,
densely coloured and somewhat melancholy style asserts itself
very well in this almost tapestry-like work. The *Madonna with
Angels* (signed and dated 1340) may be attributed to his brother
Pietro. His is a cooler, smoother art of very much greater psychical
introspection, which in its accuracy of composition appears to
anticipate the work of Masaccio and Masolino. The *S. Umiltà*
(with scenes from the saint's life) on the wall opposite is by the
same master. This work is only partially preserved; the frame in
particular, which we know from a later drawing of the work, is
missing. In the gables were the Apostles and Madonna now in the
Uffizi repository. A youthful work, this must be presumed to
date from *c.* 1325.

On the right, in the next room, is Ambrogio Lorenzetti's *Madonna*
(once in the Berenson collection) with the two saints Procolus and
Nicholas, parts of a triptych which, like all the master's works on
show in the Uffizi, dates from the period of his maturity, coincid-
ing with his second stay in Florence. – In immediate line of
succession to Giotto stands *Bernardo Daddi*, whose *Madonna between SS. Nicholas and Matthew*, dated 1328, was painted at the
same time as the S. Croce frescoes. Particularly delicate are the
portions of the large *S. Pancras' panel*, which probably dates from
a somewhat later period when artists were beginning to be aware
of developments in Siena. – Another successor to Giotto was *Taddeo Gaddi*, as his *Madonna in Glory* testifies. – The identity of
the master who is known by the name of *Giottino* is by no means
certain. His *Lamentation* reveals a powerful and individual artistic personality. Elements of the art of northern Italy have been
discovered in his work, and this is taken to show that there
existed a degree of exchange between the artistic milieux of Tuscany and the North. This applies also to the work of *Giovanni
da Milano*, who came from Como. His *Saints, Martyrs and Vir-
gins* (on the left wall, painted for Ognissanti) strikes a slightly
foreign note in Tuscany with its more intense colouring, stricter
sense of form and high level of quality.

Gentile da Fabriano and *Lorenzo Monaco*, the authors of the most
important works in the next room, belong to that soft, extremely
refined Gothic style that spread through the artistic centres of
Europe in the late fourteenth and early fifteenth centuries. Gentile's *Adoration of the Magi* is one of the principal works of this
period. Incredibly fresh in feeling, it was probably painted when
the master was over sixty. The fantastic costumes and occasional

S. Lorenzo, dome of the Old Sacristy (Brunelleschi)

S. Lorenzo, Old Sacristy, capital and entablature above the portal of the left side chapel

relief details inserted into the painting reveal something of the splendour of northern Italian and particularly Venetian art. Its formal maturity is expressed in the skilful composition of the procession approaching the crib, and in the masterly distribution of caesuras and centres of gravity, suggesting that this Gothic master was not unaware of Classical group composition. Gentile was in fact one of the first artists who have painted from Classical models. The frame is splendid, a superb surround of flowers and plants, all accurately depicted; it is signed and dated 1423. The predella is particularly lovely, with its pale landscape and colourful buildings (the *Presentation in the Temple* is an excellent copy of the original now in the Louvre). – *Lorenzo Monaco*, who was a Camaldolense monk, painted even larger panels, like his *Coronation of the Virgin*, in the style of book illustrations. Coolly refined colouring and a delicately stylized play of line give his paintings a slightly Mannerist atmosphere. The predella depicting the story of S. Benedict, and the *Annunciation* in the gables of the (damaged) Gothic frame are particularly well-preserved. – The panel by *Starnina* is of more modest dimensions. This 'easel painting' depicts the lives of saintly hermits in a landscape which, in the delicate differentiation of its shading, shows the artist to have had a highly developed understanding of nature. In content, the picture is closely related to the *Thebaid* theme. The colourfulness and the strange atmosphere, with those wispy clouds on the horizon, are reminiscent of Franco-Flemish book illustration. Some of the groups are recognizable as quotations from books of models. The attempt to attribute this picture to the young Uccello was never convincing.

In the next small room we find works by *Masaccio* and *Piero della Francesca*. Masaccio's *S. Anne with Mary and the Christ-Child* must date from *c.* 1423. It is one of the principal works of this master who, together with Brunelleschi and Donatello, was a pioneer of the Renaissance (1401–28). Opinions differ as to whether Masolino also had a hand in this work. No one, however, doubts Masaccio's authorship of the two central figures with the child's regal gesture and his face mysteriously illuminated as if from within. On the arms of the throne are spindle-shaped spiral knobs such as are otherwise found only on tombs at that time. There is a heroic quality about the hieratic serenity of the composition. – *Piero della Francesca*, rigorously self-taught, achieved such clarity of vision and by his long study of mathematics and geometry brought such strength of definition to his art, that almost every one of his works has the stamp of finality about it. The small double panel, painted on both sides, in its ingenious frame (free-standing), depicts Federigo da Montefeltro and his wife Battista Sforza. On the rear side, they are seen riding in triumphal chariots through the sort of expansive Urbino landscape that Piero could paint better than anyone else. Federigo is being crowned by Fame and is accompanied by the four cardinal virtues; Battista is seen with two allegorical figures that have not been clearly identified, and the three theological virtues (a bit of inscription appears to have survived above the head of the one on the left). Below each, as if chiselled in stone, is a monumental text. From these, we are led to assume that the wife was already dead, since her text is in the perfect tense ('TENUIT') while the duke's is in the present tense. This would place the picture after 1472. The intention of the work was to glorify the duke and extoll his wife's feminine virtues.

The *Rout of S. Romano* by *Paolo Uccello* was originally accompanied by two panels (now in Paris and London) in praise of the Condottiere Niccolò da Tolentino and his victory over Siena. His studies of perspective led the artist to place the fragments of lances and other weapons strictly along the perspective lines. The whole composition is effectively based on the five horses in the foreground. The impression of crowded confusion is achieved by filling in the remaining spaces piece by piece. The colouring is typical – earthy and rich, with occasional blue and red horses. The landscape in the background has darkened with age. The panel was painted during the years when Piero was working on the frescoes at Arezzo. – *The Madonna with Saints* by *Domenico Veneziano*, a particularly beautiful work, appears to anticipate Piero in the lyrical quality of the lighting and the purity and freshness of the colours. (The delightful predella has unfortunately been broken up; part of it is in Cambridge and part in Berlin. Known also as the *S. Lucia altar-piece* (from its original position on the high altar of S. Lucia dei Magnoli; S. Lucia is on the far right), this picture was painted *c.* 1445, and came to the Uffizi only in 1862. Here it is not perspective that is used to create the feeling of space, but a new kind of lighting. The stream of light which descends into the courtyard from above in fact constitute an epoque-making motif. Most of the colour is concentrated in the centre. A subdued blue, a soft green, a pale pink were the colours Domenico liked best. Unfortunately, some rather over-zealous cleaning in the nineteenth century removed the overall harmony. The architecture – half 'Renaissance' (round arches and half 'Gothic' (pointed arches) – cannot be identified clearly key points are concealed by figures. The statuesque saints accentu ate the composition. The figure of S. Zenobius (on the right) wa inspired by Donatello's *S. Louis*. The profile of S. Lucia, con ceived in Pisanello's medallion style, is important as representin a new ideal of beauty.

The predella on the entrance wall belongs to the Barbadori alta painted for S. Spirito (now in the Louvre) and is the work of th young *Filippo Lippi*. The *Miracle of S. Fredianus* (left) an *S. Augustine in his Study* (right; his chest pierced by the arrow of God's love) frame the unusual theme of the annunciation o the Virgin's death. This quiet scene, sustained by deep emotion, takes place in a courtyard with columns in two planes making a strong play of light and shade. The memory of Masaccio is more present here than it is in the later pictures to be found in the next room. This room contains the *Enthroned Madonna with Saints* (c. 1442; right wall, set back) from the Medici chapel in S. Croce. The drawing is firmer, the presentation more daring and realistic. The accompanying predella (on the end wall) is by Pesellino, a pupil and assistant of Lippi (the two pieces on the left are copies, the originals being in the Louvre). It depicts the *Nativity*, the *Martyrdom of SS. Cosmas and Damian* and the *Miracle of S. Anthony*, and occupies an intermediate position between Lippi himself and Fra Angelico. The *Madonna with S. Bernard* is among the last works painted by Filippo Lippi, commissioned by Lucrezia Tornabuoni in 1463 for the hermitage at Camaldoli. Its wooded, mountainous landscape with flying angels and light shining through it is reminiscent of the *Adoration of the Christ Child* on the opposite wall; this panel, painted after 1453, depicts penitents, with S. Hilarion on the left in a hole in the ground, in an atmospheric setting of dense, romantic wood-land. – One of the master's best-known pictures is surely the *Madonna and Child and Two Angels*. It is an intimate scene. Round about 1465, after many disturbances, the artist entered a calmer period of his life, and a feeling of peace and inner cheer-fulness is echoed in this panel with its stone window-frame giving on to a clear view of distant, fairy-tale mountains and a twilight horizon.

For an example of *Fra Angelico's* work, the visitor must turn back to the small room which contains Uccello's cavalry battle. There, on the entrance wall, is the only genuine Fra Angelico that the Uffizi possesses. Against a golden background formed by beams of light gathered into a sheaf, the enthroned Madonna intently and lovingly embraces the Child. The inscription on the steps of the throne probably refers to the donors. This panel, which has only been known to art historians since 1930, is from Pontasieve, where it originally formed the central panel of a polyptych. It was painted possibly c. 1445. The impressive *Coro-nation of the Virgin* in the Filippo Lippi room (immediately to the right of the door) is of uncertain authorship. This delicate and beautiful work with its gold halo is attributed by some authorities to *Zanobi Strozzi*, who was closely associated with Fra Angelico (opinions differ as to the date). – Of the two bro-thers *Piero* and *Antonio Pollaiuolo*, Piero, the younger, is the less important. The panel (from S. Miniato) depicting *SS. Eustace, Giacomo and Vincenzo* was painted by both of them together. It is appropriate that Baldovinetti's *Madonna with Saints* and *Annunciation* hang near this picture. In their austerity and spaciousness, they resemble the work of the Pollaiuolo brothers, though in their elegant use of line they are far more advanced.

The next room contains further pictures by Piero Pollaiuolo, including six Virtues which originally decorated the backs of the seats of the 'Mercanzia' judges. The visitor can turn the first panel over and will find on the back Antonio's charcoal drawing of *Caritas*. To the left of the doorway to the next room is a portrait of Galeazzo Maria Sforza, by Piero. — The seventh of the 'Mercanzia' virtues is by *Sandro Botticelli*. Also by Botticelli are the three particularly beautiful Madonnas in their remarkable frames on the opposite wall, and the two (free-standing) smaller panels telling the story of Judith and Holofernes. Strongly and brilliantly coloured, they have a touch of Verrocchio about them. They may possibly have been designed as decorations for pieces of furniture. All the Botticelli pictures here date from the period around 1470 when the artist was between 22 and 25 years old. His remarkable, soulful sensitivity and richly harmonious use of colour are already apparent. However, it is not until he enters the next room, which is devoted to Botticelli's work, that the visitor encounters the full mastery of this artist, a mastery that left his precursors Lippi and Pollaiuolo far behind. The works assembled here are famous the world over. They illustrate various different aspects of the master's mature approach, which covered the whole spectrum of feeling from melodious lyricism to Christian remorse. Immediately to the right of the entrance is the *Madonna with Saints* (altar-piece of S. Barnaba). This masterpiece — one of the most impressive altar-pieces painted in Florence in the fifteenth century — was completed after the artist's return from Rome in 1483. Rich and colourful, the picture is given a calm solemnity by the symmetry of its elevation. The Madonna looks out at the visitor as if she were lost in a dream; John, olive-coloured, deeply marked by self-denials, directs the visitor's attention to the throne. The bronze plaque on the top step bears an inscription from Dante's *Paradise*: 'VERGINE MADRE FIGLIA DEL TUO FIGLIO'. Though still conceived in Botticelli's splendid manner, this work already stands on the threshold of his late, ascetic phase, when he came under the influence of Savonarola (parts of the accompanying predella are to be found in the other room: *Salome with the head of John the Baptist, Martyrdom of S. Ignatius, Pietà* and *S. Augustine and the Christ Child at the Sea*). On the other hand the *Primavera* (1477–8) and the somewhat later *Birth of Venus*, painted for the villa in Castello, are completely different. The various discussions which have arisen over the contents of these pictures, particularly of 'Primavera', concern the world of humanistic ideas. In the centre stands Venus, with Amor shooting his fiery arrows over her head at the dancing Graces towards the left. On the left is Mercury, dispersing the mists that hang in the treetops with the Caduceus. On the right is Flora, completely covered in flowers.

Flowers are also sprouting from the mouth of a nymph who is fleeing from a zephyr. – In the other work, Venus is depicted in a shell being blown by zephyrs towards the shore, where a servant awaits her with a cloak. Botticelli's connections with the Medici family, which at times were very close, led him over and over again to include in his works portraits of members of the family and allusions of an allegorical nature. The *Adoration of the Kings*, painted in 1474, depicts several members of the family: the kneeling king is Cosimo the Elder (who had been dead for ten years at the time), and together on the left are his sons, Piero and Giovanni, and his grandsons, Lorenzo il Magnifico and his brother Giuliano, while on the extreme right is the artist himself, wearing a wide coat and turned towards the spectator. In this 'ex voto', the artist appears together with the donors. – Botticelli's delight in allegories appears again in his *Pallas and the Centaur*, one of the few pictures on canvas. The goddess, a beautiful, slender maïden, bears the Medici device of the linked rings on her white dress. The meaning is clear: Pallas, goddess of art and science, armed with an enormous halberd and wearing the emblems of the Medici, penetrates the rocky strongholds of the wild horse-people in order to tame them. – The meaning of the *Calumny of Apelles* in the next room is more difficult to unravel. In this revival of a famous Classical painting described by Lucian, 'Calumny', together with 'Hatred' and 'False Testimony', is seen dragging the victim before a judge with ears like an ass, into which 'Stupidity' and 'Suspicion' are whispering their lies. Some way off, to the left, stands 'Truth', naked and accompanied only by 'Grief', who is dressed in black. – Among the round pictures in this room, the visitor will recognize such well-known works as the *Magnificat* and the *Madonna of the Pomegranate*. The rectangular *Annunciation* was painted for S. Maria Maddalena dei Pazzi in 1489–90.

Tuscan agents (Portinari, Arnolfini, Tani) followed with particular attention the new realistic art of the Netherlands. This movement, which was relatively free of Classical tendencies, developed in parallel with the 'Rinascimento'. A certain interchange took place which proved beneficial to both sides. That the artists of the Netherlands were able to learn from the Italians is clear from *The Entombment* by *Rogier van der Weyden*, which was probably painted for Lionello d'Este (in the side room on the right). This panel was for a long time in Ferrara. Originally it had two wings (now lost); in composition, it returns to a type conceived by Fra Angelico (his *Entombment* in Munich). – Urbino, Genoa and Naples all bought works of art from Flanders and Burgundy. *Hans Memling* – represented here by a number of portraits, amongst other pieces – once sent an important work for delivery by ship to Tani, who had commissioned it, and it was captured by pirates and taken to Danzig, where it has remained ever since.

– The climax of this phase of Netherlandish influence on the art
of the Renaissance was the arrival of *Hugo van der Goes's* Portinari Altar in S. Egidio, Florence. This monumental *Adoration of
the Shepherds*, the largest work van der Goes ever painted,
dominates the next room. On the left-hand wing, Tommaso Portinari can be seen kneeling with his two sons; on the right-hand
wing is his wife Maria Baroncelli with one of their daughters.
The work, painted *c.* 1475, dates from the end of the artist's
Ghent period, immediately before he entered the monastery. In
the central panel, the shepherds are seen crowding in from the
right, their faces expressing utter astonishment, their coarse,
peasant features touched by wonder. How different are the angels
– the two kneeling in the background, dressed in blue, the two in
white in the foreground, and the richly dressed ones on the right,
floating in the air. A delicate, almost timid still-life fills the
centre foreground: lilies, violets, a sheaf of corn, the beautiful
glass and the delightful jug. An old German building of some
kind surrounds the scene, and in the shadows on the left can be
seen the ox and ass. In the middle of the bare stone floor is the
slight figure of the Christ-Child, the centre of the adoring worship of those who surround him, who keep their distance with a
certain shy wonder. The floor is seen from a high angle of vision,
the figures merely from medium height. This duality, together
with the erratic intervals of the proportions, provokes a kind of
tension which gives the overall composition a somewhat frag-
mented appearance, and may have been a symptom of the inner
disturbance of the artist, then beginning to suffer from depression.
The procession to Bethlehem on the left-hand wing and the arrival
of the Magi on the right-hand one give a broad, epic background
to the whole. The distant landscape spans both the central panel
and the wings like a panorama. On the outside of the wings is an
Annunciation, painted in grisaille; the figure of the angel Gabriel
on the right is very graceful.

On the opposite wall is a (considerably smaller) altar-piece by
Nicolas Froment, dated 1461. This masterpiece, by one of the
finest painters of southern France, is thought to be from the
small church of S. Francesco al Bosco in Mugello, a Medici
foundation probably built by Michelozzo. It is one of the gems
of the collection, and it, too, speaks of the affluence of the North.
The panels are filled to the maximum, with the heads strongly
characterized. The central panel depicts the *Raising of Lazarus*;
on the left-hand wing is Martha, announcing Lazarus' death, and
on the right, Christ in the house of Simon. On the outside is a
standing *Madonna and Child* and a cleric (the donor). – Compared with the minute verisimilitude of Ghirlandaio or the firm
brilliance of *Lorenzo di Credi* (who studied with Leonardo under
Verrocchio), the works of *Filippino Lippi*, Filippo's son, are
characterized particularly by a strong inner emotion. The *Adora-*

Signoria District: The Uffizi

tion of the Magi (right-hand end wall) is dated 1496 (on the back). This pupil of Botticelli's here combined elements of Masaccio's style (he completed Masaccio's Brancacci chapel) with a strength of expression learned from Hugo van der Goes, producing an extremely forceful work. It was originally designed to take the place of Leonardo's *Adoration*, which was never finished. – The *Sacra Conversazione* on the wall opposite is dated 1485 and came from the Palazzo Vecchio. An extremely interesting feature of this painting is the rich ornamentation, derived from the work of Donatello.

Signorelli and *Perugino* grace the walls of the next room. These two great masters from Umbria represent two different poles of Renaissance art. Signorelli's static, bronze-like strength, his nobility of conception and his decisive execution have been taken to be an anticipation of Michelangelo's *Terribilità*. There is a suggestion of pagan innocence about his work. Perugino, on the other hand, was of a gaily Christian disposition, aiming for harmony in his work and paving the way for Raphael. The *Crucifixion with Saints* was painted by both artists together. Signorelli's round painting of the *Holy Family* is a mature work, combining Classical allusions (nude youths, architectural features) with a Christian message. It was an important forerunner of another round painting, Michelangelo's *Doni Madonna*.

Verrocchio began his artistic life as a goldsmith, and later continued as a sculptor. That he equally painted we know from his *Baptism of Christ* (c. 1470), in which his pupil Leonardo also had a hand. Leonardo painted the angel kneeling on the left and also parts of the landscape; the attentive spectator cannot fail to notice the difference between the two hands. – *Leonardo's* greatness, however, did not really assert itself until his *Adoration of the Magi*, though the painting was never completed (it was commissioned in 1481 by the monks of S. Donato a Scopeto). Mary is seated in front of a hill which separates the foreground from the background, surrounded by a rich entourage of youths and old men. They crowd with forceful gestures around the classic triangular composition (the first of its kind). In the background, various groups are clustered around a fragmentary staircase, including galloping horsemen – even an elephant can be seen between the mountains. The whole is depicted in that state of heroic elevation which is characteristic of Leonardo's ideal universe. From the unfinished state of the painting (the light areas were to have been the most colourful), we can gain an insight into Leonardo's chiaroscuro. Initially he marked out the areas of light and shade with sepia lines. The many designs and suggestions, as well as the completed portions, make this work a veritable microcosm of Leonardo's painting technique. The wide-ranging contents, from profound, mythical reflection to the most crystalline rationality (namely the coolly constructed flight of stairs), have

led this to become one of the world's most celebrated paintings.
– The next room is known as the 'Sala delle Carte Geografiche'
from the beautiful sixteenth century maps of Tuscany (the ceiling
was painted by Jacopo Zucchi). It also contains a further work in
which Leonardo participated – the *Annunciation*. According to a
recent theory, this picture originated in the workshop of Ghirlandaio and was touched up by Leonardo.

This ends the first part of our tour of the Uffizi. The second part
begins in the curious **Tribuna**, a kind of 'temple of art' which
constitutes the original core of the Medici gallery. Built in 1580–8
by Buontalenti and decorated by Bernardo Poccetti, this octagonal
domed centralized structure was designed to house the finest
treasures of the collection of Duke Francesco I. The 'Urbino
inheritance' which Vittoria della Rovere brought to her husband
Ferdinando II, added a number of masterpieces from Venice to
the collection, among them Titian's *Venus*. Half a century later
the famous antiquities which still form the major part of the
display were brought from the Villa Medici in Rome. Architecturally, the 'Tribuna' represents a variant of the Florence Baptistery, even down to the inclusion of a sort of sanctuary, complete with lateral niches and indirect lighting, for works of
particular value. Today the magnificent late Pergamenian *Torso
of a Satyr* stands there. The idea of treating works of art like
sacred objects is derived from Tuscan Mannerism. – The dome is
inlaid with mother-of-pearl seashells, and inside the lantern can
be seen a device which gives the direction of the wind. The richly
inlaid floor is worthy of particular attention. In the centre stands
the *Medici Venus* (Greek, marble, height without base 1.53 m),
a well-preserved work – only the right arm and part of the left
are missing – which was found near the Ghetto in Rome. It has
stood in this place ever since, with the exception of the years
1802–16 when, together with a number of other works of art, it
was carried off to the Musée Napoléon, Paris. The statue dates
from the Hellenistic period and is a descendant of Praxiteles'
Cnidian Venus. The base bears the signature of Cleomenes, son of
the Athenian Apollodorus, and it would appear that this is a
replica of an earlier, possibly genuine signature. – Grouped around
the Medici Venus are a number of equally important works – the
well-preserved *Apollino* (slight restoration to the right arm, left
leg, hair and base), the *Knife-sharpening Scythian*, a fine intact
Pergamenian work of the third century B.C. (possibly a pendant
belonging to a hanging 'Marsyas'), the two *Wrestlers* (a copy of a
Pergamenian bronze original; neither of the heads belongs to it),
and the *Faun with Cymbals*. This last, a copy of a Hellenistic
original, is restored on the head and arms, and it used to be said
that the restoration was by Michelangelo. Originally the figure
probably held flutes instead of cymbals.

The pictures on the walls of the 'Tribuna' are mostly Medici portraits. Two works by *Pontormo* deserve particular attention. *Cosimo Pater Patriae*, an early work, is a powerful piece of idealization. Next to it *Maria Salviati*, wife of Giovanni delle bande nere and mother of Cosimo I, dates from his late period. It would be difficult to find another picture to match this magnificent work in the whole of Florentine portraiture during the sixteenth century. The heroic character of this great woman has been captured by the simplest of means. – *Bronzino*, a pupil of Pontormo, shared his master's precision of observation, but not his power to portray the depth of the soul. Several pictures here testify to the skill of his brush. Particularly moving in its innocence is the child portrait of Garzia Medici, a son of Cosimo I who died young, with the bird in his hand and the piece of coral to yard off evil on his necklace (the subject may possibly be Giovanni, another son who also died in childhood). – *Vasari's* idealized portrait of Lorenzo the Magnificent is full of clearly decipherable symbols. – The *Portrait of a Man* by Georg Pencz, signed and dated 1544, is an example of Bronzino's influence on a German painter.

A series of smaller rooms follows. The interesting ceiling decoration is all that remains of the sumptuous fittings of these once comfortably furnished apartments. They contain Italian, Dutch and German works of the period around 1500. These pictures are sometimes rearranged, so it is best not to describe them in their hanging order.

First come works by masters from Emilia, Umbria and the Romagna (Maineri, Araldi, Caporali, Antoniazzo). – Works by *Signorelli* include a grisaille depicting an allegory on fertility. – *Perugino's* splendid portrait of Francesco delle opere (signed and dated 1494) is a particularly energetic work. – One of *Francia's* most important pictures is his portrait of the Evangelist Scappi, an individually conceived and firmly drawn piece of work. – *Lorenzo Costa* painted his portrait of Giovanni Bentivoglio c. 1490 at the beginning of his stay in Bologna. – *SS. Benedict and John* by *Melozzo da Forlì* shows the personal style of painting developed by this master from the school of della Francesca and Mantegna. *The Annunciation* on the back is a work by his school. – *Giovanni Bellini*, patriarch of Venetian painting, is represented by three works of his mature period. One is an allegorical picture, apparently portraying souls in Purgatory. The *Portrait of a Man* was for some time thought to be a self-portrait (erroneously). The monochrome *Lamentation* is the kind of picture which influenced Dürer. – *Cosme Tura's* 'San Domenico', a fine late work by the master, originally formed part of a larger polyptych. – Works by *Carpaccio*, *Cima da Conegliano*, *Vivarini* (S. Louis), *Leonbruno* (Mercury holding a caduceus shaped like a crozier and accompanied by a nymph), *Giorgione* (i.e. attributed to him) and *Correggio* show various aspects of Italian painting.

Mantegna's triptych, with the *Adoration of the Magi* in the centre and the *Circumcision* and *Ascension* on the wings, and the two rather poorly preserved portraits of Guidobaldo Montefeltro and Elisabetta Gonzaga, with the scarab on her forehead, are among the most outstanding works of the Italian school. These two portraits are attributed to the young Raphael, still under the influence of Marchigian art. Mantegna's triptych in its old frame is a charming gem, its light delicate colours reminiscent of miniature painting. The central panel is curved to give an impression of space. This picture, together with the *Madonna of the Rock* beside it (notice the group of labourers on the right hauling structural fragments from the quarry, and the tiny figures on the left, including a shepherd with his flock), were probably painted for the Medici *c.* 1468 when Mantegna, who was from northern Italy, is thought to have been staying in Tuscany. – *Correggio's* 'Madonna adoring the Christ Child', a most sensitive work, was painted 1522–4 and donated in 1617 by the Duke of Mantua. The *Rest on the Flight into Egypt* may date from shortly before the Camera di S. Paolo in Parma i.e. *c.* 1514.

A number of works by *Albrecht Dürer* show the lasting influence which Italian art exercised on the most important Renaissance artist of the German-speaking countries. The *Portrait of his Father* with rosary, dated 1490, still remains completely within the Nordic school, with its finical manner and extreme concern for accuracy, but the *Adoration of the Magi*, dated 1504, particularly in the architectural details (e.g. the round arches), shows a debt to Italian influence. The richly ornamental work, with the butterfly, the stag-beetle (bottom right) and the beautiful and very 'German' Mary, was originally in the church of Schloss Wittenberg and may have had side panels. The quiet group of adoring Magi approaching with their gifts displays his considerable skill in figure drawing, and the mountainous background rising behind reveals Dürer's passion for detailed landscapes. According to ancient sources, the donkey with teeth bared (left) is a symbol of the relentless severity of the Old Testament covenant. – The two enormous apostles *James and Philip*, dated 1516 and painted on canvas, are full of a kind of inner tension. – The *Madonna with the Pear* is a late work, 1526. – The *Great Calvary*, drawn in black on green paper and mounted on white, belongs to the so-called 'Green Passion'. The reverse is by an unknown hand. Possibly a sketch for an altar-piece, this very large but unfortunately rather badly damaged sheet (1504) illustrates Dürer's way of composing masses within a large area. – A number of pictures by *Lucas Cranach*, among them a miniature-like *S. George* (with a 'S. Veronica's veil' on the back) and a self-portrait of the artist at the age of eighteen, *Albrecht Altdorfer* (represented by two groups of eight pictures on the legend of S. Florian), *Hans von Kulmbach* and two portraits from the

ate period of *Hans Holbein the Younger* complete this series of
orks by German artists.

utch painters are represented by *Gerard David*, a pupil of and
uccessor to Memling (the *Entombment*, with a scratched *Adam
nd Eve* on the back, and the *Adoration of the Magi* are among
is finest works), *Quentin Massys*, *Joos van Cleve* (a double
ortrait with his wife), the *Master of the Virgo inter Virgines*
nd *Bernard van Orley*.

n the left at the end of this wing of the Uffizi is a room con-
aining numerous miniatures, mostly of more recent date.

rossing the loggia which overlooks the Arno and enjoying the
iew of the town and the mountains and, to the right, down the
orridor formed by the Uffizi, to the Palazzo Vecchio, the visitor
ill find in the first room in the opposite wing some master-
ieces by *Raphael* and *Michelangelo*. Michelangelo's round picture
f the *Holy Family* (on the right-hand wall) was painted in 1504
or the marriage of Angelo Doni and Maddalena Strozzi. It is
he only panel painting attributable with certainty to the master,
nd one of the few datable works of his early period. The firm-
ess of the contours, the cool clarity of the colours and the
xtreme complexity of the movements (the mother is lifting the
hild over her shoulders from behind) show a marked tendency
owards formalization, a turning away from Leonardo's 'sfu-
ato' and from the direction followed by Andrea del Sarto.
eonardo is strongly present, nevertheless; wealth of movement
ombined with the closed formation of the group (characteristics
f Leonardo's *S. Anne with Christ and the lamb* in the Louvre)
ere what principally occupied Michelangelo. The heroic form
f the bodies, on the other hand, together with the firmness of
he drawing, reveal the teaching of Signorelli, whose *Madonna
ondo* (in the first section of the Uffizi) also influenced the
ontent of this picture. The figures in the background correspond
o those in Signorelli's work. Here a group of naked, almost
agan youths are portrayed against a wall which is articulated
ith pilasters and appears simply to have grown out of the
arth, part of a centralized structure that cannot be further re-
onstructed. The infant S. John turns as if to leave. The time for
lay is past. The Passion is beginning and with it the building of
he Church. The richly carved original frame takes up this mean-
ng. The heads of Christ, two prophets and two sibyls allude to
he path from ancient heathen times to redemption through the
on of God.

ext come three originals by Raphael. The *Madonna of the Gold-
inch* (Madonna del cardellino) was painted for the marriage of
orenzo Nasi in 1506, the first years of Raphael's extremely
roductive stay in Florence. It was the first of a series of paintings
f Madonnas in a free landscape. Michelangelo's Bruges Madonna
as probably the model for this picture, not only in view of the

similar relationship between mother and child but also in view of
the quiet, peaceful contours. This charming but unfortunately
poorly preserved work is full of poetic feeling. The misty landscape reveals a typically Umbrian love of nature. In the background, on the right, is a town with a centralized building reminiscent of the Consolazione church at Todi, and on the left is
a rivulet with a bridge over it. The timid gesture of the Christ
Child, making as if to caress the bird and holding his saving hand
over it as if to protect it, is full of Franciscan tenderness. – The
powerful *Portrait of Pope Leo X, with Cardinals Luigi de' Rossi
and Giuliano de' Medici* (the latter, on the right, later became
Clement VII) was painted in 1518–9 during the last two years
of the master's life. The figures are set before an architectural
background painted in very restrained colours, which has been
identified as the old Vatican Library, now the 'Floreria'. In
front of the pope lies an identifiable illuminated volume of the
gospels, with a reading glass. There is also a table-bell, an-
mirrored in the knob on the arm of his chair is a rectangular
window. This feeling for the minutest detail was one aspect of
the master's late work. The other was an extremely refined
almost impressionistic way of painting (e.g. the red damask of
the pope's chair, the velvet of the tablecloth, the material of the
pope's cloak as it picks up the light) which pervades the picture
as a whole. – Raphael reached artistic maturity very early on, as
we can see from his *Portrait of Francesco Maria della Rovere*,
the heir to the reigning prince of Urbino (painted before
Raphael's arrival in Florence). The assurance of the drawing
gives clarity to the face, and the skilful use of colour perfectly
captures the softness of the fur. The right eye is touched by
reddish reflection and the left is fixed and blueish. The significance of the apple in the subject's hand has never been explained.
– Recently experts have again come to regard the *Portrait of
Pope Julius II* as an original. Numerous copies of the work,
which was painted in 1511 and shows the Rovere acorns on the
throne, have been preserved. – The so-called *Portrait of Perugino*
is also among the disputed works. Baldinucci believed it to be a
portrait of Luther by Holbein, and consequently it had hung in
the 'Tribuna'. Later it was thought to be by Credi. The work's
inherent qualities, however, together with a certain kinship with
the portrait of Francesco Maria della Rovere, and finally the
revealing discovery that the subject was Perugino, have justifiab-
led to a tentative attribution to Raphael.

Michelangelo's *Doni* tondo hangs between two works by *Bronzino*
which illustrate very clearly two quite different styles. The signed
Holy Family (on the right, painted for the Panciatichi, c. 1534;
the family's coat of arms can be seen on the flag on the tower in
the left background) is cool and clear, with pale flesh tones, and
represents a certain academic tendency (namely the Madonna's

air, which recalls Classical portrait heads; apart from that, an affinity with Michelangelo's work can be felt), while the more passionate *Pietà* (on the left, *c.* 1528), reverting to a type associated with Fra Bartolommeo (compare his 'Lamentation' in the Palazzo Pitti), possesses greater emotional tension. The colouring is recognizably that of a pupil of Pontormo. – *Granacci*, who came from Ghirlandaio's workshop, was a very versatile artist stylistically. The figures in the large-format *Story of Joseph* are close in style to Andrea del Sarto; the fan-like tree in the left background resembles similar creations by Pontormo. In the centre are the beginnings of a centralized structure which is utterly Italian. The rhinoceros indicates that we are none the less in Egypt. – *Mariotto Albertinelli's* painting of the *Visitation*, beneath the arch dated 1503, is close to the work of Fra Bartolommeo.

The next room is dedicated to the Tuscan art of the second and third decades of the sixteenth century, a period which has been given the extremely uninformative label of 'Mannerism'. Such a revolutionary period in art, and one which was so rich in varied impulses, can hardly be assembled together under a single, slightly derogatory title. What this period certainly did bring with it was a tremendous blossoming of Florentine art, together with a strong involvement with influences from abroad. The authority of Venice and Parma became acknowledged, Dürer received a passionate disciple in Pontormo, and the result was a certain eclecticism. The fertile temperament of *Andrea del Sarto* has often been praised. Warm shadows glow through his new, chromatic play of colour. A real 'professional' (Vasari referred to him as a 'faultless painter'), he aimed at a perfection of form verging on grandeur. The climax was the *Madonna of the Harpies* (so-called from the fabulous creatures on the throne) of 1517 (signed and dated). The total mastery displayed in the elaborate folds of these crisp robes, the perfect command of colour, and the incredibly assured formal construction (notice how in the figure on the right the arm, hand and book are developed without interruption to form a remarkable gesture) made this a most popular work. The strict triangle of figures is balanced by the animated group of putti. The restricted space, with its simple architectural termination, is symbolically conceived to show Mary on the altar raised up as the object of adoration. – Other pictures are from the master's best years – the altar-piece for the convent of Vallombrosa (1528) with *S. Giovanni Gualberto and other Saints* (their martyrdoms are depicted on the predella), and the *S. Giacomo with Two Boys*. – *Pontormo* came under Andrea del Sarto's influence, but his own character led him in a rather different direction. A painter of deep seriousness and powerful impact, he was forever experimenting and often left his works unfinished. He was an individualist to the point of eccentricity. Wrestling with the legacy of tradition

and at the same time adopting a uncompromisingly independe
line, he was the last outstanding representative of the Florentin
Renaissance. He created many works of lasting value, particular
as a portraitist. Notice his *S. Anthony*, dramatically conceive
and with a sort of demoniac undertone, holding a scroll which
full of tense force. – With Pontormo, form was the ultimate, an
he used it with invariably successful suggestive force. The sma
Martyrdom of S. Maurice is full of novel animated figures s
against a stylized background. The almost expressionist art o
Dürer's woodcuts inspired Pontormo to such paintings as th
Adam and Eve (to the left of the door). – *Rosso*, a pupil o
Andrea del Sarto, took a similar direction to Pontormo. He wa
a problematic, nervous, intellectual man, deeply imbued wit
humanist culture. He experimented with dissonance in his use o
colour, and purified his style until it bordered on the abstrac
and in France his work became of international significance. H
Moses and the Daughters of Jethro belongs to that phase whi
culminates in the *Descent from the Cross* in Volterra. The creativ
impulse is free of any restraint through convention – althoug
subject to a strong discipline of its own – not only in the decora
tion but also in the magnificent play of gesture, the plasticity o
naked bodies and the silent display of simple profiles (top right
The reclining nude (below) was copied by Géricault in his 'Ra
of the Medusa' (Louvre). – Two female portraits, one by Po
tormo and one by Rosso, hang side by side in the corner by th
doorway, summing up the artistic temperaments of the two me
– *Salviati* (whose real name was Francesco de'Rossi; he assume
the name of a Roman cardinal who was a friend of his) develope
a style that found few successors, being eclipsed by the popularit
of the school of Vasari. *Caritas*, an example of his masterly b
relatively unaffecting work, clearly illustrates the rather speci
position he occupies.

On the right wall of the next room, the visitor finds Pontormo
Last Supper, a work in the magisterial style of the lunettes o
the Certosa di Val d'Ema, not very well preserved. The colou
appear to be transparent. The eye of the Trinity looks down fro
the triangle. Giving a picture of the Madonna this disturbing glan
of a cat was something that had already been undertaken b
Giulio Romano. Further works are by Rosso, Andrea del Sart
Puligo, who was a disciple of Andrea and an important portra
painter, *Beccafumi*, the leading artist of Siena, and finally *Bac
chiacca* (Francesco Ubertini), to whom few pictures can be a
tributed with any certainty, among them this predella depictin
scenes from the life of *S. Acacius* (formerly in S. Lorenzo). In
spired by Andrea del Sarto and also later by Lucas van Leyde
and Dürer, this cultured artist painted small narrative scenes o
great charm in a popular style, with a delicate precision of colou
ing that is full of character.

Light and shade and a rich, 'atmospheric' palette remained the prerogatives of Venice, and above all of *Titian*, the master of them all. The following room is dominated by the overwhelming richness of his art. The *Venus of Urbino* (on the right wall) was painted *c.* 1538, and the *Venus with Amor* (entrance wall) probably about ten years later. The varied brushwork, the different kinds of background (in the one, a servant tidying a chest, in the other a landscape) speak eloquently of a power of expression that was equally at ease in the picturesque and in the human element. *Flora*, one of his best-known pictures, painted when he was still a young man, became the symbol of Titian's ideal woman with its soft lighting and shimmering gold. The *Maltese Knight* may have been painted while Giorgione was still alive (*c.* 1508–10). The portrait of the *Duke of Urbino* is not unlike the 'Venus of Urbino' in manner; the staff of the commander bearing the Papal keys and the green twig with the device 'se sibi' are revealing symbols. The power of the synthesis and the play of iron-grey and silver-grey tones place this work slightly above the *Portrait of the Duchess*, with the clock and the little dog. – *Catarina Cornaro* appears in the picture of S. Catherine of Alexandria (the wheel was the instrument of her martyrdom). – There are two impressive panels by *Palma Vecchio* (1480–1528) – *Judith*, a mature work, and a *Madonna with Saints*.

There follows a series of smaller rooms where the visitor can admire works by Lotto, Sebastiano del Piombo, Parmigianino, Savoldo, Dosso Dossi, Mazzolino and Girolamo Campi, among others. These were the artists, together with a number of lesser names, who had such an influence on Venice, bringing that city to the artistic hegemony that was to culminate in Tiepolo. First, the large *Madonna del Collo Lungo* ('Madonna with the Long Neck', so-called because of a not particularly characteristic feature of the picture) by *Parmigianino*, a late masterpiece (incomplete) of which numerous sketches have been preserved. On the right is a shadowy row of columns. Two feet next to the prophet with the scroll indicate a further figure towards whom the prophet is turning. Parma was the geographical and Raphael the artistic point of departure for this master, who rapidly achieved fame and whose work, particularly in portraiture, reached a very high level. With his more modern conception of form and his balanced compositions, he was able to realize a whole new figurative canon of slender, almost exaggeratedly long proportions. A noble gracefulness and an elevated sense of beauty characterize his art. – *Amico Aspertini* worked mainly with his left hand; his brush is somewhat unsteady. He was fond of bizarre shapes and of antiquities, as can be seen from his *Adoration of the Magi* (notice the torso on the altar on the left). It is a typical late work with its 'romantic' landscape and its deliberately archaic high horizon (from the Berenson collection). –

The *Annunciation* by *Garofalo* may date from this master's early
period; Garofalo went blind in 1550. — The attribution of the
Portrait of a Man to *Dosso Dossi* is entirely justified, not least
because of the thundery light, which was peculiar to this artist's
work. Also by Dossi is the *Galant Company*, a large work from
his late period in which all 'romanticism' is abandoned in favour
of firm shapes and very concrete colours. — *Sebastiano del Piombo*
is represented in the Uffizi by three pictures — the *Death of
Adonis*, with Venice in the background, is carried along by a
Giorgione-like lyricism, while the influence of the school of
Raphael can be seen in the women. The so-called *Fornarina* is
closer to the work of Titian. The third picture, the *Sickly Man*
is of great intimacy but unfortunately is not very well preserved.
— The *Lorenzo Lotto* pictures exhibited here give a rather in-
adequate impression of this important master's great artistic
qualities.

The visitor comes next to a sort of blocked-up passage (Room 33)
Immediately on the right is a portrait of a woman which is (not
with any certainty) attributed to the mysterious *Jean Perréal*
— The armour in the small but magnificent picture of *François I*
on horseback is particularly beautifully painted. — *Anthonis Mor's*
self-portrait depicts him as a humanist scholar; on the easel is a
Greek poem, in his hand a palette with four brushes. The picture
is dated (1558) and signed on the edge of the board on which the
glass of water is standing. — *Amberger* painted the portrait of the
goldsmith Cornelis Gros, who also worked in Florence. — The
visitor's attention is drawn particularly to the three small panels
by *Jacopo Zucchi* which have as their theme the three ages;
Egypt with the crocodile and the Sphinx, the peace of the
animal kingdom and the invention of calligraphy refer to the
Golden Age. The Silver Age announces that man shall earn his
bread by the sweat of his brow (on the 'Justitia' panel); to this
age belong house-building and the tilling of the fields, as well as
the bat, the owl, night, cold and fire; up in the sky the hours
dance around the chariot of the sun. The Iron Age gives to each
his due; man has learned commerce and art but also war. — Further
pictures here (particularly those by *Vasari*) represent the more
intellectually orientated schools of Florentine painting in the sixteenth century. One exception is *Allori's* large *Abraham's Sacrifice* (1606, signed) with its farm cottage on the left and its
Netherlandish influence.

The so-called Veronese room also contains works by Moroni,
Giulio Campi and Savoldo. The *Annunciation* by *Veronese* (on
the left wall) continues the tradition of the fifteenth century
not only in the deep shaft-like perspective between Mary and the
angel (Piero della Francesca, in Perugia, was the first to paint in
this manner) but also in the light, almost silvery colouring. The
Holy Family with S. Barbara is different. Here a golden hue

S. Lorenzo, New Sacristy, capitals

Loggia dei Lanzi, detail of a fresco in S. Trinita (Ghirlandaio)

lows over delicately graded folds and trimmings as if the whole picture were steeped in some luminous medium.

A few words are necessary about *Barocci*, author of the principal work in the next large room. His contemporaries found him somewhat difficult to understand. He belonged to an intellectual circle whose members aimed at the expressive rather than the Classical, who sought not stability but a kind of exciting, self-generating strength, whose colours glowed and in whose masterly draughtsmanship there burned a fire that seemed to hollow out forms from the inside and even to pierce through them. Barocci was certainly among the most remarkable Italian painters of the sixteenth century. His long life-span (1528–1612) brought him to the threshold of the Baroque and beyond. The often copied *Madonna del Popolo* dates from his middle period, *c.* 1575 (it was painted for the Pieve in Arezzo). – The *Noli Me Tangere*, 1590, is a sketch for a picture now in Munich.

Bacchus, the *Shield with the Medusa's Head*, and next to it the *Sacrifice of Isaac* (notice the similarity of facial expression between the Medusa and Isaac!) by *Caravaggio* illustrate various aspects of the art of this great revolutionary, in whom a profound realism was coupled with a feeling for the most delicate shades of colouring. Further Baroque masters are exhibited here, with the *Carracci* representing their forebears and *Guercino*, with his very characteristic small landscape, charming in its utter simplicity, representing their feeling for nature. – A number of artists from the Netherlands represent spheres of influence which were to become important for the South. One master not present here is *Rembrandt*, in whose work Italians appear to have taken no interest at all. The breadth of development between the young master with the hauberk and the late self-portrait was so unique and unrepeatable that no Italian – almost until the present day – could comprehend it.

Finally a word about *Rubens*. Deeply influenced by Italian culture and with his roots firmly planted in the soil of Classical antiquity, he had as a copyist made the acquaintance of all the great masters of the Apennine peninsula. This great transformer is represented principally by two enormous compositions. *Henry IV at the Battle of Ivry* (on the left) and the *Entry into Paris* (opposite) form part of an incompleted series; like the Paris Medici cycle, it was intended to glorify the king. It would be hard to imagine a greater contrast than exists between these frieze-like monuments and the intimate portrait, full of inner wisdom, of his first wife *Isabella Brandt* (no. 779).

The Uffizi is of major importance not only as a picture gallery, but also as the home of the richest *collection of antiquities* in Italy. Most of these are exhibited in the corridors. At the far end of the west corridor (from the café the visitor can go out onto the roof of the Loggia dei Lanzi; there, at the back on the left, he

will find the fountain basin for Giovanni da Bologna's *Morgante*
now in the Bargello; further sculptures include a pseudo-Clas-
sical relief by the school of Cellini) stands *Bandinelli's* copy
of the Vatican *Laocoön*, made for Clement VII (whose device car
be seen on either side of the base) and much admired in Florence
as the first concrete example of the Classical style, then only
recently discovered. To the left is the *Nymph with Panther*, pro
bably from Alexandria, third century B.C.; the head, neck and part
of the arm have been restored. To the right, a bust of *Caracall*
which may have provided the model for Michelangelo's 'Brutus'
(Bargello). – Beside it, the *Wounded Warrior*; the head is ol
but probably does not belong to it; a fine piece, Roman, thir
century A.D. – Diagonally opposite is a *Nereid on a Wate*
Horse; among other parts the head of the nereid and the base o
the group are restored; the piece is Hellenistic, with the nerei
probably modelled on an earlier muse-type. – Further to the righ
is *Athena*, a statuette of Grecian marble; the head is Classical bu
does not belong to it; a late copy of a fifth century type. – T
the left, *Apollo*, a fragmentary copy of Praxiteles' *Sauroktonos*
the restorations, including the head, date from 1565 and ar
probably by Caccini. The 'pietra dura' work on the lyre and
base are early seventeenth century.

On the right, the visitor enters the huge **Room of the Niobide**
(decorated in 1780: architect G. M. Paoletti, stucco-work b
G. Albertolli). It houses the group of the *Niobides* discovere
in Rome in 1583; this and the 'Medici Venus' are Florence's mos
precious Classical possessions. Besides the statuary there are pic
tures by Nattier, Watteau, Chardin and Liotard, whose figur
is reading a book of virtue. – The 'Niobides' probably decorate
the gable of a temple. These pieces are thought to be copies o
fifth century models. – In the centre of the room stands th
famous *Medici Vase*, in the family's possession (in Rome) fron
the sixteenth century onwards. The scene depicted on the vase ha
never received a satisfactory explanation. Does it represent Cas
sandra, or is it the sacrifice of Iphigenia? It is thought to be
late Attic piece of the first century B.C. – The *Leaping Hors*
dates from the early imperial period.

Returning to the **corridor**, the visitor will find *Leda* immediatel
to the right of the entrance to the Niobides Room. The head an
neck are modern; the piece is a copy of a Greek original attribute
to Timotheus. – Opposite is a seated *Apollo*; the head is moderr
and the figure has one foot on a tortoise's head. – Next on the
window side is a *Dionysus with Satyr*, found in Rome befor
1550; this beautiful and particularly well-preserved group i
thought to be Hellenistic. – On the right, *Athena* by Timotheu
a Greek figure from the circle of Lysippus. – Further right, th
Omphalos Apollo, a second century A.D. copy of an origina
possibly attributable to Callimachus. – Further to the right, *Mer*

ury, Greek, fourth century. – On the left, a copy of Myron's *Discobolus*. – The female *Peplos* statue on the right, sometimes referred to as a 'Demeter', is from the circle of Alcamenes. – At the end of the passage, to left and right, are two *Marsyas* figures. The theory that one was restored by Donatello and the other by Verrocchio is untenable.

In the **Loggia** overlooking the Arno the visitor will find among other things a beautiful copy of the Borghese *Ares*, a *Boy pulling out a thorn* [Lo Spinario], and on the left the lovely *candelabrum base* of Italian marble, part of a larger series (the remainder are in Venice and the British Museum). It is probably from Rome, and is an example of the decorative art of the period of Trajan. Above is a triangular base of somewhat eclectic character; despite the apparently early date of the elongated female figures, this work dates from the time of Augustus. – The visitor should not miss the *Wild Boar*, a particular favourite of Florentines. It was found in Rome, and together with the 'Molossian Hounds' in the entrance hall was given as a present by Pius IV to Duke Cosimo I. This powerful animal, 'picking up the hunters' scent', inspired many artists of the time of Vasari by virtue of its strong realism. The bronze copy near the Mercato Nuovo is said to be by Pietro Tacca.

Turning into the **east corridor**, the visitor will see on the right wall what is probably the best-known series of tapestries in the Uffizi – the eight pieces of the so-called *Valois* series. They came to Florence in 1589 in the dowry of Christine of Lorraine. The central figure is Catherine de'Medici. In the background of the tapestries – which were created by Lucas de Heere – are depicted court banquets after designs by the Frenchman, Antoine Caron. The banquets illustrated here, at Fontainebleau and Bayonne, were essential ingredients of a policy which sought to inspire William of Orange to put the Valois on the throne of the Netherlands. The tapestries thus form an artistic reminder of the French attitude towards the revolt of the Netherlands against Spain. – Among the other noteworthy tapestries in the collection are those by Bacchiacca depicting the months of the year. – Returning to the antiquities, the visitor will find here the *Phaeton sarcophagus* (no. 251 a). The picturesque composition is matched on the other side by a bas-relief depicting a Roman chariot race, drawing an interesting parallel between the fall of a mythological figure and the fall of a historical charioteer. – The *Lares altar*, which is decorated on all four sides, dates from about the time of the birth of Christ; it was an official monument associated with the family of the emperor Augustus. – The statue of *Asclepius* on the right may be attributable to Alcamenes, though some authorities consider it to be the work of Calamis. – Opposite is an *Apollo*, a Hellenistic interpretation of a Lycean type; the restorations (including the head) are by Flaminio Vacca. – On the right, a

Meleager sarcophagus dating from the first half of the thir
century A.D. – Further to the right is a *Venus* which was restore
by Ferrata. The *Venus* opposite was heavily restored by Silla. –
On the right, an *Apollo sarcophagus* with the Muses. Nov
damaged, this piece from the time of Hadrian was once extremel
fine. – On the left, a statue of a *Hera*; among other elements, th
head and neck are modern. This piece was listed by Vasari a
being in the Palazzo Pitti; it dates from the second half of th
first century A.D. – Opposite, a copy of the Farnese *Hercules*
– Further along on the right, a second century A.D. *Meleage
sarcophagus*. – On the left, *Ganymede* with the eagle of Zeus
extensive restorations, including the boy's head; late Hellenistic
– Further along on the left is *Apollo*, a copy of a work by Scopas
– *Ariadne*, on the right, bears a certain similarity to the 'Nike o
Samothrace' in Paris. This rich piece, with its original Classica
head, is particularly worth studying. – The *Hercules sarcophagu
on the right has hardly been restored at all. It dates possibly fron
the early Antonine period. – The *Hippolytus sarcophagus*, how
ever, on the left, has been more heavily restored; it dates fron
the early third century A.D. The sarcophagus with the *Rape of th
Leucippides* is a beautiful piece dating from the time of Hadrian
it also shows (on the left) Hermes with Alcestis and (on the right
Hercules with Alcestis. Other authorities interpret these scenes o
the sides as depicting the marriage of the abducted Leucippides
– The handsome *Satyr with Grapes* on the left belongs to a typ
that was widely popular for its decorative splendour. – The *Rap
of Proserpina* – on the sarcophagus (right side) – has always bee
regarded as symbolizing return; hence, on the right, Hercules i
depicted bringing Alcestis back to life (Antonine period). – On th
left, a figure restored as a *Nike*. – Further along on the left is
copy of a *Pan and Daphnis* group by Heliodorus. – On the sam
side, further along, is *Attis*, wrongly restored as a barbarian (th
head is modern). This enormous votive statue dates from th
period of Hadrian.

Finally, the Uffizi possesses a famous collection of artists' self
portraits which is currently on exhibition in a part of the pas
sage leading to the Palazzo Pitti (ask for the times of opening o
the **Galleria degli Autoritratti**). Begun in the time of Cardina
Leopoldo Medici, the collection now comprises almost eigh
hundred self-portraits.

The entrance to the **Archivio di Stato** is in the east wing
a few doors beyond the portal leading to the Uffizi gallery.
On the north or Via Lambertesca corner of the building is th
stylistically important *Porta delle Suppliche* ('Door of th
Petitions'), a piece of pure Mannerism that continues th
tradition of Ammannati in the layered construction and th
inclusion of windows between the two pediment segments.

SACRED BUILDINGS

S. Agata (Via Sangallo 110)

A convent for nuns was founded here in 1211. It was enlarged in the fourteenth, fifteenth and sixteenth centuries, particularly in the sixteenth century when a nuns' gallery and a new flat ceiling were erected inside the church and the façade was built (1592–3) to a design by Alessandro Allori. The interior was painted in the eighteenth century.

The **façade** merits attention as an example of Mannerist architecture. As was fairly common practice at the time, it was designed by a painter (Allori, who also served for a while as Cathedral architect). The articulation consists of a (schematic) division by means of strips of macigno into nine compartments, with niches and oval and rectangular windows; a certain tension is evident in the positioning of the individual forms within the total composition. Today the building (usually closed) has a rather neglected appearance. Notice the carved *wooden door*. – The painted simulated architecture of the interior dates from 1780.

S. Ambrogio (Piazza S. Ambrogio)

One of the oldest foundations in Florence, this church was rebuilt towards the end of the thirteenth century and subsequently renovated inside, most recently by Foggini in 1716. The simple façade was reconstructed in 1888. During the nineteenth century, an attempt was made to restore the medieval form of the interior. The open frame roof may originally have been painted. The church is particularly revered as being the last resting-place of many Renaissance artists, including Cronaca, Granacci, Leonardo del Tasso and Verrocchio.

The north side of the church being obstructed by monastery buildings, the interior is illuminated only by four windows in the south wall; also in the south wall is a walled-up portal dating from the old building. The visitor enters the church through the portal in the new façade. – The rich **decoration** of the interior spans the period from the fourteenth century to the present day. The painting on the ceiling was completed in 1833. Down each side of the nave are four late fifteenth century altar tabernacles. On the first one on the right is a beautiful *Annunciation* (fourteenth century) with a remarkable angel. In the floor in front and to the right of it, the visitor will find a memorial tablet to Cronaca, who is buried here. – Nardo di Cione is assumed

to have been the author of the next picture, the *Madonna
del Latte*. – The fresco on the next altar (a *Deposition*
damaged) is by a follower of Niccolò di Pietro Gerini. – On
the wall to the right of the high altar, in the ante-bay of th
right-hand chancel chapel, is a triptych attributed to Bicci
di Lorenzo. To the right of that is a fine early fifteenth-
century sacrament tabernacle. – The left chancel chapel is
known as 'del Miracolo' because of a miracle alleged to
have taken place here in 1320; some wine left in the chalice
which is kept here is said to have turned into blood. The
beautiful *marble tabernacle* around the chalice is one of th
principal works of Mino da Fiesole (1481–3); the terracotta
candlestick angels on either side are by the school of della
Robbia (1513). On the north wall is a *fresco* depicting th
procession with the ampulla containing the blood; the procession is passing before the church and one can see the old
Gothic façade. The fresco was painted in 1486 by Cosimo
Rosselli. Notice the faces, which are particularly animated.
They include portraits of the artist himself and of Pico
della Mirandola. They were unfortunately damaged in a
fire and are consequently rather dark. – In the floor is the
tomb of Mino da Fiesole.
In the ante-bay is a composite painting: angels and saints
by Alesso Baldovinetti surround a *Nativity* by his pupil
Graffione, painted in 1484 to replace the original tabernacle
for the relic of the blood. Verrocchio is buried in front of
the next altar (lunette and painting by Raffaello dei Carli)
– The next picture, a *Madonna in Glory with Saints*, is by
Cosimo Rosselli. – The wooden statue of *S. Sebastian* (pre
1500) stands in a handsome niche above the tomb of its
creator, Leone del Tasso. The (damaged) medallion of th
Annunciation on the bottom part of the surround is thought
to be a late work by Filippino Lippi. – On the façade wall
to the right of the entrance is a strangely rigid fragment of
a *Martyrdom of S. Sebastian*, uncovered in 1888; it is
attributed to Agnolo Gaddi. – The *Visitation* in front is by
the remarkable Andrea Boscoli, an excellent draughtsman
whose work is full of character (signed and dated 1597).

SS. Apostoli (Piazza del Limbo)

*This is one of the rare examples in Florence of an early medieval
building which has been preserved virtually unaltered. The first*

mention of a building on this site dates from 1075. Excavations under the chancel have uncovered remains which go back to Classical times (a Roman crematorium below thermae below Classical and Early Christian graveyards). The legend that the church was founded by Charlemagne seems to be without foundation. It was based on a faked inscription dating from the sixteenth century (today this can be seen outside the church above the portal on the left-hand side) which convinced even Vasari himself. At the beginning of the fifteenth century, five chapels were added to the left-side aisle, and around the middle of that century chapels were added to the right-side aisle, which was vaulted at the same time. Early in the sixteenth century, Benedetto da Rovezzano built the handsome main portal and what is now the canonry. Beginning in 1546, the left side aisle was also vaulted with domes. These alterations were instigated by the Altoviti – first Bindo Altoviti (whose presumed portrait, now in Washington, was for a long time attributed to Raphael) and then his son, Archbishop Antonio Altoviti, who is buried in the chancel. The Altoviti had been patrons of the church since the fourteenth century.
In the latter part of the sixteenth century, certain decorative additions were made to the apse (by Dosio) and a considerable amount of Baroque decoration was added to the whole building during the eighteenth century. In recent years, however, and most recently in 1930, a great deal has been done towards restoring the original appearance of the church. In 1930, for example, the first chapel in the left-side aisle was reconstructed and the original wall replaced.

The impressive **piazza** (called **del Limbo** after a cemetery for unbaptized infants, who were thought to be burning in the fires of Hell) charmingly enhances the **façade** in which the basilican section of the church is clearly reflected. The central portion is more recent: above Benedetto da Rovezzano's beautiful portal is a modern double window. Moving a few paces to the left, the visitor can look down the length of the north wall (the front part is restored) to a chapel wall (also restored) containing neo-Gothic windows. The clerestory, however, still has its original masonry. Notice how in the window arches stones of different colours were used alternately, showing a certain affinity with the style of incrustation, then just beginning (early eleventh century). – The simple *campanile* was built by Baccio d'Agnolo. Only the upper part can be seen, at the south-east corner of the church.
The **interior** (*ill.* facing p. 225), with its antique dignity and

austerity, is not only one of the most effective in all Florence; it is also, in its Classical control, a typical example of post-1050 Tuscan architecture. The ground plan – a three-aisled columnar basilica with a semicircular apse and no crypt – follows the ancient Christian tradition. This is expressed most clearly in the nave, with its rather narrow arcades, its small clerestory windows and its beautiful open frame roof – one of the finest of its type in Florence. Each rafter is meticulously painted with motifs that appear to be derived from textile decoration. – The last two bays of the nave are slightly higher, and it may be assumed that they originally formed a canons' choir. The floor is a reconstruction, but in the style of the original floor. The arcades of columns put one in mind of the Baptistery, which dates from about the same time. The shafts consist of blocks of black-and-green marble. The classically styled capitals each comprise three pieces of marble, so carefully assembled that the joints are almost invisible; Vasari himself admired their craftsmanship.

The dome-vaulted side aisles owe a stylistic debt to Brunelleschi. Most of the altars down the right side date from the High Baroque period. The picture on the second one, *Peter at the Gate of the Temple*, is by Pomarancio. The next chapel contains a large picture by Vasari, the *Conception of the Virgin*, 1540–1, a highly complex allegory which may be regarded as the prototype of the Baroque 'Immaculata'. – The tomb above the sacristy door dates from *c.* 1570 and is by the school of Ammannati; the attribution to Calamech is not conclusive. – The *Madonna* at the end of the side aisle is from the circle of Nardo di Cione. – The lower part of the apse was decorated by Dosio in 1573–83. In the middle, behind the high altar, is the Michelangelo-style *sarcophagus of Archbishop Antonio Altoviti*. The two busts (on the left, in accordance with the legend of the church's foundation, is Charlemagne) are by Caccini, *c.* 1583. The high altar is modern (1901). – A very beautiful *terracotta tabernacle* by Giovanni della Robbia has been erected at the top end of the left-side aisle. Below are fragments of the *tomb of Donato Acciaiuoli*, with the figures of Mary and John in relief (1333). Against the longitudinal wall is the *tomb of Oddo Altoviti* by Benedetto da Rovezzano. On the base is an inscribed plaque in the Roman manner. The style of the piece is somewhat cold, with some of the symbols of death – such as the rotting skull with snakes – anticipating the Baroque (c. 1512). – On the first altar in the aisle is a *Nativity* by Maso da San Friano. – The last bay before the façade wall contains a tomb of a woman (it was originally situated inside the south portal of the façade) with a bust by Foggini (1698). Before that, in the fourth chapel, the visitor can admire a miraculous Cartapesta crucifix, donated in 1690. – The *aspersorium* on the last pillar is attributed to Benedetto da Rovezzano.

SS. Apostoli possesses some stone *fragments of the Holy Sepulchre*, brought back from Jerusalem by a member of the Pazzi family after the First Crusade. On Easter Saturday, a fire is lighted from them which is then carried to the Baptistery. – An artists' mass takes place in the church every Sunday at 11.45 a.m.

The Badia (Via del Proconsolo)

The oldest and most important monastery within the city walls has always been known simply as 'la Badia' – 'the Abbey'. This famous Benedictine abbey, the only official abbey in the city, was at the same time the noblest. It was founded in 978 by Willa of Tuscany. She was the mother of the Marchese Ugo to whom Dante mistakenly attributed the foundation in his 'Paradiso'. In 1285, Arnolfo di Cambio began to enlarge the building in the Cistercian manner. During the Early Renaissance, plans were made to replace the church with a new one. In 1432, Cosimo Medici wished to commission Brunelleschi to produce an entirely new design. The monks, however, were unwilling to accept the plan, and Brunelleschi's wooden model was apparently kept in the monastery right up until the seventeenth century.

Instead of an entirely new building, smaller alterations were undertaken by such masters as Bernardo Rossellino, Giuliano and Antonio da Sangallo the Elder, and – between 1503–11 – Benedetto da Rovezzano. A more radical project emerged in the seventeenth century when Matteo Segaloni suggested turning the building round through ninety degrees and orienting it in a north-south direction. This was undertaken in 1627, making the existing church into a transept and necessitating a new chancel. Originally the façade faced west; now the entrance to the church is at the north end. – The monastery was abolished in 1810, and since then the church has served the local parish. – The frescoes in the Chiostro degli Aranci were taken down in 1957.

Altogether three separate stages of construction can be distinguished: the Ottonian church (969–78), the chancel of which now leans against the old city wall which followed the line of the

Badia, portal

present Via del Proconsolo; then Arnolfo's Gothic basilica (1284–1310), the outer walls of which are largely preserved, a richly decorated church with, in particular, frescoes by Giotto; and finally, Segaloni's seventeenth-century alterations and further additions.

The visitor approaches the church from the side of the original *chancel*, attributed to that great architect, Arnolfo di Cambio. The articulation is even and flat, with individual motifs going back to Classical tradition. An interesting feature here is the connection of the two windows by means of a dosseret. – Climbing the steps, the visitor passes through Benedetto da Rovezzano's magnificent *portal*, decorated with a beautiful terracotta *Madonna and Child* (early sixteenth century, placed here in 1871; some fragments seem to have been added around the outside). The entablature of the portal has been renewed (the original is in the Bargello). The vestibule is also by Benedetto da Rovezzano. It opens up into a small courtyard.

The visitor then enters Matteo Segaloni's splendid building (erected at right angles to the original church), with its carved wooden ceiling by Felice Gamberai (1629–31). The chancel is articulated with a sort of Palladian motif. The light inside the church is best in the morning. Immediately to the left is one of Filippino Lippi's most beautiful early works – the *Vision of S. Bernard* (c. 1480, *ill.* facing p. 240). The figure at the bottom, right, is the donor, Domenico del Pugliese; the figures of Mary and the angels portray members of the donor's family. The work still retains its original frame. – On the entrance wall immediately to the right, the *wall-tomb of Giannozzo Pandolfini* from the workshop of Rossellino catches the eye. This 'lunette-tomb' has its prototype in that of Orlando de'Medici in SS. Annunziata, and represents the Arcosolium-tomb in its most classic form. The base, with its pilaster articulation, is particularly fine. The incorporation of coloured stone throughout the elevation is reminiscent of Late Classical usage. – On the right wall is an early work by Mino da Fiesole. This attractive relief, depicting *SS. Lawrence and Leonard* standing on either side of the Virgin, was originally an altar dossal (1464–9). – Turning the corner to the right, the visitor will find another work by Mino da Fiesole, the *tomb of Bernardo Giugni* (c. 1468). The composition is rather wooden, but individual parts are of great elegance. It is modelled on the Bruni tomb in S. Croce. Above the figure of the deceased is 'Justice'; right at the top of the arch is 'Faith'. The tomb is signed on the medallion in the lunette. A few traces of colour have survived. – The chapel in the (west) end wall is dedicated to S. Maurus; its decoration is Baroque. The small door of the little holy oil cupboard on the left of the altar is decorated with an unusual fifteenth century engraving. On the left wall of this western arm of the church is a remarkable altar-piece by G. B. Naldini, the *Outpouring of the Holy Spirit* (c. 1570). In the corresponding position in the eastern arm is *Christ Carrying the Cross with S. Veronica*, painted by the same master at about the same time; there is a sketch for this painting in London. – Turning into the left arm of the church, the visitor will find on the east wall the fine *tomb of Marchese Ugo*, who was wrongly supposed to have been the founder of the Badia, and died in 1001. The tomb is by Mino da Fiesole and was constructed between 1469 and 1481. It is a masterpiece of simple Classical forms, with architecture and ornamentation in beautiful harmony. The sarcophagus appears to stand in an open doorway which is decorated with a light curtain. The figure of 'Caritas' is particularly interesting, with her strangely animated children modelled apparently on fourteenth century sculptures (compare, for example, Tino da Camaino's 'Caritas' in the Bardini museum). – It should be added that none of the tombs in the Badia occupy their original positions; they were all displaced in the seventeenth century. Since they all follow prototypes, they offer an excellent opportunity to study the later effects of certain pioneer creations. – Above the tomb of Marchese Ugo is a lovely *Assunta* by Vasari, c. 1566. – Once this wall was decorated with an *Annunciation* from Giotto's first Florentine period. Remains of this fresco were discovered in 1959, but they are now once more covered with plaster. – The frescoes in some of the side chapels have recently been taken down. – The apse of the church was frescoed by Ferretti. The (restored) choir stalls were made by the del Tasso brothers (1501). The canvas depicting *SS. Benedict and Maurus* is by Curradi, 1638.

Through the sacristy, which lies to the west of the chancel, the visitor enters the so-called **Chiostro degli Aranci**, a cloister built in the transitional style of c. 1400. It is an evocative area, containing some interesting old tombs. Some particularly beautiful frescoes by an unknown master which were taken down from here are now exhibited in the Fortezza. Worth particular attention are the remains of a *fresco* by Bronzino, on the east wall above the marble *tomb of Francesco Valori* with its bust of the deceased (erected after 1550; it was brought here from S. Procolo), and also, built into the walls of the east and south wings respectively, two portions of a sacramental tabernacle (bracket and the eagle) possibly attributable to Bernardo Rossellino. Lower down on the east wall the façade of the old chapter-house can be seen.

Leaving the cloister once more and passing through the church, the visitor reaches an **atrium** with an exit on the Via Dante Alighieri; looking back, one can see the original façade of the Badia, with the *campanile* at the right-hand corner. The lower storey appears Ottonian; the upper part was built after 1330 (in 1307 the citizens had half-destroyed it to punish the monks for insubordination!) and provides the city with one of its most distinctive landmarks. – Two chapels in this atrium merit particular attention: the *Chapel of S. Stephen* in the west wing, built by Benedetto da Rovezzano in 1503–11, with a fragment of a Romanesque incrusted altar-table (the altar-piece, *Martyrdom of S. Stephen*, is by Biliverti), and the smaller *Chapel of the Holy Cross*.

S. Carlo Borromeo (Via Calzaioli, opposite Or San Michele) *The building was begun in 1349 by Neri di Fioravante and Benci di Cione and completed by Simone Talenti towards the end of the fourteenth century. It is a small Gothic hall-church belonging to the same stylistic type as Or San Michele. Altered in the seventeenth century, it was restored to its original state in 1931. – It is also known as* **S. Carlo dei Lombardi.**

The **façade** with its splendid portal rises above a tall base with a Classical profile. Powerful corner abutments. On the south side, the Baroque windows have been preserved. A particularly beautiful feature of the **interior** are the terminating chancel chapels. The *Lamentation* behind the high altar is an accredited masterpiece by Niccolò di Pietro Gerini; it came from Or San Michele. The frescoes in the chancel chapels, depicting the miracles of S. Charles Borromeo, are by Matteo Rosselli.

S. Elisabetta delle Convertite (Via de'Serragli, between Nos. 122 and 124)

The first mention of this foundation occurs in an early fourteenth-century reference to the wide-ranging influence of the Augustinian nuns here with respect to the conversion of fallen girls. It was continually necessary to enlarge the buildings. In 1490–4, the church was renovated and a cloister with columns erected. Further alterations and additions in the sixteenth century gave the church its present façade and a nuns' gallery inside. In the eighteenth century the ceiling, which until then must have been an open framework, was covered with a simulated vault. – The site passed into secular use during the nineteenth century, but in this century it was given over to the training of clergy. Later it became an oratory (which it still is today). Some renovations in the style of the fifteenth century are to be found.

Experts name Alessandro Allori as the author of the *façade*. The simple decoration of the interior is dominated by an eighteenth century ceiling painting. In the nuns' gallery (closed to visitors) are some frescoes of *c.* 1585 based partly on Dürer's woodcuts of the Passion; they are by the young Poccetti. Above the arcade on the west wall is a *wooden crucifix*, possibly by Permoser, which once stood on the high altar. This quiet, relaxed figure with its fine loin-cloth can only be seen clearly when the light is good.

S. Felice (Piazza S. Felice)

The shrine of S. Felice, one of the oldest parishes on the left bank of the Arno, has seen the passing of several owners. The first mention of the church is in 1066, when it belonged to a family. Monks from Nonantola arrived in the twelfth century, and in the fourteenth century they extended the building towards the west and added three chancel chapels. In 1413, the church came into the possession of the Camaldolensian Order. In 1450 the façade was rebuilt in the style of Brunelleschi. Dominican nuns moved in in 1557, and a nuns' gallery was erected inside the church. Other orders arrived during the eighteenth century and converted the monastery buildings into schools. – In 1897 a good many of the disfigurements of the Baroque period were removed from the church and the façade restored to its original state.

Exterior   Facing an intimate little piazza which in the sixteenth century contained a column (now removed) commemorating the Battle of Marciano is one of the few really complete fourteenth century *façades* in Florence. Resembling the wall of a house or a simple temple, it consists of a portal, windows, and a strongly profiled roof gable. The craftsmanship is of the highest order: notice the volutes

S. Felice, façade

which stand out clearly from the surround of the tympanum
above the portal. Its calm, serene mastery and clearly conceived proportions give it an impression of relaxed assurance. – On the corner abutments on either side appears the
coat of arms of the sponsor of the façade. – On the north
wall, beside the three more recent rectangular windows, are
five Gothic windows (restored; the Baroque contours can
still be seen in the masonry) and a door which bears the
date 1700. The position of the old side entrance can still be
seen in the wall to the right of this door. – The western end
of the north wall may well be the oldest part of the building (notice the vertical joint below and to the left of the

second window from the western end). – The west end of
the building, on the Borgo Tegolaio, consists of three chapels
built in the style of Brunelleschi and a campanile. – The
significance of the curious recess in the north wall (near the
façade) is not clear.

Interior   Entering the church, the visitor will find himself
in an unusually deep Gothic hall, with the view upwards
blocked by a gallery. Further on, the open framework of
the roof can be seen, as well as the square main chancel and
chancel chapels. – The **decoration** of the inside of the façade
wall is a typical combination of fifteenth century frescoes
(originally such frescoes may have covered more or less the
whole of the interior) and Baroque tombs (both of them
eighteenth century). – On the right in the nave is an aspersorium of 1460 (the one on the left is sixteenth century).
Most of the altar tabernacles are Baroque. The *Lamentation*
in the niche behind the fourth altar on the right is a characteristic terracotta group from the circle of Giovanni della
Robbia (early sixteenth century). – The altar-piece on the
fifth altar is a *Madonna with Saints* by Ridolfo Ghirlandaio, *c.* 1520. – Turning round, the visitor will find on the
front of the nuns' gallery an important *monumental crucifix* (painted over later) by an artist close to Giotto. – The
first altar on the left, starting from the chancel, belonged to
the Parigi, a family of architects. In Giulio Parigi's tabernacle of *c.* 1635–9 is a fresco by Giovanni di San Giovanni
dating from about the same period, *S. Felix comforts
S. Maximus of Nola* (the angel with the grapes was painted
by Volterrano). – The fifteenth-century tabernacle of the
next altar contains a particularly valuable *triptych* by Neri
di Bicci, 1467, still in its beautiful original frame. The
lunette fresco dates from *c.* 1400. – In the next tabernacle
is a characteristic work – unfortunately spoiled by faded
varnish – by Jacopo da Empoli, *The Virgin appears to Two
Saints*, 1595. – The next picture, the *Vocation of S. Matthew*,
is a typically colourful work by Matteo Rosselli, 1619. –
Salvator Rosa's *Rescue of S. Peter*, in the next tabernacle,
has unfortunately become very dark. Painted after 1645,
when the artist was at the height of his creative powers, it
shows an intimate feeling for nature, though at the same
time there is a disturbing quality about this 'lakescape'. –
Let into the small door behind the next altar is an attractive

Loggia dei Lanzi, 'Perseus and the Medusa' (Cellini)

Palazzo Vecchio, column in the courtyard

plaque adorned with foliage, c. 1400. – The last altar before the façade wall has a triptych by a disciple of Filippino (shortly before 1500).

S. Felicita (Piazza S. Felicita)

On this site near the Ponte Vecchio there was once an Early Christian cemetery (discovered, interestingly enough, by Vincenzo Borghini) with a small church dedicated to S. Felicita. Amongst the inscriptions found were some dating from the fifth century. Some of the most interesting pieces have been set into the wall of the passage down the south side of the church (the passage leads to a cinema). A congregation of Benedictine nuns is thought to have settled here about 833. After a somewhat chequered history (the inhabitants were expelled several times by secular priests), a church was consecrated on 8 November 1059, the day after the consecration of the foundation stone of the Baptistery. This building, which was oriented towards the south at right angles to the original (and also to the present) building, stood until the fourteenth century. Afterwards a Gothic building was erected on the site of the first permanent church.

During the fifteenth century, a small chapel was added at the south-west corner of the nave, and in 1470–3 the sacristy was renovated. In 1564, Vasari concealed the old façade behind a structure which included a part of the passage connecting the Uffizi with the Palazzo Pitti. This ran along above an open vestibule and opened into the interior of the church through small windows rather like a theatre box. The main chancel was decorated in 1610–20 after designs by Cigoli. Then, in the eighteenth century, something most unusual occurred: the entire church was pulled down with the exception of the additional structures, which were left standing. Consequently, Ruggieri's new building (begun in 1736), which turned out to be slightly wider than the old Gothic church, re-assimilated all the old additions, i.e. the chapel in the south-west corner and its counterpart opposite, added in 1589, Vasari's vestibule, the sacristy and the main chancel. The convent attached to the church was altered at the same time. There has thus been a church on this site for more than a thousand years. The present building has served as a parish church since 1821, and the convent buildings are now used for secular puposes. Excavations in 1934–5 revealed further information about the Early Christian origins of the site. The original decoration of the south-west corner chapel, overlaid by Ruggieri's decoration, was rediscovered in 1936 and restored in 1957.

The architectural history of the site can be briefly summarized as follows: the first building, a small columnar basilica, was replaced by an Early Romanesque church (the capitals of which are unusual examples of Florentine architectural sculpture of the eleventh century, with thick, fleshy leaves dating apparently from a period

*before the Proto-Renaissance and incorporating motifs of great
antiquity derived from Aquileia; two of these capitals are in the
sacristy, others can apparently be seen in one of the walls) which
gave way to a third church in the fourteenth century, which was
then in turn replaced by the present building.*

From the busy little piazza with its *granite column* (erected
in 1381, apparently replacing a Classical burial pyramid),
the visitor has a view of Vasari's vestibule with the passage
above it, and beyond that the relatively low gable of the
façade. – On the right, inside the *vestibule* is the marble
tomb of Cardinal Luigi de'Rossi, with a reclining figure of
the deceased attributed to Raffaele da Montelupo (this is
the same cardinal as Raphael depicted beside Leo X in his
painting in the Uffizi). On the left are two tombs; the one
at the bottom is of Arcangela Palladini, with the figures of
'Painting' and 'Music' in relief (early works by Antonio
Novelli) and between them a bust of the deceased by
Agostino Ubaldini. These two tombs, as well as the third
one (above, with reclining figure, 1416), were originally
situated inside the church.

The **interior** was modelled throughout by the architect Ferdinando Ruggieri, and represents one of his most important
works. The fundamentally Florentine schema (it was begun
in SS. Annunziata, developed in S. Salvatore al Monte and
taken further in Ammannati's S. Giovannino) is expressive of
a certain Classical serenity and overall balance. On either
side of the tunnel-vaulted nave are three chapels. The transition to the transept is achieved in an interesting way by
means of a graduated bay. At this point, there are balconies
supported on columns, with volutes and cartouches impart-
ing a deliberate tension. The crossing is crowned with an
oval dome on pendentives. One of the older parts of the
church and a remarkable masterpiece in its own right is
Ludovico Cigoli's *main chancel* (1610–20), an example of
a decorative style of architecture that was derived in a strict
manner from Buontalenti. Two columns frame the chancel
façade like a tabernacle; in the open gable is the coat of
arms of the Guicciardini. The vault was painted by Michelangelo Cinganelli, 1617–20; on the right wall, the *Resurrection* by A. Tempesta; on the left wall, an early eighteenth
century *Crucifixion*; on the rear wall, an early painting by
Santi di Tito, *c.* 1565.

Some remarkable works of art are in the late fifteenth

entury **sacristy** (entrance in the right transept arm). Apart from the two eleventh-century *capitals*, there are an *Adoration of the Magi* by a master close to Pesellino (to the right of the door), a five-part panel, the *Madonna with Saints*, a masterpiece by Taddeo Gaddi painted *c.* 1353–5 during the last years of his life, and *S. Felicity Enthroned with her Seven Sons* (interesting costumes) by Neri di Bicci (still painted on a gold background). The *Lamentation* dated 1470 is attributed to the Master of the 'Castello Nativity', the painted crucifix to Pacino di Buonaguida. The epitaph to the left of the entrance, with a mosaic portrait of Cardinal Alessandro Barbadori, uncle of Urban VIII, is by Marcello Provenzale (1639).

Returning to the church and looking up at the façade wall, the visitor can see the two openings through which people using the passage from the Uffizi to the Palazzo Pitti were able to gaze into the church. The chapel on the left is known as the **Barbadori chapel**. The fluted pilasters and the rosettes in the arch spandrels give it a certain resemblance to Masaccio's painted architecture in the Trinity' in S. Maria Novella. The capitals are like those used by Donatello in the side portals of the Old Sacristy in S. Lorenzo. It was these features that threw doubt on the early theory that this small building might be attributable to Brunelleschi, favouring instead an attribution to Buggiani. The date would be some time during the 1530's. The *Annunciation* fresco on the window wall, with its painted vault brackets matching the Early Renaissance style of the chapel, is by Pontormo. Its pale harmony and voluptuous beauty make it one of the most pleasing of all his works. The visitor's glance, however, is diverted by the large *Entombment* (cleaned in 1937) by the same master on the south wall (*ill.* facing p. 241). This entrancing, ecstatically spiritual picture (1526–8, still in its original frame) is painted in ethereal colours with virtually no shadows. – The figures in the spandrels are by Pontormo and Bronzino and must date from the same period.

In the opposite (north) corner is the **Canigiani chapel**, an interesting example of stylistic imitation, *c.* 1589. While adopting many of the forms used in the Barbadori chapel, it refers back at the same time in a more general way to the style of the Early Renaissance. B. Poccetti's fresco on the

window wall depicts the *Miracle of the Snow on Mt. Aven-
tine*; in the *Assumption* by the same master on the altar, the
heads of the Apostles are portraits of members of the Canigiani family who donated the picture. – The rest of the
decoration dates from 1739 (Gherardini); there is a fif
teenth-century tombstone in the floor.

The remaining side chapels contain a remarkable series of
paintings illustrating the changes which took place in
Florentine painting up until the nineteenth century. In the
first chapel on the right, S. Felicity is shown encouraging
her sons to accept their martyrdom (Giorgio Berti, 1822–4)
In the picture in the second chapel, Pope Gregory is seen
pointing out to a person who has come to him to beg for
relics a piece of Roman soil from which pours the blood of
martyrs (Ferdinando Villani, 1747–50). The next picture is
the *Martyrdom of the Maccabees* (Antonio Ciseri, 1860–3)
Further pictures are: on the end wall of the right transept
arm, *God the Father in Glory, with the meeting of
SS. Joachim and Anne beneath the Golden Gate, and Saint*
(Poppi, c. 1570); in the first chancel chapel on the right, the
Adoration of the Magi, Nicola Cianfanelli's first work
(1828); in the second chancel chapel the *Vision of S. John
on Patmos* by Lorenzo Cambi (1786); in the first chancel
chapel on the left, the *Betrothal of the Virgin* by Gaspare
Martellini (between 1828 and 1842); in the last chancel
chapel a *Trinity with Adoring Saints* (in the middle) by
Carlo Portelli, a pupil of Ridolfo Ghirlandaio who was
influenced by Rosso, Bronzino and also Vasari (the addi
tions around the edge were painted by the Englishman
Ignazio Hugford, eighteenth century). On the right wall
are fragments of a *Nativity* fresco by a disciple of Taddeo
Gaddi.

The large, very dark picture on the end wall of the left
transept arm is one of the solemn works of Volterrano's
late period. – Turning into the ante-bay, the visitor will see
on the left wall of the altar niche (partly obscured by a
confessional) an epitaph dating from 1695 that incorporate
parts of a fourteenth-century sarcophagus. The wooden
crucifix on the altar was made by Andrea Ferrucci, c. 1500
– The series of large altar-pieces continues in the chapels of
the side aisle: first, *S. Louis feeding the Poor*, 1682, by
Simone Pignoni (a talented disciple of Furini); next, *Tobia*

healing his Father, 1776, by the English aristocrat Ignazio Hugford, a pupil of Gabbiani; and finally, Fabrizio Boschi's Martyrdom of S. Sebastian (shortly after 1600).

The **cloister** (now walled in, but the elevation is still clearly recognizable) is one of the most interesting pieces of Gothic architecture in Florence, with bevelled corners and arcades of differing heights and widths. In some of the details, the artist's free formal imagination approaches the ideals of the Renaissance, though he was working in the 1370's and the result is impressive.

S. Firenze (Piazza S. Firenze)

The tradition contained in this piazza goes back a very long way. There was already a church here in the thirteenth century, a Romanesque building which stood on this site until it was removed in 1772.

The history of the complex with which we are concerned here begins in the year 1640 with the arrival of the Brothers of S. Filippo Neri. An inscription on the right side wall (Borgo dei Greci), probably the oldest inscription from this Baroque period, bears the date 1643. This history falls into two distinct phases. Initially Pietro da Cortona was elected architect and great plans were laid; numerous studies in the Uffizi – if they do in fact refer to these plans – give us an idea of their scope. The first designs were for a domed church, and a large wooden model in the Bardini museum may be connected with this original phase. Financial problems, however, imposed modesty. The second phase began under Pier Francesco Silvani (Gherardo's son) who was able to complete the present oratory in 1696. The interior was entrusted to Gioacchino Fortini and the façade was added in 1715 after a design by Ruggieri.

The new oratory was called S. Firenze Nuovo to distinguish it from the old Romanesque church, S. Firenze Vecchio, which still stood beside it. The two disparate buildings could not be connected because there was a row of houses between them. Nothing, in fact, was done to connect them until towards the end of the eighteenth century, when Zanobi del Rosso replaced the Romanesque church by a second oratory with a replica of Ruggieri's façade. At the same time the row of houses was pulled down and replaced by a monastery. – In 1865 the second building was given over to the Italian government, who used it for the Ministry of the Interior. Today the monastery and the right-hand oratory house a law court, while the first building, the one on which Pietro da Cortona and Silvani both worked, still belongs to the monks of S. Filippo Neri. – The whole complex was entirely restored in 1931.

The visitor enters the **older oratory** (i.e. the one on the left in the Via dell'Anguillara) through Ruggieri's façade of 1715, with sculptures by Fortini dating from the same period. – The tall, almost precipitous **interior**, with its particularly fine wooden ceiling, is abundantly decorated with paintings and sculptures dating principally from the seventeenth and eighteenth centuries. The *sacrament chapel* (on the south side) was added in 1772 by Zanobi del Rosso; the schema of the Old Sacristy of S. Lorenzo is here extended in a curious way to form a lateral oval. Notice the panel on the entrance wall, a *Martyrdom of the Ten Thousand* which contains numerous portraits of members of the Medici family. This important picture, from Bacchiacca's last stylistic phase, represents as it were the transition to the art of Vasari.

In what are now the **law-courts**, the visitor will find one of the grandest Baroque staircases in Florence, as well as a stately courtyard.

S. Francesco de'Macci (Via de'Macci 17)

This originally Gothic church, which is reckoned to date from 1344, was altered in the mid-sixteenth century and then, starting in 1683, modernized. G. B. Foggini changed the old west-east orientation to north-south. – There is no façade, but in the dilapidated side wall the remains of an old palace can be seen. On the same wall is the foundation inscription dated 1344 (with a damaged coat of arms). After Foggini's Baroque decoration of the interior, nothing remains of the original Gothic. Andrea del Sarto's *Madonna of the Harpies*, now in the Uffizi, once graced the high altar.

S. Francesco di Sales (Viale Ludovico Ariosto 13)

Erected by A. M. Ferri, the buildings were occupied in 1700 first by a girls' school and later by a kind of religious community for ladies. The architecture is poor, the decoration meagre. Inside is, among other things, a picture by the Englishman Ignazio Hugford.

S. Francesco dei Vanchetoni (Via di Palazzuolo 17–21)

The foundation stone was laid in 1602, with Matteo Nigetti in charge of the work, and the church was consecrated in 1603. The vestibule and the side buildings were added in 1620. – The large oratory (if closed apply to the curator) is an exciting construction by a follower of Buontalenti. The whole of the decoration is designed to glorify Blessed Ippolito Galantini, whose bust can be seen outside above the central portal. This portal, together with the window, develops an idea pioneered by Ammannati. The vestibule contains some particularly fine confessionals; the frescoes are by J. Ligozzi (c. 1620). The interior of the church is somewhat bourgeois. The two heads to left and right above the doors in the chancel wall are copies of pieces in the style of Desiderio; the originals were sold to America. – The small museum once housed in the rooms at the rear has now been dispersed.

S. Frediano in Cestello (Piazza del Cestello)

Founded by Carmelite nuns; their first church, the small church of S. Maria degli Angioli near S. Maria del Carmine, was erected in 1450–60. The subsequent history is remarkable: after S. Maria Maddalena dei Pazzi had resided in the monastery, two nieces of Pope Urban VIII felt it was beneath their dignity to remain there as nuns, and so an exchange was agreed with the Cistercians. The latter left their more airy domicile (now S. Maria Maddalena dei Pazzi) in the Borgo Pinti to the Carmelites and took over this site. They immediately began building extensively. Gherardo Silvani, brother of the Cistercian abbot, designed the complex, and his son Pier Francesco began laying the chancel foundations of a large church along the Arno. This plan, however, was dropped. Another architect, Cerutti (known as 'Colonnello'), was called in and he designed a north-south orientated building with a façade towards the Arno (like Brunelleschi's ideal plan for S. Spirito, only on a smaller scale). The foundation stone of this building was laid in 1680 and it was completed by 1698, when Antonio Ferri added the splendid dome.

This is without question a most beautiful piece of architecture. The additions and restorations of later periods have not contributed to spoiling an intimate and at the same time magnificent complex of buildings. – The church has been known as S. Frediano since the demolition of the old clergy house of this name which stood on the corner of the Piazza del Carmine.

The visitor is recommended to approach the church across the small piazza from the direction of the river. The bare *façade* of rough dressed stone is, like all the other walls of the church, entirely without decoration. From the other side of the river, the silhouette of the church is dominated by the tall *dome* and the beautiful Baroque *campanile*.

The **interior** is laid out in the form of a hall with transept and chancel structures. The nave is flanked by rows of chapels. The solemnity of the proportions is unusual for Florence; the subdued grey and white colouring, however, corresponds to the local style of the period. All the decoration dates from the period around 1700, except for a few nineteenth century pieces such as the two altar tabernacles in the transept arms; some of the older pieces were brought here from other churches. – The first chapel on the right, dedicated to S. Maria Maddalena dei Pazzi, was decorated by Matteo Bonecchi (frescoes) and Giovanni Sagrestani (altar-piece). The decoration of the two following chapels is centred on the *Triumph of the Cross* and the *Life of the Virgin* respectively. – The *Paradise* fresco in the dome is one of Gabbiani's masterpieces (1702–18); the allegories in the pendentives were added by Bonecchi. The wooden cross on the high altar is thought to be by the school of Baccio da Montelupo, as are many others like it.

The sacristy (the *Assumption* in the vault was painted *c.* 1700) contains some remarkable works of art, among which the large and unusual panel on the right wall, *Crucifixion with Eight Saints* (S. Lawrence reclining in the foreground), by Jacopo del Sellaio occupies a special place. The sombre colours may have darkened with age, but they serve to emphasize this richly inventive master's powerful and sensitive melancholy. In this work, which dates from his last creative phase (1490–3), Jacopo achieved a monumental grandeur. The picture was brought here from the demolished clergy house of S. Frediano. Next to it hangs a copy of Raphael's *Canigiani Madonna*, now in Munich. An interesting feature here is the halo with seven angels in the upper part of the picture; in the original this has been painted over. The sacristy also contains a *Madonna with Saints* by Curradi (above the entrance), and a small bronze crucifix by a pupil of Bologna.

The chapels down the left-hand side of the nave, like those on the right, each have a particular theme. The first is devoted to S. Bernard of Clairvaux (Piero Dandini), the second to John the Baptist (Antonio Franchi) and the third to S. Anastasius (G. Ciabelli). In each case, the artist was responsible for both frescoes and altar-piece. On the altar of the first chapel is the venerated *Smiling Madonna*, a painted wooden sculpture of the mid-fourteenth century in the style of Nino Pisano. Less valuable is the sixteenth century figure of S. Roch on the altar of the second chapel.

The monastery, one of the most important Baroque complexes of its type in Florence, extends far to the east. The entrance is through the large, interesting *portal* in the Borgo S. Frediano (no. 20), the mellow forms of which represent a highly personal variant of the style of Buontalenti. The monastery buildings (the courts are magnificent) are not usually open to visitors.

S. Gaetano (Piazza degli Antinori)
The church lies to the right of a small piazza of which the left side is dominated by the exceptionally beautiful Palazzo Antinori.

Roman remains have been found on the site, and there is mention of a church here as early as the eleventh century. This was completely rebuilt, beginning in 1604, by Nigetti and the Silvanis. Since 1553 it had housed a community of Olivetans; they were followed by Theatine monks. and finally in 1786 the monastery was given over to secular use and the church became a parish church.

The splendid **façade** in the style of the Late Baroque followers of Buontalenti is richly adorned with sculptures (*ill.* facing p. 256). The figures of *Spes* and *Caritas* above the main portal, early works by Balthasar Permoser, are particularly noteworthy. The *S. Andrea Avellino* above the right portal is by the same German sculptor; the figure in the corresponding position on the left is by Francesco Andreozzi. Entering the church through the right portal, the visitor will find directly in front of him in the porch a *bust of Orazio Piattesi* by Volterra, signed and dated 1557.

The **interior**, with its single aisle, was decorated during the seventeenth and eighteenth centuries. The contrast between the dark, almost black stone and the lighter, almost white figures and reliefs produces a strange effect. The large marble statues above the architrave represent the twelve Apostles and the Evangelists Luke and Mark. They date from the late seventeenth century and are by various hands. SS. Peter and Paul on either side of the triumphal arch are by Foggini. – Among the paintings, particular mention must be made of the *Martyrdom of S. Lawrence* in the second chapel on the left by that great Baroque painter Pietro da Cortona. In the first chapel on the right is a terracotta *Madonna* from the workshop of della Robbia. – Right and left, on the walls of the transept arms, are two identical tombs; their rich and characteristic use of 'pietra dura' decoration reveals the stylistic influence of the Cappella dei Principi in S. Lorenzo.

On the left of the church is a smaller **oratory** (usually closed) and the quite elaborate **monastery buildings** extending some way to the east. The 'Sala Theatina' on the first floor has a fine *Crucifixion* from the circle of Filippo Lippi, unfortunately not in a very good state of preservation.

S. Giorgio e Massimiliano dello Spirito Santo (Via Costa di S. Giorgio 33)

The convent church of S. Giorgio 'on the Costa' (the name of the steeply ascending street) was first mentioned c. 1000. It grew to

*become a large complex. The principal enlargements were made
around 1700, when Foggini extended the convent. It has been
used as a barracks for almost a hundred years now.*

The church has survived and lies on a tiny piazza that constitutes the entrance to an army medical school. The main
portal dates from 1705. – The **interior** (open only on rare
occasions) is a simple hall terminating in a semicircular
apse. In the chancel, there is an important picture by the
Master of S. Cecilia, a *Madonna with Angels*, heavily cut,
however, at the sides and bottom. The rest of the decoration
is Baroque (the paintings include works by Passignano, Gabbiani and Gherardini).

S. Giovanni Battista della Calza (Piazza della Calza)

1362 is the date of the first mention of a hospital of the Knights of
Malta at the southern exit of the city. In 1392, a community of nuns
moved in, but they left in that year of crisis, 1529, because they were
dangerously close to the city wall. The Gesuati who arrived in 1531
gave the building its present name, 'della Calza', derived from their
long stocking-like hats. Around 1600, the chancel end of the church
was extended and the monastery expanded towards the south. The
campanile was erected in 1649. In 1668 the Order of the Gesuati was
abolished. Today the complex houses nuns of the order of Perpetual
Adoration. – The chief features of the exterior are the plain, plastered
façade and the campanile. The simple interior is Gothic in its proportions. The present decoration has been very much purified; the
finest piece is the picture on the high altar in a typical tabernacle
frame from the period around 1600.

S. Giovanni dei Cavalieri (Via Sangallo 66–70; entrance to the cloister, 68)

*This complex was founded in 1323 as a home for fallen girls and
was consequently first named 'S. Maria Maddalena'. Then in
1551 nuns of the Order of the Knights of Malta moved in, rearranged the buildings according to their needs, and re-named
the church after the patron of their order. In 1553 it temporarily
received a third name when it was dedicated to S. Nicholas of
Bari. – The monastery was abolished in 1808, and the church
turned into a clergy house. It was restored in 1924 with the aim
of re-establishing the original appearance after many alterations,
while preserving the sixteenth-century additions.*

*The architectural history of the site falls into three distinct phases:
the small hall which was the first oratory (1322–7), the larger
fourteenth-century church (begun in 1329) which forms the substance of the present building, and the convent of the Maltese
nuns (begun in 1551) with its nuns' gallery and tunnel vault (now
removed).*

The façade with its Maltese Cross (framed by angels bearing
the crown of the Grand Dukes of Tuscany) and its applied

strips of Baroque decoration dates from 1699. A large vestibule as wide as the nave, with cupboards for vestments let into the walls, leads to the spacious and attractive **interior**. Four pillars similar to those of S. Trinita divide the church into three aisles. The wide nave has an open frame roof. An interesting feature here is the length-wise extension of the bays. The *first altar* on either side has a round-arched stone surround with crockets in the transitional style between Gothic and Renaissance. Both are attributed to Piero di Giovanni Tedesco. On the *second altar* on the right is a late work by Santi di Tito, the *Birth and Naming of John the Baptist* (1603, with self-portrait, completed by the master's son). Further on is an *Annunciation* altar-piece which still retains its original frame; the artist was either the so-called Master of the 'Castello Nativity' or, as some authorities believe, Jacopo del Sellaio (*c.* 1475). The *Coronation of the Virgin* on the last altar on this side is by Neri di Bicci (*c.* 1450). – In the small **sacristy** is a sawn-out *Crucifixion with Mary and John* attributed to Lorenzo Monaco. – The main chancel was once flanked by chancel chapels, but these have been walled up. Alessandro Gherardini painted the frescoes. – Two noteworthy pictures on the left side of the church: the *Nativity* by Bicci di Lorenzo (dated 1435 on the frame) and the *Presentation of the Virgin* in its old frame. – Turning back towards the façade wall, the visitor will find a beautiful mid-sixteenth century organ screen on the nuns' gallery. The gilded wooden bust of S. Peter to the left of the entrance dates from a slightly earlier period. – The adjacent clergy residence contains further works of art. – The **cloister** offers a typical example of the architecture of the fourteenth century.

S. Giovanni di Dio (Via Borgo Ognissanti, next to no. 20)
The Augustinian hermit followers of the Portuguese Saint John of God moved into this hospital in 1587. The hospital had been in existence since the fourteenth century. Today it is run by nuns. – The architect responsible for the church (which is usually closed) was Carlo Andrea Marcellini, a pupil of Cirro Ferri and Ercole Ferrata. Hence the unusually rigid façade, which in its details is modelled on Florentine examples. – Inside the church there is, among other things, a stucco *Madonna* by the young Luca della Robbia (second altar right; on the socle is the *Eve* from the Paradise Doors of the Baptistery).
Amerigo Vespucci was born in a house (now demolished) that stood in the grounds of the monastery.

S. Giovannino degli Scolopi (corner of the Via Martelli and the Via de'Gori, opposite the Palazzo Medici)

In 1505 a plan was drawn up to replace a small Gothic oratory on this site by a large domed church dedicated to S. John the Evangelist, thus invoking Christ's favourite Apostle as a sort of second protector of the city after John the Baptist. It was hoped that Cronaca would be the architect. The plan came to nothing, however, as did a second plan of 1526 to erect here, in the immediate vicinity of the Medici Palace, a centralized funeral chapel for the two Medici popes, Leo X and Clement VII.

At the request of Cosimo I, the site was offered to the Jesuits, who came to Florence as early as 1547. In 1579 enlargements were planned which were to include an important college. The chief sponsor of this plan was not a Jesuit but an artist, Bartolommeo Ammannati, who devoted the last years of his life to religious contemplation. He and his extremely gifted wife (the poetess Laura Battiferri) concentrated all their efforts on an architectural undertaking that was to provide a home for them in their declining years and offer their bodies a final resting place. – The great artist's extensive literary remains were also kept here in the Jesuit college; only recently were they transferred to the State Archives.

The form of the church was determined by the older building, and represents an effective union of original architectural ideas with the given Gothic conditions. The adjacent college buildings posed a different problem: here the site had to be bought up piece by piece after laborious negotiations. At the time of Ammannati's death in 1592, the long façade on the Piazza S. Lorenzo was probably complete.

The work was continued by Giulio Parigi, who erected the large courtyard and the part of the Via Martelli, and his son Alfonso who was at last able to erect the façade of the church, faithfully reproducing Ammannati's model (1656; see the relevant inscription in the lower part of the left-hand niche). At the same time, Alfonso replaced the original flat, carved wooden ceiling with a vault.

The completion of the whole complex, however, was only achieved in the eighteenth century after a generous donation by the pious Cosimo III. – In 1773 the Jesuits were expelled and their place was taken by the Padri Scolopi with a

*school. Further extensions (an observatory in the south
wing) and restorations ensued. In 1842 the façade was renewed (an elaborate inscription in bronze lettering below
the gable refers to this). In 1907 so much plaster had peeled
off the north wall that some Gothic forms reappeared. The
façade was cleaned once more in 1960, and the soft sandstone renewed in several places. – The former college building now houses a secondary school.*

In front of the church is a small piazza which was once
entirely occupied by houses, which is the reason for the
delay in the erection of the façade. Before this was completed in 1656, the church had only a side entrance. Alfonso
Parigi followed Ammannati's design for the **façade** (which
dated from the period after 1580) very faithfully, with the
result that it is one of the finest pieces of Mannerist architecture in existence (*ill.* facing p. 257). The dissolution of the
wall into individual blocks of masonry follows the style set
by Michelangelo; the structural paired columns (single
columns at the sides) are let into box-like recesses like those
of the vestibule of the Laurentian Library. The sections of
wall which protrude between the columns are hollowed out
with niches; Ammannati's individual style is evident in their
surrounds (notice the pairs of narrow horizontal slots beneath the entablature between the storeys) as much as in the
cornice above the central window and the Jesuit symbol
flanked by volutes in the gable. The three-dimensional,
stratified elevation of the niches and the wall panels of the
storey above represent an independent continuation of
Michelangelo's ideas.

On the left, near the corner of the college building, is an
extremely good *Madonna with Child* relief (under glass) in
the style of Desiderio da Settignano. – On the north wall of
the church, on the right, remains of the Gothic windows and
the old portal can be seen, as well as the newer windows
above.

The bright and extremely harmonious **interior** is in two
storeys, the lower rather heavier than the upper. The articulating order more or less dictated to Alfonso Parigi the form
of his shallow tunnel vault with its pointed heads. Ammannati extended the Gothic church by adding his chancel at
the west end. He also made it narrower by drawing up an
inner layer of wall (containing statue niches) which he then

punctuated with his tunnel-vaulted side chapels, all of which were originally decorated uniformly with distinctive stucco ornaments. He thus made possible this 'pulsating' articulation of space, with each chapel followed by a massive block of masonry. At the west end, on either side of the chancel, two large niches of the same size as the chancel arch give a kind of lateral movement. He may have had in mind here the first Jesuit church in Rome, Il Gesù.

The beautiful **decoration** provides a rich and positive complement to the architecture (*ill.* facing p. 272). To obtain an impression of the original appearance, the visitor should mentally subtract a number of eighteenth century works, e.g. the life-sized Apostles with John the Baptist by G. C. Cateni, the remarkable carved confessionals below, Agostino Veracini's vault fresco depicting the apocalyptic vision of S. John the Divine and its stucco surround by Bartolommeo Portogalli (both the latter works date from after 1759). Coloured murals were part of Ammannati's plan, and the panel-like clerestory frescoes in their gilded stucco frames depicting scenes from the lives of Christ and the Apostles belong to the original decoration (*c.* 1584–90); they are by Alessandro Fei 'del Barbiere' (a pupil of Ridolfo Ghirlandaio who had become connected with the school of Vasari) and Bartolommeo Carducci. Equally part of Ammannati's plan was the application of rich stucco decoration to his chapels, and here the bare and economical architecture of his late period suddenly bursts into bloom. This decoration was derived basically from the style of Vasari, but there was also a certain impulse from secular architecture, e.g. palace decoration. Unfortunately only the first side chapel on the right has preserved more or less its original appearance. The altar picture in this chapel, a *Crucifixion* of *c.* 1590, is by Girolamo Macchietti, one of Vasari's assistants in the Palazzo Vecchio. – The next chapel was decorated in the eighteenth century (altar-piece of 1936), as was equally the next, although a few traces of the stucco are left here on the inner face of the arch at the top (by Carducci). – The next piece of stucco decoration (in the right 'transept' arch) was donated *c.* 1700 by Cosimo III (the artist was Ticciati). There is an important (though very dark) altar-piece depicting S. Francis Xavier preaching to natives in the Far East, a masterpiece by Francesco Corradi who was probably the most remarkable artist of the large Corradi family.

A small passage leads to the **sacristy**. On the west wall, between the windows, is a beautiful *alabaster crucifix* of the period around 1600. To the left of the entrance, a late-sixteenth century wall font. Another door communicates with the chancel, with its modern choir stalls and wall decoration (1954).

Returning to the church, the visitor will find on either side of the chancel two very fine painted *wall cupboards* which formed part of the original decoration. – The other side of the church begins with some pompous Baroque decoration (post-1775), remains of slightly earlier decoration and three all-grey frescoes of scenes from the life of S. Ignatius in the arch. The altar-piece, *S. Ignatius*, is by A. Puglieschi, 'a pleasing eclectic, old-fashioned in style', *c.* 1718. – The following chapel (nineteenth century marble decoration) contains, apart from some traces of earlier decoration, Curradi's *Immaculata* of 1635. – Ammannati and his wife are buried in the next chapel, their names inscribed on a simple plaque. The marble decoration dates from the early nineteenth century. Alessandro Allori's *altar-piece* depicts the story of the Canaanite woman; the bearded old man leaning heavily on his stick is a portrait of Ammannati, and the woman in the white veil with a book in her hand is his wife Laura. It is an interesting work, painted around 1587. – The last chapel contains some pictures by J. Ligozzi which formed part of the original decoration. Notice particularly the imposing altar-piece and *Jacob's Dream* on the left (cleaned).

The adjacent **college building** is elaborate and palatial in character, its dry style typical of Ammannati's last phase. A number of extremely disparate elements are combined to form the homogeneous façade which dominates the Piazza S. Lorenzo. The austerity which is particularly noticeable here may have been specifically demanded by the Jesuits. – In the entrance to no. 6 stand two beautiful spiral columns with gilded Corinthian capitals; their origin is unknown. – Inside (no visitors are allowed) the decoration is Baroque. The most remarkable feature are the **underground oratories**, reached through the small door in the forecourt to the left of the church façade.

S. Giuseppe (Via di S. Giuseppe)

This is Baccio d'Agnolo's most important sacred building, erected in 1519 on a quiet street almost in the shadow of S. Croce. The wooden model (preserved in the Museo Topografico) was rather more elaborate, and included a lateral portion which was never built. The motive for its foundation was a miraculous image, the 'Madonna del Giglio', which stood on a street corner on the way to the place of execution and from which condemned prisoners derived consolation on their final journey. The church was 'modernized' in the eighteenth century; the ceiling was raised and painted and the façade improved (it was renewed in the nineteenth century). The campanile is modern and dates from 1933.

Vasari expressly mentions the beautiful *portal* as being Baccio d'Agnolo's last work. The **interior** – a rectangular, tunnel-vaulted hall with side chapels – has a communicative simplicity that shows a feeling for the effects of the Classical style. Together with the large arch before the chancel, it reveals the continuing influence of Cronaca's S. Salvatore al Monte. Notice, too, the inclusion of a half-bay between the last of the side chapels and the chancel; this was to recur quite frequently in later Florentine churches. – The **decoration** includes some more recent works. In the third chapel on the right is a Raphael-like, almost 'academic', painting by Santi di Tito, the *Nativity*. Born in Borgo of a patrician family, Santi di Tito showed himself here, in one of his first major works (1564), to be a simple and clear Mannerist (he was a pupil of Bandinelli and Bronzino) whose objectivity eminently qualified him to take over the legacy of the High Renaissance – namely, nature and harmony. The last picture on the right, the *Miracle of S. Francesco di Paola* is by Vignali, as is the picture opposite. Above the pulpit on the left is a painted *crucifix* by Lorenzo Monaco. – On the middle altar on the left is the miraculous image (heavily overpainted) of the *Madonna del Giglio*.

S. Jacopo sopr'Arno (Borgo S. Jacopo 34)

Entering the little street from the Via Maggio (on the corner of the Via dello Sprone is an interesting fountain by Buontalenti, its beautiful plastic impact vividly embodied in a mask), the visitor will find this twelfth century Romanesque **church**, several times enlarged and altered, immediately on his left. The Romanesque **vestibule** is

Palazzo Vecchio, the Studiolo of Francesco I

SS. Apostoli, interior

*Buontalenti's fountain,
corner of the Via dello
Sprone and the Borgo S. Jacopo*

orized as the only surviving example of its type in Flo-
ence. The attic storey dates from a later period. Potential-
y Classical column shafts with capitals of the period
around 1000 support three arches. The decoration consists
of a fine Classical-style cornice with sculptured heads and
white and green incrustation. This vestibule has an interesting history. It stood originally in front of the church of
. Donato in Scopeto, which had to be demolished in 1529
o make room for fortifications (it was re-erected in 1580).
The Augustinian monks moved here to S. Jacopo and
rought their vestibule with them. – The **interior** (usually
losed) is entirely overlaid with Baroque decoration. The
hurch was renovated in the eighteenth century, involving
in 1709) the demolition of the dome of the Ridolfi chapel.

This, according to Vasari, had been erected by Brunelleschi in 1418, without the use of scaffolding, as a sort of dress rehearsal for his Cathedral dome. – From the Ponte S. Trinita, the visitor has a fine view of the rear of the church with Gherardo Silvani's beautiful *campanile* (1660).

S. Jacopo in Campo Corbolini (Via Faenza 37–39)

According to early accounts, this church was consecrated in 1206. The vestibule must date from around 1290. Probably during the Gothic period, the church was vaulted and given a chancel.

In front of the church and jutting out into the street is an important *portico* of three arcades supported by octagonal pillars. This is the only instance in Florence of a Gothic church with a portico. On the fascias of the cubiform capitals are coats of arms. There is a fine coat of arms on the corner. The windows of the upper storey date from the seventeenth century. – There are some interesting capitals in the **interior** of the church, and to the right of the high altar is the tombstone of Prior Luigi Tornabuoni, the only work which can definitely be attributed to the sculptor Cicilia of Fiesole.

S. Jacopo tra'Fossi (Via de'Benci 11)

This extremely ancient foundation apparently received its name from the sewers which used to flow into the Arno at this point. Three phases can be distinguished: a Romanesque church with a westward orientation followed by a second, Gothic church using the same walls; the third and present church is Baroque, and has an eastward orientation. From the rear the visitor can see that the church originally had two façades; the walled-in portals and windows are clearly recognizable. The interior is without interest; in 1849 the building (which is now a Protestant church) suffered the degradation of being used as a barracks for Austrian troops, and the whole of the decoration was either lost or given away to museums.

SS. Jacopo e Lorenzo (Via Ghibellina 33)

1363, foundation of a convent for the nuns of S. Clare; 1543, a new building of which the architect was Antonio Lupicini, otherwise known only as a writer, who later went to Prague to the court of Rudolph II. 1584, consecration of the high altar. – The last restoration took place in the eighteenth century and the building is at present extremely neglected.

S. Leonardo in Arcetri (Via di S. Leonardo)

Founded in the eleventh century, this small and much restored church stands in a delightful narrow street. Today visitors mainly come to see the Romanesque *pulpit*, brought here in 1782 from the church of S. Pier Scheraggio which

was incorporated into the Uffizi. This pulpit is supported
by two columns and decorated with reliefs depicting (from
left to right) the *Adoration of the Magi* and *Nativity*, *De-position* and *Rod of Jesse*, *Baptism* and *Presentation in the
Temple* (an *Annunciation* belonging to the series is now in
New York). On the high altar is a triptych by Lorenzo
Gerini; on the left a *Madonna with Four Saints* (*c.* 1469)
and on the right an *Annunciation*, both by Neri di Bicci.
Above the door to the sacristy on the right, *Tobias and the
Angel with Two Saints*, a triptych by the Master of
S. Miniato.

S. Lucia dei Magnoli (Via dei Bardi, between 22 and 28)
Above the portal in the otherwise bare façade of this tiny church is a
touching figure of S. Lucy between two glazed terracotta angels
(B. Buglioni? Around 1515). Inside, on the first altar on the left, is a
beautiful panel by Pietro Lorenzetti depicting *S. Lucy* against a gold
background (touched up). The angels and the figure of Mary on the
wings are attributed to Jacopo del Sellaio. On the second altar on the
left, a *Madonna with Saints* by Empoli, *c.* 1620. On the immediate
right, next to the façade wall, is the Loreto chapel of the Alamanni
family. It dates from 1712–15 and is modelled on the Casa Santa,
Loreto; it was restored in 1961.

S. Margherita de'Ricci (Via del Corso 6)

*The foundation stone was laid in 1508. The columnar vestibule
was erected in 1611 by Gherardo Silvani. Alterations were made
in the eighteenth and nineteenth centuries, e.g. the erection of the
vaults within (1707). – The motive for the foundation was a
popular miraculous image. The building has been restored, par-ticularly the vestibule (1924).*

The **façade**, which is flush with the row of houses, opens
up at the bottom through three arches into a vestibule. In
the spandrels are relief busts of the Madonna and the Angel
of the Annunciation. The capitals and the elaborate win-dows of the upper storey are delicately decorated. In the
gable above the entrance is a contemporary bust of the
Annunziata to whom the church is dedicated (see the in-scription on the cornice of the vestibule). – The interior, its
few windows casting a dim light, consists of a single **aisle**
terminating in a slightly narrower section which is vaulted
with a dome. On the high altar, surrounded by some ex-cellent Baroque carvings, is the miraculous image, the
Madonna de'Ricci, which was brought into the church in
1769 (the artist was Giovanni da Milano, *c.* 1360; it is some-times covered up). In the tunnel vault above the nave,

which seems to correspond to the original plan, is an eighteenth century fresco of the *Assumption* by Lorenzo del
Moro. The dome (on spandrels) above the altar is by
Zanobi Rossi (1769) and is the most recent part of the
building. The church is articulated by means of a system of
pilasters between alternately wide and narrow round-
arched openings. These arches may originally have been
derived from Classical triumphal arches, but in this case the
inspiration probably came directly from Ammannati's S.
Giovaninno degli Scolopi in the Via Cavour. The architect's
decorative taste is evident in the stately formation of
balusters, screens and cornices. The visitor should not miss
the *altar-piece* in the first chapel on the right, with its predella in the style of Bicci di Lorenzo relating the story of
S. Margaret (*c.* 1450).

S. Maria degli Angeli (Via degli Alfani, on the corner of
the Via del Castellaccio)
The beginnings of the site date from around 1300. More than a
century after that date, Brunelleschi began to build a chapel for
the heirs of Pippo Spano in the extensive grounds of the
monastery here. It was never completed and is now used for
secular purposes. The date 1437 chiselled in the north wall at eye-
level shows that the building had reached at least this height by
then. In 1563, Cosimo I decided to complete the centralized
building as the seat of the Accademia del Disegno, but this plan
was never realized. The upper part of the church was completed
in 1934–40 after a drawing which may possibly have been made
by Brunelleschi, though this is doubtful. Certain restorations were
made during the 1950's.
Today the building's effect is unfortunately somewhat reduced by the fact that it houses an automobile club. It has
sixteen faces outside and eight inside, with a modern portal
at the corner of the street (above it, a bust of the Madonna
by Caccini), and is one of Brunelleschi's most important
later works. Having begun with buildings in which each
wall was a separate entity and every joint sharply delineated, the pioneering architect had progressed to a stage
where the eight chapels of this monumental building appear
to have been carved from a single block. The pillars stand
there resembling left-overs from the mass of the masonry;
they have become three-dimensional sculptural elements.
The architect may have derived this style from his study of
Classical buildings in Rome. – The **cloisters** attached to the

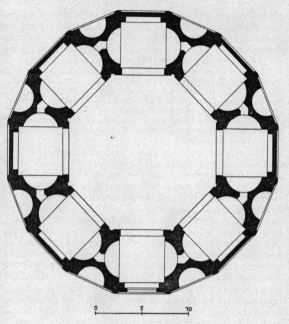

S. Maria degli Angeli, ground plan

chapel (the second one on the Via Alfani is by Ammannati) were changed and in parts demolished during the war.

S. Maria in Campo (Piazza S. Maria in Campo)
This little church, first mentioned in 1137, was extended eastwards in 1279; in 1358 the woodwork of the roof was renewed, and some time after 1550 the church was modernized. – The simple late sixteenth century façade overlooks a small lively piazza which lies to the east of the Via del Proconsolo near the Cathedral. Inside the church, the chancel is given emphasis by a triumphal arch in the style of Santi di Tito or Dosio. At the near end of the right-hand wall is a large fifteenth century wooden crucifix.

S. Maria del Carmine (Piazza del Carmine)
Nos. 3 and 5 of this very wide **piazza** constitute a long,

palatial façade which is all that remains of the once extensive **monastery of S. Frediano**. It is a beautiful piece of Florentine Mannerist architecture. The window surrounds contain masks in the style of Buontalenti. The church of S. Frediano, demolished in 1787, stood on the corner.

S. Maria del Carmine was begun in 1268, completed in 1475 and 'modernized' in 1568 by Vasari, who pulled down the monks' choir and applied uniform tabernacles down both sides. In 1771 the church was destroyed in a fire started by a careless carpenter. Only the façade and the chapels at the ends of the transepts were spared. The new building, which incorporated what remained of the old walls, was completed in 1775 under the direction of Ruggieri and Mannaioni.

The bare **façade** (only the base is dressed; the rest is still in its rough state) with its tall Gothic proportions conveys some idea of the vast size of the church. The Early Gothic portal of dressed stone was restored in the nineteenth century. On the left side of the church is a small piazza.

A few steps lead the visitor up into the **interior** of the church, which is in the Tuscan High Baroque style. The very long, hall-like nave is tunnel-vaulted; a dome crowns the crossing. The shallow nave chapels form part of a system of articulation which is basically derived from Ammanati's pioneering church of S. Giovannino. The greater part of the decoration dates from the eighteenth century. The *Ascension* fresco in the vault is by Giuseppe Romei, and the architectural painting by Domenico Stagi (1782). The altar-pieces, however, are of an earlier date. Bernardo Monaldi's *Burial of S. Albertus* on the second altar is from 1613, Vasari's *Crucifixion* on the next altar from 1560. The *Visitation* on the fourth altar is by Aurelio Lomi (1595), easily recognizable by his piercing colours. The fifth altar, too, is worth studying for its Baroque tabernacle with a covered half-figure of the *Madonna and Child* (stucco, early fifteenth century, style of Ghiberti). Romei also painted the dome, glorifying various Old Testament figures; in the pendentives are Isaiah, Jeremiah, Ezekiel and Daniel (1780).

Standing under the dome, the visitor will see to his right in the end wall of the transept a chapel which formed part of the old Gothic building and miraculously survived the fire. It was saved from demolition during the Baroque period through the intercession of Vittoria della Rovere, the mother of Cosimo III. This is the world-famous **Brancacci** chapel, whose murals by Masolino and Masaccio have made it one of the most important turning points in the development of Western art.

The entrance arch (1748, by the Lorraine architect Joseph Chamant) is Baroque, as are the vaults (painted by Meucci and Sacconi, 1765), the window, the altar tabernacle (inside is the late thirteenth century *Madonna del Carmine*; restored) and the altar-rail. They contain the ancient walls like a precious casket.

The Brancacci family had had a chapel in the church since 1386, but it was not until Felice Brancacci returned from a diplomatic mission to the Far East in 1423 that it became known as the Brancacci chapel. In the next year, Masolino began the paintings which he was to continue with Masaccio, who was eighteen years younger than himself and a boyhood companion from the tiny village of S. Giovanni Val d'Arno where they were both born. As to how Ser Felice got hold of the two artists, we can only hazard a guess. In 1422 Masaccio painted a picture in the Carmelite monastery of the consecration of the church, which took place in that year, and we know from documents that Masolino painted stage-machinery for a S. Peter play produced in the monastery in 1425. It may be, then, that they entered Felice Brancacci's employment through the recommendation of the Carmelite monks.

The best time to study the *murals* is on a sunny morning. On the pillar, top right, is *The Fall*; to the left of that, in the large panel, S. Peter is depicted raising Tabitha and healing a cripple. People can be seen walking about on a broad piazza (probably the Piazza della Signoria here in Florence), amongst them a young man wearing a garment of costly brocade. – To the right of the window (above) is S. Peter baptizing a neophyte who is deep in meditation; a further neophyte can be seen waiting to one side, appearing as if he were cold. Below, SS. Peter and John distribute communal possessions while Ananias, having wrongly witheld his portion, sinks down dead at their feet. How humanly the artist has portrayed the tact with which the mother and child are given their gift! The colouring anticipates something of the spirit of Piero della Francesca. – To the left of the window (below) the cripple is healed by S. Peter's shadow (Acts. 5); notice the marvellous contrast between the quasi-divine assurance of the chief Apostle and the lame man's look of watchful scepticism. The figure on S. Peter's left wearing a peaked cap is traditionally thought to be a portrait of Masolino. Above, S. Peter preaches a sermon. –

The upper part of the left wall tells the story of the tribute money. Jesus, entering the town, is stopped by the tax collector who demands the tribute money (*ill.* facing p. 273). The Apostles, who have no money, are utterly at a loss, but Jesus promises Peter that he will find the money in the mouth of a fish. In the left background, Peter is seen kneeling at the water's edge and extracting the promised coin from the fish's open mouth, and on the right he is seen handing it to the tax collector. The whole scene takes place partly at the town gate, and partly before a vast mountainous landscape which has the effect of stressing the paucity of detail. – At the top of the pillar on the left, Adam and Eve's expulsion from Paradise. The last golden beams of bliss can be seen breaking through the gate. The angel – a pre-echo of Leonardo – points to the earthly wilderness. – Below, S. Paul visits S. Peter in prison; in the corresponding place opposite, S. Peter is released by the angel. – The lower panel on the left wall, which was completed only in 1483–5 by Filippino Lippi, shows S. Peter raising the emperor Theophilus' son who has been dead for fourteen years; on the right, S. Peter is seen enthroned at Antioch addressing the Carmelite brethren gathered around him. As was his habit, Filippino Lippi included a number of portraits; the youth being raised from the dead is apparently a portrait of the young Granacci. – The mural in the lower part of the right wall is also for the most part by Filippino Lippi. On the right, SS. Peter and Paul before the proconsul Agrippa (the old man with the cap is thought to be Antonio Pollaiuolo, the figure on the extreme right a self-portrait of Filippino); on the left, S. Peter's crucifixion (the figure seen in profile on the left is Sandro Botticelli).

Not everything has been preserved. The four Evangelists are missing from the ceiling, as are the lunette paintings, which were probably among the earliest pictures. The paintings on the upper part of the window wall (Masolino's on the left, Masaccio's on the right) which dated from their first period of collaboration (1423–5) are equally no longer there. In 1426, Masaccio spent some time in Pisa but then resumed work here until 1427. He probably painted the *Tribute Money* at that time, as well as the architectural decor for the *Raising of Tabitha*, completed by Masolino on his return from a visit to Hungary in 1426–7. By that

ime Masaccio was already working on the lower scenes on
he window wall. Then both masters worked together on
he entrance pillars, Masolino on the *Fall*, Masaccio on the
Expulsion. Here the difference between the older man's
softer, gayer style and the volcanic temperament of the
younger Masaccio is clear. Masaccio's last contribution was
part of the panel below the 'Tribute Money', i.e. the emperor Theophilus, the Apostles, some of the people in the
crowd and, on the extreme right, S. Peter on his throne. In
1428, he went to Rome, where he died shortly afterwards.
The rest of the panel was painted by Filippino Lippi fifty-
five years later.

As in Romanesque buildings, Adam and Eve appear to the
right and left inside the entrance arch. They have no immediate bearing on the principal theme which is the story of
S. Peter, told according to the Golden Legend. The core of
the narrative is expressed in the figure of S. Peter on his
throne – the chief actor, as it were, of the whole drama. He
is seen here in his three-fold function as ruler of men,
priestly shepherd of the community and teacher of Christianity. Adam und Eve belong to the theme only in so far as
they symbolize sinful mankind towards whom Peter's three-
fold function is directed. (It is worth mentioning here that
another S. Peter cycle – there are not many of them – is
preserved in the Early Christian church of S. Pietro at
Grado, on the coast not far from Pisa.) – A closer study of
the surface of the paintings is extremely interesting, for one
can distinguish the different patches of plaster, each of
which presents a day's work, as well as perspective lines
and, in the 'Tribute Money', vertical axes for the figures
(the earliest authenticated example). – The individual paintings together comprise a total composition which is held
within a frame of painted Classical architecture, with
pilasters and bands of denticulation, so that the visitor has
the impression of being in a kind of pillared hall. The
perspectives are not always uniformly consistent, but the
illumination is treated throughout in such a way that all the
painted light appears to come from the window. – The visitor should imagine the colours as being rather lighter and
more fifteenth century (the way they are in the small portion of the 'Shadow' picture that has recently been restored).
The present darker shade comes from eighteenth century

over-painting. The window wall has suffered particularly from damp.

One can sum up by saying that the Brancacci chapel frescoes constitute one of the climactic moments of post-Giotto European art. They still contain certain fourteenth-century elements (e.g. in the 'Raising of Tabitha') but out of these they forcefully evolve the image of a new type of man. The strength and power of imagination that informs these figures with vibrant life also brings to their emotional situation a degree of tragic grandeur that was to pave the way for the creations of Michelangelo. It is little wonder that artists through the ages have sought out this phenomenal achievement of Masaccio and Masolino like some mysterious teacher, silent yet eloquent. Castagno, Botticelli and Leonardo sat as long before them as did Michelangelo himself who once flew into such a passion in their defence that as a result, he obtained that broken nose which was to disfigure his face for the rest of his life.

To the left of the Brancacci chapel is the entrance to the **sacristy** (1394). Only the walls are old; everything else was restored after the fire of 1771. Above the portal in the vestibule is a standing *Madonna* which is sometimes attributed to the young Michelozzo. In the sanctuary, *frescoes* by Bicci di Lorenzo (after 1394) depicting the life of S. Cecilia and a *crucifix* by a disciple of Cimabue. Mementos of S. Andrea Corsini, pictures of scenes from his life, including an early work by Poccetti (healing a blind man at the gate of Avignon). On the altar, a panel in the manner of Sellaio (the predella depicts among other things the Battle of Anghiari, c. 1440). Also a small stucco *Madonna and Child* statuette in the style of Desiderio da Settignano. – From the vestibule, the visitor can enter the **cloisters** (permission is necessary), renovated in 1612 using the old remains. They contain some fourteenth century frescoes. In the adjacent refectory, Alessandro Allori's *Last Supper* 1581 or 1582.

Returning to the church, the visitor will find on the right in the **apse** (behind the curtain) a monument to Piero Soderini the last Gonfaloniere of the Republic, who is buried in Rome (the monument is by Benedetto da Rovezzano). The screen of the enormous organ was designed by Mannaioni On the altar is the small *Crocifisso della Provvidenza* which

reputed to have worked miracles. Beneath the apse is a
room (usually closed to visitors) containing some very late
fourteenth century fresco remains as well as some murals
by Ulivelli.

At the end of the left transept arm is the **Corsini chapel**
with its beautiful façade. This firmly articulated structure
was built in 1675–83 by Pier Francesco Silvani. The fresco
in the dome, the *Apotheosis of Andrea Corsini*, was painted
in 1682 by Luca Giordano. Above the altar is the saint's
sarcophagus, decorated with a silver relief (Foggini, c. 1680);
the powerful marble relief depicts the saint's ascension. The
popular belief that the author of the latter was Balthasar
Permoser has no foundation in fact; this work, too, was
designed and executed by G. B. Foggini (1677–83), as were
the reliefs on the sides (right, the Battle of Anghiari,
1685–7; left, the saint's altar miracle, 1685–91). That the
rich decoration of the chapel was not all planned at the
same time is demonstrated on the right, where the lower
edge of the enormous and very lively 'painting in marble'
does not meet the architectural frame exactly. It was
originally intended only to have a portrait bust between the
volutes of the sarcophagus and, behind, a painting on canvas. – The chapel as a whole, coldly splendid, is quite unlike anything produced by the Baroque period in Rome.

Of the altars on the left-hand side of the nave, notice
particularly the fourth with its *Annunciation, with God the
Father* by Bernardo Poccetti (1601). – Some remains of frescoes by Starnina in smaller rooms off to the side have been
taken down.

S. Maria della Croce al Tempio (Via di S. Giuseppe)
Founded in the fourteenth century, this church is now almost completely
renovated. It was used for the administration of spiritual consolation
to condemned prisoners before their execution. Inside are some fresco
remains, as well as the cross which used to accompany the processions to
the place of execution.

S. Maria Maddalena dei Pazzi (Borgo Pinti 58)
The convent was founded by Cistercian nuns in 1257, and has
been altered several times, notably by Giuliano da Sangallo. In
1669, Maria Maddalena dei Pazzi, who is buried here, was
canonized, and as a consequence the chancel was enlarged. The
dome, the lantern and the floor were designed by Cirro Ferri
and executed with some alterations by P. F. Silvani. This phase

of the construction, which produced some of the best work of t
Baroque period in Florence, was completed in 1685. – When t
Via Colonna was extended in 1885, it cut down the northern ed
of the site. Today the building houses a community of Fren
Augustinian monks.

The beautiful Baroque *portal* on the Borgo Pinti bears t
coat of arms (weathered) of Pope Urban VIII, who in 162
persuaded the Cistercians to vacate the convent in favour
the Carmelite nuns. – Inside the vestibule, on the right,
the **Neri chapel** (Cappella del Giglio, usually closed; bu
in 1505 and redecorated more richly in 1598) with fresco
by Poccetti (there is a particular abundance of figures in t
dome) and on the altar a *Martyrdom of a Saint* by Pa
signano. – The visitor then enters Giuliano da Sangallo
atrium-like **cloister** with its characteristic Ionic pillars, n
all of which, however, are original. The whole cloister
not unlike that of SS. Annunziata as Michelozzo first plan
ned it. However, the period is later and the style mo
Classical, with more precise references. – The few fresco
brought here from other parts of the convent during th
nineteenth century, are of no particular artistic valu
(M. Rosselli, Fontebuoni).

It is advisable to visit the **church** only when the light
good. Chapels have been added on either side of the single
aisled nave. The substance of the nave walls is still Goth
(post–1257); the chapels were added in 1480–1500. Th
capitals, designed by Giuliano da Sangallo, are particularl
beautiful. The Baroque decoration is by L. Arrigucci; th
ceiling was frescoed by Chiavistelli, the side walls by Ul
velli. The fourth chapel on the right contains a notab
Madonna and Child and Saints by Puligo. In the next chape
is the original frame of Botticelli's *Annunciation*, now in th
Uffizi (and replaced here by another picture), and som
stained-glass windows from the period around 1500.

The **sacristy** (1526) was decorated in the eighteenth cer
tury, and offers one of the few examples in Florence
something approaching Rococo. The crucifix on the lef
wall is thought to be a youthful work by Bernard
Buontalenti.

The sixth chapel has been dedicated by the Augustinians
Joan of Arc (modern). – The visitor then comes to the mai
chancel, richly decorated after designs by P. F. Silvani an

Cirro Ferri (the dome was painted by Dandini). To right and left are scenes from the life of S. Mary Magdalen by Luca Giordano (1685). The altar-piece is by Cirro Ferri, the statues by Spinazzi (right, 1781) and Montauti (left, 1690). The decoration is particularly rich on the lower part of the walls; especially fine pieces are the large marble putti and the six bronze reliefs depicting scenes from the life of . Maria Maddalena dei Pazzi by Carlo Marcellini (*c.* 1685). The third chapel on the left-hand side contains an exciting wooden statue of *S. Sebastian* by Leone del Tasso; the saints on either side are by Raffaello dei Carli: the window still retains some of its original glass. – In the following chapel, the visitor will find Santi di Tito's *Mount of Olives*, 1591, derived from Albrecht Dürer's 'Little Passion'; the figure of Peter is derived from the copper engraving on the same theme. – The beautiful *Coronation of the Virgin* (1505) by Cosimo Rosselli in the next chapel is worth study equally for its old frame.

The rest of the **monastery grounds** are either closed to visitors or are used for various other purposes (the northern section houses a school). In the old **chapter-house**, though, a marvellous fresco by *Perugino* has been preserved (best seen in the morning light; entrance at Via Colonna 7 or 11). Executed in 1493–6, i.e. during the period when the master was at the height of his powers, this fresco will impart to the visitor one of the happiest impressions to be gained anywhere in Florence. It is on the end wall of the hall, divided in three parts corresponding to the three divisions of the arcade, yet at the same time held together by one continuous serenely peaceful landscape. In this way, the horror of Christ's martyrdom on the cross (with Mary Magdalen, and on the left S. Bernard of Clairvaux and Mary, on the right John and S. Benedict) is removed. – On the left are some further pictures by *Perugino* (the fresco of *Christ helping S. Bernard* is probably from his workshop), and on the right, a beautiful *pulpit* in the style of Benedetto da Maiano.

. Maria Maggiore (corner of the Via Cerretani and the Via de'Vecchietti)

This is one of the most delightful medieval churches in Florence, probably going back to Early Christian times. Whether the name implies a connection with the church of the same name in Rome

remains an open question. The building was renovated during t
Romanesque period, and some remains of this renovation a
preserved beneath the present chancel. The church was subsequent
enlarged in the Gothic style. According to some authorities, t
architect was Arnolfo; others (Vasari) say it was a master calle
Buono. The sacristy was built in 1449, and in 1596 Buontalen
added the inner wall of the façade. Further small alteratio
were carried out in the seventeenth century, and in 1912–13 t
entire complex was thoroughly restored.

Exterior The visitor should picture this corner, now s
heavy with traffic, as it once was – a quiet little piazz
with, projecting into it, the small vestibule that once forme
part of the façade (some of the holes for the entablatur
can still be seen). The scaffolding of a huge triumphal arc
was regularly erected for royal weddings on the north sid
along the present Via Cerretani. The original pre-Roma
nesque *campanile* is incorporated in the part of the façad
on the left of the nave. It is among the earliest examples o
its kind, resembling the one in Ravenna in its masonr
technique and its small windows (except that here the win
dows are round). High up on the side of the campanil
facing the Via Cerretani is the delicately chiselled bus
known as the *Berta*, a late Romanesque (if not Classical
marble with a certain stylistic relationship to the school o
Nicola Pisano. The Baroque portal in the style of Buonta
lenti on the north side should also be mentioned, as well a
the small addition which projects slightly on the extrem
left and of which the purpose is not clear. Nor do we ye
have a satisfactory explanation of the fourteenth-century
fresco remains that can just be distinguished within th
upper part of the arch.

The visitor will have no difficulty in distinguishing the sec
tion of the former Romanesque basilica in the structure o
the façade wall. Passing through the lovely *portal* with th
Virgin standing in the arch (c. 1330–40) and the beautifully
carved doors with saints (1686), the visitor enters a three
aisled hall of the Cistercian Gothic type, with square pillar
and polygonal projections on the side-aisle walls. Denticu
lated mouldings and covering plates form extremely rudi
mentary capitals on the pillars. The slight dimension of the
church – only three bays long – is striking, though it is no
unusual for Tuscan Gothic. – The *inner façade wall*, erectec
by Buontalenti in 1596, is rather heavy compared with his

isual style. On the right of the portal, the *Outpouring of
he Holy Spirit* by Passignano (1596); above the portal a
beautiful organ surround (modern mechanism), and to the
eft of the portal, *S. Albertus Rescues Drowning Jews* (by
Cigoli, 1596). Here, too, one can see some remains of late
ourteenth-century frescoes.
The vaults and windows of the side aisles are Baroque;
many of the decorative elements too date from the seventeenth century, including some of the side altars (the first
wo are by Gherardo Silvani, c. 1630; the last altar on the
right is by Alessandro Allori and slightly earlier). On some
of pillars, there are further traces of fourteenth-century
frescoes. The two statues by Caccini on the third altar on
the right (*S. Bartholomew* on the left, *S. Zenobius* on the
right) are particularly worth the visitor's attention. The
ceiling was decorated by Poccetti c. 1590 with stucco and
frescoes depicting the deeds of S. Zenobius. – The main
chancel contains a small, old organ surround and some much
damaged remains of frescoes in terra verde painted by
Spinello Aretino (uncovered in 1901), the subjects of which
– Herod receiving the Wise Men from the East, ordering
the massacre of the Innocents, and the Massacre itself – are
barely recognizable. The windows and the altar are neo-
Gothic.
In the *left-hand chancel chapel*, the visitor will find a
brilliantly coloured thirteenth-century relief known as the
Madonna del Carmelo. Actually only the central figure is
carved in relief; the rest of the panel is painted. The combination of painting and relief makes the work quite unique.
Mary's head sits on the frame and is slightly bent forward,
as in crucifixes; her shining golden halo extends far above
the frame. In the frame are the twelve Apostles (four of
them only busts). Mary and the Child, seen full-face, are
depicted according to the oldest known Byzantine type,
both monumental and ceremonial. Two full-length adoring
angels can be seen on the gold background behind Mary,
and below are two scenes from the Gospel: the *Annunciation* and the *Three Maries at the Sepulchre*. The author of
this impressive work must be assumed to have been Coppo
di Marcovaldo, the most important artist before Cimabue
and probably the latter's teacher. A comparison with other
examples of his work in Siena, Orvieto and San Gimignano

confirms this attribution. – On the right wall of this chapel
are portions of the tomb of Brunetto Latini (originally
decorated with small columns; they have been here only
since the end of the last century). On the left wall is a
fourteenth century tomb with a figure presumed to be that
of Salvino Armato degli Armati, who was once thought
– without foundation – to have been the inventor of spec-
tacles. Above is a Roman bust. – The ceiling of the first
chapel on the left was decorated by Volterrano. Large crucifixion sculpture with two attendant figures. – On the third
altar, *The Virgin hands the Christ Child to S. Francis*
(painted by Matteo Rosselli, who was also responsible for
the pictures on either side). On the next wall is a (restored)
fourteenth century fresco, a *Madonna del Latte*.
The sacristy contains a *Madonna* panel by the school of
Verrocchio; also the entrance to a small cloister (now a
boys' school).

S. Maria Novella (Piazza S. Maria Novella)

In the irregular polygonal **piazza** before the church are
two **obelisks** (1608) supported by tortoises and crowned
with lilies, bronze works attributed to Giovanni da
Bologna. They served as the turning-points in the horse
races which Cosimo I introduced into Florence in imitation
of Classical cavalry entertainments.
The south side of the piazza is formed by the **Spedale
S. Paolo dei Convalescenti**, which was also used as a pilgrims' hostel. It is a pleasing sixteenth century imitation
of the Innocenti hospital. In the spandrels of the arcade
are terracotta medallions of saints by Giovanni della
Robbia. The corner medallions, which are cut into by the
pillars, contain portraits that have been variously interpreted and are now both thought to represent the warden
of the hospital, Benino Benini; they are attributed to Andrea
della Robbia, who was also responsible for the handsome
lunette above the west door inside the vestibule (depicting
SS. Francis and Dominic). – Outside, above the central
arch, is a bust of Grand Duke Ferdinando I by Giovanni
dell'Opera.
S. Maria Novella, situated on the north side of the piazza,
is the principal Dominican church of the city.
It was built to replace the old S. Maria delle Vigne, a tenth-

Badia, 'The Vision of S. Bernard' (Filippino Lippi)

S. Felicita, Barbadori chapel, 'The Entombment' (Pontormo)

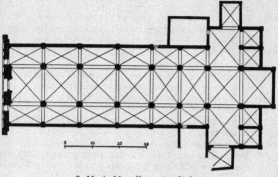

S. Maria Novella, ground plan

century oratory which lay among vineyards and was enlarged in the eleventh and twelfth centuries. Remains of the
old church can be seen in the Bardi chapel. The present
building was begun in 1246. By 1360, the principal parts
– including the campanile and the sacristy – had been completed by Fra Jacopo Talenti da Nipozzano. The history
of the site can best be recounted with the help of a list of
dates.

983 Earliest mention of the first oratory.

1094 A new parish church is consecrated by Bishop Rainer
(who is buried in the Baptistery); church and oratory
then stood side by side.

1221 The whole complex comes into the possession of the
Dominicans (John of Salerno).

1246 The extremely gifted Prior Aldobrandino Cavalcanti
begins the erection of the transept and chancel of a
new church that, both in size and in its use of the
hitherto unknown monumental Gothic style, is unprecedented in Florence.

1279 The foundation stone of the campanile is laid by the
Papal Legate, Cardinal Latino Frangipani, Bishop of
Ostia, to commemorate the reconciliation between
Guelfs and Ghibellines which has been brought about
by his efforts.

1287 The initial laying-out of a large piazza in front of the *church.*

1300 This is the probable date of the façade, and also of
     the completion of the whole building in its rough
     state.

Between 1303 and 1325, the Rucellai chapel is added at the
     east end of the transept.

Around 1350, the lower part of the façade is incrusted; the
     erection of the sacristy and campanile follows.

After 1456, the decoration is continued up to the top of the
     façade; Giovanni di Paolo Rucellai persuades Alberti
     to provide an architectural articulation for the entire
     façade (this is executed by Giovanni Bettini).

1470 Inscribed as the date of the final completion of the
     façade decoration. Of the two large volutes, only the
     one on the left dates from this period (the right-hand
     one is fairly recent).

In the fifteenth, sixteenth and seventeenth centuries, further
     extensions are made; for example, the addition – com-
     missioned by the Ricasoli family – of the so-called
     'Cappella della Pura' in the corner between the nave
     and the eastern transept arm.

1565–72 The church is thoroughly 'restored' according to
     plans by Vasari, altering much of the medieval de-
     coration. The monks' choir is removed and large altar
     tabernacles erected along the side walls, as in S. Croce
     and the Cathedral.

During the nineteenth century, the windows are reduced by
     raising the sills to make room for the neo-Gothic altars
     which replace Vasari's tabernacles.

1922 Erection of the right-hand volute of the façade to
     match the left-hand one.

Exterior   In the *façade* of this north-south orientated
three-aisled basilica, older elements mingle with newer ones
introduced by Alberti. Essentially the whole structure of the
lower storey is old. Alberti's original contributions were the
magnificent portal (*ill.* facing p. 288) and the terminal
pilasters at either side. The upper part with the gable also
goes back to his design (the right-hand volute of 1922 is an
exact copy of the left-hand one), and the architrave between the storeys may be attributed to Alberti as well. The
'sails' on it are the emblems of the Rucellai. At the top of
the façade, the donor's name and the date of completion

(1470) are written in large Roman letters. A further inscription referring to the Rucellai is to be found on the doorstep of the central portal. Vasari mentions this specifically because the porphyry lettering constitutes the earliest example of the use of this incredibly hard material during the Renaissance. – The tympani above the three portals are decorated with frescoes. In the centre, S. Thomas Aquinas kneels before the crucifix, while in the background the Corpus Christi procession is seen arriving in front of S. Maria Novella. Aaron with the manna in the left tympanum and Melchizedek with the loaves of bread in the right are symbolic references to the sacrament of the Eucharist. All three frescoes are by Ciocchi, 1616, and are extremely faded. The astronomical instruments on the façade were the gift of Cosimo I (inscription); they were made in 1572 by the court astronomer Ignazio Danti, a brother of the sculptor.

The visitor is recommended to walk first around the exterior of the church. A particularly interesting feature are the 'avelli' or tomb niches for individual families grouped along the (now neo-Gothic) wall extending from the façade towards the right. This wall originally enclosed the cemetery. Similar tomb niches were once also to be found in the wall on the left, leading towards the cloisters. – The brittle and yet at the same time so powerful yellowish brickwork has tremendous dignity. Standing slightly to the east of the transept and looking back, the visitor can see how the edge of the façade sticks out beyond the Gothic building. The traveller who arrives in Florence by train will have a particularly fine view of the *chancel end* of the church as he leaves the station. The precisely ornamented masonry, the small groups of three-quarter columns, the triple windows with their Gothic tracery, the campanile – all these combine to create a brilliant impression of the severe and yet so Italian Gothic style that first took shape in this building. – The gable, like those on the east and west sides and on the campanile, once contained a cross (we do not know of what material). During the course of time these have fallen out, leaving only empty cruciform spaces.

Interior   Entering the church from the façade end, the visitor will find himself in one of the most remarkable Gothic interiors in the whole of Italy. Large expanses of

wall stretch out on either side, capturing areas of light and
shade. The firmness and solidity of the architecture seem to
contain more than a suggestion of the Romanesque period:
the pillars, too (a square core with four half-columns)
follow a native tradition (S. Miniato). A pillared, rib-
vaulted basilica with transept and five square chancel
chapels, the church is an example of that Cistercian variant
of the Gothic scheme which the monks of Fossanova and
Casamari introduced as early as 1187 in the neighbourhood
of Rome and also in Tuscany (the romantic S. Galgano,
south of Siena, 1218). The interior appears slightly more
'French' than the exterior. It eschews both the delicacy of
the Florentine Proto-Renaissance and the style of incrustation, which was applied only to the façade. None the less
one cannot really speak here in terms of 'imported' architecture, for there is an evident preoccupation with Italian
architecture not only in the monumental corporeality of the
building, but also in the expansive proportions. It is
questionable whether the comparison that has been made
between the measurements of these arcades and those of the
arcades of the Upper Church at Assisi is justifiable, but the
Umbrian churches of the Order of the Mendicant Friars
certainly had some influence, and the tomb niches of the
outer wall were modelled on examples in the architecture
of northern Italy. That so 'nationalist' artist, Michelangelo,
was particularly fond of S. Maria Novella.
The first quality to impress itself on the visitor is the spatial
simplicity of the interior. The third bay on the east side
contains a remarkable fourteenth-century *portal*, walled in
by Vasari (the best view is from outside, in the former
cemetery to the east of the church). The nave suffered most
from the changes of later epochs; the present neo-Gothic
altars were erected in 1861 (at the same time even the
tombstones in the floor were lined up in a row!), and the
impression has been further falsified by the neo-Gothic confessionals and windows. The interior as a whole, however,
has not suffered excessively. Almost 100 m long, it is made
to appear even longer by the fact that the spaces between
the pillars supporting the marvellous pointed arches diminish
towards the north or altar end.

Decoration   Inside the façade wall, above the portal, is a
fresco by Botticelli, the *Nativity*, which was subsequently

brought to the church. The rose-window – the earliest
extant example in Florence – depicts the *Coronation of
the Virgin* surrounded by dancing angels and framed by an
ornamental band of heads; the design is attributed to
Andrea da Firenze. To the right of the portal is a late
fourteenth century *Annunciation*, set in a slightly oblique
room with, in the background, the bed-chamber or 'Thala-
mus Virginis'.

Moving over to the *right side aisle*, the visitor will find on
the first altar a highly praised and often copied masterpiece
by Girolamo Macchietti, the *Martyrdom of S. Lawrence*,
1573; the work is stylistically superior to that of the Vasari
school proper. To the right of the second altar is a monument to *Beata Villana*, a pious townswoman who died in
1360; the monument, which is only partially preserved,
dates from 1451 and is by Bernardo Rossellino and assistants. It stood originally against the choir-screen (now removed) and was placed here in 1579. Slightly to the left of
it is the last resting place of *John of Salerno* († 1242; see in
the list of dates above); it is from the workshop of Danti.
On the altar is a *Nativity* in Naldini's 'sfumato' style. –
Two further pictures by Naldini adorn the third and fourth
altars – the *Presentation of Mary in the Temple* and the
Entombment, 1577. On either side of the fourth altar are
two sixteenth century tombs (the one on the right is dated
1530) of the Minerbetti family, the work of Silvio Cosini
da Pisa, a pupil of Andrea Ferrucci da Fiesole. – The floor-
level rises by two steps at this point; this was where the
monks' choir once began. On the pillar on the outer wall to
the right is a fine *aspersorium* in the shape of a ship
(1412).

The following door leads to the **Cappella della Pura** of
1472–97 (decoration largely renovated in the nineteenth
century). The most important piece here is the lovely fourteenth century miraculous image immediately on the left,
a *Madonna and Child, with Saint and Donor*. Its appeal is
so direct that one has no difficulty in understanding the
beautiful legend according to which, in 1472, the Madonna
called out to two boys playing in the churchyard in front
of the open door and told them to go and wash. The mothers of the city have come in pilgrimage to this memorable
spot ever since. The fresco prompted not only the building

of the chapel but also the construction of this tabernacle,
which is similar to the one in SS. Annunziata. Today it is let
into the neo-Classical arcade which, together with the
matching one on the other side, was erected in 1841. On the
main altar is a large early fourteenth century *cross* (with a
Baroque base) before which 'Beata Villana', whose tomb
by Rossellino the visitor has just seen, is said to have prayed
every day. – The adjacent side rooms are all closed to visitors.

Returning to the church, the visitor will find on the next
altar immediately on his right a huge picture by Jacopo
Ligozzi. The artist was fond of adding curious details to
his paintings occasionally, and in this depiction of *S. Ray-
mond raising a Boy*, we find a black and white dove up in
the window on the left, an allusion to the monk Raffaello
delle Colombe who never tired of urging the artist to hurry
his work. Next to it is the wall tomb of a Ricasoli bishop
(† 1572). – In a small, late sixteenth-century tabernacle in
the *right transept arm* is a distinctive bust of S. Antonio
(terracotta, *c.* 1460). There are also three important *Gothic
tombs* here. On the right above the door is the tomb of
Bishop Tedice Aliotti who died in 1336; it is by one of
Camaino's later pupils. On the left is the famous tomb of
the young prior Aldobrandino Cavalcanti who died in 1279;
it is still very 'Romanesque' in style, including the way the
deceased is depicted in a reclining position on the front of
the sarcophagus. Finally, below these and to the left of the
door, we find the tomb of the Patriarch of Constantinople
who died in 1439 here in the monastery (Gozzoli painted
his portrait in the chapel of the Medici Palace on the occasion of the patriarch's visit to the Council in Florence). The
fresco depicting the venerable man between two angels was
painted by a contemporary Byzantine artist (it has been
restored). The marble arcade is an excellent example of the
transitional style of these early years, with its retention of
the old medieval 'avelli' form.

The chapel at the end of the transept arm was built in
1303–25. It is known as the **Rucellai chapel** after its
patrons. The floor was raised in 1464 to match that of the
corresponding chapel in the western transept arm. Climbing
the staircase, the visitor will find on the landing a (fourteenth century?) sarcophagus that was placed here in 1510

to serve as an altar (notice the three round slabs of porphyry on top). This handsome, tall room once housed Duccio's great 'Madonna', now in the Uffizi. Today a bronze work by Ghiberti is protected here from further wear; this is the *tomb-plate of Leonardo Dati*, 1423, which originally lay before the main chancel. It is a subtle piece of draughtsmanship, the elegant folds of the cassock merging into the distinctive features of the death mask to form a delicately smoothed surface. Ghiberti discusses the work at some length in his autobiography. It shows the same preoccupation with the problems of shallow relief as the lions' heads on the insides of the two leaves of the north doors of the Baptistery. The tomb-plate has become quite heavily worn over the centuries, as can be seen in the only partially preserved pattern of the lovely pillow. – On the left wall of the chapel, the visitor will find a remarkable picture with an interesting story attached to it, for Bugiardini's *Martyrdom of S. Catherine* is said to have been painted with the assistance of Michelangelo (they studied together in the Ghirlandaio workshop), the latter being responsible for the foreground. – The walls bear indistinct traces of fourteenth century frescoes uncovered in 1912. – On the altar is a *Madonna* (originally painted) of the French type, probably an early work by Nino Pisano (Andrea's son). It stood on the Cavalcanti tomb for many years.

Returning down the stairs, the visitor will find in a niche on his right a large late eighteenth century *clay crib*. Below the chapel is a burial vault, reached from the Cappella della Pura. On the wall above the crib is the tomb-plate of Corrado della Penna, Bishop of Fiesole. The original elevation was like that of the Cavalcanti tomb.

The first of the chancel chapels on the north side of the transept is the **Bardi chapel**, with its beautiful seventeenth century screen. At the top of the right-hand entrance pillar is a pretty little relief (dated 1335) depicting S. Gregory blessing the founder of the chapel. Inside on the right-hand wall is a small Renaissance tabernacle and – more important – a remarkable *double niche*. This belongs to the oldest part of the building, and it is not entirely clear whether or not it was originally designed as a window. Another interesting fact is that such niches featured in the Hohenstaufen architecture of southern Italy. In the spandrels is the *Tree* *of Paradise*, with birds and apples. The frescoes in the lunettes are rather difficult to decipher. The older one on the right is from the circle of Cimabue (late thirteenth century). More recent frescoes attributed to Spinello Aretino depict the legend of S. Gregory. The altar-piece, the *Madonna with a Rosary*, was painted in 1570 by Vasari with the assistance of Jacopo Zucchi. The ceiling and the left-hand tympanum were decorated by P. Dandini.

In 1487, Filippo Strozzi commissioned Filippino Lippi to decorate the **next chapel** as soon as he had completed the frescoes (by Masolino and Masaccio) in the Brancacci chapel (in S. Maria del Carmine). However, in 1488 Filippino had to leave for Rome (to do some work for Cardinal Caraffa in S. Maria sopra Minerva) with the result that his Florentine commission could not be completed before 1502 (inscription on the 'Drusiana' picture). The four panels of the ceiling depict the patriarchs Adam, Noah, Abraham and Jacob. On the right are scenes from the life of S. Philip as recounted in the Golden Legend. The principal scene shows the episode in which the saint, forced by the heathens to sacrifice to an idol, tames a dragon which has killed the priest's son. The lunette depicts the saint's sacrificial death at the age of 87. The opposite wall shows scenes from the life of S. John the Evangelist. In the lunette, the saint is boiled in oil at the order of the emperor Domitian; in the principal panel below, he is seen raising Drusiana after his return to Ephesus. Filippino was a gifted master of decoration. The work as a whole displays an expression of piety clothed in a Classical style. Numerous details borrowed from archeology have been discovered, particularly in the architecture. Below, integrated into the whole, is a *tomb* (the spandrels depict the spirits of death). Here, in a sarcophagus by Benedetto da Maiano (1491–3; the bust belonging to it is now in the Louvre), rests Filippino's employer, Filippo Strozzi. Stylistically the tomb stands on the threshold of the High Renaissance, notably in the splendid frieze of round arches. There are not too many examples of this type of sculpture in Florence (one thinks of the chests in the vestibule of the sacristy of S. Spirito).

A further word must be added regarding the *window wall*, where the incorporation of musical symbols and allegories in a burial chapel raises certain questions. In the composition of his work, the artist had to take into account a tall, narrow Gothic window with stained-glass depicting in the upper part the *Madonna* and in the lower part *SS. John the Evangelist and Philip*. This provides the strongest colour accent in the room. The frescoes themselves are almost monochrome, painted in blues and greys with an occasional gold overlay singling out objects of symbolic importance. The slender columns that accompany the window were derived from the Arch of Constantine; on the socle zone which supports them appear the figures of *Caritas* and *Fides* and, in the spandrels above the sarcophagus, angels holding skulls. In the main zone, at the bottom, left, is *Parthenice* with a stringed instrument, accompanied by two putti with wind instruments; bottom, right, stand two female figures with between them a kind of tall lyre. Above each of these two groups is an inscription plaque. The one on the left reads 'Sacris superis initiati canunt'; the one on the right is rather damaged, but from a drawing in the Uffizi we know the inscription reads 'Quondam nunc Deo op. max. canimus'. In both cases the alternative meaning of 'canere' is used, 'to play an instrument' (no one depicted in the fresco is singing). – The inscription above the head of the Madonna in the stained-glass window reads 'Mitis esto' ('be at peace'). In the upper part of the wall hang circular discs bearing the words 'Si scires' and 'Donum Dei', a reference to John 4. 10, where Christ, speaking to the Samaritan woman, refers to the Word of God as the water of life; these inscriptions thus allude to the promise of eternal life. The inscription panels are connected by a complex system of bands. – Above the marble arch, between angels of death painted in the spandrels, another inscription panel reads 'Ni hanc despexeris vives' ('If you do not reject this, you shall live'), where 'hanc' refers to 'hanc aquam' (i.e. the 'donum Dei'); the panel thus represents a paraphrase of 'Spes', and together with the personifications of 'Caritas' (right) and 'Fides' (left) completes the trio of virtues.

The stringed instrument in the hand of the 'Parthenice' is a cross between a lyre and a guitar; the artist, misunderstanding the Classical lyre, has changed it by adding a fingerboard beneath the strings. The instrument is played with the bone plectrum in the shape of a deer's foot; this, like the instrument itself, also goes back to the Classical period and

testifies to the artist's interest in archeology. One of the
putti is blowing the syrinx with seven pipes; the other is
playing an instrument which represents an imaginative reconstruction of Classical depictions of the aulos. A third
instrument is lying on the floor. All these instruments
appear in very similar versions in Filippino's 'Allegory of
Music' in Berlin. – The two women on the right are taken
from a Classical sarcophagus – formerly in Rome and now
in Vienna – with Minerva, Apollo and the nine Muses. The
third Muse from the left has been faithfully reproduced
here, even down to the bone plectrum; the one on the far
left has been reversed. The instrument on a tall socle between the two women is also an imaginary creation, derived
from the tripod cithara that appears on Classical Muse-
sarcophagi.

The meaning of this whole complicated combination of
muses and music with symbols of death and eternal life is
to be found in the ideas of the Florentine Platonic academy
(Marsilio Ficino), according to which the muses are also the
guarantors of the immortality of the soul, their music being
the image of the harmony of the spheres (Winternitz). At a
later date, Raphael was to paint his 'S. Cecilia', based on
the same assumptions.

On the left-hand pillar of the triumphal arch of the main
chancel, there is a remarkably beautiful candlestick in the
shape of a spiral column; it is for the Easter candle, and is
attributed to Piero di Giovanni Tedesco (late fourteenth
century). The candlestick opposite is a modern copy. There
is an early sixteenth-century crucifix on the altar. Visitors
are allowed to go round behind the altar from the side,
where some beautiful choir stalls (partly by Baccio d'Agnolo,
c. 1490, partly from Vasari's period) and a powerful lectern
are to be found. – However, the principal work of art here
is the famous cycle of frescoes which Domenico Ghirlandaio
painted in 1485–90 with the help of pupils, including the
young Michelangelo. In his precise, confident narrative
style, Ghirlandaio has given us here a picture of the life of
his period, enlivened by portraits of many contemporaries.
The biblical story is told in firm contours and clear, bright
colours, making use of numerous localities, personalities and
events taken from Florentine life. In detail: on the ceiling,
the four Evangelists. On the left wall (bottom to top): left,

Joachim's expulsion from the Temple; right, the Birth of the Virgin (in the background is the signature 'Bigordi Ghirllandai'). In the second strip: left, the Presentation in the Temple; right, The Marriage of the Virgin. In the third strip: left, the Adoration of the Magi; right, the Massacre of the Innocents. In the lunette, Death and Assumption of the Virgin. – Turning to the window wall we find, in the lunette, the Coronation of the Virgin. The paintings on either side of the window depict (starting at the top): left, S. Dominic burning heretical books, right, the Death of S. Peter Martyr; left, the Annunciation, and right, John the Baptist in the Wilderness; then come two portraits of Giovanni Tornabuoni and his wife Francesca Pitti. – The beautiful stained-glass window was also designed by Ghirlandaio. – On the right wall (starting from the bottom): right, The Angel appears to Zachariah (in the background is the date 1490); left, the Visitation. In the second strip: right, the Birth of John the Baptist; left, his Circumcision. In the third strip: right, the Sermon of John the Baptist; left, the Baptism of Christ. In the lunette, Herod's Banquet. – Some time ago, some remains of Orcagna's frescoes were discovered beneath Ghirlandaio's work. They were taken down and are occasionally on show in the Fortezza.

To the left of the main chancel is the Gondi chapel, decorated by Giuliano da Sangallo in 1508. This is probably the earliest tangible evidence of the advent of Mannerist architecture in Florence. On the rear wall is Brunelleschi's famous wooden crucifix. According to a story which Vasari relates, this was expressly intended to provide an exemplary rectification of Donatello's figure of the Crucified Lord. Compared with Donatello's work, it is more 'idealized', the surface animated organically with a greater delicacy of differentiation. Nothing positive can be said about the date of this crucifix. The ceiling of the chapel is decorated with extremely ancient frescoes, possibly by one of those Greek artists mentioned by Vasari (c. 1270; uncovered in 1932). A closer study of these frescoes, which are now barely distinguishable, reveals certain stylistic similarities with the dome mosaic of the Baptistery. In the niches on either side of the altar are two stucco angels by Francesco Gargiolli, c. 1602. – Next comes the Gaddi chapel, decorated by G. A. Dosio. The ceiling was painted in 1577 by Alessandro

Allori. The altar-piece, the *Raising of Jairus's Daughter*, is the last work painted by Angelo Bronzino. On the walls to right and left are the delicate, discreet and slightly Classicistic *Marriage of the Virgin* and *Presentation in the Temple* by Giovanni dell'Opera. The two tombs at the sides are those of the cardinals Taddeo (1577) and Niccolò Gaddi (1578). On the rear wall, almost completely hidden, is the tomb of the wife and child of another member of the Gaddi family. The 'pietra dura' floor is beautiful.

At the end of the left transept arm is the **Strozzi chapel** (in the niche under the stairs are some fourteenth century *frescoes* in the style of Orcagna; very early relief figures in the spandrels). It represents one of the few examples in Tuscany of this type of large and gloomily monumental fourteenth-century interior. Nardo di Cione's *frescoes*, painted *c.* 1357 and restored in 1950, are famous. In detail: on the inner faces of the pilasters and the arch are saints. In the four medallions on the ceiling, accompanied by S. Thomas Aquinas, *Faith* and *Obedience*, *Hope* and *Fortitude*, *Charity* and *Chastity*, *Justice* and *Peace*. – On the window wall, the *Last Judgement*; Nardo di Cione also designed the windows. – On the left wall, the *Mystic Paradise*; the group in the bottom left includes a portrait of Dante. – The right wall depicts *Hell* after Dante's description. There is an interesting difference in colour tones from the *Paradise* opposite. – On the altar in an old frame is *Christ in Majesty with Saints* by Andrea di Cione, known as Orcagna; the work is signed and dated 1357. This is one of the earliest attempts to overcome the limitations of the polyptych by treating the five panels as a single, coherent composition.

On the right at the bottom of the stairs, beneath the campanile, is a (closed) chapel with fourteenth century frescoes: outside, the *Coronation of the Virgin*, inside, *S. Christopher*. – The next entrance leads to Jacopo Talenti's generously designed **sacristy** which contains some beautiful works of art. By the entrance, there is an important *wall font* by Giovanni della Robbia (1498), a decorative, architectural design executed in glazed terracotta. Opposite is an eighteenth century lavabo (Gioacchino Fortini, 1721), and nearby a panel depicting Dominican saints standing on either side of an enthroned Madonna and Child, painted by a contemporary of Bernardo Daddi (*c.* 1360). The particularly fine *wall cupboards* also catch the eye; designed by Buontalenti, they are decorated partly with eighteenth century inlaid work (by Guerrino Veneziano) and partly with paintings by Camillo Perini, dated 1693. On the right wall are pictures by Ligozzi (*Conversion of S. Paul*) and Stradanus (*Baptism of Christ*), and on the left wall pictures by Dandini (*S. Vincent Ferrer*) and Vasari (*S. Anselm's Vision of the Crucifixion, with Virtues und Vices*, 1566). The cross on the altar is attributed to Maso di Bartolommeo. The most important piece in the sacristy, however, is undoubtedly the large painted *wooden cross* above the entrance. It was brought here from inside the façade wall, but its original position was probably on the (demolished) monks' choir. It is an important early work by Giotto. The arms with their bird-like hands unfold like huge wings. The body is conceived elementally, with the eyes of a sculptor, with enormous and rather 'unclassical' forms; a great intensity and a penetrating feeling for reality make the anatomy appear somewhat crude.

Returning to the church, the visitor will find near the corner of the transept an *aspersorium* by the school of Cellini. The vessel of Asia Minor granite probably came from among the possessions of Lorenzo il Magnifico, who had a collection of them. Silvani's portals in the south wall of the transept represent a distinctive continuation of the style of Buontalenti. – On the first altar in the *left side aisle* is a picture by Allori, the *Vision of S. Hyacinth.* – Masaccio's fresco of *God the Father, with the Crucified Christ and Mary and John* beyond the third altar is not only one of the most valuable treasures in this church, but also occupies an extremely important place in the history of art. On either side, in front of the pilasters of painted Renaissance architecture, kneel the two donors; below them is a skeleton on a sarcophagus. No document referring to the painting has come to light. By indirect means, the date 1425 has been arrived at, which makes the picture one of the very earliest works in the Renaissance style. The donor was the Florentine Gonfaloniere Lenzi, who is buried just in front of it. Never before had anyone painted a picture similar to this. God the Father is holding the Cross on which his Son hangs; at the foot of the Cross the hill of Golgotha is suggested

The group is set within a quite remarkable piece of architecture which is part chapel, part mausoleum and part triumphal arch, all at the same time. Taken in detail, it illustrates in an almost canonical manner the vocabulary of forms that Brunelleschi introduced into architecture; the low angle of vision and the consequent perspective foreshortening of the room may also be regarded as a perfect demonstration of the great architect's optical theories. The technical execution of this perspective construction is no less interesting; even today, the guidelines are still visible on the fresco. Easiest to follow is the centralized perspective of the tunnel vault with its vanishing lines. Rather less clear is the network of verticals and horizontals placed over Mary's majestic and splendid face; experts are still undecided as to whether these were intended to facilitate the exact reproduction of a draft or whether – and this seems more likely – they constituted a kind of 'horizon system' by which the artist achieved exactly the right degree of foreshortening sloping away to the right. The picture's inner meaning is certainly clear enough to the faithful: the two donors, kneeling before the real 'sanctuary', pray to the Throne of Mercy (as well as to Mary and John as intercessors) for life after death, the skeleton beneath the painted altar table (a dubious reconstruction which was based on the old altar table of the stylistically similar Barbadori chapel in S. Felicita has now been removed) providing the reminder of death – the 'memento mori' – with the clear message (written above the skeleton), 'I was what you are, and what I am you shall be'. – The fresco was covered up by Vasari, transferred to the inside of the façade wall in 1861, and only returned to its original place in 1952; at that time, the lower part with the skeleton, which had been left here, was discovered and re-united with the rest of the fresco.

On the altar to the right of Masaccio's masterpiece is Vasari's *Resurrection* of 1568. The *Annunciation* on the altar on the left is Santi di Tito's last work, dating from 1603. The *pulpit* on the last pillar but one was designed by Brunelleschi in 1443 and made by his pupil Buggiani. The partly gilded white marble is beautifully effective. The surrounds of garlands were inspired by Trajan's Column in Rome. The reliefs depict scenes from the life of the Virgin. – One's attention is attracted by the serene picture on the

fifth altar, the *Samaritan Woman at the Well*, by Alessandro
Allori, 1575. To the left of this is an *Annunciation* in the
style of Bicci di Lorenzo, 1455. To the right of the sixth
altar is the *tomb of Ant. Strozzi* (1524) by Andrea Ferrucci
da Fiesole; the figurative details are by a pupil. One of
Santi di Tito's most remarkable works is to be seen on the
last altar, the *Raising of Lazarus*.

Leaving the church, the visitor will find the extensive
cloisters lying to the west (entrance fee). The first is the
Green Cloister (Chiostro Verde), built after 1350, probably
by Fra Jacopo Talenti; it is a harmonious and elegant structure, with four tall severe-looking cypress trees in the middle
surrounding a fountain which was restored in 1859. Before
the cloisters were built, the walls of the monastery grounds
had already been decorated with Old Testament frescoes
by Turino Baldese, who died during the plague of 1348.
Later the cloister was redecorated. The most important
pictures were in the east wing (on the church), including
those painted in 'terra verde' (whence the name 'Green
Cloister') by Paolo Uccello; in the south wing were frescoes
by a master of the Lorenzo di Niccolò circle (c. 1430; the
first five bays only), while the west wing contained some
frescoes from the fourteenth century and some by a contemporary of Uccello, possibly Dello Delli. Almost all these
frescoes have today been taken down; the most important
ones by Uccello are currently in the monastery **refectory**,
reached through a small passage in the west wing (ask the
curator for the key). On the inside of the entrance wall is
a fresco of the *Gathering of the Manna* by Allori which
incorporates a fourteenth-century *Madonna with Saints* in
the style of Starnina. The vestibule contains some ecclesiastical vestments. On the east wall of the three-bayed main
room is a *Last Supper* by Alessandro Allori (1583). Apart
from this and the tables, the principal pieces here are some of
Uccello's frescoes from the cloister, of which the most
powerful is the *Flood*, with the ark and the drowning
people, some of whom are trying to find refuge on an island.
The colossal figure on the right with his right hand meaning-
fully raised has recently been thought to be a portrait of
Pope Eugenius IV. The work dates from after 1447.

The adjacent **large cloister** to the west houses a college for
Carabinieri and is not open to visitors. It is decorated with

late sixteenth-century frescoes, as can be seen through the screen. It is not, however, possible either to see or to visit the **Papal chapel of Leo X** on the first floor of the north wing. This contains paintings by Pontormo (including the *Veronica*) and Ridolfo Ghirlandaio (a *Coronation of the Virgin* on the end wall) and some stylistically important decorative grotesques by Andrea di Cosimo Feltrini; all these works were completed c. 1515.

On the north side of the 'Chiostro Verde' is the **Spanish Chapel**, built as a chapter-house for the Dominicans. The cost of the building and the decoration was borne by a private individual, Buonamico di Lapo Guidalotti, and consequently he and his family were allowed to be buried in the sanctuary. The chapel was begun in 1348 after the great plague (which had included among its victims the donor's wife) and completed in 1355. Andrea da Firenze completed the murals in 1365, ten years after Buonamico's death. It has been known as the 'Spanish Chapel' since 1540, when Eleonora of Toledo chose it for the church of her Spanish entourage, and in 1592 it was dedicated to the patron saint of Spain, S. James of Compostela. – The architecture is distinctive and of particular interest. Notice the beautiful double windows with their small central columns resting on expressive lions. Inside the chapel, the vaults rise steeply from short octagonal pillars set partly within the wall and occupy most of the height of the room. The distinction between base and vault is thus blurred. The same applies to the bevelled platforms on which the pillars rest. There are thus no right-angles in the floor.

The *murals* – real 'idea pictures' – are extremely important. They are among the very finest fourteenth century works in Tuscany. Their theme, probably laid down by Jacopo Passavanti, a famous preacher and prior of the Order from 1354 to 1357, is the Sufferings and the Imitation of Christ, the latter part being depicted by means of the major figures of the Dominican Order. To the left of the sanctuary, we see the path winding up to Golgotha; above the arch is the *Crucifixion* and on the right Christ is seen climbing down among the sinners in Purgatory. In the vault sections are the *Resurrection*, *Ascension* and *Pentecost*, as well as the *Navicella* on the Sea of Galilee. The remaining walls are devoted to Dominican subjects. On the entrance wall are

*S. Gaetano, detail of the façade with a window
and the Medici coat of arms*

S. Giovannino degli Scolopi, façade (Ammannati)

six scenes from the life of S. Peter Martyr, probably the most famous Florentine Dominican. The right wall depicts the difficulties encountered on the road to salvation. It begins at the bottom left with the Church of Christ, here represented by Florence Cathedral which was under construction at the time (*ill.* facing p. 289). Beside the Cathedral sits the statuesque figure of the Pope, flanked by his secular (on the right) and his ecclesiastical (left) assistants like buttressing pillars. Grouped around these dignitaries are the lower clergy and the laity. The black and white hounds – 'domini canes' – wear the same 'habit' as the Dominicans who convert sinners and banish heretics (the dogs, too, are chasing away wolves). S. Thomas Aquinas, S. Peter Martyr and S. Dominic are seen at work here. Farther up, on the right, some young people are seen dancing and ladies and gentlemen savouring the pleasures of life. A monk hears confession and absolves a penitent woman; S. Dominic points the way to Paradise, which can be seen a bit farther up on the left; the blessed ones are received at the gate by S. Peter and given crowns by two angels. At the top, Christ appears in glory above the empty throne with the Lamb, accompanied by choirs of angels.

The opposite wall depicts the *Apotheosis of S. Thomas Aquinas*. The hero of the faith is seen enthroned as a theologian and conqueror of heretics, between Evangelists and Prophets who are depicted considerably smaller than himself. Seven flying Virtues look down at him, and at his feet crouch the conquered heretics Sabellius, Averroes and Arius. Below, in a Gothic pew, are fourteen female personifications – the seven theological sciences and the seven liberal arts. At the feet of each one sits a scholar representing her particular subject: (from right to left) Priscianus with *Grammar*, Cicero with *Rhetoric*, Aristotle (?) with *Dialectic*, Tubalcain with *Music*, Ptolemy with *Astronomy*, Euclid with *Geometry*, Pythagoras with *Arithmetic*, S. Augustine with *Theology*, S. John Chrysostom with *Ethics*, Dionysius the Areopagite with *Dogma*, S. Jerome with *Canonical History*, Hippocrates with *Natural Philosophy*, Innocent IV (?) with *Canon Law* and the emperor Justinian with *Civil Law*.

The paintings in the vaults are thematically related to those on the walls. Above the S. Thomas Aquinas picture is the

Pentecost (strange iconography; highly animated figures in front of the house) with the outpouring of the Holy Spirit over Christ's disciples; above the opposite wall, the storm-tossed *Navicella*. The right side clearly represents the *vita activa* and the left side the *vita contemplativa* of the Christian faith. The same blurring of divisions applies to the painting as was noted earlier in the architecture. Indeed it goes as far as to affect the pictorial form, for each wall is treated as a single unit with no frames dividing the individual episodes. – The overall impression conveyed is that of some great ceremonial – a mixture between a Passion play and a courtroom. In fact, sentences were passed by the Inquisition in this chapel.

The sanctuary walls were once decorated with scenes from the Passion, but the sanctuary was completely remodelled during the sixteenth century by the Spaniards. Arch and pilasters were removed from the entrance side, the vault ribs taken out, the window altered and the paintings replaced by others. Today the visitor will find pictures by the school of Allori (Battle of Clavigo, Saints; grotesques on the ceiling by Poccetti, 1592). Behind the altar is a panel by Allori (*S. James Healing a Cripple*), on the altar is a fourteenth-century polyptych and on the left wall a crucifix by Pieratti (seventeenth century).

A small passage containing a number of tombstones leads to the smaller **Cloister of the Dead** (Chiostro dei Morti) which lies to the north. Around the small courtyard are several chapels which were originally clearly defined by dividing walls, since pulled down. The **funeral chapel of the Strozzi family** is in the left corner. The frescoes (*Nativity* and *Crucifixion*) are today attributed to the circle of Orcagna; notice particularly, in the *Nativity*, the delightful 'Annunciation to the Shepherds' with the frightened dog. – The scenes from the life of the Virgin on the right are attributed to Nardo di Cione. In the lunette of the central arch of a (closed) door under the right portico is a fresco with a half-figure of S. Thomas Aquinas; this work was awarded particularly high praise by Ghiberti, who named a certain 'Stefano' as the author. Right, at the rear, is a small chapel containing a polychrome terracotta from the della Robbia workshop (*Noli Me Tangere*). From here, the visitor can enjoy a last view of the church.

S. Maria Nuova (Piazza S. Maria Nuova)

The principal hospital in Florence and also the oldest one, it was founded in 1287 by Folco Portinari, the father of Dante's Beatrice. It was originally on the other side of the piazza, where the Topographical Museum is situated today, i.e. in the former Convent of Oblates with its church of S. Maria *(on the corner, closed; the crutches above the bricked-up door and the window are the insignia of the hospital).*

At the beginning of the fourteenth century, the hospital was transferred to its present position, the site of S. Egidio which belonged to an order of mendicant friars. It was subsequently enlarged, and the new part was called S. Maria Nuova to distinguish it from the old part. The large portico that surrounds and defines the whole site was added in 1611–18 by Giulio Parigi (except for the west wing, which was only added in 1960; it is dated on the keystone with a reference to an endowment from the Florence Savings Bank) after Buontalenti's extensive designs. At first, only the eastern part of the central building was built. Pietro da Cortona was working on the interior of the hospital in 1650. G. B. Pieratti was retained here at the same time, and by 1666 he had altered some of the parts already begun and had removed some of Buontalenti's buildings. In 1660–99, the loggia was extended westwards, and in 1708 the lateral east wing was added. The entire upper storey was added at the same time.

This extensive site contains many architectural and decorative delights, but because of the busy life of the hospital, it can only be visited exceptionally.

Standing before the **loggia**, which is a good example of Buontalenti's style, the visitor will see in the middle Bicci di Lorenzo's church of S. Egidio (1418–20). Above the central arch and below the balcony is a bust of Ferdinando II by Bartolommeo Cennini (seventeenth century). On the right is *Cosimo II* by Caccini, dated 1620, and on the left is *Cosimo III* by C. Marcellini (1690); above the centre of the right-hand lateral wing, *Giangastone di Montauti* (eighteenth century). In the arch panels are frescoes by Pomarancio, and on the right-hand end wall is an *Annunciation* fresco by Federico Zuccari, *c.* 1579, which is badly damaged. The visitor then comes to the church of

S. Egidio

The *Coronation of the Virgin* by Dello Delli above the portal of the church is a particularly beautiful work of art. There are traces of an old painting known to have been by Bicci di Lorenzo (1424). The interior consists of a single

aisle, with side altars attributed to Giovanni da Bologna.
The altar-like structure in front on the immediate right is
the tombstone of old Folco Portinari. On the high altar is a
large papier-mâché, cross made from a model by Susini
(1594) and beyond it on the right-hand wall of the nave is
an early terracotta *Madonna and Child* by Andrea della
Robbia. The stairs up to the chancel are easily recognizable
as a simpler version of Buontalenti's stairs in S. Stefano
(and originally in S. Trinita). – The visitor should not miss
Bernardo Rossellino's beautiful fifteenth-century *tabernacle*
to the left of the high altar. On the little door, the enthroned Christ is seen giving a blessing. This is a copy (the
original is in the possession of the hospital management) of
the last authenticated work of the old Lorenzo Ghiberti. –
Behind the choir stalls are remains of frescoes by Domenico
Veneziano, Castagno and Baldovinetti, but they are so fragmentary that the visitor misses nothing by not seeing them.
– The two pictures on the left by Alessandro Allori (*Pietà*,
1579) and Volterrano (*S. Louis Healing the Sick*, c. 1675) have
become very dark. – On the right of the façade wall is the
tomb of Lemmo Balducci, reassembled in 1845.

This site once housed an extremely valuable collection of
art treasures, most of which have now been scattered. Some
have been preserved in the Hospital, but only a few of
them are accessible to visitors. Lying to the east is a handsome fourteenth century **cloister** with a *Pietà* (c. 1425)
modelled on Luca della Robbia's 'Corsini Madonna'. The
Madonna and Child and Angels in a stucco lunette is attributed to Nanni di Bartolo. – Near the last entrance on
the left, which leads to the so-called 'old cemetery', is the
tombstone of Monna Tessa, the servant-girl who is said to
have persuaded Portinari to found this hospital of S. Maria
Nuova. She is seen wearing the habit of an Oblate nun.

S. Martino della Scala (corner of the Via della Scala and the Via degli
Orti Oricellari)
The old 'della Scala' hospital, named after its famous superior opposite
the cathedral in Siena, was founded in 1313. In 1531, it was converted
into a monastery and in 1873 into a home for educationally subnormal
children. – From the outside, one can still recognize traces of the
church – a number of columns and a niche pillar added at the corner.
The frescoes by Botticelli and Uccello which are sometimes mentioned
as being here have recently been taken down.

S. Michelino (S. Michele in Visdomini; Piazza S. Michele in Visdomini)

This small church is situated on a lively and attractive little piazza surrounded by splendid palaces. It once stood on the site now occupied by the Cathedral, and had to be removed when the Cathedral chancel was built. It was re-erected here in the four-teenth century. The original establishment was founded by the Vicedomini family, probably even earlier than the eleventh cen-tury. The building was renovated in 1660 by Michelangelo Pacini. The façade, in the style of Ammannati, dates from the late sixteenth century. The neat **interior** consists of a single aisle. On the second altar on the right is a *Holy Family with Saints* by Pontormo (1518, dated on the Evangelist's book); on the first altar is Empoli's *Nativity with Saints and Donor*, begun in 1618. The left-hand side chancel con-tains a notable piece: the early fourteenth century German wooden crucifix brought here by pilgrims from Nuremberg (or Paris?) and known as the *Crocifisso dei Bianchi*.

S. Miniato al Monte

This gem of Tuscan Romanesque architecture represents one of the most memorable experiences Florence has to offer, not least because it stands on a hill from which the visitor has a uniquely beautiful panoramic view of the city. The first mention of the church dates from the time of Charle-magne. Bishop Hildebrand began to renovate it in 1018, and this renovation was almost complete by the early thirteenth century. The clearest system will be to take the dates in chronological order:

Around 250 Emperor Decius has the Christian Minias be-headed. Possibly the earliest sanctuary in Florence is erected over his grave.

971 The church is given to the nun Hermengard.

1018 Foundation of the Cluniac Benedictine abbey. The bones of Minias – who has been canonized in the meantime – are laid to rest in a crypt built especially for the purpose, and this triggers off a period of energetic building.

1207 is the date on the floor of the nave and the church must have been complete by this time.

Between 1294 and 1320, the bishops Andrea di Mozzi and Antonio d'Orso build an episcopal palace not far from the church.

1323 *The painted incrustation is applied to the interior.*

1373 *The Cluniac monks give the monastery and the church to the Olivetans.*

1387 *The sacristy is built by Benedetto di Nerozzo Alberti. Renovations to the cloisters and monastery are undertaken.*

The Renaissance style brings with it a series of important changes.

After 1447 Piero de'Medici not only renovates the chancel stairs (by B. Rossellino), but also employs Michelozzo to erect a marble tabernacle before the crypt.

1459 *Cardinal James of Portugal, a member of the Portuguese royal family, dies in Florence.*

1460 *Manetti builds a burial chapel for him in the left side aisle.*

1495 *The campanile collapses; the commission set up to supervise the erection of a new one includes among its members Leonardo and Giuliano da Sangallo.*

1518 *Baccio d'Agnolo draws up a plan for the new campanile.*

1527 *Work on the new campanile is held up; Florence is under siege, and as the area around S. Miniato forms a key position, it is heavily fortified. Michelangelo has the campanile protected with mattresses.*

1553 *The entire monastery is turned into a fortress and soldiers move in.*

1633 *The church is used as a hospital for victims of the plague, and later even as a hostel for the homeless.*

1854 *The cemetery is laid out; some Germans, too, are buried here, including the art historian Werner Cohn.*

1858–61 *The church is extensively restored; during this period, the columns of the nave are covered with marble stucco.*

After 1902 and 1924, further restorations are undertaken.

The church looks out over the city. The façade is covered with white and green incrustation, and is in three distinct sections. The *lower storey* (c. 1075) consists of half-columns with delicate blind arches of an almost Classical character. Notice the continuous door surrounds, the bottom edges of which at the same time form the doorsteps. The Renaissance was later to adopt this motif for its own use (e.g. the loggia of the Innocenti hospital and Alberti's doors in the Palazzo

Rucellai). – The *upper storey* is richer and more sophisticated, with sculptures (heads with arms), a beautiful tabernacle window and a mosaic (extensively restored) depicting Christ with Mary and S. Minias. Here, too, notice how the architraves bend at right angles, continuing vertically downwards until they meet the capitals. The beginnings of an astragal show that originally an intermediate storey, as in S. Maria Novella, was planned. – The richest part of the whole façade ist the *pediment*. Figures support it on either side, in the upper triangle is a cross with six candlesticks, and on top is the eagle of the Calimala guild (1401) which for a long time owned the patronage of the building. – A memorial slab in front of the right-hand portal indicates the spot in the cemetery of the first Florentine Christians where relics of martyrs were found in 1707.

Passing into the **interior** of the church, the visitor is immediately surrounded by that feeling of harmony and quiet dignity which results from a totally balanced treatment of space; it is almost like entering a comfortable home, although one becomes aware at the same time of the courtly splendour and institutional function of the building. A kind of music pervades it – these rich gradations of space unfold almost like a chord, and the articulation is brilliantly rhythmic. The columns (some of the fluting has worn away) have interesting capitals including some Classical pieces, not all of which have the same diameter as their shafts. Others are Byzantine (the last but one on the right in the chancel) and further ones were left unfinished (on the left in the chancel). Covering the interior is a magnificent open frame roof; although this dates from the Gothic period, the impression it transmits is Romanesque (except that in the Romanesque period the rafters were placed closer together; compare the row of brackets on the inner walls of the side aisles). The painted decoration has been touched up according to original remains.

The side walls and floors have been embellished with old tombstones; the nave has a luxurious 'carpet' of inlaid marble, in which can be seen a number of oriental motifs, including a zodiac, elements of a zodiac and the date 1207.

The **decoration** of the right side aisle is confined to murals. Each picture frames a painted tabernacle, and the whole

S. Miniato al Monte, capital

was executed between the early fourteenth and the fifteenth centuries (saints, including Nicholas, Minias and John the Evangelist; a simulated triptych attributed to Spinello Aretino). – In the nave, before the chancel, stands Michelozzo's precious *Altar of the Crucifix*. The crucifix is said to have bent down towards S. Giovanni Gualberto as he was adoring it, which moved him to forgive the murderer of one of his relatives. The crucifix itself is today in S. Trinita, but in 1448 Michelozzo erected his altar on this memorable spot for Piero di Cosimo Medici. The altar is enclosed by an iron screen with diamond rings (emblem of the Medici) forming the joints, and above it stands a tunnel-vaulted marble ciborium. The splendid capitals are among the most beautiful we have from the fifteenth century; each one represents a 'variation' on the basic theme, whereas a master like Brunelleschi always used more or less the same form. The base is still the old Romanesque altar, but turned round in the longitudinal sense; the top and the surround stick out through the rear wall of the ciborium. Remains of the old floor can be seen in the present floor and the inside rear wall. The Medici device is everywhere, and round the back we find even the falcon (tondo in the round gable) and the word 'SEMPER'. The tunnel vault is decorated on the inside with particularly beautiful glazed coffers and on the outside with colourful tiles; both are the work of Luca della Robbia. The bronze eagle on top again refers to the Calimala guild. The altar itself and the outer rear wall are decorated with incrustation. Mounted on the inside of the rear wall and adjusted to fit the measurements of the ciborium is the beautiful old *altar-piece* painted by Agnolo Gaddi probably shortly before his death; he was assisted here by the 'Master of the Madonnas', who was responsible for the standing saints and parts of the 'Scourging'. The altar itself is adorned with a gilded wooden reliquary bust of S. Minias, attributed to Cozarelli (fifteenth century). Climbing the stairs to the right, the visitor will find at the top on the immediate right the entrance to the **sacristy**. Outside, between the second flying buttress and the sacristy door, eight narrow *rectangular panels* can be seen, each depicting a saint, and on the left a ninth panel in which all that can be distinguished is a woman stretching out an arm and a very delicate hand *(Annunciation?)*. These are the oldest frescoes (*c.* 1210) in Florence.

The *fresco cycle* in the square, rib-vaulted sacristy is one of the principal works of Spinello Aretino and his school. On the ceiling, Evangelists; in the lunettes, scenes from the life of S. Benedict (whose rule the Olivetans followed). The whole cycle was restored *c.* 1840. Beginning in the left-hand corner of the side opposite the entrance (South wall): The saint leaves his family. – He mends a bucket that the nurse has broken. – (West wall): He retreats to Subiaco to be with the monk Romanus. – God sends a monk to visit him at Easter. – (North wall): The saint overcomes temptation by rolling naked among thorns. – The brothers of Vicovaro elect him abbot; some malcontents attempt to poison him, but he shatters the murder vessel with the sign of the cross. – (East wall): He leaves the brothers and receives the Romans Maurus and Placidus into the Order. – The story continues in the lower part of the walls: (West wall): S. Benedict founds Monte Cassino and raises a monk who has been killed by a collapsing wall. – He flogs a monk who has been tempted away from the service of God by the devil disguised as a monkey. – (North wall): He makes a scythe appear out of the water. – He commands Maurus to rescue Placidus who has fallen into a lake. – (East wall): He drives out a devil who has made a stone very heavy. – He recognizes as Totila's shield-bearer a person who has come to him pretending to be Totila himself. – (South wall): Totila comes to the reconciliation. – The saint's death. – The fine *wall cupboards* were made by Jacopo Legnaiuolo *c.* 1472 (some neo-Gothic additions were applied in 1860). The two statuettes, *S. Benedict* and *S. Minias*, are by the school of della Robbia. Inside the wings of the fairly recently painted tabernacle is an *Annunciation* by Giovanni dal

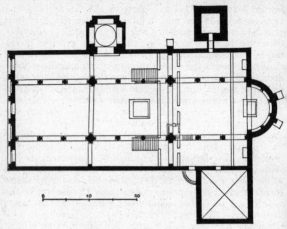

S. Miniato al Monte, ground plan

Ponte. On the right is a coloured terracotta half-relief of
the Madonna by the late fifteenth-century Lucca school. –
The little *side-room* contains a beautiful lavabo; the *Isaiah*
in the lunette is from the circle of Cosimo Rosselli (the
customary attribution to Castagno is obviously incorrect).
Returning to the church and to the frescoed right side aisle,
the visitor will find against the back wall an incrusted altar
table dating from *c.* 1100; on it can be seen S. Gualberto
and the donor (in the red coat), and on the predella scenes
from the saint's life, including – next to the murder of the
brother – the miracle of the crucifix of S. Miniato (*c.* 1370).
The remarkable **chancel** is in three aisles and is separated
from the church by an extremely interesting screen. The
incrusted *pulpit* (*ill.* facing p. 304) on the right-hand pillar
is of the very greatest delicacy; a lion at the bottom
supports a man who supports an eagle which in turn
supports the reading desk (*c.* 1200). Inlaid choir stalls
(1466–70, by Giovanni di Gaiole and Francesco di Domenico) and the old Romanesque altar together with the crucifix from the della Robbia workshop (*c.* 1470) complete the

furniture. The lower part of the beautiful semicircular apse has a Classical columnar arcade. According to very ancient practice, the windows are filled with thin, transparent slabs of marble (compare e.g. the Galla Placidia tomb in Ravenna). The powerful *mosaic* represents a variant on the theme of the mosaic in the façade, with the addition of symbols of the Evangelists. Dating from the late thirteenth century, it was restored in 1491 by Baldovinetti; then in 1860 it was taken down and completely renovated according to the original design. The painted inscription (now damaged) on the entablature below the mosaic bore the date 1297.

In the rear of the left side aisle on the altar (a modern copy of the corresponding one in the right side aisle), the visitor will find an important work by Jacopo del Casentino, painted *c.* 1340, depicting numerous scenes of martyrdom (principally that of S. Minias). The frescoes on the wall above the stairs include a *S. Jerome* by a disciple of Castagno (*c.* 1460).

Descending the stairs, the visitor will see the famous **chapel of the Cardinal of Portugal** on his right. Consecrated in 1466, this centralized structure with three short side arms is one of the most interesting Florentine buildings of its period. It was built between 1461 and 1466 to provide a dignified home for the tomb of James of Lusitania, nephew of King Alfonso V of Portugal and Cardinal Archbishop of Lisbon; the architect was Manetti, Brunelleschi's heir, and the basic form in fact goes back to the Old Sacristy of S. Lorenzo. Above the entrance arch outside are the consecration inscription and the cardinal's coat of arms. The modern iron screen (1930) is a reconstruction of the painted screen in the picture on the high altar (a copy of the original by the brothers Antonio and Piero Pollaiuolo which is now in the Uffizi). The two figures of *prophets* in the outer spandrels were painted by Baldovinetti. On the left outside is a beautiful *aspersorium* (*c.* 1460). The *ceiling* of the chapel is covered with painted tiles and contains five large terracotta tondi (the four cardinal virtues with the Holy Ghost in the centre). There are a number of interesting references to Classical and Early Christian styles. The *mosaic floor* reproduces similar Classical forms to those found, for example, in the Bishops' Palace in Ravenna and even in the chancel of Westminster Abbey. The sarcophagus of the cardinal's *tomb* (by Antonio Rossellino, assisted by his brother) was modelled on a Classical porphyry sarcophagus which stood near the Pantheon at that time, and was later taken into the Lateran as the tomb of Clement VII. On the base, apart from some particularly beautiful inlaid decoration, we find a Classical Mithraic sacrifice. A stone curtain adorns the niche; in the tympanum is a beautiful *Madonna and Child* (tondo). On the opposite side is an empty throne with costly inlaid work of porphyry and serpentine – an idea derived from Early Christian tradition. The *Annunciation* above it is by Baldovinetti (painted on wood and let into the wall; the trees and sky 'al fresco'). Beneath the Madonna is an inscription in praise of the King of Portugal; the inscription beneath the angel refers to the privileges conferred on the chapel by Pope Paul II.

The left side aisle, like the right, is decorated with frescoes (some taken down), including a *Crucifixion with Saints* and a *Coronation of the Virgin, with Saints* which are attributed to Mariotto di Nardo.

The broad eleventh-century *hall-crypt* was restored in 1930. The seven aisles are spanned by groin vaults supported by columns (some fluted) of various origins; they were all modified during the fifteenth century, and some of them have Classical capitals. The fragments of frescoes on the ceiling and in the lunettes (Saints and Prophets) are attributed to Taddeo Gaddi (1341). The altar, on which the bones of S. Minias were laid to rest in 1013, is the original one. The iron *screen*, signed and dated 1338 (in the middle), is by the Sienese artist Petruccio di Betto. The visitor should not leave this underground crypt without first attempting to observe the columns of the chancel above, and the way in which they appear to break through the ceiling here and continue down to the floor.

Adjoining the sacristy is a picturesque and very beautiful **cloister**. This is particularly worth visiting at Christmas time, when the visitor can admire the church's magnificent Crib. On the upper storey of the north side are the much faded remains of a fresco cycle by the circle of Uccello, and also the earliest known painting by the young Poccetti (beside further sixteenth and seventeenth century fragments).

The former **Bishops' Palace**, which served for a long time as the summer residence of the bishops of Florence, was much altered during the sixteenth century by the Spanish troops of Cosimo I. It was only joined to the rest of the monastery complex in 1594. In the seventeenth century, it was used as an infirmary for plague victims, and in the eighteenth century it housed a community of Jesuits. This imposing building, now occasionally used as a concert hall, is open to visitors.

Passing through the cemetery, the visitor comes to the **campanile**, erected in 1518–27 according to designs by Baccio d'Agnolo after the old tower had collapsed in 1499. The upper storey was never completed and is still missing today. The campanile dominates this whole fortified area which once stretched as far as the Arno.

S. Monaca (Via S. Monaca 6)
Convent of Augustinian nuns founded in 1444. The small church was completed in 1460. Façade restored in 1906. Interior (usually closed) in the form of a rectangular hall. Fine altar with an **Entombment** attributed to Bronzino.

S. Niccolò sopr'Arno (Via S. Niccolò)

This twelfth century church was rebuilt in the fifteenth century and embellished during the sixteenth. The Romanesque building lay on an east-west axis (i.e. at right-angles to the present church) and had a crypt. The late Gothic building, from the period around 1400, is interesting as an example of the kind of architecture among which Brunelleschi grew up. A particularly fine feature is the incredibly precise jointing of the masonry.

The **interior**, a large wide hall, was made slightly higher towards the end of the sixteenth century. The **decoration** throughout dates from that period. On the first altar, immediately to the left of the portal, is a late work by Alessandro Allori, *Abraham's Sacrifice*. Also attributed to Allori is the second altarpiece on the left side wall, the *Martyrdom of S. Catherine*. Paintings by Poppi (third chapel on the left) and Empoli (chapel on the left of the high altar) are also of interest. The sacristy contains a beautiful aedicula in the style of Michelozzo. The lunette frames a *Madonna* fresco by Piero Pollaiuolo; both landscape and figures have a realistic freshness about them. – The room off the sacristy beneath the campanile is where the verger hid Michelangelo from his pursuers after the capture of Florence in 1530.

S. Niccolò del Ceppo (corner of the Via Giuseppe Verdi and the Via de'Pandolfini)
This little church was built in 1561–3 after designs by Giovanni da Bologna. The entrance is on the Via de'Pandolfini. The very plain exterior conveys nothing of the beautiful Vasari-style architecture of the interior (visits only by permission of the curator). The fresco on the back wall of the vestibule is by Pieter Candid (de Witt, dated 1585); this *Madonna and Child and Saints* is one of the few pictures by this master in Florence. – On the back wall of the church is a life-sized stucco *Madonna* by Francavilla, who was also responsible for the *Annunciation* relief on the façade wall, *c.* 1600. – A *Crucifixion* in the sacristy is close in style to Fra Angelico.

Ognissanti (Piazza Ognissanti)
All Saints' church, which grew from modest beginnings into the present richly decorated building, was founded by the Humiliati, an order of monks from northern Italy which concerned itself with the artistic weaving of wool, with trade and with teaching. The original church was erected between 1252 and 1257 on a site near the river (the water of the Arno was utilized in the weaving process), and formed the centre of an extensive complex of workshops and monastery buildings. This church still constitutes the substance of the present building. – In 1561, the Humiliati left their elaborate site and in their stead came Franciscan Minors who renovated the neglected church to meet their own requirements. Between 1564 and 1566, parts of the medieval decoration were removed, altar tabernacles were placed along the side walls, organ and pulpit were elaborately and tastefully decorated and a large chapel was built on beyond the Gothic chancel; this was consecrated in 1582. – After that it was not so much a question of alterations as of concealing more and more of the church's medieval character beneath Baroque decoration. Between 1593 and 1615, the old chancel was vaulted and decorated with 'pietra dura' work, statues and paintings. In 1627, the architect Bastiano Pettirossi da Fiesole (quite unknown in another context) articulated the lower storey of the side walls with an entablature and an order of pilasters (the upper order of pilasters of wood and stucco was added later, in 1687–91, as were the Baroque windows). Matteo Nigetti erected a new façade wall in 1637 (the date can be seen on the outside beneath the left-hand upper storey window). Around 1700, the chancel chapels were given a Baroque stucco coating. In 1737 Bernardo Ciurini replaced the painted open

*frame roof of the monks' choir with a dome. The flat
painted ceiling of the nave was erected in 1769. Previously
a simple open frame roof had covered the equally simple
ground plan of this hall-church with main chancel and side
chancels. In 1871–2 the dangerously worn façade was pulled
down and replaced by an accurate copy.
The three medieval cloisters and their courts were extensively altered in the fifteenth century. Today only the first
is open to visitors, the other two being used for secular
purposes.*

Exterior   The façade, which runs flush with the adjacent
buildings on either side, is relatively small, like the rest of
the building. It is in two storeys, though the enormous gable
makes it appear to have three, and projects some way above
the roof of the church. Stylistically it stands in line of
succession to Buontalenti and the circle of architects associated with the Cappella dei Principi in S. Lorenzo. Com-
paring it to a somewhat similar composition – the façade of
S. Stefano dei Cavalieri in Pisa (by Don Giovanni Medici,
with the collaboration of Vasari) – one becomes aware of
its peculiar density of expression; yet, on the other hand,
the ornamentation clearly reveals the debt to Buontalenti,
several of the details inviting comparison with the façade
of S. Trinita, e.g. the splayed lamellae beneath the side
niches (the two opposing pediments of the upper storeys were
influenced by Buontalenti's 'Porta delle Suppliche' in the
Uffizi). The influence of Michelangelo, too, is evident in
the way the columns on either side of the main portal are
let into hollowed-out pilasters; obviously the thought of the
staircase of the Laurentian Library still preoccupied architects even in the seventeenth century. The glazed clay relief
in the tympanum was taken over from the old façade, and
has consequently been patched around the edge; it depicts
the *Coronation of the Virgin* with choirs of angels playing
musical instruments and busts of saints, some of whose faces
are seen in profile and some turned towards the visitor
(*c.* 1515, probably by Giovanni della Robbia). In the tympanum above the main portal is the dove, symbol of the
Holy Ghost, set within a lovely cartouche. A remarkable
feature of the façade is the continuous vertical axis. It is as
if the whole middle section were being thrust upwards by
forces emerging from the ground. In the gable is a powerful

coat of arms cartouche with the lily of Florence. – The niches on either side of the entrance should be understood simply as architectural forms; they were not intended to contain figures.

On the right, the visitor can see the (restored) **campanile** just as it appeared in the thirteenth century, with its beautiful acoustical openings which increase in number towards the top, and the powerful, aggressive cornice situated slightly below the termination of the tower. – On the left, at no. 42, is the entrance to the **cloister**, the principal feature of which is the chapel against the end wall of the left transept arm of the church. It is built on three solid octagonal pillars and roofed with a weighty and robust rib vault, and with its beautifully shaped Gothic windows, it recalls the impression which was once conveyed by the whole church. We have here an early example of Florentine Gothic (comparable features are to be found in S. Maria Novella). From the west side of the cloister, the visitor can just perceive in the high wall of the nave the beginnings of three walled-up Gothic windows beside the present Baroque ones.

Interior   The visitor can see here an example of the extent to which the height, width and depth of a building determine the stylistic impression it conveys. Beneath the overlay of later additions, the Gothic proportions live on, for in Florence length and breadth are of the essence of the Gothic architectural style and the impression they convey here is a strong one. One feature of the interior, however, is distinctively Baroque, and that is the view through the chancel into the second, late sixteenth-century chancel beyond, with the triumphal cross picturesquely silhouetted in the enormous opening. – The raised transept, which is paved with numerous tomb slabs, has almost the proportions of a corridor. The change in height in the openings of the side chancel chapels is due to the fact that the original building had a single main chancel (square) and only two side chancels half the size of the main one; the two adjacent side chancels with their taller arches were added later. All the other chapels in the transept date from the Late Renaissance or Baroque periods with the exception of the very much higher one at the end of the left transept arm which is reached by stairs; one of the earliest sections of the building.

S. Giovannino degli Scolopi, pulpit

S. Maria del Carmine, Brancacci chapel, detail of
'The Tribute Money' (Masaccio)

Decoration Beginning at the entrance wall, the visitor will find on the right the earliest known copy of the frequently reproduced and deeply venerated miraculous image of SS. Annunziata; this frescoed *Annunciation* was once inscribed with the date 1369. – Above the portal and difficult to see is a *Madonna and Child and S. Francis* by Ulivelli (1662). – The large 'pietra dura' coat of arms in the floor marks the grave of the donor of the façade, Antonio Vitalis de Medici (1656). – The painting on the ceiling of the nave depicts the *Glory of S. Francis* (1770), framed by a painted loggia in simulated perspective. – The much darkened half-figure paintings beside the windows depict saints of the Franciscan Order. They date from 1687–91, as does the stucco surround belonging to them.

The series of *altars* begins on the right with an *Ascension* by Ludovico Buti, *c.* 1581. A disciple of Santi di Tito, he took as his principal figure the Christ of the latter's 'Resurrection' in S. Croce; in its colourfulness, the painting exemplifies the school of Andrea del Sarto. – The door beyond leads into a side room which is all that is left of a chapel donated in 1597; it now serves as the vestibule of an eighteenth-century oratory (at Christmas a beautiful Crib can be seen here). The tomb of the painter Agostino Veracini dates from 1762. The oratory of the lay brothers was decorated during the eighteenth and nineteenth centuries. – Returning to the nave, the visitor will find on the second altar the oldest tabernacle in the church (1472); the others were modelled on this one during the sixteenth and seventeenth centuries (the last ones before the transept on either side date from 1627). The frescoes are by Domenico Ghirlandaio. In the lunette is a *Madonna of Mercy* with members of the Vespucci family who sponsored the work. In its strong concentration on physiognomy, its emphasis on spatial composition and its precision of line, it is a typical example of the master's early work; it is also of great interest as containing the only extant portrait of the young Amerigo, the Florentine discoverer of America (mentioned by Vasari; no longer identifiable with certainty today, but commonly assumed to be the young man on the right of the Madonna). – Below is a rather later *Lamentation*, an austerely expressive work. The poor state of preservation, particularly of the fragments of angels on either side, is due to the fact that a coat of whitewash was applied in 1616 (the frescoes were uncovered in 1898 and have recently been restored and some small sixteenth-century additions removed). The round plaque in the floor before the pilaster to the left of the altar (bearing the date 1471) marks the tomb of the Vespucci family. – The third tabernacle contains a youthful work by Santi di Tito, a *Madonna with Angels and Saints and God the Father.* – On the wall before the next altar on the right is a masterpiece by Botticelli, *S. Augustine in his Study.* This fresco once adorned the screen of the monk's choir (now removed), and was placed here in 1564. It was donated by the Vespucci, whose coat of arms appears in the picture. The 'interior' atmosphere of this little room, with its delicate paraphernalia of spiritual pursuits, reveals something of the Netherlandish influence which pervaded Florence during that period. The date of the fresco is assumed to be 1480. – The *pulpit* between the fourth and fifth tabernacles is an example of the artistic trend which was current around 1565 and which drew its inspiration from fifteenth century forms. Excellent relief panels on the sides of the polygon depict the legend of S. Francis. The pulpit is supported on curious volutes and imaginary beasts which suggest the influence of Benedetto da Rovezzano. They were probably made by the school of the Lorenzi. The colour harmony – pale marble, greenish-grey macigno, gold frame and painted ornamentation – is characteristic. – The sixth and last altar has one of the few extant pictures by Domenico Pugliani (very stained). Above it, in the upper storey, is a seventeenth century clock.

All the chapels in the right transept arm are decorated in the Baroque style, and furnished with a quantity of pieces which from the artistic point of view are not worth mentioning in detail. The two similar fourteenth and fifteenth century tomb-slabs, one in the floor of the chapel at the east end of the transept and the other in the adjacent first chapel on the north side, belonged to the original building. Anyone who is interested in the painter Rosselli will find in this latter chapel two good pictures with his characteristic brilliant blue (on the right, *S. Elizabeth of Portugal Blesses a Child*, 1625; on the left, *S. Andrew being led to his Martyrdom*, 1620). – In the right-hand side chancel is a recently renovated statue of the Madonna (fifteenth century?).

Every piece contained in the *main chancel* (1593–1616) is well worth the visitor's attention. In the vault are some early paintings by Giovanni da San Giovanni (*c.* 1616), though their poor state of preservation makes it impossible to assess their quality. The four niche figures depicting Franciscan saints are the only known works by the sculptor Giovanni Simone Cioli. Excellent 'pietra dura' work adorns the side walls and the elaborate high altar. The inlaid *Legend of S. Francis* on the top of the altar is by Francesco Gargiolli. The whole thing is reminiscent of the monks' choir in the crossing of S. Spirito (compare, too, the two adoring angels in the background to right and left which were influenced by Caccini's figures). The powerful bronze crucifix on the altar is the most recent piece of all; Bartolommeo Cennini executed it in 1669–74.

Baroque decoration predominates in the left transept arm too, except for the sacristy. In the vestibule of the sacristy is a *crucifix* by the school of Veit Stoss, the head and the straightened legs being especially typical of this German style. On the right in the main room is a *monumental painted crucifix* by a disciple of Giotto (a similar piece is in S. Marco), and on the wall opposite the entrance is a slightly renovated *Crucifixion* from the circle of Taddeo Gaddi. – Under the stairs leading up to the war memorial at the end of the transept is a tomb niche with very archaic paintings of prophets in the spandrels. It now contains a Holy Sepulchre (Baroque). – Up in the chapel at the end of the transept is a *Madonna* altar-piece by the school of Baldovinetti, remarkable for its very late use of a gold background. – The tunic which is kept under glass near the corner of nave and transept is said to have been worn by S. Francis in La Verna on the occasion of his receiving the stigmata.

Turning back into the nave, the visitor will see high up in the window zone on the left side an interesting *tomb* of the style of *c.* 1410 with the figure of Cardinal Luca Manzoli lying on the sarcophagus in a sloping position. Placed here during the Baroque period, it is, of course, far too high up. A little farther on towards the façade, the visitor will find Ghirlandaio's *S. Jerome in his Cell*, a pendant matching Botticelli's 'S. Augustine' opposite. More brooding but rather less emotional than Botticelli's work, it shows just as great a degree of Netherlandish influence (van Eyck). It was painted for the Vespucci and is dated 1480; like 'S. Augustine', it was originally on the screen of the monk's choir. – The following *Assumption* is by Maso da San Friano; it is a somewhat characterless composition in terms of colour, but the spirit of Rosso is still present in the robes. The angels in the semicircle above were added by Santi di Tito. – The next altar (the second one before the façade wall) has a *Trinity* and in the arch panel a *Coronation of the Virgin* by Ridolfo Ghirlandaio (early sixteenth century).

The **cloister**, which the visitor reaches from the street along a passage which incorporates parts of the original (Gothic) court, once housed one of the most important fresco cycles painted in Florence in the period around 1600. The most important frescoes have been taken down because they were showing signs of serious decay (the damage was caused by children playing). The ones that can still be seen here today are by disciples of Jacopo Ligozzi and Giovanni da San Giovanni. In the places where the others were taken down, one can see some interesting traces of sketches on the plaster and the closely meshed grid.

The **refectory** (entrance in the cloister; ask the curator) contains a masterpiece by Ghirlandaio, his famous *Last Supper* dated 1480. Approaching it from the opposite end of the room, the visitor captures immediately the illusion of space which the master obtained by extending the actual window wall and the central vault bracket into the simulated interior of his painting. The work stands between Castagno's Last Supper in S. Apollonia and Leonardo's 'Last Supper' in Milan. The details are extremely charming – the glasses, bottles and fruit, the beautiful border of the tablecloth and the birds and trees seen between the terminal wall and the arch. Having overcome Castagno's 'heroic bluntness', the work has not yet attained Leonardo's inner fire. The master's realism here unfolds in a climate of bourgeois art in the best sense of the term. The picture is in an excellent state of preservation; only Christ's head has been renovated (by Carlo Dolci in the seventeenth century). – For the rest, this impressive room contains a lectern (1480), two wall fonts on the entrance side and a collection of fresco fragments. The right wall is dominated by some crude pictures by Vasari; the left wall includes two pieces by disciples of Castagno, the *Crucifixion* and the *Madonna*, the *Workers in the Vineyard* by Andrea del Sarto, and a number of pieces by disciples of Perugino. – The anteroom contains a Baroque table font.

S. Onofrio di Fuligno (Via Faenza 40–48)

The first mention of a small hermit chapel here was in the early fourteenth century, and from this developed a convent of Franciscan nuns 'from Foligno'. The façade of this church was where no. 42 is today. Later a new church was built (today no. 48; previously the site of the enclosing wall).

From outside, it is impossible to reconstruct the appearance of the former complex, and even inside numerous alterations have very much confused the design. The most interesting things here are Perugino's *Last Supper*, discovered in 1845, and the **Ferroni Museum**, a private collection of pictures from the fifteenth to the eighteenth centuries which has been bequeathed to the city. This, however, is at present being reorganized and is therefore closed to visitors.

The curator (entrance at no. 42) shows the visitor into a large hall on the end wall of which he will find the *Last Supper*, set in a pillared hall. In the background, against a pale horizon, is the scene on the Mount of Olives. A striking feature of the fresco is its strict symmetry, even down to the arrangement of the objects on the table (notice the bowls of figs!). The work may have been painted *c.* 1490, and in it Perugino followed the iconographic tradition laid down by Castagno and continued by Ghirlandaio. – The hall also contains at present some extremely rare cartoons for sixteenth century tapestries that were restored here, and some large plaster casts of fragments of the Ponte S. Trinita. After this marvellous bridge had been destroyed in the war, it was possible, thanks to these casts and to the portions of the bridge that were still standing, to reconstruct it exactly.

Or San Michele (Via Calzaioli; *ill.* facing p. 305)

The name probably derives from S. Michele 'in Orto', i.e. 'in the gardens', an eighth century oratory which stood on this site. In 1285, a corn market was built here, of which the architect was probably Arnolfo di Cambio. This was burnt down during a feud in 1304. A new building was begun in 1307, but soon afterwards a larger complex with the present dimensions was planned and the foundation stone of this was laid in 1337. The design for the new building was probably drawn up by Francesco Talenti, Neri

di Fioravante, Benci di Cione and very likely also the painter
Taddeo Gaddi working together. The vaults of the market hall
were closed in 1357. In 1367–80, Simone Talenti filled the arches
between the supporting piers – open until then – with masonry
and very delicate tracery work (as they are now). The reason for
this modification was a miraculous image which adorned one of
the piers and which had been responsible for miracles as early as
1292. Crowds of pilgrims began to arrive, and the market hall
became more and more a place for prayer and virtually a kind of
church. Finally, it was in fact consecrated, and it thus constitutes
a unique combination of market hall and place of worship. Some
of the channels in which the corn was poured down from the
upper storey can still be seen inside the church (in the inner face
of the arch in the north-west corner; in the pillars of the north
side). The cornice was erected in 1404. Shortly before that date,
the importance of the church finally superseded the importance of
the corn market, and the latter was moved elsewhere. In 1569 the
legal archives were moved into the free upstairs rooms. – The
entire building is in an immaculate state of preservation.

Or San Michele is very tall and provides one of the
dominant accents in any view of the city. The warm colour
of the sandstone, the white marble filling of the upper storey
windows, the charming delicacy of the cornices and the
almost dreamlike assurance of the proportions combine
with the sophisticated treatment of the masonry to give an
impression of the very highest quality, placing the building
on a level between the popular art of the Palazzo Vecchio
and the new patrician style introduced by Brunelleschi. The
round arches of the pillared arcades (originally open) are
filled with some of the richest tracery work produced in
Florence in the fourteenth century, a final blossoming of
Late Gothic (the sharpness of some of the details has unfortunately become blurred through the action of the
weather).

The **niche figures** on the pillars are of the utmost importance
as supreme examples of the development of the Renaissance
sculptural style. Each niche was erected, decorated and
maintained by one of the guilds, the intention being that
mass should be said from a portable altar before each one
(hence the corbels for candlesticks, etc. on either side of
some of them). The wool-weavers and cloth merchants began the cycle in 1339–40, but since their figures were lost
and replaced during the Renaissance, there is now no longer
any trace of Gothic influence (except in the seated *Madonna*

on the south side) among the monumental sculptures of Or
San Michele. The result is an almost incredibly pure stylistic
harmony.

The figures on the **east side** are in bronze. On the left is
John the Baptist by Lorenzo Ghiberti, signed and dated
1414, in a contemporary inlaid niche which is picturesquely
colourful. This figure, the first large bronze statue of the
newer Italian art, was excellently summed up by Jacob
Burckhardt in the words 'a work of harsh forms and unaffected inner power'. Next is a masterpiece by Verrocchio,
Christ with Doubting Thomas (1465–83), a clearly articulated work planned on a large scale. Possibly inspired by
Bicci di Lorenzo's fresco on the same theme in the Cathedral, the group was carefully prepared in drawings and in
a clay model which was considered very valuable. The
niche is considerably earlier in date. The mixture of scalloped
niche and tabernacle, the detail (e.g. the billowing cushion
between the supporting bracket and the niche socle) and the
sensitive relief work with its play of light and shade identify
this as a characteristic work by Donatello (1422). It originally contained his gilded 'S. Louis', which was subsequently
moved to the façade of S. Croce and is now in the museum
there. The third niche, by Niccolò Lamberti (1403–6), is
slightly too narrow for Giovanni da Bologna's radiant
S. Luke (1600).

The first figure on the **north side**, *S. Peter*, unmistakably
breathes the spirit of Donatello. Its niche is one of the oldest
on the building. *Philip*, the next figure, is by Nanni di
Banco (*c.* 1412), as is also the following niche with the
Martyrs Castor, Symphorian, Nicostratus and Simplicius,
known as the *Quattro Coronati*. Niche and figures were
carved probably *c.* 1415 in the relaxed Classical spirit that
was prevalent in the early fifteenth century (*ill.* facing
p. 320). On the west corner of the building is Donatello's
S. George (a modern bronze copy of the pre-1417 marble
original now in the Bargello), a tribute to the knight
and martyr by the armourers of Florence. Seen from
the front, the statue offers the eye a series of clearly defined
forms; the contours – as sharp as if they had been drawn –
reveal the master's breakthrough to the purity of conception
of the new style. It is not by chance that the relief on the
socle depicting the fight with the dragon occupies such a

special position in the history of centralized perspective representation. The fourteenth century character of the niche makes it probable that it dates from the first few years of the fifteenth century. The north wall as a whole has the most homogeneous decoration of the entire building (originally all the figures here were marble).

The first figure on the **west side** is Ghiberti's *Matthew*, probably his most important monumental figure and one which proved extremely difficult to cast. The niche is particularly interesting, combining Gothic motifs in an order which differs from the traditional arrangement. The rectangular frame and the extreme shallowness of the niche reduce the space within which the statue stands, so that it no longer contains the statue so much as provides a background architecture that optically supports and enhances the sculpture. Niche and figure date from 1419–22, as does the very fine *Annunciation* flanking the gable (possibly by Michelozzo). Next comes Ghiberti's unaffectedly beautiful bronze statue of *S. Stephen* (1427–8). The niche is one of the older ones (1339–40). On the southern corner pillar is Nanni di Banco's *S. Eligius* (c. 1415–20), patron saint of smiths, viz. the decoration of the niche with tongs and the shoeing of a horse in the socle relief.

The **south side** begins with an early masterpiece by Donatello, *S. Mark* (*ill.* facing p. 321), begun in 1411 together with the niche, although this was not designed by Donatello. The figure was originally entirely gilded. Donatello is said to have designed it especially for this niche, and indeed figure and surround form an extremely happy combination. The following apostle, *S. James*, dating probably from after 1422, is by Niccolò di Pietro Lamberti; on the socle is the beheading of the saint. The *Madonna delle Rose* is the oldest figure of all (inscribed with the date 1399). She is seated in a round tabernacle which was modelled on Orcagna's tabernacle inside the church. The last niche (1339–40) contains one of Baccio da Montelupo's most beautiful works, a *S. John* (1515) which is curiously close in style to Donatello.

In the wall above each niche is a round space, and in some of these spaces the visitor will find the coat of arms of the guild for which that particular niche was designed. They are of glazed clay and were made by Luca della Robbia around the middle of the fifteenth century. Figures in the style of Francesco Talenti stand on top of all the tracery columns in the arcade arches; some of these are nineteenth century copies (the west side has most originals; the rest are in the Bargello). The small reliefs (half-figures) let into the solid masonry of the lower part of the arcade date from c. 1340, but they came from elsewhere and were probably placed here at a somewhat later date.

The **interior** is a pillared hall with two aisles, the west wall being particularly strong on account of the staircases which it contains. Each bay forms a square. The central supports are beautifully articulated with tall socles, foliate capitals, engaged columns at the corners and niches with pointed arches. They carry broad, powerful semicircular arches. Decorative elements are flat with bevelled edges, precise without there being any sharp corners. The painted decoration has unfortunately suffered very heavily. During the Renaissance, some of the *frescoes* were covered up with paintings on wood and others with whitewash. The original appearance has today been more or less reinstated, except that some more recent panel paintings are hung inside the arches. The whole of the old decoration dates from c. 1400. Most of it consists of individual figures, with larger scenes appearing only on the central pillars (e.g. the *Pentecost* on the western one, where the visitor will also find Andrea del Sarto's *Ecstasy of S. Mary Magdalen* in a hexagonal panel). The programme for the decoration of the *vault* was drawn up by the short-story writer Francesco Sacchetti, who was also the captain of the Compagnia dell'Or San Michele. He divided the history of the world into three phases – 'ante legem', 'sub lege' and 'sub gratia' – and embodied this typically Renaissance idea in a series of monumental figures which are not in every case clearly identifiable, but which were probably inspired by a cycle of 'viri illustres'. The contemporary stained-glass are among the most precious in the city. They depict the miracles of the Virgin; the iconography is derived from book illustrations.

The church's most valuable possession is surely the *tabernacle* in the south aisle (it can be illuminated) which Orcagna made for the ancient miraculous image which adorned one of the pillars; it is dated 1359. The structure develops out of a socle storey and terminates in a cupola.

The whole is covered with decoration including incrustation, enamel-work and reliefs and was originally richly gilded. It is virtually a compendium of every form known to the fourteenth century; the Ionic-style capitals are a particularly interesting feature. The cyclical programme is devoted to the glorification of the Virgin. On the socle are scenes from the life of the Virgin together with Virtues. The small columns of the principal storey are crowned with statuettes of the Apostles. On the back is an important relief by Orcagna together with his assistants depicting (above) *The Virgin giving the Girdle to S. Thomas* and the *Death of the Virgin*. The man wearing a hood on the right in the lower relief is a self-portrait of the brillant master, the earliest known self-portrait of the newer art (except for one example on the Novgorod door, 1135). This rich and fabulous piece of work calls for long and careful study, nor should the visitor overlook the surrounding marble rail with its beautiful bronze grilles by Pietro di Migliori, 1366. The whole tabernacle represents the most decisive stylistic step in the direction of the Renaissance. Daringly imaginative, it takes shape in an almost matter-of-fact way with the free corporeality associated with the style of Giotto. The panel which is kept in the tabernacle is by Bernardo Daddi (1347).

Finally, the visitor should look at the *Altar of S. Anne* in the north aisle, erected to commemorate the banishment of the Duke of Athens in 1343 (on S. Anne's Day). Francesco da Sangallo's group replaced an earlier painting on wood in 1526. It was obviously influenced to some extent by Leonardo's cartoon of 'S. Anne with the Virgin and the Christ Child'. The complexity of the task accounts for the somewhat mannered traits. A certain tendency towards poverty of decoration remained characteristic of the master throughout his life.

S. Pancrazio (Piazza S. Pancrazio)

This church, which was probably founded on an Early Christian site, is today partially in secular use. It contains the Holy Sepulchre made by Leon Battista Alberti, who also gave the whole building a new appearance. The late sixteenth century and the seventeenth and eighteenth centuries brought about so many alterations that the church has completely lost its old character. Only the Rucellai chapel is open to visitors (key from the porter of the Palazzo Rucellai).

The **façade** is simple. On the right is a curious circular form. The tympanum has been described as being part of a door added by Alberti (?). The whole building, which opens up in a very successful way into a small piazza, may be re- garded as a late example of the stylistic trend known as 'Arnolfian' (*c.* 1375). The old façade was breached in 1809 to form the present entrance hall; this was then articulated with Alberti's arcade which had previously stood between the Rucellai chapel and the nave. The arch cuts sharply into the round Gothic window. A pair of weathered lions flank the stairs.

The visitor enters the **Rucellai chapel** from the north. Alberti designed this tunnel-vaulted hall in 1460. The walls are articulated with Corinthian pilasters which continue up into the vault as transverse arches. The wall opposite the entrance once opened up into the church (here stood the arcade now in the entrance hall); it was filled in 1809, following the same system as the rest of the chapel.

The *Holy Sepulchre* (*ill.* facing p. 336) has a story attached to it. Giovanni Rucellai had the original measurements of Christ's sepulchre brought from Jerusalem, so that he could erect a reconstruction of it in his new chapel. This was probably envisaged in connection with the marriage of Bernardo Rucellai to a niece of Cosimo de'Medici in 1461 (the only explanation of the combination of the Rucellai sail with the Medici emblem of the plumed rings (*ill.* facing p. 337). However, this small structure which looks like a model of itself bears no resemblance to the sepulchre of Christ either in size or shape. Box-like, with a round apse that curiously enough achieves impact only from the outside and not inside, Alberti's work of art stands in the middle of the chapel. The inscription on the entablature turns corners even in the middle of words, and the date of completion, 1467, is to be seen above the door. The fine capitals are all uniform. There are some exciting medieval features – the inlaid pattern borrowed from the Proto-Renaissance, the cruciform flowers (originally gilded) on the cornice. Why these 'Romantic' touches? Which 'tempi bassi' (the eccentric entrance is another example) did Alberti wish to recall? Why did he make use of such an ancient sepulchral form as the tiny wooden tabernacle on the roof with its spiral dome

(another example in Florence is in Brunelleschi's Old
Sacristy – also an 'Entombment')? The only way to do
justice to these features is to regard Alberti's work not as a
(poor) architectural copy but as a kind of ideal reconstruction which attempts to capture the spirit of its ancient prototype by means of details which themselves go back a very
long way. There are other instances of this great architect
making use of similar 'paraphrases' of ancient monumental
structures. – Entering the sepulchre through the door, the
visitor will find that the interior is lit by means of a circular
hole in the tunnel vault. The principal item of furniture is
the sarcophagus-like altar. On the right is a heavily damaged
fresco, the *Risen Christ with Two Angels*, which dates from
the same period as the sepulchre, and the *Corpse of Christ*
(plaster cast). An almost square block of stone near the
entrance represents the block on which the angel is supposed
to have sat.

To the east is the adjacent **Chapel of S. Jerome** (1485; style
of Giuliano da Sangallo); the tomb of one Bernardo Rucellai who died in 1656 adorns the western end wall.

The **cloister** of the church has a fresco by Neri di Bicci in
the south-east corner (*S. Giovanni Gualberto and Saints*).

S. Paolino (Piazza S. Paolino)

*The foundation goes back to Early Christian times when, on the
model of the basilica of S. Paul in Rome, it was situated outside
the city near the former west gate. It was completely renovated
in the Gothic period, and again in 1669 by Giovanni Battista
Balatri. Today the former monastery is used for secular purposes
and the church is a parish church.*

This pompous building is situated on a little piazza in a
charmingly animated district inhabited by various artisans.
The present orientation is north-south; originally it was
west-east, but in 1669 Balatri turned it round through
ninety degrees. From the outside, the various different stages
of the building at different epochs can be clearly distinguished. The domed interior is wide and pleasantly spacious, but
contains few items of any interest. Immediately on the right
in the first chapel are a few fragments (inscription plaque)
of a fifteenth century sarcophagus; the decoration of the
chapel itself is Baroque (partly modern).

S. Pier Gattolini (Via Romana, between nos. 74R and 38, on the Via
Serumido)

This tiny church is first mentioned in 1050. It was demolished and rebuilt in 1544–52, enlarged in 1572, and in 1603 it received a new chancel, donated by Giovanni Serumido.

S. Pier Maggiore (Piazza S. Pier Maggiore)
Only the entrance hall has been preserved of this church which was finally demolished in 1783 after half of it had collapsed. A late work by Matteo Nigetti, it takes the form of a tripartite portico. Today it stands in a charming market district, and a street runs through the arch, giving it more the character of a gateway.

Chiesa dei Pretoni (Via Sangallo 20)
This simple little building was erected by Giovanni'Antonio Dosio. The painted decoration of the interior was executed c. 1590 by the extremely prolific Giovanni Balducci, one of the artists who worked on the Studiolo in the Palazzo Vecchio. The open frame ceiling dates from as early as 1312 (the painting is modern). The church has beautiful wooden doors, as do many of the Florentine churches of the sixteenth century.

S. Remigio (Piazza S. Remigio)

Founded during the Carolingian period, this small building was first a pilgrim hostel and then, from 1040 onwards, a seminary for canons. Later it was completely transformed into a Gothic hall-church which, however (and this is its special charm), is still utterly Italian. The campanile and the adjacent buildings for the canons were erected after 1581.

The church is a simple rectangular structure. Traces of the **old building** can be seen on the exterior, in the small added portal on the right of the façade (round arch and architrave) and in the rear part of the north wall (embrasure-like window with a round arch consisting of a single piece of stone).

The articulation of the **façade** is vaguely reminiscent of S. Stefano. The traces of plaster and paintings date from 1821, the fresco in the tympanum depicting *S. Remigius* from 1818. – The **interior** is harmonious though a trifle rustic, consisting of three aisles of three bays terminating in rectangular chancel chapels with a continuous rear wall. It resembles S. Maria Maggiore in character, and the visitor will also find here a clear example of the Florentine Gothic style as it appears (albeit on a different scale) in S. Croce. Certain details (pillars, capitals) are not unlike those of the Badia. The stairs before the chancel were built in 1589. The decoration of the main chancel is relatively recent (1821). – Behind the high altar is an important though much darkened picture by Jacopo da Empoli, the *Immaculata*, depicted according to Dante's description. The altar tabernacles in the side aisles were made in Rome and only erected here in the seventeenth century. Behind the first one on the left is a *Madonna* from the circle of Cimabue; it may originally have stood on the high altar, but it was moved here from the façade wall. – The plaster crucifix on the left wall dates from the fifteenth century; it was damaged in 1912 and has been touched up.

S. Salvatore al Monte (also known as S. Francesco; below S. Miniato al Monte)

This is one of the most fascinating late fifteenth-century buildings in Florence. Michelangelo called it affectionately 'la bella villa-nella' (the pretty country lass). Franciscans from Fiesole took up residence here in 1415, the Della Tosa family having bequeathed them an oratory dedicated to S. Damian. The monks began to enlarge their little monastery, and in 1419 their first church was completed. Later, under the sponsorship of Castello Quaratesi, a new and more sumptuous building was planned. The monastery itself was prepared to provide the labour under the leadership of Brother Leone di Lorenzo, but the church – with eastern chancel and west façade – only started to take shape after Lorenzo the Magnificent, that generous Medici patron, began to take an interest in the project in 1475. He donated money and was successful in his attempt to promote a grander, even magnificent plan, which meant that work did not in fact begin until 1487. Cronaca was chosen as architect. Initially, he had to overcome enormous difficulties. The chief obstacle was the instability of the ground, due to which the already completed east end collapsed in 1500. (In 1529 Michelangelo surrounded the site with a bulwark to support the precipitous terrain; the foundations of the church had to be further strengthened in 1555, and in 1562 considerations of statics gave the builders no choice but to shorten the campanile by sixteen metres. Giuliano da Sangallo and Leonardo, among others, had given expert advice about the danger in 1499.) – The consecration of the church took place in 1504. In 1561 the brothers had to leave the monastery because of the renewed danger of collapse (they went to Ognissanti). Since 1705 Franciscans 'del Ritiro' have once more occupied the site.

Approaching from the south, the visitor has a clear view of the simple **exterior** of the nave with its rows of low chapels on either side. The clerestory windows have alternately round and pointed pediments, a procedure which was much admired and which was probably derived from the Proto-Renaissance (the Baptistery). This was probably the earliest appearance in the fifteenth century of a feature that was to become part of the canon of architectural motifs, particularly in Rome (viz. Raphael's palaces). –

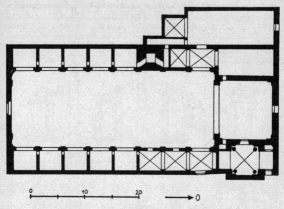

S. Salvatore (S. Francesco) al Monte, ground plan

Walking round to the left, the visitor will find on the
façade the eagle of the Calimala guild who, as Castello
Quaratesi's executors, were responsible for having the
church built. A beautiful and strongly Classical pedimented
portal, three windows in the upper storey and cornices
constitute the articulating elements.

The building belongs in type to a larger family which
includes Michelozzo's SS. Annunziata, Sangallo's S. Maria
Maddalena dei Pazzi and the little known cathedral in
Città di Castello. Is one perhaps right in sensing something
of the spirit of early Christendom in this hall-like interior
with its open frame roof and rows of chapels down either
side? For all its initial appearance of simplicity, the interior
is in fact very skilfully designed; after the first five chapels,
there follows on both sides a piece of solid wall (the campanile adjoins here on the north side, which may have been
the origin of the 'idea'), with the result that the last chapel,
which is open again, gives the effect of a sort of transept-
like extension, all the more so as the one on the right
contains the side entrance to the church. – One's eye is
arrested by the remarkable beauty of the noble articulation
of the nave walls. It has been said that this represents a

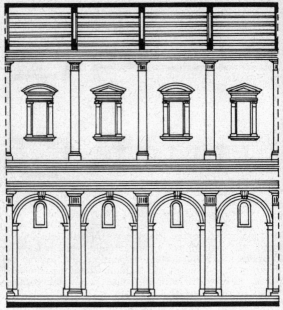

S. Salvatore (S. Francesco) al Monte, bays of the nave

revival of the Classical motif of the two-storeyed theatre
façade, but this does not explain the curious and very pronounced symmetry. The only explanation of the fact that
the triumphal arch before the chancel is repeated in a kind
of shallow projection on the inside of the façade wall lies
in the Renaissance concept of the centralized structure,
to which all other motifs have had to submit. Apart from
the architect's overall design, the visitor should not fail to
notice the masterly quality of the workmanship with
which that design has been executed, and which is expressed particularly well in the fine cut of the contours.
The side chapels are vaulted with tunnels and illuminated
by means of small, Brunelleschi-like windows situated high

S. Maria Novella, the middle portal of the façade

S. Maria Novella, Spanish chapel, detail of 'The Church Triumphant' showing Florence Cathedral (Andrea da Firenze)

up; some of them (six in all) contain some fine old stained
glass. Lying like a second, smaller church on the south side
of the main building, from which it is quite separate except
for the connection through the last side chapel on the
right, is the interesting **Tanai de'Nerli chapel**. It comprises
four spaces which, in their severe and massive strength,
strike an unusual note in the architecture of the Early
Florentine Renaissance. Particularly interesting is the centralized chancel with its remarkable Corinthian columns at
the corners, and the dosserets and pieces of entablature
projecting directly from the wall.

The **decoration** of the church is rather less rich. On the left,
on the façade wall, is Ferrucci's bust of the secretary of
state Andriani who signed Savonarola's death sentence; he
died in 1521, and his tomb is just in front in the floor. The
decoration of the side chapels, with the exception of the last
one on the left before the chancel, dates from the eighteenth
century. The coloured terracotta *Lamentation* group above
the rich portal in this chapel dates from the early sixteenth
century, and the small stone gallery in the nave before it
bears the date 1615. – In the fifth chapel on the right is a
Pietà with Saints from the circle of Neri di Bicci. On the
left wall of the Tanai de'Nerli chapel, there is a particularly
good 'Sacra Conversazione' by an unknown late fifteenth-
century Portuguese artist who was obviously not without
some experience of Italian art.

Chiostro degli Scalzi (Via Cavour 69)

Passing through a vestibule (entrance fee), the visitor enters
a small elegant **court** which is today roofed with glass. The
walls are decorated with scenes from the life of John the
Baptist and with the four Cardinal Virtues.

Andrea del Sarto painted the frescoes c. 1511–26 for a brother-
hood of S. John whose crucifers used to go barefoot in processions
(whence the name 'degli Scalzi'). The frescoes were cleaned in
1617 and restored again in 1720. When the brotherhood was
dissolved in 1785, this gem of Renaissance painting came under
the supervision of the Accademia di Belle Arti.

These pale *murals* are among the most famous grisaille
paintings of the Renaissance. Detailed investigation has revealed that they were transferred to the walls from cartoons
(of which, however, no trace has survived). In the course of
the eleven year working period, *Andrea del Sarto* was able

to achieve a balance between certain differences in colour (the earlier scenes have a golden warmth; the Virtues, on the other hand, are cool and greenish) and in the size of the figures (at the beginning there is a difference in height between the Virtues and the figures in the scenes). – Starting on the right, the visitor will find *Faith* (1520), *The Appearance of the Angel to Zachariah* (1524), *The Visitation* (1524), and the *Birth and Naming of John the Baptist* (1526). The next two scenes (showing John going out into the wilderness and meeting Christ) were executed by *Franciabigio* during Andrea del Sarto's stay in Paris in 1518–19. The *Baptism of Christ*' which follows had, according to Vasari, already been completed by Andrea in 1511. *Caritas* and *Justitia* are particularly beautiful; they were both painted *c.* 1515. Next comes the *Sermon of John the Baptist* (1515) followed by *John Administering Baptism* (1517), the *Arrest* (1517), *Herod's Banquet* (1522), the *Beheading* (1523) and *Salome with the Head of John the Baptist* (1523). *Hope* was also painted in 1523. – The visitor should bear in mind that this small court was rebuilt by Giovanozzi in 1722. Originally, it had a simple open frame roof; the present arcades and vaults contradict the master's intentions. When they were erected, the lunettes which they created had to be filled, and Giovanni Panaiotti added the urns above Andrea's terminating ornamental frieze.

The sculpture in the gable above the entrance (1722) is an idealized portrait of Andrea del Sarto.

S. Simone (Piazza S. Simone)

Founded in the twelfth century and extended in the thirteenth century, the church was further enlarged in the seventeenth century by Gherardo Silvani (c. 1630), who altered the chancel end and dressed the walls of the nave with blind arcades following a system inspired by Ammannati's S. Giovannino.

The medieval portions of the **façade** which are now visible were uncovered when the church was restored in 1897. Thus. Silvani's beautiful *round-arched portal* with its two columns (and its curious stylistic harking-back to the Renaissance) frames the old neatly executed medieval portal. – The **decoration** of the interior breathes the spirit of 1630. Particular mention must be made, however, of a number of earlier works. The fresco above the portal inside, a *Lamentation with S. Jerome*, was moved to this position in 1660

from the right-hand wall opposite the side entrance. It is
the earliest known work by Giovanni Battista Naldini
(c. 1570), an apprentice of Pontormo who subsequently
went to Rome and who worked with Vasari (his colours,
however, are sometimes more violent, and more biting than
those of the master), reaching fame as an accomplished
draughtsman. The fresco is unfortunately rather damaged.
– On the first altar on the right is a work by the Master of
S. Cecilia (an assistant of Giotto) dated 1307. The monumental figure of *Peter* may possibly have been inspired by
the very ancient bronze statue in S. Peter's, Rome. – The
two life-sized *marble figures* to right and left of the chancel
arch are the only known large-scale works by Orazio
Mocchi. – The small sacrament tabernacle is attributed to
Francesco Laurana. – The attractive terracotta tabernacle
decorated with little angels and garlands above the side
door on the left is by Andrea della Robbia (c. 1470). In it
is a small Gothic *marble altar* containing a late fourteenth
century marble bust of S. Ursula; this bust enjoys a certain
fame as being one of the earliest known examples of highly
realistic portraiture.

S. Spirito (Piazza S. Spirito)

*The history of this marvellous church, which is such an
exemplary embodiment of the style of the Renaissance, is
also an example of the extraordinary vigour with which the
new style thrust forward towards its incomparable achievements. In 1250, a modest but soon to be enlarged Augustinian church was erected beside an older small portico-chapel,
but as early as 1269 it had to give way to a more elaborate
new building, which made this the most important sacred
complex on the left bank of the Arno. In 1397, spontaneous
rejoicing over some local victory in battle found expression
in a plan for yet another extensive new building which was
to surpass everything that had gone before. Although the
project was supported by the clergy, it was not until 1434
that a building commission was set up with the active cooperation of several noble families. The commission turned
immediately to the most famous architect in Florence – Brunelleschi. Unfortunately his plan – to turn the church round
so that the façade looked north towards the Arno – was
not accepted, though its rejection was soon to become a*

matter for regret. Obviously the time was not yet ripe for the novel solution of building a church with a large square piazza giving on to the river and integrating this, from the point of view of town planning, with the mass of residential buildings which was old Florence. In one respect, however, all tradition was here thrown overboard, for whereas up until then the architect had always complied with his employer's wishes, in this case he was given a completely free hand in the formation of his architectural ideas.

Brunelleschi explained his plan by means of drawings and a wooden model, and a start was made on the foundations of the new church in 1436. It lay on a southward orientation in front of and at right-angles to the old church, which was still in use. After initial financial difficulties, work was resumed according to a modified plan (the idea for the rows of chapels in the side aisles does not seem to have come up until later). In 1446 the first column was delivered and the vaulting begun. A few days later, however, Brunelleschi died, and with his leadership removed, work on the building came to a halt (the column just mentioned was not erected until 1454). From then on, the building progressed only hesitantly; certain aspects of its creator's singular vision posed great difficulties for his successors (Manetti, who was the one most conversant with the basic conception, until 1460, and then until 1471 Giuliano Sandrini and Giovanni di Domenico da Gaiuole). In 1471, on the occasion of the performance of a religious play in honour of the Duke of Milan, the old church (with its rich thirteenth, fourteenth and fifteenth century decoration, including a masterpiece by Brunelleschi, his Magdalen) burned to the ground. At first, attempts were made to restore the ruin, but soon all efforts were concentrated on the new building. With the completion of the dome over the crossing in 1479–82 by Salvi d'Andrea, who kept to Brunelleschi's design, the church could be taken into use. The remains of the old building were demolished immediately afterwards.

The most important deviation from Brunelleschi's basic conception is probably the inclusion of the side chapels – which were originally rounded on the exterior – within the straight line of the wall. This was probably done shortly after his death (and before 1457), abandoning a lively, vibrant and varied exterior view in favour of plain stereometry. The man responsible for this major alteration may be assumed to have been Manetti, who thus robbed the building of one of its most original features. Although bulging niches are not unknown on the side walls of churches (S. Anastasia in Verona, Orvieto Cathedral, S. Claudio al Chianti, Carmine in Padua), the continuation of this feature around the entire church would have made this building quite unique. The extent to which this idea interested the next generation of architects is shown by a number of sixteenth-century drawings which reconstructed, at least on paper, Brunelleschi's original plan. On the north side of the church (in the corner of the Via dei Coverelli) one of the rounded chapels, with a beautiful socle cornice, has been freed from Manetti's coating wall.

The name 'Santo Spirito' covers not only the church but the whole complex including sacristy, campanile, monastery buildings and three cloisters. The sacristy was built shortly after the church had been completed; it occupies the site which became free when the old church, which had been destroyed by fire, was demolished (begun 1488). Giuliano da Sangallo furnished the design. Several important masters contributed to this tiny building. After the death of Lorenzo the Magnificent, who had devoted particular attention to its construction, the octagonal room was left for a while without a dome. The vestibule was built after a model – so it is said – by Cronaca. In the absence of Giuliano, the dome of the sacristy was erected by Antonio Pollaiuolo, whose understanding of the principles of construction was evidently slight since it collapsed two months after its completion (1496). It was re-erected immediately.

The foundations of the campanile – one of the most beautiful in Tuscany – were laid at the same time as those of the sacristy, though it was not completed until the late sixteenth century, with Baccio d'Agnolo (so Vasari tells us) being responsible for the upper storeys. An inscription below the pyramidal top has the date 1566. – In 1601–02 Caccini's steep, stylized lantern set the finishing touch to the dome above the crossing of the church. – The large cloisters were added to the medieval complex in the late sixteenth century. The architects were Ammannati, followed by Alfonso and Giulio Parigi. Only the first cloister can be visited freely (murals begun in 1639); to see the second (now an army depot), *the visitor must obtain permission from the officer in charge, while the third (a private store-room) is inaccessible.*

Exterior   There is a story behind the fact that this Renaissance basilica, which is otherwise thought out down to the last detail, has nothing but a pseudo-façade, which is completely unarticulated and as flat as a board. Building obviously began at the chancel end, and at the time of Brunelleschi's death, least progress had been made on the parts towards the entrance. The first mention of a model for the façade is in 1475. A quarrel broke out over this, however, which has a great deal to do with the present fragmentary condition of this end of the building. The argument was whether Brunelleschi intended to take the arcade which runs round the rest of the interior across the façade as well, or whether, as is the case today, it was to have ended against the façade wall. In the first case, two bays of the arcade would have stood before the façade wall (the same solution as was adopted for the ends of the transept arms), necessitating two entrance portals for the nave. In the latter case, a central entrance portal (as we have it today) would suffice. Counting the side aisle portals as well, the problem thus lay between having a four- or three-portal façade. Though Giuliano da Sangallo was passionate in his support of the four-portal solution, basing his appeal upon Brunelleschi's own intentions, his opponents decided upon a three-portal structure; this was begun from the inside in 1487, but was not completed outside as it did not prove satisfactory. During the late Baroque period, the upper part was 'beautified' with a pair of lateral volutes and the bare plane was decorated with a painted architectural simulation which was still visible until fairly recently. The present smooth plaster coating is modern (1957).

The smoothness of the **side walls** is, of course, a quite different matter. These walls absorb the burgeoning strength of the rounded chapels inside, making them completely indistinguishable from the exterior, but at the same time they emphasize one of the most important and fundamental features of the building – its stereometric order. Their bareness is also very well suited to the extremely economical style of Brunelleschi's late period. The visitor

will find it a particularly rewarding experience to walk
along the outside of the side aisles looking upwards, taking
in the impressive way in which the simple and harmonious
strata of articulating forms progressively increase. In this
way, it becomes clear with what masterly skill this cruciform building is designed to culminate in the dome. – The
side wall is enlivened only by the tall windows, almost
Gothic in their proportions, with a colourful coat of arms
above each one. One can explain from earlier examples, like
the chancel of Pisa Cathedral, the fact that the window
bays are rounded and the arches above them form spherical
recesses (with the exception of the first two bays where the
arches above the windows are flat) corresponding to the
chapels inside. The rigorous logic of the building leads to a
surprise as far as the windows are concerned, for in the
corners between nave and transept two windows meet and
join – inevitably, since inside two chapels are situated at
right angles here and their windows, being at the crown of
the curve, must reach the exterior at the same point. – The
best view of the exterior is from the broad piazza-like street
(Via del Presto di S. Martino) running down the east side
of the church (the visitor is recommended to stand at the
corner of Borgo Tegolaio, 2). The building rises with great
dignity on a platform several steps above street level. The
round windows in the upper part of the side wall, which is
set back from the lower part, are there purely for their
effect upon the external appearance; they open on to the
framework above the side aisle vaulting, and consequently
let no light into the interior of the church. – Left of the
façade is the entrance to the first *court of the monastery*,
a beautiful example of the work of a successor of Vasari,
probably Alfonso Parigi the Elder, *c.* 1580. The large building that sticks out on the left with two tall Gothic windows
(tracery and glass renewed) was originally the **refectory**;
in the nineteenth century, it became the studio of the
sculptor Raffaello Romanelli (inscription plaque), then it
became a garage, and now it is a museum. The building has
been much restored. On the entrance wall are some family
coats of arms. – The **campanile**, undecorated except for the
upper storeys, uses motifs taken from the repertoire of
the Sangallo family (drawings for S. Peter, S. Biagio in
Montepulciano).

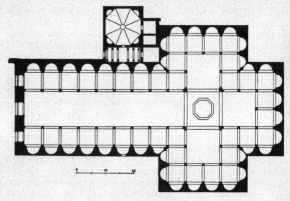

S. Spirito, ground plan

Interior (*ill.* facing p. 352). The first impression that greets the visitor as he enters the church through the façade is one of the strictest and most thorough organization. The arches are supported by columns and are based on squares, forming cubic units of space. Strips of grey macigno repeating the squares of the ground plan are let into the floor of diagonally laid square red tiles, revealing at a glance that the central axes of the column shafts stand on the corners of the basic square units. If the word 'classical' can be applied to an Early Renaissance building, it is certainly appropriate to this disciplined interior. The continuation of the columns in uninterrupted succession down one side of the nave, round the transept arms and chancel and back down the nave to the façade wall was something quite new in the history of architecture. Unlike the Christian basilica in which the columns form as it were a solemn procession from the entrance to the altar, here the chancel end is given the same order of columns as the chancel arm and the transepts. The crossing thus constitutes a kind of centralized structure, gathering the whole building together in a way which draws a further specifically Renaissance quality out of the old motif of a system of arches supported on columns. For this interpenetration of longitudinal and centralized

S. Spirito, bays of the nave

structures by means of the most economical of formal repertoires, indeed using the same forms in the one as in the other – an artistic achievement of the very highest order – can only be appreciated fully when it is seen as arising out of the Renaissance style.

The columns as well as the *chapels* which can be seen along the outside of the side aisles (raised up on two steps) are continued around the whole interior. Here a further factor comes into play which is not explicable simply in terms of

the basically geometrical composition of the building. It is
as if space has here become a living thing, as if forces
radiating outwards from the interior have caused the walls
of the church to bulge out in each bay. Similarly, in the side
aisles, each bay bulges upwards like a balloon. The contours
themselves are alive with flexible and malleable elements,
breaking like waves from the calm solidity of the dividing
half-columns to introduce the roundness of the chapels.
Notice particularly the dosserets above the capitals of the
half-columns, the capital superstructures above the dosserets,
and finally the broad springer plates cutting into the curved
contours like some harder material. Forms which are
already complete encounter others which still seem to be in
the process of growing, creating a marvellous interplay of
static and dynamic forces, both supported by an abundance
of sculptural means, revealing the masterly hand of the
church's architect-in-chief.

With such emphasis being laid on the articulation of the
larger forms, it is hardly surprising that decorative forms
are pushed into the background. The architectural members
– columns, arches and entablature – create their own effect.
Whether the capitals in fact go back to Brunelleschi's models
is questionable, but they do follow a Brunelleschian type.
(The oldest capitals are in the crossing, including three
which use actual objects as motifs. The column shafts here
are slightly narrower at the neck. These are obviously the
oldest columns – some of them being secured with metal
rings – and among them is presumably the one that was
delivered first, ten days before Brunelleschi's death in 1446.)
– The decoration of the dome with egg and dart and cyma
mouldings is too crude, clearly reflecting the style of Salvi
d'Andrea who was responsible for the erection of this
shallow melon-like structure, apparently a faithful execution of the model left by Brunelleschi (very probably Brunelleschi did not give any directions as to the decoration).
The *dome* consists of two shells, the outer rising considerably
higher than the inner, and was carefully calculated by the
architect to give the maximum effect both inside and outside. Examples were provided by Brunelleschi's Cathedral
dome and the domes of the Baptistery and S. Mark's,
Venice. The difference in height between the two shells
meant that the lantern opening was extended downwards

by means of a channel surrounded by pairs of pilasters
– an important preliminary stage towards Michelangelo's
dome of S. Peter's, and also towards the identically constructed dome of the sacristy of S. Spirito itself. – A
bright light pours through the windows of the drum. The
clarity of the architecture obviously demands a brightly lit
interior. Unfortunately, some of the tall chapel windows
have subsequently been partially or wholly covered up; the
visitor should try and imagine the building even lighter
than it is today (although Brunelleschi would have reckoned
with the first three windows on the west side being blind
because beyond them is the adjacent cloister). The clear,
graphic style of the architecture is enlivened by the colour
contrast of white and green, harmonizing with the reddish
tone of the Tuscan earthenware floor-tiles.

The *inner façade wall*, begun in 1486, is by Salvi d'Andrea.
Tall rectangular panels reminiscent of the style of Antonio
da Sangallo provide the background for the central portal,
crowned with curiously metallic-looking, springy palmettes.

Decoration It would represent a very serious misunderstanding of Brunelleschi's disciplined architecture to feel in
it the cold breath of pure rationality. On the contrary, not
only is the whole interior alive with dynamic forces, but
also with rich decoration, and where, as in the left transept
arm, this has been preserved in its original state, it creates
an impression almost of comfort. Paintings, altar-frontals
(paliotti), old frames and stained glass all evoke the visitor's
admiration, and in addition there are some elaborate pieces
from the sixteenth and seventeenth centuries. – The *round
window* in the façade wall depicts the *Outpouring of the
Holy Spirit*, c. 1500; it was made to a design by Perugino
and the faces and hands may be by his own brush. Apart
from this, the **nave** contains the least original pieces, although it has some remarkable works none the less. In the
second chapel on the right is an early marble copy of Michelangelo's *Pietà* in S. Peter's (by Nanni di Baccio Bigio,
erected 1549, signed on the band draped over the Madonna's
shoulder, with an indication that it is a copy; 'Lippi' was
the copyist's family name). – The third chapel, which is inlaid with coloured marble (the lower part 1607, the upper
early eighteenth century), contains a simple wooden statue
of S. Nicholas of Tolentino, unsuitably illuminated so that

it looks like a sort of idol. The theory that it was made to a design by Jacopo Sansovino is somewhat unlikely, as is the attribution of the two angels on either side to Franciabigio (c. 1510). In the fourth chapel is a picture by Stradanus, the *Expulsion of the Money-changers from the Temple*, signed and dated 1572. Stradanus, the first artist from the Netherlands to settle in Florence, was particularly interested in applied art (tapestries), a talent which is revealed in the genre-like details on the toppling table (compare Dürer's woodcut, B. 23). There is a sketch in the Uffizi. This composition, important for the effect of depth which it achieves and which interested Rembrandt in 1626, was engraved by Philips Galle. – The *seventh chapel* (after the side door) was decorated throughout by Passignano and is well worth attention. The altar tabernacle is one of his few architectural works. The *Martyrdom of S. Stephen*, with its smoky, atmospheric colouring (the picture is in poor condition, as are many of Passignano's pictures), is a characteristic example of the style of this late Renaissance artist, the most 'Venetian' of all Florentine painters (altar and picture dated 1602). – The eighth chapel contains Giovanni Baratta's *Tobias and the Angel*, completed in 1698, and some elaborate marble and stucco decoration. – The second chapel on the *left side* contains another copy of a work by Michelangelo, the *Christ* in S. Maria sopra Minerva, Rome, made by Taddeo Landini in 1579. – In the fifth chapel on the left is one of the numerous testimonials to the successful cooperation of Michele and Ridolfo di Ghirlandaio, *S. Anne with Mary and the Christ Child and Adoring Saints*, dating from the mid-sixteenth century.

Passing beneath a very beautiful, black tinted wooden organ gallery (second half of the sixteenth century) in the next chapel, the visitor comes first to a vestibule and then to the **sacristy**. A surprising feature of the lateral *vestibule* are the twelve Corinthian columns set very close to the wall (an idea derived from the Baptistery) and supporting a vast tunnel vault articulated with strongly sculptured coffers (containing classically-styled motifs which were originally painted). Vasari praised this ceiling decoration as being something new in Florence. The architect is presumed to have been Cronaca, but with the cooperation of Giuliano da Sangallo who built the sacristy itself, an octagonal

centralized structure which also owes a debt to the Baptistery.
In fact, the earliest exact ground plan of the Baptistery to
have survived was drawn by Giuliano. The original intention of this impressive building has been somewhat marred
by the fact that the apses on the oblique sides are covered
by enormous wooden cupboards (1584). The ground plan,
reminiscent of certain Early Christian sites (the Arian Baptistery in Ravenna), is thus no longer clearly distinguishable.
Both storeys are articulated with pilasters, and the upper
storey contains aedicule windows, all but three of which
are blind; it was the first appearance of this type of window in the Renaissance. The magnificently carved *capitals*
constitute some of the noblest decoration which the Renaissance produced (*ill.* facing p. 353). It is as if every decorative impulse in this otherwise so economical interior has
been concentrated on these small areas. They are designed
to present the broadest possible viewing surface. On the
ground floor, it is the pieces that are situated close together
that have a similar decoration and not – though this would
also make sense – those which carry a section of the entablature together (this feature, too, was inspired by the Baptistery). Individual parts of the capitals – leaves and above
all figures – are treated so independently that one is justified in speaking here in terms of the emancipation of decoration. Anyone who wishes to gain an idea of the formal
vocabulary of highly developed Renaissance decoration
should carefully examine each piece individually (binoculars
are essential!). The *sanctuary* of the sacristy constitutes an
independent centralized structure, complete in itself and
with its own articulation, added on to the main space – an
example of the Renaissance tendency towards individuality
in spatial articulation, where half-measures were unknown.
On the altar is a Cross with Mary by Butteri, *c.* 1590. The
altar-piece in the main room is by Allori, 1596.

Returning to the church and turning left, the visitor comes
immediately to the place for which Raphael created his
'Baldacchino Madonna' (for the Dei family; it is now in
the Palazzo Pitti). Today the chapel contains an eighteenth
century copy of a *Madonna* by Rosso (also in the Pitti).
There is some good *stained glass* in the window (but only
the upper part depicting *S. Bernardino* is visible). – The
next *chapel*, the last on this side of the nave, is important

S. Spirito, sacristy

as it is said to be the earliest example of the technique of inlaid work known as 'pietra dura'; it is dated 1562 on the altar
(covered by an overhanging cloth). The inscription tells us
that the stone used for the decoration came from Egypt and
England. It was the beginning of a trade in such stone which
was later to make possible the imposing Cappella dei Principi in S. Lorenzo. The originator of this art was Vasari,
with his keen interest in mineralogy. The two busts above
the inscription panels with their delicately rounded volutes
are (right, 1562) by Angelo Montorsoli, who may have been
responsible for the whole of the decoration of the chapel,
and (left, 1581) one of Montorsoli's followers.

The **crossing** is occupied by a centralized sanctuary structure which absorbs all the space and spoils the stylistic unity
of the interior, but which on the other hand does present
one of the most sophisticated examples of the 'pietra dura'
technique. The date is given as 1600 on the front corners of
the balustrade and the middle posts on the sides, but in fact
planning began in 1599 and the work was not completed
until 1609, the date in the richly inlaid floor in front which
was donated by Cosimo IV and beneath which are monks'
tombs. The design was furnished by Caccini, to whom we
also owe the choir stalls, the tall bronze candlesticks (the
round bulbous ones are by Cosimo Merlini, 1708) and most
of the figures. His four candlestick angels on the front part
of the balustrade are well visible and most impressive (the
four at the back are very much drier works by the young
Silvani). With their flat backs, their robes flowing principally in triangular folds, and the Ammanati-like innocence
of their faces, they represent particularly picturesque examples of the work of the Giovanni da Bologna succession.
The *tabernacle*, shaped like a small temple, which stands on
the altar table is by Giovanni Battista Cennini (not to be
confused with the author of the treatise on painting,
c. 1400!). The bronze *Evangelists* in the niches of this beautifully decorated little structure are from the school of Caccini, possibly by Susini. – The theory that the crucifix above
the rear of the balustrade is an early work by Michelangelo
(there is evidence that he made one for S. Spirito) is definitely wrong; this crucifix dates from the late sixteenth
century and has no connection at all with the work of the
great sculptor.

Turning to the decoration of the **left transept arm**, the visitor will find in the first chapel a beautiful *stained-glass window (Doubting Thomas, 1485–90)*, and in the second a picture by Raffaellino del Garbo in a richly carved frame. – The altar-piece in the fourth chapel, the *Trinity*, with its delicate shimmer of gold, was attributed by Jacob Burckhardt to Filippo Lippi but is more likely to be by one of the followers of Raphael. – The fifth chapel contains the *Corbinelli altar* (named after the patrons of the chapel), an important early work by Andrea Sansovino dating from *c.* 1490. The 'triumphal arch' theme of this sacramental altar was something new in Florentine art, indicative of the transition to 'classical' art. A sketch in Munich shows that initially the artist departed from the traditional idea of the altar with a tall, isolated tabernacle. The pediment, the volutes and the cleverly imitative sections on the sides are later additions (1642), as is the very fine balustrade at the front which divides off the sanctuary. In the niches on either side stand SS. James and Matthew (whose presence here in the vicinity of a sacramental altar is unusual, incidentally), and below each apostle is depicted his martyrdom. In the centre of the predella is the *Last Supper*; in the upper part, in two medallions, an *Annunciation*. Here the curious hollowing-out technique of the chisel-work is particularly evident; and certain features of the 'Virgin' (on the right) reveal the strange kinship between this style and Mannerist art. In the lunette is the *Coronation of the Virgin*, and on top is a statue of Christ flanked by candlestick angels, their garments swirling as if a storm were blowing. Two interesting features are the decoration of the pilasters and surrounding panels with instruments of torture treated ornamentally, and the dressing of the niches with porphyry – a material which at that time was only rarely used. Two small porphyry plaques also adorn the sarcophagus from which the nobly modelled *Man of Sorrows* rises in front of the altar table. – In the seventh chapel, *S. Monica* is depicted teaching some Augustinian nuns the rule of the order; both picture and predella are attributed to Botticini, end of the fifteenth century. – The altar-piece in the eighth chapel is by the same (anonymous) master as was responsible for the picture in the third chapel, and one's attention is caught by the fact that the same figure is seen standing on the left in both

S. Miniato al Monte, pulpit

Or San Michele, exterior from the north-west

pictures. This is typical of the extremely homogeneous
decoration of this transept arm, creating an atmosphere of
great intimacy.
The chancel is different, however. Here the decoration is
dominated by a feeling of lofty solemnity. Particular mention must be made of the four large late sixteenth century
altars with their imposing surrounds. In the chapels in the
end wall, from left to right: *S. Clare Communicates before
Christ* (Vignali), *Christ and the Woman taken in Adultery*
(Alessandro Allori, 1577, a work of simple clarity and full of
meaning), *The Martyrdom of the Ten Thousand* (by the
same artist, this work being characterized by the violence
of a follower of the later Michelangelo; the *predella* is
interesting because the visitor will find on the left the
Palazzo Pitti depicted in its original form with only seven
bays) and finally *The Adoration of the Magi* (by Aurelio
Lomi, its coldly venomous, glistening colourfulness betray-
ing no hint of the artist's origins in the school of Allori). –
The next chapel (in the right-hand wall) houses the only
fourteenth-century work in the church, a polyptych with a
Madonna and Child at the centre.
Turning into the **right transept arm**, the visitor will find
in the second chapel a niche, covered with a screen and
painted inside (a torch is necessary), containing the *marble
sarcophagus of Neri Capponi* (by Antonio Rossellino). The
date – 1457 – is interesting because it signifies that the
erection of the outside of the chapels must have been complete by that time, the niche occupying the dead space between the rounded chapels and Manetti's straight outer wall.
– The bright red portrait bust of a Capponi cardinal on the
left dates from 1659. – In an old frame in the fourth chapel
is a rich and colourful *panel painting* by Filippino Lippi
(*c.* 1488). – The *fifth chapel*, with its remarkable architectural decoration, is a late work by Buontalenti (1601).
Sketches in the Uffizi tell the story of its creation. Characteristic details include a pediment consisting of distorted shells.
The whole work has tremendous dignity.
The **first cloister**, erected *c.* 1580 by Alfonso Parigi the
Elder, can usually be reached from the vestibule of the
sacristy by means of a double staircase reminiscent of
Michelangelo and Vasari. Strolling through these severely
simple stylized halls, the visitor has a view of the

tortoiseshell-like dome of the sacristy which its beautiful Florentine tiles, and also of the campanile which can be studied particularly well from this vantage-point. The chapter-house on the north side, the Renaissance refectory on the west and the Augustinian 'clausura' are not open to visitors. – The remarkable **second cloister** (entrance by permission only) was erected by Ammannati on the system of the Palladian motif.

The church of S. Spirito, Brunelleschi's last work and the gem of the whole monastery complex, is a notable piece of European architecture. Inspired by the Classical period and achieving an almost physical corporeality, architecture here completes the conquest of the Middle Ages as represented by the longitudinal church building.

The **Gothic refectory** (accessible only from outside, on payment of an entrance fee) houses a small **museum** presented to the city of Florence in 1946 by Salvatore Romano.

On the right-hand wall inside are a *Crucifixion* and below a *Last Supper* (both severely damaged) by Orcagna (the right-hand section of the 'Crucifixion' and the lower parts; after 1360) and Nardo di Cione (the left-hand section). Also to be pointed out are two sea lions (no. 3) from the altar of S. Restituta in Naples, thirteenth century; the ornamental portions (foliage and details taken from architecture, bead moulding) are of great delicacy. – A Florentine vestment table (sixteenth century) stands on a modern base (no. 4). The polychrome stone *Madonna of Mercy* is an early fifteenth piece from Siena (no. 5). – The polychrome *Madonna and Child* in stone by a follower of Quercia dates from the mid-fifteenth century (no. 8). – Two Donatello-like fragments of a screen from Padua, considerably cut for re-use as steps, represent S. Prosdocimo and S. Massimo (?); once coloured, with a delicately patterned background with green inlaid enamel (no. 21). – Between them stands a remarkable portal by Natale di Ragusa, signed and dated 1471, with a beautiful frieze with portrait-like heads (no. 23). – The head of a Capuan lioness (no. 28) is extremely majestic and expressive. – There are two figures by Tino da Camaino: a somewhat weathered caryatid minus right arm, holding an eloquent pose (c. 1322, no. 38), and a similarly fragmentary adoring angel (no. 44). – The fountain surround with the Gonzaga coat of arms (1460–70, no. 41) is particularly fine.

S. Stefano (Piazza S. Stefano)

Legend has it that the first church on this site was founded by Charlemagne. The history becomes clearer from the year 1116, the date of the earliest mention of the church; by 1140 this church had a cloister. – Around 1233, what was obviously a more elaborate façade was erected and a little later the small basilica became a hall-type church of Gothic character with a tripartite chancel. – In 1585 Augustinians of the Congregation of Lecceto

*moved in, and during the seventeenth century they undertook
a thorough renovation of the church. Whether or not the man in
charge of this operation was Ferdinando Tacca, we cannot say
with any certainty. The somewhat unusual nature of the chancel
decoration makes it unlikely that he was. The Augustinians left
the building in 1783, when it became a parish church. Restorations
undertaken during the last years of the nineteenth century freed
parts of the façade which had become covered up; at the same
time Buontalenti's chancel stairs were brought here from S. Trinita and Giovanni da Bologna's high altar from S. Maria Nuova.*

Exterior Stylistically, the façade is divided into a lower
part which is Romanesque and an upper part which is
Gothic. The lower part is a simple three-portal structure
erected *c.* 1233; around the main portal is some incrustation
of a type which is unusual for Florence. An attractive
double window above each of the side doors completes the
decoration. The upper part consists of finely worked dressed
stone and contains three lofty Gothic windows (the middle
one with a beautifully graduated profile). The two side
windows are not properly coordinated with the axes of the
lower part. An original feature is the broad shallow niche
above the central window with small slender columns
supporting a pointed arch over it. All the elements – including the mask on the roof-ridge bracket – are traditional
late thirteenth century motifs.

Interior A large hall with an open frame roof, higher
towards the rear. The Baroque chancel decoration is well
worth seeing. On the left wall of the nave is an altar niche
with pointed arch uncovered in the nineteenth century. –
The decoration of the nave is predominantly seventeenth
century in character. On the right, however, beyond the
door there is a panel of the *Martyrdom of S. Peter* which is
attributed to the Master of S. Cecilia (early fourteenth
century). – On the fourth and last altar, there is a good
picture by Francesco Corradi (*Urban I and the dying
S. Cecilia, c.* 1642). – Next is a beautiful tabernacle dated
1576 with a sixteenth century wooden crucifix beneath it;
above is the organ gallery. – The rear third of the church is
higher than the rest, and consists of a square main chancel
accompanied on the right by a side chancel (the corresponding side chancel on the left has been walled in to form a
tomb). As in Ognissanti, there is another square chancel
chapel beyond the main chancel. For all the apparent

orthodoxy of the system of articulation in the chancel
(triumphal arch with Corinthian pilasters and a pediment),
the bizarre decoration is most unusual for Florence. The main
chancel arch is broken in a curious way, forming seven sides
of a twelve-sided polygon, and angular and broken elements
predominate in the other parts as well; all the mouldings
are polygonal and there is a generous use of interlocking
right angles. The constantly recurring pattern of the lily
on a chequered panel is the coat of arms of the Marchese
Bartolommei, the builder and possibly also inventor of this
decorative scheme, which reaches its curious climax in the
overloaded coffers of the monks' choir in the rear. The
chancel articulation is continued in the first bays of the side
walls, where it incorporates on either side an older round-
arched tabernacle. – The uncompleted vault of the main
chancel was closed somewhat summarily.

The chancel contains two first-rate works of art, of which
the first is the *staircase* which leads up to it. This consists of
a central portion with a flight of steps on either side, and
is one of Buontalenti's masterpieces. An interesting feature
is the way the shell forms situated to right and left of the
pilasters, with their characteristic masks which enclose the
central cartouche, approximate so closely to steps that, seen
from a distance, they seem themselves to constitute the ascent
(whereas in fact the ascending flights go up from either
side). The visitor finds it as difficult to gauge the spatial
impression of the staircase as he does the design and even
the material used, for the marble steps appear to have been
reduced to an almost doughy consistency – a characteristic
of the Florentine art of the period around 1600. Like the
staircase, which came from S. Trinita, the second masterpiece in the chancel, Giovanni da Bologna's free-standing
high altar with its tabernacle (1591), also originated from
elsewhere (S. Maria Nuova). The brightly gleaming white
marble, sparingly inlaid with colour, represents the same
flat, slender and unusually finely cut architectural style as
characterizes the architectural forms of the master's reliefs,
approaching here the style of Dosio. – Apart from these
two pieces, the visitor will find a marble sarcophagus (1642)
at the top of the chancel steps on the right (with a corresponding piece on the left, neither of them made for this
church). Above the door, in the right-hand side chancel, is

a large wooden statue of S. Thomas of Villanova (*c.* 1650).
– In the monks' choir are a lectern and (in a niche) a wooden
statue of S. Stephen, both *c.* 1650. – Descending the stairs
and turning to the left side of the nave, the visitor comes
first to an important late work by Santi di Tito, the *Donation of the Girdle by the Virgin*, 1585. In a spacious Gothic
niche on the same side stands the former high altar of the
church (decorated with inlaid 'pietra dura'), with, as a
frontal, an important *bronze relief*. This enormous unframed
panel represents as it were the stylistic extension of the
'Porta del Paradiso' (Baptistery) into the picturesque. Made
in 1656, it depicts the *Martyrdom of S. Stephen* and is one
of Ferdinando Tacca's finest works. Above the altar is
a particularly good relief, a *Madonna and Child* accompanied by angels, from the latter fifteenth century.

On request the sacristan will admit the visitor to the small
cloister where he will find a number of tombstones, a
chapel dedicated to S. Eligius and a meeting-room of the
Florentine goldsmiths.

S. Tommaso d'Aquino (Via della Pergola, between nos 8 and 12)
Santi di Tito began building this small oratory in 1568 in the middle of
an extensive site comprising living quarters and workshops and it was
soon the centre of one of the largest pilgrim hostels in Florence. During
alterations *c.* 1700 the church was given a tunnel ceiling and stucco decoration was applied to the walls. Today the church is partly given over to
secular use and only the façade can be seen – a picturesque, loosely
jointed structure, the individual parts of which appear to have been stuck
together at random without any mutual support.

S. Trinita (Piazza S. Trinita)

*S. Trinita is one of the most famous churches in Florence,
and like so many of the city's churches, it successfully con-
ceals its ancient wall behind a late sixteenth-century façade.
According to a legend which is without any evidence to
support it, the first foundation dated from the Carolingian
period; the earliest mention, however, is in 1077. This
original building was granted to the Vallombrosan Order in
1092 and it is still their principal house in Florence. In the
middle of the thirteenth century, they began to rebuild the
church in the Gothic style, but by the time the work was completed, the sixteenth century had almost run its course, so that
the last part to be built – the façade – is a typical example of
the transitional style between Renaissance and Baroque (1592).*

The story of the Gothic building is an incredibly complicated and as yet unfinished chapter of architectural history. Recent researches have still not succeeded in providing a definitive solution. The following summary should therefore only be taken as tentative. The new building (this much is certain) was begun between 1250 and 1260. By 1300 part of it was in use and there is mention of a consecration by Pope John XXII in 1327. The period from 1360 to 1405 is better documented. The erection of the chancel chapels falls into this period, so there is something to be said for the theory that the church was built from east to west. The transept and campanile must date from around 1400 and the sacristy a little later. The identity of the architects is still uncertain. The name of Nicola Pisano has been put forward, on somewhat shaky evidence, as the author of the plan.

Later changes included first of all the conversion of the sacristy into a family chapel for the Strozzi in 1418–23; this deserves particular attention as an early monument of the Renaissance style at the period when it was still struggling to shake off the Gothic past. In 1574, Buontalenti made extensive changes to the original chancel decoration and designed a more elaborate one; this was later removed and all that remains of it is an interesting staircase, re-erected in the corresponding position in S. Stefano where it can still be admired today. Buontalenti was also the architect of the façade, and between 1584 and 1593 he rebuilt the monastery buildings. — The decoration of the church was continually being modified throughout the seventeenth century and the original Gothic appearance suffered considerably in the process. In 1820 the level of the nave was raised, which entailed digging up the entire floor and destroying almost all the tombs; several windows were blocked up and some of the chapel openings were filled in with high walls. A thorough restoration became more and more urgent, and in 1881 this was undertaken, continuing until 1897. It was carried out under the auspices of the Vallombrosan Order and was done with such care and discretion that the church was given back a great deal of its former beauty. — Excavations by an American team in 1957 resulted only in the (disputed) hypothesis of a third church to be interpolated between the Romanesque and Gothic buildings.

Exterior   Judgements of Buontalenti's façade (1593–4)
vary very considerably, ranging from the highest praise to
the severest criticism. However, leaving aside the question
of its value and concentrating only on its distinctive characteristics, we must draw attention to the charming contrast
between the smooth and delicately treated articulation of
the wall surface and the projecting entablatures, throwing
caesuras of shadow across this façade which is so lively with
decoration and so strongly independent in its detail. Behind the pilasters and rising between the main portal and
the pediment are delicate band-like layers which reveal the
master's training in the school of Ammannati. Some of the
ornamental forms can be traced back to Buontalenti's earlier
work, e.g. in Pratolino, or to his drawings, as for example
the scroll-work on surrounds and cartouches that splays out
from the wall in the form of lamellae. The upper storey is
supported on either side by double volutes with feathered
wings. Two herms support the pediment. In the central panel
is a large round window. The façade is heavily weathered and
many of the details have become impossible to distinguish.
Above the middle of the three portals, in an elaborately
decorated cartouche, is a relief depicting the *Trinity*; it was
executed by Caccini with the assistance of Pietro, father of
the great Roman sculptor and architect Lorenzo Bernini.
Beyond the left-hand portal, in a niche let into the diamond-
pointed rustication of the wall of the first projecting chapel,
is a statue of S. Alessio, also by Caccini, c. 1595. The noble
wooden doors (seventeenth century) merit particular
attention.

Otherwise the building is completely surrounded by houses.
On the north side, on the Via del Parione, all that can
be seen is a dressed stone portal of 1394 with beautiful
foliate brackets in the corners and coats of arms and the
'Lamb of God' in the architrave.

The high wall to the right belongs to the **sacristy** and is
one of the most interesting examples of the beginnings of the
Renaissance style affecting a still Gothic building. Deeply
ed stone with tracery and pointed arches are set within
classically styled tabernacles crowned by pediments (1418–23).
From the first **cloister** (next entrance), the visitor has a
view of the simple rear end of the church and the main
chancel window which, although not erected until 1463,

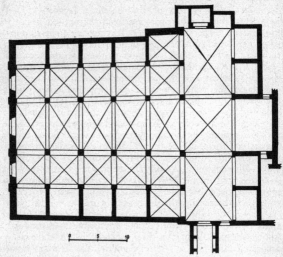

S. Trinita, ground plan

combines a Gothic scheme with Renaissance round arches.
– The short **campanile**, built 1395–6, rests on the corner
supports of the main chancel.

Interior   Inside, the church constitutes a three-aisled
pillared basilica with rows of chapels down each side and a
transept with five rectangular chancel chapels. All the vaults
are rib vaults and all the arches pointed. The painting of
the keystones of the arcades in black and white was done
only in 1885 (possibly following old traces). The five bays
of the nave grow slightly wider and higher towards the
chancel and the pillars stand fairly close together, so that
the building does not develop any great feeling of depth.
The lateral development, however, is extremely effective
by virtue of the fact that the last chapel on either side opens
not only into the nave but into the transept as well, so that
very soon after entering the church the visitor has a view of
the whole width of the richly designed chancel structure.

The rows of chapels down the side aisles – the oldest of their kind in Florence – are raised two steps above floor level; the transept is one step above, the chancel chapels another six steps and the main chancel a further seven steps above the nave floor, thus adding a precisely calculated effect of height to the impression of breadth. The whole structure is composed of austerely graceful parts. Particularly attractive is the articulation of the pillars with their bases and the simple semicircular dividing mouldings around the shafts. – The trapdoor-like grating slightly to the left of the longitudinal axis of the nave covers a staircase which leads down to a kind of crypt (see below).

Interior Decoration   On the inside of the façade wall to the right of the main portal is the very fine tombstone of *Dr. Antonio Amato* (originally it was in the nave). The deceased (with skull) is seen beneath a classically-styled baldacchino. The work is by the school of Donatello (*c.* 1440). The subject of the traces of fresco above the northern portal (by Uccello) can hardly be distinguished today. – Part of the articulation of the wall consists of the old *Romanesque façade* with its projecting frieze of five arches and the old walled-up round window. – Before each of the first two pillars is a beautiful late sixteenth-century aspersorium. **Right side aisle:** The first chapel has a Baroque decoration in the style of Silvani. On the inner face of the arch are remains of a fresco of *c.* 1400. – Second chapel: characteristic Baroque decoration in the style of Matteo Nigetti, 1642 or 1645; the painting on the altar (the *Sermon of John the Baptist*) is a late work by Corradi, *c.* 1650. – Neri di Bicci's altar-piece in the third chapel was brought here from the Uffizi in 1890 along with a number of other pieces, in order to restore something of the atmosphere of the original Gothic decoration. – The fourth chapel, the **Bartolini chapel**, is the most important one on this side. Beyond the beautiful cast-iron *screen* (*c.* 1420) is the most important *fresco cycle* by Lorenzo Monaco, painted probably between 1422 and 1425; it was covered with whitewash in the seventeenth century and is consequently damaged (the visitor can turn on the light-switch himself). Outside, in the panel above the entrance to the chapel, is the *Assumption of the Virgin*. The saints depicted on the inner face of the entrance arch are Bartholomew, John the Baptist, John the Evangelist and Paul. The seated figures in the vault segments are identifiable as Moses, Daniel, Isaiah and David. The sequence of scenes begins in the panel on the left wall with the (heavily damaged) *Expulsion of Joachim from the Temple* and his *Retreat into Solitude*. Next, in the main panel below, comes the *Meeting at the Golden Gate* before a fantastic town gleaming in reddish gold. One can only guess at the *Foundation of S. Maria Maggiore, Rome* in the lunette of the altar wall. On the left of the altar is the *Birth of the Virgin*, on the right her *Presentation*; in the main panel of the right wall, the *Marriage of the Virgin* is depicted and in the lunette her *Death*. All the painted surfaces are framed with the most delicate borders, their ornamental foliage familiar from Lorenzo Monaco's miniatures. A dentil frieze painted in perspective in the style which had been explored in Assisi leads into a terminating socle of (painted) marble. The buildings depicted in these scenes are more decorative than realistic and lend a considerable fairy-tale atmosphere to the action. It would be wrong, however, to regard this cycle as a work of pure poetic inspiration, overlooking the fact that each picture is exactly calculated as to its effect in relation to the others. Indeed, all the pictures in the bottom row (as well as the dentil frieze) are directed at a single point of view; the visitor will receive their full effect only when he stands in the middle of the entrance. This was something quite new in painting, making Lorenzo Monaco the immediate precursor of Masaccio, and the Bartolini chapel the forerunner of the Brancacci chapel (in S. Maria del Carmine). On the altar is an *Annunciation* in an old frame; it is a late work, also by Lorenzo Monaco. – In the next (i.e. corner) chapel, on the wall on the right in a former tomb niche, is a frescoed *Man of Sorrows between Mary and John* of c. 1430. The *tabernacle* on the north wall, with capitals modelled on those of the sacristy of S. Spirito, is by Benedetto da Rovezzano. It may be a fragment of an uncompleted tomb; in any case it was not brought here until 1887. The altarpiece, a *Resurrection with Saints*, is by Maso da San Friano.

In the end wall of the **right transept arm**, a simple portal with a segmental arch opens into the passage leading to the Via del Parione (in the sides of the passage are niche tombs;

paintings restored). – Left of the portal is the entrance to the sacristy, a particularly fine marble interior which is half-Gothic and half-Renaissance, using the delicate formal repertoire so characteristic of the transitional period (it was built 1418–23 for Onofrio Strozzi). The proportions, however, are still completely Gothic. A three-bayed hall, with the last bay taken up by the chancel, the sacristy gives the impression of being another, separate church. The tall walls and the triumphal arch before the chancel bay date from the period 1390–1405, while the vault is usually dated c. 1418 on account of the strange 'pyramid brackets' which support the ribs and transverse arches, and which belong to the 'transitional' style (the same feature appears in Michelozzo's work, e.g. the chancel of S. Francesco al Bosco, the vestibule of SS. Annunziata). The lovely floor is from the same period. In the first two bays this is surrounded by the girdle of the Order, delicately drawn and leaving room for the choir stalls (now cupboards). The handsome crowns of Anjou with red feathers on the sanctuary steps belong to the coat of arms of the Strozzi family. – A monument particularly worth noticing is the *lunette tomb* of the donor, Onofrio di Palla Strozzi, which is let into the left-hand wall of the altar bay and can be viewed from both sides. Possibly designed by Donatello, this work introduced an important development. It was probably the first time since the Classical period that putti were used as the principal decoration of a burial monument. Here, in the immediate vicinity of the altar, they represent angels, and the arch on which they are situated is like the vault of Heaven. In the intrados of the arch, like a still-life painting, are bunches of lilies, some opening and some still closed, in sgraffito vases (probably the earliest existing example of this technique). These, too, have a sacred connotation: they symbolize the Resurrection. The side facing the altar is the more elaborate one, with a richer cornice supported by brackets; it is this element particularly which may constitute Donatello's contribution. The rear side, however, is no less impressive, and here the visitor should not miss the solemn, weighty, heroic undertones of Piero Lamberti's style. – There is an interesting example of early Florentine weaving under glass in the sanctuary opposite the Strozzi tomb: a pluvial, a chasuble with a Byzantine-style silk lining, and the mitre

of S. Bernardo degli Uberti († 1133), a Vallombrosan
monk and bishop of Parma. In the side room is the so-
called S. Giovanni Gualberto fountain (fifteenth century);
in 1580 the water from this fountain healed many Florentines of a malignant fever.

Returning to the church, the visitor will find on his right
one of the most important pieces of Early Renaissance
architecture in Florence, the famous **Sassetti chapel**. The
fresco cycle of legends of S. Francis was begun by Ghirlandaio in 1479 and completed in 1486. The date beneath
the portraits of the donors was altered and completed at
a later date. The paintings, which are among the artist's
most successful works, combine for the first time religious
themes with motifs from contemporary Florentine life,
thus paving the way for the frescoes in S. Maria Novella.

Starting on the *outer wall*, the visitor will see above the entrance the
Sybil of Tibur expounding the majesty of Christ to the emperor
Augustus. At the top of the painted pillar on the left is the figure of
David (the female saint painted at the bottom of the pilaster on the
left belongs not to this chapel but to the next one). In the vaults are
four sibyls. – *The legend of S. Francis:* In the lunette on the left:
Renunciation of the Worldly Life. Main panel: the *Gift of the Stigmata.*
In the lunette of the altar wall: *Confirmation of the Rule of the
Order by Pope Honorius,* the event taking place on the Piazza della
Signoria (*ill.* facing p. 193). Lorenzo il Magnifico's sons Piero, Giovanni
and Giuliano, accompanied by their teacher Poliziano, are seen ascend-
ing the stairs in the foreground. On the right stands the donor Francesco
Sassetti with his younger son Federigo, the poet Antonio Pucci and
Lorenzo il Magnifico; opposite him are his three older sons, Galeazzo,
Cosimo and Bartolommeo Sassetti. This type of parallel presentation is
derived from Ambrogio Lorenzetti's fresco of S. Louis before Boniface VIII (S. Francesco, Siena). Sassetta then introduced it into the
iconography of S. Francis; he probably knew about Giotto's fresco in
Assisi of the 'Appearance of S. Francis to the Brethren at Arles'. In the
main panel: the *Raising of a Child of the Spini Family.* The event has
been transferred to the piazza in front of S. Trinita, and the visitor
can here study the Romanesque façade. A number of portraits of distinguished citizens is included, as well as a self-portrait of the artist (far
right). Below, the donor Francesco Sassetti and his wife Nera Corsi are
seen kneeling on either side of the altar. Right-hand wall: in the lunette, the *Ordeal by Fire before the Sultan,* in the main panel, the
Death of S. Francis. – In the niches on either side are two splendid black
sarcophagi in the style of Giuliano da Sangallo. – The *altar-piece* (dated
1485 on the dosseret of the left-hand pillar) depicting the *Adoration of
the Shepherds* is one of Ghirlandaio's most important works.

It is only when the visitor has gained some idea of the
inventory of the chapel decoration that he can achieve any
clear impression of its meaning and interrelation. Apart
from the exuberant inclusion of portraits of the donors,

their relations and their Medici friends, the most important
feature to be pointed out is the juxtaposition of religious
themes (in the S. Francis cycle) with pagan Classical decoration and even heathen sarcophagus demonology. The tombs
are decorated not with Christian motifs but with profane
ones. The whole of the lower part of the chapel must be
understood as a 'Classical zone'. Above a stone base with
ornamental bands are the tomb niches, and in the spandrels
of the arches above them are shadowy grisaille paintings
depicting scenes from the lives of Roman emperors copied
exactly from old coins: left of the right-hand niche, com-
manders in conference, right, an address to the troops
('allocutio'); left of the opposite niche, a triumph with
quadriga, right, troops on the march ('discursio'). In addition, there are a number of small medallions and scenes on
the niche surrounds, particularly in the case of the sarcophagus of the man on the right where centaurs are seen
gambolling and where the visitor will find, on the lower
frieze (left), putti playing and (right) a wake which is
modelled on a Meleager sarcophagus in Florence. The bull
skulls on both sarcophagi are references to the cult of the
dead. However, although many details can be explained on
a personal level (such as that the centaurs are taken from
the Sassetti device and the wake scene is a symbol of the
death of the deceased), the root of this strangely hetero-
geneous decor lies deeper. It signifies an ideology which,
making a complete break with medieval tradition, has
accommodated the world of Classical ideas within the
framework of Christian thought. Even the Sybil of Tibur's
allusion to Christ on the outer wall of the chapel is properly
speaking a scene from Classical antiquity. So are the sybils
in the segments of the vault. The key to this is to be found
in the altar-piece: in this *Adoration of the Shepherds*
(where, incidentally, figures from Hugo van der Goes'
Portinari Altar in the Uffizi have been used for the shepherds crowded together on the right) the manger for the ox
and ass is demonstrably a Classical sarcophagus, with an
inscription that reads (translated): 'Fulvius, augur of Pom-
pey, falling by the sword of Jerusalem, announces that a
godhead will arise from the coffin that houses his body.'
Here the Christian church triumphs over the heathen world.
Similarly, the two people buried here hope to rise from

their 'Classical' sarcophagi into the saintly world that unfolds above them in Ghirlandaio's colourful legend of
S. Francis. Such a train of thought was completely original,
and in fact one of its results was that the Sassetti chapel
came to be built here in S. Trinita and not in S. Maria
Novella where the family had always had their chapel before, for the monks of S. Maria Novella would not tolerate
such a heretical intrusion of Classical culture. The attitude
of the Vallombrosans was somewhat freer, and thus it became their privilege to assist in the realization of this novel
decor, and to bring into being one of the most astonishing
artistic manifestations of the new mentality of the Renaissance. – A further remarkable feature of the chapel is
how close the decorative scheme remains to the formal
framework of Lorenzo Monaco's Bartolini chapel in the
right side aisle. – The altar-piece appears slightly too large,
covering as it does part of the lower panel of the frescoed
wall. Possibly a smaller altar-piece was originally planned,
which would also explain the presence of the rather low
niche on the rear wall (behind the present altar-piece) otherwise unexplained.

In the *second chancel chapel* on this side (painted 1881–97)
the visitor will find – apart from some remains of a fresco
behind the modern altar-piece (1932) – S. Giovanni Gualberto's crucifix, a painted panel which was originally in
S. Miniato al Monte and from which the figure of Christ is
said to have bowed down towards the saint in 1003 to
approve the saint's charitable forgiveness of his brother's
murderers (only visible on Easter Day; heavily overpainted. For a long time the crucifix stood on the high
altar of the church). – In the *main chancel* is an Old Testament fresco cycle by Alesso Baldovinetti (1471–91) which
has almost completely faded. The *high altar* is an excellent
work by the school of Donatello (in the centre is the three-
headed symbol of the Trinity; the two wooden figures
standing on fifteenth century marble pillars on either side
are modern). – Next is the colourful *Usimbardi chapel*,
named after the two brothers, both bishops, who are buried
here (their busts can be seen on either side above the black
sarcophagi which in colour were inspired by the Sassetti
chapel and in form by Michelangelo's New Sacristy in
S. Lorenzo). The architecture, begun shortly after 1602 by

Ludovico Cigoli, represents a variant of the Gaddi chapel in
S. Maria Novella. It was not completed until 1638. The
fresco in the panel of the right-hand wall (the *Crucifixion
of S. Peter*) is by Giovanni da San Giovanni; the painting
below (*Peter Walking on the Water*) was begun by Cristofano Allori (the figure of Peter) and completed by his pupil
Zanobi Rossi (the picture has darkened a great deal). The
panel on the opposite side was also painted by Giovanni da
San Giovanni; below it is a characteristic work by Jacopo
da Empoli. The remarkable *bronze paliotto* on the altar is
by the northern Italian sculptor Tiziano Aspetti, whose
work was close in style to Giovanni da Bologna. – The next
chapel (decorated like the others with very faded fifteenth
century fresco remains and repainted in the nineteenth century) contains an important marble work by Luca della
Robbia, the tomb of *Benozzo Federighi* (1455–6). Made
originally for S. Pancrazio, it was brought here in 1896
(traces of the move can be seen in the slightly shortened
coffers with heads of putti in the upper intrados of the
niche; obviously the original niche was slightly deeper). A
brilliantly coloured frieze of flowers in glazed terracotta
tile surrounds the recess. On top of the sarcophagus lies the
deceased (the head was modelled from a death mask) and
on the front two angels hold a wreath bearing a funeral
inscription. Above, in three panels framed by Classical
profiles, a *Man of Sorrows* accompanied by Mary and
John, both the latter characterized by a heraldic severity.
Turning to the end wall of the **left transept arm**, the visitor
comes first to a chapel which was built by Caccini in 1593–4.
The subject of Passignano's fresco is S. Giovanni Gualberto,
whose relics are housed in an extremely distinctive shrine
(by G. B. Puccini, 1584) in the altar (usually closed). The
piece of incrustation in the floor in front is a remnant of a
Romanesque antependium. – The altar-piece of the next,
smaller chapel (built 1506–10) is a venerated picture of
Christ Carrying the Cross, with Mary, painted in the style
of Cosimo Rosselli, *c.* 1470. – If the visitor steps backwards
a little at this point and looks up, he will observe at the
onset of the vault on either side that the ribs are supported
not by brackets but by powerfully modelled busts of strong
men (there are similar ones on the inside of the façade
wall).

Turning to the first chapel of the **left side aisle**, which also
opens into the transept, the visitor will find above the altar
a wooden *Magdalen* which Desiderio da Settignano left
unfinished and which was completed by Benedetto da
Maiano (*ill.* facing p. 368), a most expressive work dating
from *c.* 1465. – On the altar of the following chapel (in
which the Florentine historian Dino Compagni is buried;
small inscription plaque lower front left) is a *Coronation
of the Virgin, with Saints and Donors* (and predella) painted
by a Florentine artist *c.* 1400. – The altar-piece of the next
chapel is an *Annunciation* by Neri di Bicci, *c.* 1450–60. Also
of interest here is the *niche tomb* of the knight, Giuliano
Davanzati, with inscription on the left wall. The figure of
the deceased (*c.* 1450) reclines on an Early Christian sarcophagus of the third century with a relief of the *Good Shepherd* in the centre and lions' heads at the corners. The
round-arched niche is framed by a pair of painted pilasters
and an arcade in the spandrels of which two angels painted
in brown on brown once prayed to a Madonna (now lost).
The niche cuts into some murals which are attributed to
Giottino (*c.* 1363). – The next chapel (by M. Nigetti, 1629–
35) is a kind of imitation of the last chapel, which Caccini
built in 1603. Nigetti's chapel was heavily damaged during
the war and robbed of all its pictorial decoration. It has
now been thoroughly restored. On the altar is a *S. Catherine
of Siena* by Ceraiolo and on the walls two handsome works
by Ridolfo Ghirlandaio (all have been well cleaned). The
picture on the left can be swung outwards, revealing a niche
with a frescoed *Man of Sorrows* (fourteenth century). –
Caccini's last chapel is architecturally much more successful.
Not only did the artist give it a beautiful inlaid floor, but
also the two marble statues, one on either side of the altar,
Peace and *Temperance*, which are among the finest works
from the period around 1600. Above the entrance arch
outside, Poccetti painted *Adam and Eve*, in the dome *Paradise* with angels dancing, and in the arch panel above the
altar *David and Elijah* (*c.* 1604). The *Annunciation* in the
altar tabernacle is by Jacopo da Empoli (signed and dated
1603). The painting on the left wall is by Pompeo Caccini
(whose family relationship with the builder of the chapel
has never been clarified); depicting the *Martyrdom of
S. Lucy*, it is one of the two works that can with certainty

Or San Michele,
e 'Quattro Coronati'
(Nanni di Banco)

Or San Michele,
'S. Mark'
(Donatello)

be attributed to this master.

The staircase in the nave leads down to a **hall-crypt** with a Gothic vault. The ground plan, a clover-leaf inside, has been built out to form a rectangle on the outside. It formed part of the Romanesque church (two old pillar bases were discovered here). In a niche in the apse is a beautiful (clay) *bust of Christ* by the school of Verrocchio, accompanied on either side by relics in strange recesses which extend as far as the outer wall layer. The little columns of Prato marble are attractive.

Leaving the church through one of the portals of the façade, the visitor will see across to the left the large **column** from the Thermae of Caracalla which was donated by Pius IV and erected in 1560 to commemorate the Battle of Montemurlo. It carries a *Justitia* by Tadda (1581; the bronze cloak is later). – The powerful **monastery buildings** erected by Buontalenti and the Parigi at the rear of the church are today occupied by university institutes and little can be seen of them. Only two **cloisters** are open to visitors.

SECULAR BUILDINGS

Bargello – National Museum (Via del Proconsolo, north of the Piazza S. Firenze)

In the heart of old Florence rises the powerful mass of the 'Palazzo del Podestà', one of the most important sights of the city. Its stout tower together with those of the Badia and the nearby Palazzo Vecchio forms a distinctive landmark in the city. This town palace surrounds like a fortress the area of an entire block.

It was decided in 1250 to erect a symbol of the defeat of the aristocracy. The building was begun in 1255, and six years later it became the seat of the 'Podestà'. The present name dates only from 1574 when the legal authorities, the 'Bargello', moved into the building. Vasari mentions Lapo Tedesco – according to legend the father of Arnolfo di Cambio – as being the architect, but there is no more precise information on the subject. The period of the Renaissance witnessed many scenes of terror, and the members of the Pazzi conspiracy met a cruel death within the palace's dark cells. In the sixteenth century, the building was restored by Baccio d'Agnolo and Giuliano da Sangallo and finally, after the Bargello administration had moved out in 1859, the National Museum was installed here to house sculptures and small works of art from the overcrowded Uffizi. Today, the architecture and the art collection form a happy combination and the visitor will find this a stimulating ambience.

Considering this enormous building – which has a threatening appearance even today – from the south, the visitor will notice two peculiarities. The palace is in three storeys clearly separated by cornices, with small pairs of windows and even smaller openings above them (we are not concerned here with the Gothic window, which was added later), and the two lower storeys are marked by double rows of powerful postholes – the remains of wooden galleries which formerly ran around the building. These constituted a characteristic feature of this hall-like building which in type was similar to the 'Pfalzen' of Germany (e.g. Goslar). The type had become popular in Italy, where it retained only one specifically Italian tradition – the tower. This brings us to our second peculiarity. There appears to be justification for the theory that this powerful tower, so restrained in its detail, belonged originally to an old family palace. Its incorporation into the new 'Pfalz'-type building was not without influence on the later development of secular architecture, giving rise to a specifically 'Italian' succession in, for example, the Palazzo Vecchio, Florence, and the Palazzo Pubblico, Siena.

Walking round the whole complex, the visitor will notice that like the later Palazzo Vecchio, it comprises several separate 'houses' joined together. The original core, which runs parallel to the Via del Proconsolo, is attached to north and south to two further buildings; the rear portion, completed in 1346, was the last to be added, creating at the same time the beautiful interior court.

The visitor first enters a huge and rather dark vaulted room which extends virtually over the entire lower storey of the original building. The extraordinary grandeur of the vaults conveys that conception of 'heroic' architecture which preoccupied thirteenth century Florence. The room is divided into two aisles by a row of pillars. The decoration is nineteenth century throughout, with the exception of a *Madonna with Saints* from the circle of Taddeo Gaddi (to the right of the door to the side room; damaged) and a fresco of the same subject (on the right at the rear).

Among the magnificent *weapons* on exhibition here are the remaining pieces of the Medici collection, one of the most important in the world until 1780 when – quite inexplicably – parts of it were sold. The gigantic cannon immediately on the right (with the head of S. Paul on the end) belongs to it. Cosimo Cenni cast it in 1638 for Ferdinando I and it was then taken to the fortress at Livorno. On the left are further cannons by Cenni, among them the *Great Falcon* with the Medici stars discovered by Galileo (made in 1620 for Cosimo II). – The majority of the remaining weapons were donated by the collectors Carrand (1888) and Ressmann (1899; he was the Italian ambassador in Paris). Among the many pieces of armour, only the most beautiful one need be mentioned, with *Neptune* and *Abundantia*, made by a Milanese master. It dates probably from the second half of the sixteenth century and can therefore hardly have been made for Charles V as has been mentioned. Some Venetian swords of the later fifteenth century catch the eye with their oriental-style shape and decoration.

The small side-room (the irregular ground plan is due to the tower which encroaches at this point) contains further weapons, including some of the heroic horsemen of Giovanni delle Bande Nere, as well as an embroidered seventeenth century saddle (middle case).

Entering the **courtyard**, the visitor will find that its archi-

tecture has a genuinely medieval stamp. The fountain in
the middle (until 1782 the town gallows stood beside it),
the pavement made up of small bricks, the staircase and the
loggia all combine to give it the appearance of a stage set.
The *staircase* (by Neri di Fioravante) once had a wooden
roof. It is interrupted half-way up by a portal; the screen
is by Giuliano da Sangallo. On the west wall of the courtyard are a number of coats of arms of the Podestà and of
the Bargello judges; inside the arcaded passage are the
(coloured) *coats of arms* of the various districts of the city
of Florence, including on the east wall a picture of the
Baptistery (under 'Cathedral district'). – Let us first have a
look at the architecture. The ground floor loggia, built
1280–90, reflects the basic Gothic style of S. Maria Novella
and S. Trinita. One antique feature is its three-sided form.
The upper storeys were erected in 1316–20, and were
modelled on the Palazzo Vecchio, then just completed. The
double windows are particularly successful, with their small
slender columns in the corners and their slightly tapering
voussoirs which provide a solid arch while at the same
time remaining an integral part of the wall. The lily in the
spandrel also derives from the Palazzo Vecchio and is equally
noteworthy.

This lovely festive frame now provides the setting for a collection
of statues. In the **lower loggia**, immediately on the left, is Danti's
portrait of Cosimo I which once dominated the south end of the
Uffizi courtyard (where it was replaced by Giovanni da Bologna's
more severe piece). It is conceived idealistically, in the manner of
Michelangelo, with the face reaching the elevated plane attained
by the seated dukes in the New Sacristy of S. Lorenzo. The ornamental armour, too, would be inconceivable without the influence
of Michelangelo. – Next comes the *funeral statue of Mario Nari*,
created by Ammannati for SS. Annunziata but never erected there
(a victory with the conquered, now in the Giardino dei Semplici,
belongs with it). The reclining figure represents an interesting
type. Using a sarcophagus to provide a kind of couch for the
deceased was a favourite motif of the Etruscans. Michelangelo
re-introduced it in his designs for the New Sacristy, but did not
in fact use it. Since Ammannati's work would seem to go back to
one of those designs, we have in fact here a Michelangelesque
concept which was not, however, executed by Michelangelo himself. Here, too, the armour shows certain similarities to that of
the 'capitani'. – Giovanni da Bologna's *Oceanus* (in the south-
east corner) once stood on the fountain in the Boboli Gardens
(where it has been replaced by a copy). One notices immediately

that each limb has its own impetus, that the body as a whole is poised in a composite movement and is not activated by a particular central force. This 'total movement' is to be understood as the correlative of the artist's 'total view', for Giovanni da Bologna was particularly concerned that a sculpture should produce a continous composition when the spectator walked around it. – Baccio Bandinelli's *Adam and Eve* group recalls Dürer's masterly engraving of the first human couple. The snake which once coiled around a tree trunk between the two figures is now missing; it is kept in the museum's repository. Each figure has its own socle and they both share a second base – a peculiarity which is difficult to account for. – Of the remaining works exhibited here, special mention must be made of three pieces by Ammannati – *Juno*, *Earth* and *Temperance*. They once belonged to an important fountain which was originally planned for the large hall of the Palazzo Vecchio (south end), was then moved to the grotto wing of the Palazzo Pitti (now occupied by the Fontana del Carciofo) and was subsequently, as we know from pictures, in Pratolino. Further pieces belonging to it are to be found in the Boboli Gardens.

On the east side of the loggia is the entrance to the **hall of Gothic sculpture**. The figures of prophets on the entrance wall were made by Simone Talenti to decorate Or San Michele. On the left wall is the original architrave of the Badia portal with the Pandolfini coat of arms at either end (by Benedetto da Rovezzano); the figure of *S. Pancras* on top does not belong to it. – In the middle of the room is a fourteenth-century Tuscan aspersorium. Beside it is a beautiful *marble support* from Pisa, consisting of three figures leaning against a column. The significance of the piece is far from clear. – At the back on the right is a very fine Venetian alabaster *Madonna and Child*. The robe is like a frozen waterfall, its gleaming gold material perfectly expressing the spirit of the early fifteenth century. – Above the entrance is the upper portion of an *avello* from S. Maria Novella.

The **next room** is devoted to Michelangelo and to the principal works of his so-called 'school'. The *Drunken Bacchus* opposite the entrance, a remarkable youthful work (1497), is the earliest extant monumental figure by the master. It was made for Jacopo Galli, who put it up in his garden of antiquities where Heemskerck came to draw it. In his right hand, the god is holding a bowl (decorated with simple rosettes; hand and bowl were broken off in the sixteenth century but the original pieces were stuck on again); on the tree stump behind him a faun is nibbling grapes. In this case, it would be wrong to look for any allusion to Classical culture beyond the actual subject itself. The visitor with a keen appreciation of artistic form will become aware of the novelty of this statue: by moving forward the shoulder above the flexed leg, the sculptor removed the supporting function of the other leg; the figure is thus uprooted, and instability takes the place of dynamic action. The result is a movement which, rather than reaching outwards, appears to circulate within the body. The body itself is at work, the search for stability entails effort; the swelling shapes are thus the expression of inner forces, the whole figure represents potential energy, and each limb is the incarnation of an impulse. Michelangelo, who was to come closer to the heart of nature and to its hidden currents than any other Renaissance master, has here given us a figure that speaks not so much of the will of man as of the unalterable character of his being, of which one aspect is his uncontrollable vitality. – The round relief with *Mary, the Christ Child and the infant S. John* must date from about seven years later. Mary's head, worked almost in the round and sitting on the top edge like the stone in a ring, anticipates the sybils of the Sistine chapel ceiling. – Two further works from the period of the sculptor's maturity complete the collection: the (unfinished) *Apollo* was made in the autumn of 1530 for Baccio Valori; the superb bust of *Brutus* was made for Cardinal Niccolò Ridolfi, *c*. 1540, probably at the suggestion of the historian Donato Gianotti. The purpose of the bust was to glorify Lorenzino, the murderer of the hated tyrant Alessandro Medici. Michelangelo probably took as his model the bust of Caracalla which is in Florence (Uffizi). – The room is further decorated with a number of late sixteenth century pieces, all of the highest quality. Particularly noteworthy are Danti's *bronze doors* for the Studiolo of Francesco I in the Palazzo Vecchio, a splendidly 'material' piece of work, and the two remarkable *marble niches* on either side of the entrance with their extremely delicate decoration (candelabra and plant motifs); they were made by Benedetto da Rovezzano for the Palazzo Salviati (Palazzo Cepparello) in the Via del Corso.

Returning to the courtyard and climbing the staircase, the visitor will come to the **upper loggia** erected above the south wing in 1320 by Tone di Giovanni (initially it had a flat wooden ceiling; when the vaulting was added later, the supporting pillars had to be strengthened inside, giving rise to this alternating order of pillars and piers which should therefore not be understood as an intentional use of the 'motif').

The principal exhibits here are works by Giovanni da Bologna, together with a number of lesser works from the same period. His *animal bronzes* are interesting; they once decorated a grotto in the Villa Castello, the villa of the Medici. There is a magnificent 'naturalism' about the eagle (falcon?) or the turkey with its picturesque plumage; the latter is surprising for the 'pastoso' style of the modelling, for Giovanni da Bologna loved a smooth finish to a greater extent than other sculptors. – In the middle of the room is the marble figure of *Architecture*, known in several copies (it also exists in bronze and gilded wax). This one was probably executed by Francavilla (compare his 'Venus' in Hartford, Conn.). One notices here a marked reduction of detail and a classicistic schematic treatment of the facial features which place the work completely outside the tradition of fifteenth century sculpture (to which Florentine artists had in one way or another adhered up until this time). A new kind of vision entered Tuscany with the arrival of this uninfluenced master from the Netherlands, a vision which saw details in a metaphorical rather than a purely concrete sense. One becomes aware of the necklace with its medallion only by suggestion; the socle on which the figure sits is not quite perpendicular; the eyes are sightless, although they are looking in a definite direction – things, rather than having a life of their own, are much more objects of the spectator's perception. The work does not take possession of the spectator but rather demands to be taken possession of by him; hence, too, the pose, 'as if for a photograph' – a characteristic of the new 'court style'. – The soaring figure of *Mercury*, famous for its solution to the problem of equilibrium, was much imitated. The figure is poised on a gust of wind perforated with a number of small holes from which originally water spouted, obscuring the optical significance of this tiny base. One can see even more clearly in this case how the work, rather than being self-explanatory, needs the spectator to interpret it. This is an excellent opportunity to study the total action of the body, which is stretched right out from toe to finger-tip, its magnificent energy developing upwards as well as forwards. The finger of the right hand is extended towards heaven, indicating the direction of the movement and at the same time terminating the vertical axis which, since it appears vertical from whichever side it is looked at, contributes greatly to the stability of this complex piece of sculpture.

The visitor comes next to a smaller room containing works by *Tuscan goldsmiths* of the thirteenth to sixteenth centuries, including processional crosses and the old base of the silver altar from the Baptistery with enamel-work by Andrea Pucci da Empoli (right), 1313. Notice particularly the lovely *reliquary cross from S. Gaggio* with the six translucent silver enamel panels on the back ('God the Father', 'Mary', 'S. John', 'S. Catherine' and two saints in episcopal dress). They are attributed to Antonio Pollaiuolo, as is the silver-plated *reliquary bust of S. Ignatius* which came from S. Maria Novella and reveals the stylistic influence of Antonio di Salvi. – The vestments for Pope Nicholas V were made in 1450 on the occasion of the canonization of S. Bernardino of Siena.

In the adjacent larger room, the visitor will find a display of *majolica*. As with the weapon collection, these pieces are all that

remains of what was once a magnificent treasure. Probably the
most important pieces are to be found in the two cases by the
window – the service with grotesques which Orazio Fontana made
for Guidobaldo II, duke of Urbino. Further pieces from Urbino
include a dish depicting the *Martyrdom of S. Cecilia* attributed
to Niccolò da Uzzano and a piece with the *Burning of Troy*
which was inspired by Raphael's 'Borgo Fire' in the Vatican
(wall-case). – Other exhibits include some Spanish-Moorish bowls
made in Valencia and some 'Medici' porcelain.

Returning to the first room and proceeding from there into the
long three-bayed room farther to the right, the visitor will find
some good fourteenth and fifteenth century *wooden figures* including (on the wall immediately on the right) a large Misericordia Madonna from Umbria, together with some smaller works of
art and the famous ivories; all these pieces are from the **Carrand
collection**. Right at the front is a fifteenth century carved ivory
chess set from Burgundy depicting scenes from courtly life. – The
following ivories are particularly worth attention: – Diptych
panel with *S. Basil* (fifth century). – A pyx with the *Adoration
of the Magi* (sixth century). – A portrait of the empress Arianna
(end of fifth century). – A *Denial of S. Peter*, a very thin panel
(with several cracks; fourth century?) depicting Christ and S. Peter
(putting his finger to his lips) on either side of an Ionic column;
above and below are some particularly fine foliage and at the
bottom there are two birds. – A book cover with the *Women at
the Sepulchre*, Ada group (ninth century), the lower part of a
Crucifixion panel in Berlin. – Two *Virtues*, Ada group (ninth
century); characteristically full forms and rich ornamentation;
probably two of the four Cardinal Virtues, holding Vice at bay
with their spears beneath a splendid arch supported by Corinthian columns. – An *Ascension* (tenth century) conceived
symmetrically and full of movement; style of the Romanos group;
the Greek inscription between the beautifully stylized trees reads:
'Men of Galilee, why stand you gazing up into heaven' – Book
cover with the *Crucifixion* (ninth/tenth century, English); on the
left, Longinus (with spear), Mary and Ecclesia; on the right,
Stephaton, John (with a beard, strangely enough) and the syna-
gogue turning away; at the bottom, six resurrected beings. – Book
cover with *King David* (ninth/tenth century), surrounded probably by his poets who are writing down the Psalms; on the right
his entourage and guard (warriors); the stars at the top on either
side are worked in an unusual way so that they are almost free
of the background. – *Peter, Preaching and Baptizing* (ninth/tenth
century, Metz style); the extremely dense lush foliage is stylistically exciting. – A diptych depicting Christ and S. Michael as con-
querors of evil (mid-twelfth century, Belgian; walrus tusk); verses
on the frame. – Pieces for a board game. – Parts of a box with
runes (other parts are in the British Museum; *c.* 800) and three

scenes from nordic mythology. – Plate with scenes from the child-hood of Christ (mid-eleventh century, Echternach) beginning with the *Annunciation* on the left. – The *Women at the Sepulchre* (eleventh century, Rhineland). – The *Death of S. Aemilianus* (c. 1070, Spanish) from the saint's tomb in S. Millan de la Co-golla; originally there were two arches but the right-hand one broke off (it is now in Boston); consequently in the spandrel only one of the two angels who receive the soul of the deceased re-mains. Above the bed-head is the cross. – The side of a portable altar with the apocalyptic Christ in the centre (eleventh/twelfth century, Italian). Christ is wearing the golden girdle, beside him are seven stars, at his feet are seven candlesticks, and in his right hand he is holding the keys of heaven and hell; the sword (now broken off) originally came out of his mouth. Plants are etched in the background of the side panels. – An *Ascension* (eleventh/twelfth century, Italian). – A French crozier (bishop with attendants, twelfth century). – An English crozier (a naked man among foliage, twelfth century). – Numerous other ivories include some from Mesopotamia and Fatimid Egypt. – A Siculo-Arabian casket of the eleventh or twelfth century (painted).

In view of the wealth of objects on display here, our survey has necessarily had to be somewhat limited, but we cannot conclude it without mentioning the famous *Tournus flabellum* which the visitor will find in a case on the left-hand window wall. It dates from the middle of the ninth century, and an inscription on the central knob gives the name of the author: 'Johel me scae (sanctae) fecit in honore(m) Mariae'. This magnificent piece of work was probably made in the monastery of Cunault on the Loire. A liturgical fan (which, however, can also be used to 'shoo away flies'), it opens in a circle of thirty-seven folds painted in three concentric circles with ornaments and saints and decorated with bands of inscription (poems). Of particular importance are the ivory carvings on the box (above) in which the fan was kept, for these six illustrations from Virgil's Eclogues point to a read-ing that must be dated earlier than all the known painted versions of the Roman poet's works; the Eclogues had always been taken to represent an anticipatory interpretation of the Christian era. – The pieces exhibited here as well as some of those in the following rooms came into the possession of the museum after 1887 through the French collector Louis Carrand. There is such a mass of material that the visitor will need a great deal of time and leisure to study it all. A notable piece from the Carrand collection is the so-called *Carrand Diptych* from the Paris School, c. 1390. Its rich tracery superstructure framing the delicate paintings (on the left, *Madonna and Child* between saints, with some interesting angels watching in the background as if through windows; on the right, the *Crucifixion*) testifies to the as yet unbroken connection – so natural to the craftsman – between painting and architecture. The whole work looks like the double portal of a cathedral, representing the way to Mary and Christ.

Through a door on the right, the visitor comes to the *chapel*, once decorated throughout with Gothic paintings. The *frescoes* recount the lives of Mary Magdalene, the dedicatee of the chapel, and S. Mary of Egypt, with additional scenes from the lives of Christ and John the Baptist. Formerly one could see 'Hell' on the entrance wall and 'Paradise' on the rear wall; in the latter the portrait of Dante was recognizable until quite recently (bottom left).

A number of other Dante pictures are exhibited here as well as some *missals* from S. Maria Nuova with extremely fine miniatures from the fifteenth century. The lower part of the walls are occupied by excellent *choir stalls* by Bernardo della Cecca (end of the fifteenth century). They and the enormous lectern came originally from the monastery of Monte Olivetano. – At the back, on the right, is the small sacristy (usually closed) containing (from Byzantium right up to the Renaissance) and, in the cases, niello 'Paces', incunabula of the art of metal engraving once attributed to Maso di Finiguerra – the inventor, according to legend, of copper-plate engraving.

The visitor then enters the long **Podestà Hall**, with a wealth of exhibits that can merely be cursorily mentioned here. Glassware, including a fourteenth century Arabian mosque lamp and a fifteenth century goblet from Murano with the *Triumph of Justice* in inlaid enamel. The cases at the sides contain ironwork, Flemish and German bronzes of the fifteenth and sixteenth centuries, oriental metalwork, astronomical instruments, jewellery (a particularly beautiful gold filigree necklace and earrings, Moslem, thirteenth century), enamel-work from the Limousin, cameos, twelfth century French gold work, fourteenth and fifteenth century Italian gold work, reliquaries – in short, such a quantity of material as almost defies description. Nor can one stress too strongly the fact that all the pieces are of the very highest quality. A particularly fine piece is the elaborate crozier signed by one Brother Willelmus.

The visitor should, however, spare a moment from the collection to look at the room itself. This was the residence of the duke of Athens. His coat of arms on the wall is a replacement, the original having been removed after the duke's banishment. The beautiful fireplace is by Lorenzo di Andrea Guardini (1478).

The adjacent **tower room** has been arranged for *tapestries* though at the time of writing only two tapestries, from the fifteenth and sixteenth centuries, are hung there.

Next comes the vast main hall which, though it forms part

of the original Bargello palace, only received its present
form after the banishment of the duke of Athens (1343).
At the same time, the magnificent south-side window, designed by Benci di Cione in the purest Gothic style, was
added. The hall was devoted to assemblies of the General
Council. It is divided by two powerful vaults resting on
wall pillars and bearing the city coats of arms. At the end
of the sixteenth century, the hall was split up into four
storeys of cells. Today the entire hall has been restored to
its original state (the last very careful restoration was in
1961) and decorated with the most outstanding pieces of
Florentine Renaissance sculpture.

In a niche on the north wall (a plaster cast of its original niche in
Or San Michele) stands Donatello's *S. George*, made in 1416 for
the armourers' guild (it was removed from Or San Michele when
it was found to be in danger of becoming dangerously weathered;
today it is replaced by a bronze copy). Donatello based his creation on a old Byzantine convention, depicting S. George as a standing figure in armour with a shield and a cloak over his left arm.
He omitted such traditional attributes as the spear and the flag,
and placed the shield not to one side but in front of the armoured
figure, which thus rises as a half-figure above a sort of bastion,
becoming fully human only in the bare unhelmeted head (above
the knotted cloak slung over the chest and partially covering the
warlike armour). The hero of the faith and the noble knight are
both represented. The compelling power that draws one's admiration derives not least from the simplicity of the statue. The
equilibrium is clear, the direction of the movement, with the bent
left arm above the shield, is distinct, the contours are unequivocal
and there is complete harmony between the body and its dress.
The significance of the term 'disegno' in the artistic world of
Donatello becomes perfectly clear when we study the almost
graphic quality of the individual limbs. – The marble *David* dates
from slightly earlier. Having been moved from the Cathedral to
the Palazzo Vecchio, it was brought here to the Bargello in the
latter part of the nineteenth century. The cloak knotted over the
chest may recall the 'S. George', yet this statue stands under other
stylistic influences than the realm of Gothic. The figure was
revised by Donatello himself. The original version may have
carried a rolled script, traces of which can be distinguished under
the right hand. In the second version, however, the idea of the
young 'prophet' gave way to that of the 'warrior': he wears a
wreath of amarant in his hair – biblical symbol of the eternal
glory of the brave – and at his feet lies the enormous head of his
enemy, the forehead split by a stone. The sling should be pictured
as connected to the hand by a rope. One cannot look at the face

without being moved to thoughtfulness; slightly cheeky, even frivolous, it is certainly Donatello's most 'restless' head. – The powerful *Marzocco lion* was created for the papal quarters in S. Maria Novella, where it was intended for the bottom of a staircase. The animal is the embodiment of controlled strength. Looking at it for any length of time, one gains the impression of being in the presence of an elder statesman, which is not so surprising when one realizes that the artist 'humanized' his lion, giving it a face in which an almost human destiny is expressed (the eyes!). – *Amor Atys* is the name given to the bronze faun-like boy with upraised hands. A later work by Donatello, it poses many a puzzling question. It represents, in any case, a Bacchic boy (it is the little ram's tail that gives him the appearance of a satyr). Originally, the outstretched hand must have held a bunch of grapes. The belt is decorated with poppy-heads (possibly an allusion to opium intoxication). – The excellent cast bronze *David* was made c. 1430–2 for a fountain in the Palazzo Medici. It is one of Donatello's most beautiful works, with a marvellous composition developing out of the circle of the victor's wreath. The head of the slain Goliath is disposed like a still-life, the plume of his helmet lapping against his conqueror's leg like a wave breaking against a cliff. The consummate craftsmanship, the thrilling inventiveness and the magnificent and meaningful decorative style of the piece all call for leisurely study. Observe, for example, the precious greaves or the triumphal procession of putti on the dead giant's helmet. – Donatello's authorship of the youthful *bronze bust* with the medallion around its neck is sometimes – and quite unjustifiably – disputed. The illustration on the medallion is based on a Platonic image of the soul: 'Psyche' is driving the chariot of life which is drawn by two horses, one full of fire and straining ahead, the other lazy and lagging behind, symbolizing the base side of man. Hence the pronouncedly Classical formation of the boy's head; Donatello probably intended his bust to be an ideal portrait in the sense cultivated by the Academy of Careggi. – Some of the works here, however, cannot be attributed with such certainty to Donatello. The walking marble figure of *John* is in fact certainly not by him; it probably belongs to the Sangallo circle. The suggestion was made in 1961 that it was by the young Michelangelo on account of the coolly precise, almost scientifically depicted anatomy (the foot, particularly). – One would be sorry to see the very realistic bust of *Niccolò da Uzzano* (on the wall next to the 'S. George') removed from Donatello's œuvre. – The *Madonna* from the Villa Goretti in Campoli is by a master who, stylistically, occupied a position between Donatello and Michelozzo. The *Dancing Putto*, however, from the baptismal font in Siena, is entirely Donatello's own.

Among the works of other masters exhibited here, particular attention must be given to Ghiberti's and Brunelleschi's famous competition pieces on the theme of the *Sacrifice of Isaac* for the Babtistery door (1402). Brunelleschi, as we know, lost the competition. If we look at his piece we can understand why: the future belonged with Ghiberti's more graphically picturesque style. The latter's reliquary of *SS. Proteus, Hyacinth and Nemesis* is also exhibited here. – Bertoldo was a pupil of Donatello. His relief with the *Battle between Romans and Barbarians* was for a long time taken as the model for many forms of movement and fighting positions; his polished craftsmanship and toy-like delicacy were also not without influence on the later sixteenth century. – Also to be pointed out are Bertoldo's *Triumph of Bacchus* and *Crucifixion,* Desiderio da Settignano's *Madonna Panciatichi,* Agostino di Duccio's multi-coloured stucco and marble *Madonnas* and the lovely *Madonna* by Michelozzo, standing out against its white and blue background. – Luca della Robbia's *Madonnas* are particularized in various different ways, but underlying each one is this artist's simultaneously grand yet simple basic conception. – Finally, we would mention Vecchietta's painted wooden statue of *S. Bernardino;* every visitor finds himself deeply moved by the naked repentance expressed in the saint's face. – By the time the visitor leaves this hall, he will have seen examples of all the many different stylistic directions – from the heroic and the Classical to the delicate and tenderly poetic – which sculpture took in the relatively short period from Ghiberti to Michelangelo. This halcyon period was not only a time of free individual development, however; it also saw the systematic formation of the sculptural style of the epoch at a time when architecture and painting had already found theirs. For sculpture can be said to have been the last of the Renaissance arts to feel the firm ties of a collective stylistic effort.

When the visitor at last ascends the stairs to the **upper floor** (from the room with the ivories), he will find first a lateral room containing masterpieces by **Benvenuto Cellini**. In the centre rise the slightly weathered figures of *Narcissus* and *Apollo and Hyacinth*. It was only in 1940 that they were found in the Boboli Gardens and recognized as being by Cellini. They are the only known large marble sculptures by the master. Wonderfully sensitive, youthful and 'romantic', they stand in the greatest possible contrast to the world of the Early Renaissance. Their dreams have a fantastic, slightly neurotic quality; the figures almost shiver as they rise. The vertical visual axis of the 'Narcissus' is a formal feature peculiar to Cellini's work. The snake on the back of the finely chiselled socle is an allusion to the youth's corruption. – The vertical visual axis also plays an important role in the two models (wax and bronze) for the *Perseus* in the Loggia dei Lanzi. – The original of the socle relief from the 'Perseus', depicting the rescue of Andromeda, is also by Cellini. Here we can point to the influence of Bertoldo's 'Battle' relief in the main hall of the museum: the idea of using vertically rising figures at the edges of the picture may have derived from there, and the standing figure with upraised arm is formally not unlike the figure at the right-hand edge of Bertoldo's work. The sudden gaping holes, however, are Cellini's invention, as are the 'eloquent pauses' full of demoniac feeling, the sudden jumps in size, the silent screams. – The large bronze *bust of Cosimo I* is a magnificent piece. It stood for a long time above the door of the fortress of Portoferraio. Many copies of it exist, including some in marble. The steely gaze of the protruding eye-balls is as suggestive as the marvellous and thoroughly elaborated decoration of the armour. – Mention must also be made of Cellini's small wax portrait of *Francesco I* (for Bianca Cappello), the bronze relief of a *dog* and the two *Ganymede* groups, incorporating portions of a Classical marble torso of Apollo. – The *della Robbia works*, embellishing the walls like beautiful colourful flowers, constitute a further attraction of this room. For the rest, we will mention only Rustici's terracotta group of fighters, which is not far from the style of Leonardo, and the same sculptor's design for Giov. della Robbia's *Noli Me Tangere*. A further room on the left contains works by the della Robbia school, those of Andrea being rather more sentimental than those of the principal master, Luca.

The adjacent Verrocchio room contains some extremely important fifteenth century works, among them Verrocchio's standing figure of *David*. In the middle of the wall opposite the window is the famous coloured terracotta *Resurrection*, made for the Medici for their Villa Careggi. The artist's power, expressiveness and verve communicate themselves directly to the visitor.

Almost an entire day is necessary for the study of the remaining pieces exhibited on this floor, and anyone who wishes to extend his knowledge of Renaissance and post-Renaissance sculptural style will no doubt want to remain even longer. Here we shall mention only the most important works. Mino da Fiesole, Antonio del Pollaiuolo and Rossellino are all represented here. In two small rooms, the visitor can admire the finest originals of Italian medals. Further on we come to works by Jacopo Sansovino and Francesco da Sangallo (notice the half-figure of Giovanni delle bande nere), then to Alessandro Vittoria's bust of *Paolo Costabili* and Bernini's splendid portrait of *Costanza Bonarelli* (the model of a fountain for Clement IX is by the same master). The famous *fireplace* on the rear wall once stood in the Palazzo Borgherini (Rosselli del Turco) (near SS. Apostoli); it was carved by Benedetto da Rovezzano. The small figure of *Morgante* for a fountain on top of the Loggia dei Lanzi has now been correctly labelled 'Giovanni da Bologna' (it used to be ascribed wrongly to Cioli).

Beyond the Cellini room, the visitor comes to a large collection of small *bronze works*, all by the finest masters. – Finally, we must not overlook *Baron Giulio Franchetti's collection* of materials in the adjacent tower room and *Gaetano Zumbo's wax sculptures* in another rather out-of-the-way room in the tower. The latter, arranged in tableaux on a sort of stage, represent scenes from the plague in Florence. Not all of them are particularly agreeable, which is why the little collection can only be seen with special permission.

Casa di Bianca Cappello (Via Maggio 26)

The house of Bianca Cappello, mistress and subsequently wife of Grand Duke Francesco I, constitutes the earliest known architectural undertaking of Bernardo Buontalenti, who gave the original building its present appearance in 1567. The grotesque bats beneath the windows are as much a part of his style as the tall elevation of the façade with the oculi beneath the roof ridge. The portal (above is the Cappello coat of arms) with its stylized rustication stands out in relief against the rest of the smooth wall, which is covered with extremely delicate 'sgraffito' decoration (designed by Poccetti).

Casa Buonarotti – Michelangelo House (Via Ghibellina 70)

Michelangelo bought this house for his nephew Leonardo; he never lived in it himself. The fact that it is still known as the 'Michelangelo house' is due to the decoration: veering between Mannerism and Baroque, it follows the traditional arrangement of the 'artist's house' and its purpose is to glorify Michelangelo. – Leonardo was the founder of a long-lived branch of the Buonarotti family whose members rose to public office and included an important literary figure (Michelangelo the Younger, 1568–1642). The last member of the family was Cosimo Buonarotti who, on his death in 1858, left the house and the collection which had been built up in the meantime to the city.

This collection, too, serves to justify the use of the term 'Michelangelo house' for it includes a number of important sculptures and drawings by the master. The decoration, however, is also worthy of the visitor's attention. Executed by Florentine artists c. 1620, it reflects in a specific way the fame which Michelangelo – as representing a certain type of artist – enjoyed during the Baroque period.

In the room where the visitor purchases his entrance ticket is an attractive della Robbia *Madonna* and a copy of the Sistine Chapel *Last Judgement* (Alessandro Allori); notice the interesting change of colouring to cooler, more clay-like tones. – The vestibule is decorated with a number of Roman fragments (note the restored *Apollo* near the stairs; on the wall opposite is an arm of the *Discobolus*), some casts by Raphael and Andrea del Sarto and a small *Cupid* by Andrea Ferrucci. Looking into the adjacent courtyard, the visitor will see on the rear wall two Roman statues of togaed figures which were found near the Porta S. Gallo.

At the top of the stairs, the visitor comes to a further vestibule containing busts of the generous donor and his wife, Rosa Ven-

dramin (by Costoli, nineteenth century). Opposite the donor's
bust is the head of an Apostle by Guido Reni. The small room off
to the left containing works by Michelangelo and followers is
dominated by Daniele da Volterra's excellent *portrait bust* of
the master. – Towards the window is the small *Madonna of the
Stairs* relief. An early work, it follows the type of the 'virgo
lactans', though it shows none of the tender sweetness of Tuscan
Madonnas, no tie of sentiment between mother and child. The
eyes of the heroine-like woman have a distant prophetic look as
if she sensed the approach of disaster. Behind her, putti are busily
occupied hanging up (or taking away?) a curtain. The halo is the
only indication of sanctity and the figure of the Christ Child
is depicted – with unusual licence – from the rear. The tragic
undertone may have been inspired by the work of Donatello, but
here it is filled with a new intensity. The low relief looks as if it
were drawn. Not all the details are complete, and the setting
remains a subject for conjecture (what, for example, is the significance of the stairs behind Mary?). The work was given to Cosimo I by Michelangelo's nephew Leonardo, and came back into
the possession of the family in 1617.

The *Battle of the Centaurs* on the opposite wall is also an early
work. At the suggestion of Poliziano, the artist depicted in this
piece the quarrel that broke out at the marriage of Pirithous and
Hippodamia. His chisel bit deeply, hollowing out the stone with
its full force. The bodies are formed almost completely in the
round. In the background, particularly near the top, are heads
with hair flying, mouths open and eyes full of terror. Here, too,
there is something of the style of the late Donatello, although
the composition as a whole is conceived on Classical lines. The
movements of the bodies demand particular attention. The visitor
should try and follow these movements through, and gain some idea
of the sculptor's aim – an aim that was to place the highest
demands upon his powers of imagination – namely, to mould all
the bodies in a single mass, and yet at the same time leave them
their individuality. The details are of the utmost charm and will
reward close study; the visitor cannot fail to be aware of the
breath of spontaneous creative strength that informs this (incomplete) piece.

The finest exhibit in the case opposite the window wall is the
model for *Hercules and Cacus* (or 'Samson with the Philistine',
a broken group of which some further fragments were discovered
recently); this may have served as the model for Bandinelli's
later group which stands before the Palazzo Vecchio. The remaining models are by disciples (based on the master's motifs).

The drawings in the adjacent room on the left by Michelangelo
have now been restored, but we will turn our attention to the
room on the right. On the window wall is the seated portrait
of Michelangelo by A. Novelli (1620). The *Apotheosis of the*

S. Pancrazio, Rucellai chapel, the Holy Sepulchre (L. B. Alberti)

S. Pancrazio, Rucellai chapel, the Holy Sepulchre,
Medici and Rucellai devices (L. B. Alberti)

Artist on the ceiling and walls was painted by various hands. On the wall opposite the windows is a *Madonna with Saints* after a design by Michelangelo. – The doors are decorated with inlaid work, using the natural grain of the wood to create fantastic figures; the artist responsible was Pietro da Cortona. – The murals, starting from the left, depict: Michelangelo presenting himself to Julius II as Florentine ambassador (A. Fontebuoni). – M. refuses to go to Constantinople (G. Biliverti). – M. shows the model of the S. Lorenzo façade to Leo X and presents him with the plan for the Laurentian Library (Empoli). – M. directs the fortification of Florence (M. Rosselli). – M. flees to Venice and is received by the doge, Andrea Gritti (V. Marucelli). – Paul III comes to M's studio to tell him to stop work on the tomb of Julius II (here fantastically depicted) and concentrate all his efforts on the Sistine chapel ceiling (F. Tarchiani; the wooden model is of the Capitoline museum). – M. shows Julius III the model for the Rota palace (F. Boschi). – M. shows Paul IV the model for S. Peter's (D. Passignano). – M. writing poetry (A. Allori). – Prince Francesco Medici allows M. to sit in his chair (C. Gamberucci). – Below this series of paintings is an equally exciting series of grisailles. Taking them in the same order, they depict: M. communicates to the ambassador of Julius II his refusal to return to Rome (J. Vignali). – M. presents himself before Charles V in Bologna (J. Vignali). – M. is jubilantly received in Florence (M. Rosselli). – M.'s mother falls from a horse (F. Furini). – M.'s death (F. Furini). – M. writing (on the left, an allegory of 'Prudence'; M. Rosselli). – M. refuses the money that Paul III offers him for S. Peter's (F. Furini). – M. lecturing to some nobles on art and philosophy (F. Furini). – Each picture reveals an element of what, in 1620, constituted Michelangelo's fame. – Equally interesting in this respect is the painting on the ceiling which celebrates the artist's genius by way of his tolerance, his four artistic virtues, his Christianity, his immortality, his capacity for work and his temperance (here, too, each picture is by a different artist). In this portrayal of Michelangelo, the emphasis is on his diplomatic character; anything which might bring to mind his 'terribilità' (such a vital ingredient in our present understanding of the man) is omitted. Next to the Studiolo of Francesco I in the Palazzo Vecchio, this room constitutes the most important and best preserved collection of the works of the Florentine masters of the period shortly after 1600.

The best way to enjoy the following rooms is to take them as a whole, savouring the atmosphere they evoke. They are full of references to and portraits of the Bunonarotti family's great ancestor, and indirect allusions to his life and work. Notice F. Boschi's beautiful paintings in the simulated doors of the first room, and also G. Finelli's bust of the poet, Michelangelo the Younger. – A small dome indicates that the next room is a chapel.

Here, too, Pietro da Cortona had a hand in the paintings. – Cecco Bravo's opportunity came in the following room. One of the finest painters of the seventeenth century, he is only now beginning to receive due recognition. In a glass case, there is a model by Pietro Tacca for the restoration of the Classical *Menelaus* group (now in the Loggia dei Lanzi). Beside it is a work from the Limousin.

Turning back, the visitor will find on the other side of the stairs two rooms containing pictures from the family's collection, including some portraits of Michelangelo, a representation of his *Leda* and two *Noli Me Tangere* after his design of 1531 (the more important one is by Battista Franco, opposite the window wall). Before leaving, the visitor should have a look at the large wooden model for the never executed *façade of S. Lorenzo*. It is attributed to Baccio d'Agnolo, but in elevation (leaving aside the detail), it comes very close to the ideas of Michelangelo.

Casa Horne (Piazza S. Jacopo tra'Fossi 6)

This Classical palace, attributed to Giuliano da Sangallo, houses the collection (now belonging to the state) of the English art connoisseur Herbert Percy Horne († 1916), comprising paintings, sculptures, furniture, drawings and a library. The beautiful capitals in the court were probably made with the assistance of Andrea Sansovino. The visitor is recommended not to miss this impressive and extremely picturesque establishment.

The three rooms of the ground floor contain small sculptures and some beautiful furniture, while the first floor comprises chiefly paintings. Particularly noteworthy are Dosso Dossi's *Allegory of Music* (with the 'ludus tonalis'; a contrapuntal work), a diptych (*Madonna with Four Saints*) by Bernardo Daddi and an unfinished *Entombment* by Benozzo Gozzoli; also further pictures by Jacopo del Casentino, Filippino Lippi, Beccafumi and Furini. – Among the drawings are some sheets by Tiepolo, a sketchbook of Salvator Rosa, some lovely drawings by Fuseli and the earliest extant sheet by Claude Lorrain. – There are also two terracotta statuettes by the school of Giovanni da Bologna. Outstanding among the pieces of furniture is an extremely rare round chair (*c.* 1350). – Catalogues (by Count Carlo Gamba) laid out in each room provide the visitor with an accurate description of every piece in this rich collection.

Conservatorio Cherubini (Via degli Alfani 80)

Founded in the early nineteenth century; rich library. The basis of the world-famous museum of antique musical instruments was the collection belonging to the unfortunate Francesco, one of the sons of Cosimo III. String instruments by Stradivari and Nicola

Amati. Instruments from the Classical period and from the Orient.
Early keyboard instruments. – Important library.

Fortezza da Basso (Viale Filippo Strozzi, north of the station)
This powerful construction (now an army barracks) was erected by
Antonio da Sangallo the Younger (who laid the foundation stone in
1534) with the help of Alessandro Vitelli and Pier Francesco da Viterbo.
The round shapes in the masonry of the outer wall are possibly either
a reference to the spheres ('palle') of the Medici coat of arms, or an
imitation of Etruscan forms such as have survived on fortresses in
Perugia, for example.

Fortezza del Belvedere
*Laid out by Grand Duke Ferdinando I and designed by Giovanni
Medici, this fortress was artistically embellished in 1590–5 by
Bernardo Buontalenti.*
Jutting like a thorn into the outskirts of the once free city,
this tyrant's fortress offers the visitor a magnificent view of
Florence. He can wander along the well-kept paths and
every now and then cast a glance into the deep vaults. The
fountain-like structure in the middle is said to have been at
one time the hiding-place of the legendary treasure of the
Medici. The graceful building at the top of the hill is laid
out quite symmetrically. A curious feature is the way the
interior is divided like a seam through its east-west axis by
the narrow staircase, an architectural principle which characterizes other Buontalenti villas such as, for example, Arti-
mino. – During the summer months, a remarkable exhibition
of frescoes is mounted here.

Hildebrand's House (Piazza S. Francesco di Paola 3)
*This is a late sixteenth century building with foundations going
back to the fifteenth century. It was purchased during the nineteenth century by the German sculptor, Adolf Hildebrand, who
created here one of the most exciting circles of German and
Italian artists. Böcklin, Fiedler and Marées (the latter sometimes
occupied a studio on the upper floor) were all habitués of the
house, as were Cosima Wagner and later the archeologist Ludwig
Curtius with his then young pupil, Wilhelm Furtwängler. Karl
Stauffer-Bern died in one of the ground-floor rooms.*
The house, with its beautiful old decoration, still belongs
to the family and can be visited on request. There is a
painting in the house chapel which stands very close to
Tintoretto. A number of reliefs by Hildebrand himself
and some paintings by his talented daughter. – In the nearby church there is a huge fifteenth century wooden crucifix which is well worth seeing.

Loggia del Grano (Via dei Castellani, at the corner of the Via de'Neri)
Built in 1619 by Giulio Parigi for Cosimo II. The market was held in
the hall and the corn was stored in the upper, enclosed part. (In 1868,
it was turned into a theatre and today it is a cinema.) The fountain
and the bust of Cosimo II above the middle arch are by Chiarissimo
Fancelli. The architecture is Mannerist, reflecting the achievements of
the school of Vasari in the flat strip-like articulation and the absence
of any other decoration.

Loggia del Mercato Nuovo – The New Market (Via Porta Rossa, at the corner of the Via Calimala)

*Originally the centre of the silk and gold trade, the New Market
became during the seventeenth century the lunchtime meeting-
place of Florentine high society. It constituted one of the focal
points of the city, being situated at the junction of several streets.
Cosimo I conceived the idea of erecting a loggia on this busy site
immediately after taking over the reins of government. The foundation stone was laid in 1547 and the building was completed
four years later. The architect was Giovanni Battista del Tasso.
– The Florentine legal archives were for a long time stored in the
rooms above the vaults. Today, the building houses a market for
goods made of straw.*

The rectangular building comprises twelve square sections
and is laid out from south to north. Twenty columns support
the vaults – domes of the type known as 'Bohemian' with
the emblems of the Medici in the keystones. Pillars stand
before the outer columns at the ends, containing scalloped
niches with pointed pediments reminiscent of Michelangelo.
The statues are modern.
The building appears rather dry from the outside, like an
overmodest piece of carpentry, but from the inside it represents a consummate use of space. Jacob Burckhardt gave
it particularly high praise in his *Der Cicerone*. The capitals
are outstanding. They occur in the same form in the tribuna
of the Palazzo Vecchio (on which del Tasso also worked).
Vasari was critical of the fact that they come too close to
the pillars at the ends (spoiling the foliage).

Bardini Museum (Piazza dei Mozzi 1)

In 1923 the art dealer Stefano Bardini bequeathed a rich collection
to the city of Florence, and it was opened to the public in his
former (nineteenth century) palace. – Surrounds from dismantled
altars from the church of S. Lorenzo in Pistoia have been placed
around the windows outside.
The collection comprises sculptures, furniture, small *objets d'art*,
paintings and tapestries, and offers the visitor the opportunity
of considerably extending his knowledge of Italian art. Here we

shall mention only a few items. In the lower sculpture room is the *Caritas* attributed to Tino da Camaino which may have provided the inspiration for Mino da Fiesole's figure of the same subject for the tomb of Marchese Ugo in the Badia; Roman marble tables; a model of the church of S. Firenze from an early stage in the planning. Beautiful wooden ceilings, some of them medieval, were brought here from other buildings.

Castagno Museum (Cenacolo di S. Apollonia; Via di XXVII Aprile 1)

The Benedictine convent of S. Apollonia, founded in 1339, is today partly occupied by the army and partly converted into flats. In the former refectory, one of Castagno's masterpieces can be seen, as well as a number of other works assembled here after the restorations of 1890 and 1910. There is a small church (closed) in the Via di S. Gallo which was extensively altered by Dosio.

If the visitor rings the bell, the curator will admit him to a vestibule containing a collection of photographs of Castagno's works and then to the tall, broad refectory with, on the right, the famous *Last Supper*. This picture came to the attention of researchers at a relatively late date, i.e. only after the secularization of the convent in the nineteenth century, when it became possible to visit it. Initially, it was attributed to Uccello, though the true author became known soon enough and the work was agreed to be one of the most important specimens of Renaissance painting. The setting goes back to fourteenth century tradition (compare Taddeo Gaddi's work in the S. Croce refectory); beneath a powerful *Crucifixion* (on the left, *Resurrection*; on the right, *Entombment*), Christ celebrates his last meal with his disciples in a box-like house painted in exactly calculated perspective, with every tile of the roof individually drawn. The picture is in an excellent state of preservation and the vivid colouring comes over clearly. The artist's energy of invention and the realistic plasticity and dramatic tension of the scene combine to make the work unusually powerful. Judas sits alone on the near side of the table, the apostles, with a great variety of facial expressions, on the other (their names are given on the steps below). The depiction of the *Passion* in the upper part shows that the artist knew of Piero della Francesca's work. This would date the fresco in the period after 1450, making it one of the master's later works.

Also to be seen here: A *wooden crucifix* by Raffaele da Montelupo (c. 1540). – A fresco (taken down) of the *Crucifixion*, one of the most important works of Paolo Schiavo. – Beside it, a lunette fresco, *Man of Sorrows*, by Castagno (c. 1450–7). – A *Crucifixion* by Castagno, an important work of c. 1453. Like the following *Crucifixion*, which is also attributed to Castagno, its original position was in the courtyard of S. Maria degli Angeli. – Along

the end wall and the opposite side wall are some *frescoes* which
were taken down from the *Villa Pandolfini-Carducci* in Legnaia,
near Florence. They depict nine famous men and women and also
count among Castagno's finest works (*c.* 1450). Those represented
are the poets Dante, Petrarch and Boccaccio, the Condottieri
Niccolò Acciaiuoli, Farinata degli Uberti and Pippo Spano, the
Sibyl of Cumae and the Queens Esther and Thomyris, regarded as
liberators of their peoples.

Andrea del Sarto Museum (Cenacolo di S. Salvi; Via di S. Salvi, in the eastern part of the city)

*This small museum is situated in the grounds of the famous
Vallombrosan abbey of S. Salvi, founded in 1048. Henry VII
resided here in 1312 during the siege of Florence. In 1529, the
abbey was partly destroyed by a riotous mob.*

The visitor first enters a long and rather dark gallery containing
numerous plaster models by the sculptor *Lorenzo Bartolini* (early
nineteenth century) which give a somewhat ghostly impression
today. Bartolini, together with Ingres and the Belgian music
historian Fétis, founded an anti-David academy in Paris. The
walls are hung with a number of sixteenth and seventeenth century pictures, including some good ones by Vasari, Rosselli and
Empoli (all labelled). On the right is a room with a large sixteenth
century fireplace; the wall font is by Benedetto da Rovezzano, as
are the numerous fragments of *reliefs* on the walls. These high-
quality pieces are from the tomb of S. Giovanni Gualberto,
destroyed by Imperial troops in 1530. – The tomb in the middle is
a plaster-cast of Jacopo della Quercia's famous *Ilaria del Carretto*
in S. Martino, Lucca. – Passing into the refectory, the visitor will
find there on the end wall one of Andrea del Sarto's principal
works, the *Last Supper* of 1522. This fresco, which counts among
the most interesting murals in Florence, is characterized by very
harmonious colouring, great naturalness of movement and an
extremely assured treatment of space. It depicts the dramatic
moment when Christ reveals his betrayer as the man who dips his
bread into the bowl together with him – Judas, the third disciple
on the right of Christ. – On the walls are some copies of works
by Andrea del Sarto, a beautiful *Man of Sorrows* (fresco) by the
master himself, and a number of works by his school, among
which Puligo's portrait of a noble lady and Sogliani's *Madonna
and Child* merit particular attention.

On the right at the end of the street is the little church of **S. Michele
presso S. Salvi.** The old building lies concealed behind a sixteenth
century portico. The panel inscribed with verses from Dante's 'Divine
Comedy' depicts the terrible death of Corso Donati, who is buried
here. – Also well worth looking at are some sixteenth century paintings inside the church, the handsome **cloister** with its fourteenth
century remains, and in the monastery area some further fragments of
reliefs by Benedetto da Rovezzano.

Museo Stibbert (Via Federico Stibbert)

*Frederick Stibbert was a Scottish officer whose collection of art treasures was presented to the city of Florence in 1906. The collection is housed in an old mansion (the **Villa Montughi**, which once belonged to the Davanzati) situated among gardens on the northern edge of the city. In the nineteenth century, the house was extended with a great display of pomp to its present palatial proportions. The collection of weapons is particularly worth the visitor's attention. The wealth and variety of the pieces here, when taken in conjunction with the Carrand and Ressmann collections in the Bargello, conjure up once again something of the splendour of the Medici armoury, which included some of the world's greatest treasures in the field of weaponry. Unfortunately this armoury, housed first in the Palazzo Vecchio and then in the Uffizi, was subsequently (in 1780) broken up and distributed by a foolish curator.*

The way the collection is presented (e.g. the massive suits of armour on their plaster horses) may seem odd to our eyes, but the visitor should bear in mind that it reflects the spirit of the period in which the collection was founded (1860), and constitutes an Italian-Scottish variant of the 'Makartstil' which has an important place in cultural history. Pictures, furniture, tapestries, musical instruments and souvenirs of war, not forgetting Marzio de Tschudy's collection of porcelain which was purchased en bloc in 1889, are all arrayed in the form of a 'display'. It is characteristic of the city's foresight that the whole collection has been preserved intact as something unique and unrepeatable.

In the entrance lobby (entrance fee) are some pieces recalling the old Pisan game, the 'bridge festival'. Continuing down the dark passage, the visitor comes to the (reconstructed) seventeenth century kitchen. Hung on the walls are harquebuses from Sardinia and swords used by the guards of the Doge of Venice. Upstairs, the visitor comes to a large drawing-room in the middle of which stands an exciting malachite table from the Napoleonic period. Like the malachite fireplace with the two candelabra (made by Thomire for the king of Westphalia), this came from the Villa Donato. The walls are hung with Flemish tapestries and a number of paintings (notably a *Susanna* and *Lot and his Daughters* by Luca Giordano, two *Flood* pictures by Jacopo Bassano and a portrait by Moroni). The condottiere on horseback near the left wall is wearing a quite unusually complete suit of fifteenth century Italian armour. – The first of the two small rooms on the right contains a choice collection of Flemish paintings (Brueghel, Ruysch, Savery, etc.) and a case of sixteenth century swords; the second, which is artificially darkened in the manner of the nineteenth century 'salon', contains some furniture and a lovely clay model. – The *Hall of the Great Cavalcade* was built during the nineteenth century in the style of the fifteenth century (architect:

G. Bianchi). Various suits of armour of Italian, German and Oriental origin are exhibited on a procession of riders; in a case at the top end of the room is the armour of Giovanni delle Bande Nere (as well as portions of the cloth lining) just as it was recovered in 1857 from his grave in S. Lorenzo. – From here, the visitor can proceed to a number of small rooms (about seventy) which are crammed with a total of more than 100,000 exhibits. The most important pieces include an *Adoration of the Child* by Neri di Bicci, two pictures by Carlo Crivelli, a portrait of a man by Cosme Tura, a sketch in oils by Tiepolo and a Roman *Caritas* by Bernardo Luini. There are a number of portraits of the Medici family and some oriental artefacts.

Museo Topografico (opposite S. Maria Nuova)

Housed in the former **convent of the Oblate nuns**, this museum provides a survey of the topographical development of the city of Florence. Numerous paintings and drawings convey an exciting picture of the city, its life and its festivals.

Opificio delle Pietre Dure (Via degli Alfani 80)

Even today, this workshop continues with undiminished activity the unique tradition of decoration known as 'Florentine mosaic' – the inlaying of precious stones. The tradition goes back to 1580, when Grand Duke Francesco I placed the Casino Mediceo, not far from S. Marco, at the disposal of some stone-workers from Milan, though the idea had already been suggested by Vasari. In 1588, under Francesco's successor, Ferdinando I, the 'Opificio' was set up as an official institution and moved to the Uffizi. In 1769, it came under the direct control of the Tuscan state and in 1796 it was moved to the former convent of S. Niccolò where it is today.

Although from the beginning the **workshops** produced tabletops, ornaments, vases and pieces of jewellery for the court, the principal object of all operations was the decoration of the Cappella dei Principi, intended to be decorated throughout with 'pietra dura' work. Today the establishment still pursues this aim, and for the rest concerns itself with restoration work which is entrusted to it from all over Italy and even elsewhere in Europe. An exciting museum provides a survey of the various possible techniques. – The still very old-fashioned workshops are grouped around a picturesque courtyard containing a vast store of precious stones, including some pieces which go back to Vasari's time.

The **museum**, which was rearranged in 1952, is on the ground floor and the first floor. It contains numerous masterpieces of the 'pietra dura' technique, to which may be added the pieces in the Palazzo Pitti, the Uffizi and the Palazzo Vecchio.

Room 1: Porphyry work. A fragment of a Roman statue (a captive), probably one of the 350 porphyry pieces that Ferdinando I had delivered from Rome in 1597 to provide material for the Cappella dei Principi. A Medici coat of arms (unfinished) supported by putti. An imitation of a Classical bust (eighteenth century) representing Alexander the Great.

Room 2: Exhibits relating to the Cappella dei Principi in S. Lorenzo. Portions of the planned but never completed high altar. An interesting model of the chapel, also a head of Cosimo I by Bernardo Buontalenti (at one stage 'pietra dura' statues were planned for the tops of the tombs in place of the present bronze figures).

Room 3: Nineteenth century pieces.

Room 4: Paintings on stone; imitations in inlaid plaster ('scagliola'). Some interesting oil paintings on a kind of marble found in Valdarno, the veining of which suggests natural backgrounds of landscapes and objects. The 'scagliola' works are the finest of their kind. The principal ones are by the Abbot of Vallombrosa, Henry Hugford. The visitor enters the next room through a beautiful portal designed by Buontalenti for his rich decoration of the chancel of S. Trinita.

Room 5: Painted models for 'pietra dura' works. A particularly fine ebony cupboard of c. 1600 (one of the earliest of the workshop's decorative pieces to have been preserved). The magnificent table near the entrance, made for the 'Tribuna' in the Uffizi, took sixteen years to complete. The central motif was designed by Bernardo Poccetti, the surrounding portions by Jacopo Ligozzi. A particularly notable piece is the so-called *Torricelli cameo* of Cosimo III in the glass case. This was cut to a drawing which can probably be attributed to Massimiliano Soldani. The model for the small relief depicting the kneeling Cosimo II is also of great interest. Designed by Biliverti and executed by Orazio Mocchi, it can be admired in its finished form (in precious stones) in the Palazzo Pitti.

Some eighteenth century sculptures decorate the **staircase** to the first floor.

The **upper rooms** contain more works including, in the middle of the room at the back, an enormous vase designed by Eduardo Marchionni. This was never completed, and was only put together in 1952 from a number of fragments. The animals, flowers and other ornaments on this vase testify to the artistic skill of the craftsmen who work here.

Orti Oricellari (Via della Scala 85)
On the site of the present **Palazzo Venturi-Ginori** are the remains of the once famous Orti Oricellari, into which (at the instigation of Bernardo Rucellai) the Neo-Platonic Academy was moved in 1498.

Both Leo X and the emperor Charles V stayed here as guests. – On written application to the porter, the visitor can inspect the large statue of *Polyphemus* (height 8.4 m) by Antonio Novelli, a pupil of Giovanni da Bologna. – On Thursdays between 10 a.m. and 4 p.m., one can visit the 'classical' sixteenth century grottoes in the Via degli Orti Oricellari; decorated with painting and sculpture in the Mannerist style, they were the scene of 'romantic' funeral cults.

Palazzo Altoviti (Borgo degli Albizzi 18)
This is of interest because of the fifteen busts of famous Florentines that adorn the façade. They were put up here *c.* 1558 by Baccio Valori. To left and right of the portal are 'Alberti' and 'Ficino'.

Palazzo dell'Arte della Lana (behind Or San Michele)
This complex, consisting of three separate houses, was begun shortly after 1300. In 1569, Buontalenti linked it to Or San Michele by means of a bridge. It housed the richest and most influential of the guilds, that of the wool-merchants, with the lamb in their coat of arms. The building was thoroughly restored in 1905. The beautiful tabernacle on the north-east corner belonged originally on the Mercato Vecchio. It contains a rather darkened picture by Jacopo del Casentino. On request, the porter will show the visitor parts of the old painted decoration of the interior.

Palazzo Bartolini-Salimbeni (Piazza S. Trinita 1)

Situated at the end of the block which lies between the Via di Porta Rossa and the Via delle Terme, this palace was begun *c.* 1520 by Baccio d'Agnolo. A certain kinship with the Palazzo Pandolfini – e.g. in the way the entablature above the windows is continued along the entire wall – suggests that Raphael's building exerted a direct influence on the design. The new and unusual arrangement of empty round niches may indeed have been modelled on Raphael's Palazzo dell'Aquila in Rome, but it may also – and this seems more likely – reflect the early stages of the Palazzo Pandolfini. The terminating cornice, as Vasari pointed out, is a faithful copy of a Classical example. With its 'Italian' (i.e. more 'Roman' than specifically 'Florentine') style, the palace is an important example of High Renaissance architecture in the period immediately preceding the intervention of Michelangelo. As such, it has always aroused particular interest among architectural historians, who have sought to recognize a certain 'Bramantesque' element in it. The columns and the pediment above the portal represented a real novelty, and one which gave rise to numerous commentaries – a fact which is alluded to in the inscription on the door lintel: 'CARPERE PROMPTUS QUAM IMITARI' (or 'It is easier

to belittle than to imitate'. According to Pliny – Nat.
Hist. XXXV. 63 – the saying was first formulated by
Zeuxis; it became well-known as a humanist maxim and
was even used, for example, by the Holbeins, father and
son). The little columns placed on top of one another in the
windows of the façade also represent an original conception. The rather flat and timid rustication is limited to the
corner pillars. Each storey recedes further from the one
below so that the corner pillars project increasingly towards
the top of the building. On the transoms of the windows
(owing to the absence of any corresponding members on
either side, the transoms appear somewhat unstable) is the
motto 'PER NON DORMIRE', a reference to the commercial
aplomb of a Siennese ancestor who had made a fortune in
silk.
The beautiful **courtyard** bears traces of 'sgraffiti' (partially
renovated). The windows on the sides have no pediments –
a further feature inspired by the Palazzo Pandolfini.

Palazzo Buini-Quaratesi (Piazza Ognissanti 2)
This beautiful early fifteenth-century building (sometimes
mistakenly attributed to Brunelleschi) is decorated with
interesting 'sgraffiti' which have been wrongly ascribed to
Andrea di Cosimo Feltrini, the leading master of grotesque
decoration in the Florentine High Renaissance.

Palazzo Canigiani (Via de'Bardi 28–30)
The site originally comprised two houses, one of which stood next to
the church of S. Lucia, in which legend has it S. Francis of Assisi met
S. Dominic. Dante, too, is said to have been the guest of the brothers
of S. Lucia on several occasions. The extremely imposing façade dates
from the fourteenth century.
The palace, together with others in the Via de'Bardi, belongs to the
transitional style between medieval and Renaissance. It is an important
building from the point of view of the history of courtyard construction, the narrowness of the site provoking an interesting adaptation of the traditional method. Once a hall stood in the courtyard
(notice on the right the walled-in octagonal pillars with their cubiform
capitals), from which an architect who was close to Michelozzo developed the present Renaissance solution.

Palazzo Castellani (Piazza dei Giudici)
This stern, compact-looking three-storeyed medieval building
(restored 1889) was from 1574 to 1841 the seat of the 'Giudici di
Rota'. Since then, it has housed the Accademia della Crusca
(founded in 1582, and devoted to the Italian language) as well as

the unique **National Museum for the History of the Experimental
Natural Sciences**, installed here in 1930. A great many of the
scientific instruments in this famous collection were once in the
possession of the Medici family.

The visit begins on the **upper storey**, where the first room contains microscopes, telescopes and some famous lenses, the manufacture of which was regarded in its day as the high point of
technical achievement. All these were used for experiments of
fundamental importance.

The next room is devoted to mathematical instruments, including
some early calculating machines. There is a fascinating eighteenth
century writing machine with an artificial hand which dips a
quill into the ink and writes a Latin sentence. In this case – and
in some others, too – it is not entirely clear whether the interest
of the piece was primarily scientific or whether a feeling for
artistic craftsmanship got the upper hand.

The third room contains electrical instruments, amongst them
some early telephones (by Reis) and the first apparatus for the
reproduction of speech (gramophone) by T. A. Edison.

The subjects of the following room are cosmography and astronomy. The central place is occupied by Antonio Santucci delle
Pomerance's huge sphere, which illustrates a certain theory concerning the planetary system; in the centre of the concentric
circles is the Earth. This priceless piece was made between 1588
and 1593 for Grand Duke Ferdinando I. Further globes and
instruments of navigation include an Arabic astrolabe from the
Carolingian period (no. 1113).

The fifth room is dedicated to Galileo and contains a number
of the great astronomer's instruments, including the lens of the
telescope with which he discovered the moons of Jupiter, which
became known as the 'Medici stars'. Preserved in a glass jar
beside it is the middle finger of his right hand (taken from the
skeleton when his tomb in S. Croce was opened in the late eighteenth century). Further extremely valuable pieces are the numerous instruments of the Accademia del Cimento, the earliest research institute for the natural sciences, founded by Cardinal
Leopoldo Medici. The extraordinarily artistic blown-glass ther-
mometers are particularly remarkable.

Further rooms contain some eighteenth century instruments for
the illustration of the laws of mechanics.

The collection continues in the rooms of the **ground floor**. The
visitor's attention is drawn particularly to the surgical instruments (notice the early pair of obstetric forceps) and the petrified
preparations of human limbs which the anatomist Girolamo
Segato produced in the nineteenth century, although the latter
will not be to everyone's taste.

Palazzo Cepparello (also known as **Salviati** or **Portinari**; Via del
Corso 4)

This spacious mansion, which incorporates some older buildings, now houses the Banca Toscana. A number of works of art decorate the interior. There is a statue of Cosimo I in armour (with an old socle; school of Bandinelli) which is well worth seeing, and also some excellently preserved frescoes by Alessandro Allori depicting the saga of Odysseus in one of the courts towards the rear; the surrounds of the frescoes are embellished with still-life motifs such as fish and birds drawn with extreme realism in the manner of Jacopo Ligozzi. The large front court (now the counter-room) reflects the architectural style of Baccio d'Agnolo.

Palazzo Corsini (Lungarno Corsini 10)

Pier Francesco Silvani and Antonio Ferri built this stately palace in the second half of the seventeenth century. Its Baroque style is closer to the Roman than to the Florentine type. The palace houses one of the richest private collections in northern Italy (part of it is open to visitors on Saturdays). Founded in 1765 by Don Lorenzo Corsini, a nephew of Pope Clement XII, the collection is devoted chiefly to seventeenth century Italian works.

Palazzo Davanzati (Via di Porta Rossa 9)

This is one of the most beautiful secular buildings of the fourteenth century in Florence. It was purchased by the state in 1950 and arranged as a museum. It offers a picture of the town-dwelling of an aristocrat during the Middle Ages. – After the Davanzati, the palace came into the possession of the Davizzi, who owned it until 1516. It was subsequently purchased by the Protonotary Apostolic, Zanobi Bartolini.

The façade is unusually tall for its width. The loggia on top wads added in the fifteenth century; the original termination consisted of a crenellated rampart projecting on corbels. The Davanzati coat of arms above the middle window of the first storey dates from the sixteenth century. Looking through the screen down the small alley which runs along the side of the palace, the visitor will see flying buttresses supporting the side walls. In the **museum**, notice particularly the *furniture*, which includes some priceless and irreplaceable pieces.

Palazzo Frescobaldi (Piazza Frescobaldi 1)

This magnificent example of Florentine Baroque architecture was designed by Cavaliere Bernardo Radi and erected *c.* 1640, along with the Baroque monastery buildings of the neighbouring S. Jacopo sopr'Arno. The ornamentation clearly reveals a kinship with the styles of Buontalenti and

Nigetti. The stately façade is decorated with portrait busts set in niches: Ferdinando I, Cosimo II, Ferdinando II (by A. Novelli, *c.* 1640) and Cosimo III (by Marcellini, 1703). – The palace was restored in 1921. During the period when Florence was the capital of Italy, it housed the Admiralty. Today it is a girls' school.

Palazzo Giacomini-Larderel (Via Tornabuoni 19)

The architect of this particularly severe palace, begun in 1580, has never been identified for certain, though critics of style agree that it may well have been Dosio. Inside, instead of a courtyard, it has a tunnel-vaulted vestibule – a solution which is unusual for Florence. The decoration of the ground floor with large windows gives the palace more the character of an imposing dwelling-house. All the detailed work is of a high level of quality.

Palazzo Gondi (Piazza S. Firenze 1)

This extremely imposing palace, begun in 1490, is one of the most important examples of the art of Giuliano da Sangallo, although it was not completed until 1874, long after the architect's death, following the example of the parts already built. Among the houses which were demolished to make way for it was the one in which the young Leonardo grew up.

Palazzo Gondi, capital

The rustication is unusual in that it becomes less pronounced with each storey, receding until it is hardly more than a kind of drawing on the stone. It appears to have been extremely carefully composed, and in the spandrels of the window arches of the middle storey the stone is cut into cruciform shapes with pointed extremities. The upper windows originally had transoms. – The **courtyard** is one of the most charming from the whole Renaissance period. The visitor will enjoy the noble, slender columns, the excellently carved capitals and particularly the staircase. The latter, ascending in two flights on the right, cleverly links the vestibule with the hall. The steps are delicately decorated, the balustrade has a delightful, balcony-like quality, and the staircase is covered with an elaborate stone ceiling. In the centre of the courtyard is an attractive fountain of the post-Vasari style (1604); the water for this fountain was drawn from the fountain in the Piazza della Signoria – a privilege granted by Ferdinando I. – Inside, on the first floor there is an important fireplace (the palace is only occasionally open to visitors).

Palazzo Guadagni (Piazza S. Spirito 7; *ill.* facing p. 369)
The palace was begun after 1503 for Riniero Dei. In 1506, it was inherited by his son Piero (who commissioned Raphael's 'Madonna del Baldacchino', now in the Palazzo Pitti but originally intended for the Dei chapel in S. Spirito). It derived its name from the Marchese Tommaso Guadagni, into whose possession it came in 1684. From the end of the seventeenth century onwards, it belonged to the Dufour-Berte family. It was the Florentine seat of the German Institute for the History of Art until 1964.
The extremely fine workmanship and the tendency towards grandeur appear to justify an attribution to Cronaca. The building is in four storeys and is dressed with plaster painted to look like masonry – a technique which remained characteristic of Florentine palace architecture from the fourteenth to the nineteenth centuries. The upper storey has been magnificently converted into an open loggia.

Palazzo Medici-Riccardi (Via Cavour, on the corner of the Via dei Gori)
Of the three monumental palaces of the Florentine Early Renaissance (the others are the Palazzo Pitti, in its original form, and the Palazzo Strozzi), this was probably the first to be built. Brunelleschi apparently furnished the first model, which was regarded as too elaborate and was rejected in favour of a model made by Michelozzo. – The simple forms of the palace have a magnificent archaic eloquence.
The history of its construction is still unclear in many details. On the basis of recent discoveries, it is thought that work began in 1444. Filarete's book on architecture, compiled between 1460 and 1464, mentions the building as being complete and decorated. Since Gozzoli painted the chapel in 1459–60, we can place the date of completion of the building slightly earlier. – Originally the palace appeared very different from the way it looks today. The two arcades to right and left of the street-corner stood open, allowing free access to the 'Loggia de'Medici' – a typical example of the

sort of semi-public room which indicated the status of the Florentine gentleman. These arcades were closed in 1517 with windows (after a design by Michelangelo) of the type known as 'kneeling windows' ('inginocchiate') because of the brackets on either side supporting the sill. — In 1659, Grand Duke Ferdinando II sold the palace to the Marchese Francesco Riccardi who extended the façade on the Via Cavour (formerly the 'Via Larga') by the addition of seven bays, modelled exactly on the existing ones. The building, which was originally square, now has seventeen windows along the front instead of ten — a fact which disturbs the general impression. A number of smaller complexes have also been added — particularly towards the rear — including what was once the gallery and is now the

Biblioteca Riccardiana, Entrance at the rear (Via dei Ginori 10) Founded at the end of the sixteenth century by Riccardo Romolo Riccardi, the library was opened to the public in 1715. It comprises more than 30,000 valuable volumes including the famous *Gesta di Francesco Sforza* with an equestrian portrait of the duke (1486), the most complete edition of the *Divine Comedy* with Landino's commentary (1481), and engravings by Baldini after drawings by Botticelli, and the *Riccardian Virgil*, an illustrated edition dating from the fifteenth century. — The adjacent **Biblioteca Moreniana** has a rich collection of ancient literature relating to Florence and numerous descriptions of festivals. — These rooms were painted by Luca Giordano and are among his most important works.

In 1715, G. B. Foggini built the main staircase of the palace. This took up a great deal of space, and involved the demolition of part of the old building.

The palace was erected on a site which belonged to the Medici family, and which extended almost as far northward as S. Marco. It has been the scene of numerous celebrations — the entry of Charles VIII in 1494, and the visits of Pope Leo X in 1515 and of the Emperor Charles V in 1536. It remained the seat of the head of the family until Cosimo I moved his household into the Palazzo Vecchio in 1540. Subsequently, it housed the mothers, widows and children of the family.

The palace was also an extremely influential centre of art and culture; the quantity of works of art lost in the successive plunderings which followed first the banishment of Piero, Lorenzo the Magnificent's son, and then in 1527 the

S. Spirito, interior of the nave

S. Spirito, pilaster capital in the sacristy

'*Sacco di Roma*' is almost unimaginable. Today almost everything has gone. A small museum attempts to revive the memory of one of the most brilliant epochs in the history of the world – an epoch of which this palace represented the hub. The chapel is the only room that still bears witness to the splendours of the past.

The palace became the property of the state in 1814, and today it houses the Prefecture. It was subjected to a thorough restoration in 1911.

The beautiful façade is an eloquent example of the nobility of the new mentality that had begun to pervade Florentine art. The three storeys are treated in a fairly individual manner, with the result that the façade can be read better in the vertical than in the horizontal sense. The lower storey of colossal rusticated blocks, some of which bear stone-masons' marks, is reminiscent of the Palazzo Pitti. A distinctive feature of the middle storey is the beautifully compact row of windows. The reason why these are not quite as high as those of the upper storey is that Cosimo the Elder, feeling himself very strongly to be a 'citizen', wished to remove the emphasis from the 'piano nobile' – the privilege of aristocrats. The small columns in the middle of the window openings bear foliate capitals of a still Gothic cut. The storeys diminish in height towards the top, and the degree of relief in the masonry becomes less marked. The façade is terminated by an enormous cornice of a distinctively 'rustic' Classical type. Most people fail to notice that the axes of the upper, windowed storeys do not correspond to those of the ground floor – a medieval touch which shows that architecture still had some way to go to achieve the fluent rhythmic and melodic qualities that characterized the High Renaissance.

Passing through the nobly constructed portal, and along a short passage, the visitor comes to the square **courtyard** with its slender columns, composite capitals and pure semicircular arches – one of the most beautiful of all Renaissance courtyards. The middle storey has three windows on either side which were obviously fitted in at a later stage of building, for the fabric of the wall still shows traces of rectangular openings with round windows above them (where these have been uncovered). The loggia at the top which is now glassed in should be conceived as being open. The wall

was painted with 'sgraffiti' by Maso di Bartolommeo; these
were restored on the basis of surviving remains, but today
they have already disintegrated again. Twelve *marble tondi*
from the workshop of Donatello (Bertoldo?) decorate the
narrow zone between the arcades and the first storey. The
one in the middle of each side represents the Medici coat of
arms; of the other eight, seven go back to cameos and the
eighth to a sarcophagus relief: 1. A youthful satyr carrying
the infant Bacchus on his shoulder; from a cameo of the
early Imperial period, now in Naples. – 2. Diomedes, with
the stolen pallium, leaping down from an altar which is
decorated with wreaths; from a chalcedony intaglio of the
early Imperial period. – 3. A bound barbarian is brought
before a commander; from the end of the Classical sarcophagus which now stands on the right before the south wall
of the Baptistery; it represents *Clementia*. – 4. A centaur
from the company of Bacchus; from a Hellenistic Roman
sardonyx cameo, now in Naples. – 5. Bacchus and his
followers find Ariadne after she has been abandoned by
Theseus; from a cameo which is now at Brocklesby Park,
Lincs. – 6. Bacchus reclining in a chariot with his arm around
the neck of a young satyr (because Bacchus is always depicted as looking effeminate, he has here wrongly been
thought to be a woman); from a sardonyx cameo of the
early Imperial period, now in Naples. – 7. A scene from the
legend of Daedalus and Icarus, shortly before Icarus takes
off (Pasiphae is seen helping on the left; the figure on the
right is a personification of the island of Crete); from a
sardonyx cameo of the Augustan period, now in Naples.
– 8. The contest between Athena and Poseidon over Attica;
from a Neapolitan sardonyx cameo. The actual significance
of these scenes was probably not clear at the time the palace
was built. Did the master of the house take such pleasure in
scenes from Classical mythology that he merely wished to
acquaint his visitors, by means of these monumental representations, with some samples of his collection of Classical cameos, without urging them to serious contemplation?
The themes depicted here, however, may have been considered suitable for the illustration of the two great Classical
philosophies – as represented by Lucretius' didactic poem
and by Neo-Platonism – which were brought to new life in
Florence by Cosimo Medici. In that case, the beginning of

the cycle (the first scene, on the right on the left-hand wall) would represent primitive man, with scenes two and three (reading towards the left) representing the ascent of the 'genus humanum' to the 'sub lege' era. The appearance of law in the third scene (with the Old Testament as the theological parallel) introduces the Neo-Platonic theme. The following scenes (up to no. 6) possibly illustrate the turning away from 'voluptas' towards 'virtus', seen reclining on a chariot which is constructed according to the symbol of the soul in Plato's *Phaidros*. The Lucretian theme reappears at the end, with the references to artistic skill and culture representing the summit of human development (E. Simon).

In the courtyard, on the axis between entrance and garden, stands Baccio Bandinelli's youthful *Orpheus* in the posture (slightly altered) of the 'Apollo of the Belvedere'. The elaborate socle is by Benedetto da Rovezzano; the symbol of the 'yoke' reveals that it was carved during the time of Leo X. – On the walls of the rooms around the courtyard is a collection of antiquities – some discovered in Rome and some in Florence – which belonged to Marchese Riccardi. According to the usual eighteenth century practice, they are set in Baroque surrounds. The most important pieces (a bearded *Head of Anacreon* after a fourth century Greek original, a bust of *Athena Parthenos* after Phidias and a *Sappho* in the style of Phidias) are currently in the repository of the Archeological museum. Of the original statue decoration, nothing remains today. This included Verrocchio's bronze *David* (Bargello), the two figures of the *Hanging Marsyas* (Uffizi; they were situated on either side of the passage to the garden) and Bandinelli's copy of the *Laocoön* group (also in the Uffizi). Cosimo I is said to have had a fountain installed in the middle of the courtyard but this has disappeared today.

The small, intimate *garden* is surrounded by a high wall; Donatello's *Judith* group once stood here, surmounting a fountain basin. It was moved to its present position in front of the Palazzo Vecchio after the 1494 expulsion of the Medici. The present layout of the garden dates from the time of the Riccardi, though the mosaic-like paving of the paths and the line of the yew hedges are restorations based on traces discovered beneath a later pavement. The four (Baroque) travertine statues in the middle are from the

Mastai-Ferretti palace in Sinigaglia; the figure above the
fountain on the right-hand end wall is Classical and the
portrait head which has been added is recent (late eighteenth century). – The loggia at the opposite end was altered
during the Baroque period, but in 1911 some old supports
were discovered in the masonry and partially uncovered.

In the main court to the right of the main entrance is the
door leading to the **Medici museum**. Founded in 1929, this
exhibition of souvenirs of the family who built the palace
and gave it its life is interesting principally for its important collection of portraits, which illustrates in a comprehensive way the somewhat confusing family tree of the
Medici (see the front end-paper of this book).

The **first room** – once Lorenzo the Magnificent's – is decorated
with tapestries made by Benedetto Squilli to designs by Stradanus;
the principal figures are Cosimo the Elder and Lorenzo himself.
On the wall to the left of the entrance is a painting by Granacci,
the *Entry of Charles VIII of France* (1494), which depicts the
palace in its original form with the open loggia on the corner.
The cases contain numerous reproductions – old views, works of
art belonging to the Medici, and inventories, particularly of the
Classical stone jars which Lorenzo had engraved with his name
(they are in the Argenteria of the Palazzo Pitti).

The **second room**, formerly the 'Loggia de'Medici' (part of the
architecture is exposed and one can see that the vault is a later
addition), contains a fountain basin by Tribolo and portraits
of the earlier members of the Medici family up to Piero and
Giovanni di Cosimo. However, the portraits are really only
faithful reproductions from Cosimo the Elder onwards. The relief
portraits in porphyry are particularly remarkable; they are by
Francesco Tadda (1497–1585), one of the first masters since the
Classical period to work this extremely hard stone. In the upper
part of the wall are two beautiful lunettes by Utens (1599) of
views of the villas at Cafaggiolo and Trebbio. – The *Madonna* in
the passage is by Filippo Lippi, an important work dating from
c. 1450. The Child is standing on a balustrade with Mary bending
down maternally towards Him (on the back is an excellently
drawn head of S. Jerome).

The **third room** honours the memory of Lorenzo il Magnifico. His
death mask (on the right wall; the inscribed and decorated base
is original) still speaks of his strong and idealistic will. In small
containers on either side are relics from his tomb (teeth) and that
of his brother Giuliano (fragments of a garment). Almost all of
the known portraits of Lorenzo il Magnifico are assembled here
(some in reproductions). The remaining portraits are of other
members of Cosimo the Elder's branch of the family. On the

window wall (left) is Vasari's famous portrait *Duke Alessandro* with its stylized pose and firm, cool colouring (powerful red). The painting in the middle of the wall (by Jacopo da Empoli) is of the marriage of Caterina Medici to Henry II of France (1533); Clement VII and François I are both present. Bronzino's *sixteen small portraits* (in copper) are particularly delicate.

The **fourth room** belongs to the grand dukes. From the strong head of Giovanni delle bande nere, the brave general who cared little for the prosperity of his house, the visitor moves past the intelligent face of Cosimo I, then that of his powerful and cunning son, coming finally to the portrait of the last male member of the Medici line, Giangastone. The curious altar-piece (by the school of Bronzino) deserves special mention: the saints in this picture of *S. Anne, the Virgin and the Christ Child* are portraits of Cosimo I and his family. The visitor will also find here the beautiful Bianca Cappello (one of the few authenticated portraits of the mistress and subsequently wife of Francesco I) and the unfortunate Margherita Louisa of Orléans (wife of Cosimo III) who, unable to forget her childhood in France, became extremely eccentric and died a lonely death in a French convent. He will also be confronted with the stupid features of Vittoria della Rovere, whose bigoted intolerance contributed to the downfall of the Medici house. Anna Maria Lodovica, wife of 'Jan Wellem' of Düsseldorf (her portrait, by Douven, hangs on the window wall), was the last of the line, and in 1743 she bequeathed all the family's art treasures to the city of Florence. Her will, containing this bequest, can be seen in the middle case; it is far and away the most important document in this room.

Foggini's staircase (with some fine statues) on the right side of the courtyard leads the visitor up to the richly decorated **chapel** on the first floor. Built by Michelozzo, this is the only room which still conveys some idea of the splendour of the original decoration of the palace. Initially, the chapel was completely square, but when the staircase was erected a second door had to be broached and this corner turned inwards. Fortunately, an important part of the frescoed decoration was preserved, although removed from its original context (the painting on the wall above the new door dates from the eighteenth century). – The chapel is decorated throughout – the ceiling with polychrome coffers, the floor with precious stones including porphyry and serpentine (the elaborately ornamented main panel matches that on the ceiling; the design leaves room for the pews designed by Giuliano da Sangallo which have been slightly altered and are today placed in a different arrangement),

the walls with Benozzo Gozzoli's *frescoes* (1459–60). Gozzoli
trained as a goldsmith, worked on Ghiberti's 'Paradise
Doors', and was at one point chief assistant to Fra Angelico.
He began these frescoes after an extended period of employment in Umbria, but at the time he was still relatively unknown in Florence. He began with the side walls of the
sanctuary, where angels, set in a paradisical landscape full
of flowers, birds, animals and some of the Medici villas,
adore the Christ Child (on the altar-piece). The *altar-piece*
itself, an early copy of Filippo Lippi's original which is now
in the State Museum, forms the focal point of the whole
decoration. The ox and ass look on from outside the
sanctuary (on the walls on either side). Around the walls of
the main room, beginning on the right of the chancel, moves
the procession of the Three Magi. Spread out up the hill is
a crowd of people with various beasts of burden including
camels. Many of the faces in the crowd are portraits (not
in every case clearly identifiable). The procession itself is
richly and elaborately accoutred and is accompanied by
exotic animals such as monkeys and hunting leopards. The
figure of the oldest king, seen riding on the wall, left is a
portrait of Josephus, Patriarch of Constantinople, who visited Florence in 1439 for the Council and died here (his
cenotaph is in S. Maria Novella). Riccardi's alterations have
cut his pale-coloured mule in half (the rest of it, together
with the page boy, is continued on the side wall of the
projecting entrance). According to an ancient tradition, the
Three Kings represented the three ages of man; hence the
one in the middle above the old entrance to the chapel (the
emperor John VIII Palaeologus, also present at the Council;
ill. facing p. 384) is a man in the prime of life, and the
youngest king (on the right-hand side wall) is hardly more
than a boy. This is Lorenzo il Magnifico, here about twelve
years old, richly dressed, preceded by two pages bearing the
sword and reliquary which symbolize the 'miles christianus',
and riding before a procession headed by Piero di Cosimo.
The crowd following him includes the painter himself, who
signed his work on his red cape: 'opus Benotii' and other
details.

These uniquely well-preserved, colourful and animated
frescoes with their lavish wealth of ornamental detail combine to make this chapel one of the most evocative interiors

in Florence. All the more astonishing is the poorness
of the lighting: not until the nineteenth century was a window broached in the rear wall of the sanctuary, sacrificing
two frescoed symbols of Evangelists (only the 'eagle'
and 'angel' high up on the left have been preserved); the
window has since been walled in again. The beautiful altar
of red marble is the original one. It was recently found elsewhere, and reconstructed according to an old description.
Opposite the chapel is the entrance to the **state rooms**,
decorated throughout in the Baroque style (not generally
open to visitors).
From the courtyard, the visitor can reach by a second
staircase the **Hall of the Seasons**, decorated during the
Riccardi period and named after an important series of
tapestries of Medici manufacture (*c.* 1650), and a **gallery**
painted by Luca Giordano which constitutes the culmination
of Florentine Baroque art. Giordano came from Naples and
preserved a Neapolitan intensity of colouring.
On the ceiling (painted 1682–3) is an *Apotheosis of the
Cardinal Virtues* and a cycle of the life of man; the latter,
with its inventive composition, its variety and its highly
developed draughtsmanship, merits a place among the very
finest examples of decorative art.

Palazzo Niccolini-Bouturlin (Via de'Servi 15)
Domenico di Baccio d'Agnolo built this palace *c.* 1550 for a wealthy
merchant, the same who was to employ Dosio to construct the Niccolini
chapel in S. Croce. Originally unplastered, the building today has a
relatively recent 'sgraffito' decoration (1854). The large loggia in the
upper storey recalls the style of Cronaca. Let into the window surrounds
are little pillars with socles and dosserets; this was the third appearance
of such a motif (after the Palazzo Pitti and the Palazzo Rucellai). – The
gentle swelling of the rusticated blocks is impressive. A lovely courtyard. – During the period when Florence was the capital of Italy, the
palace served as the British Embassy; today it houses the Chamber of
Commerce.

Palazzo Nonfinito (Via del Proconsolo 12)
Begun in 1593 for Alessandro Strozzi but left incomplete.
The ground floor is by Buontalenti and is an excellent
example of his powerful, one might almost say 'vital' style.
The portal and the upper storeys were built by Giovanni
Battista Caccini; for the second storey, he used a design by
Vincenzo Scamozzi. The courtyard was designed by Cigoli,
the staircase by Santi di Tito. – Today the building houses
the **Ethnological Museum**, founded in 1869.

Palazzo Pandolfini, system of the top storey

Palazzo Pandolfini (Via S. Gallo 74)
This unique example of Raphael's architecture in Tuscany was never completed. We know from Vasari that Raphael drew a design for the Archbishop of Troia, Giannozzo Pandolfini, to be executed by Gian Francesco da Sangallo who was sent to Florence for the purpose. When this architect died in 1530, Aristotile da Sangallo attempted to complete the work.

This unusually noble palace differs markedly from every other building in Florence. The motifs it employs, from the 'running dog' ornamental band to the shape of the windows, are Roman. The cornice is regarded as one of the most beautiful in all Italy (from the underside of the row of dentils onwards, it is made of wood). – One of the questions that puzzles researchers is whether it was intended to continue the building in this manner only above the left side of the ground floor, or whether it was to be continued correspondingly on the right, so that the door – as would be natural – should form the centre. The inscription can give us a clue: on the street side (beneath the cornice) is written the archbishop's name and on the rear side, where it can only be seen from the garden (closed to visitors), the date 1520 is given for the erection of the building 'a fundamentis'. However, we know that this cannot refer to the date of completion because of the inscription on the end, which mentions not only Pope Leo X but also Clement VII ('LEONIS X ET CLEMENTIS VII PONTT. MAXX. BENEFICIIS AUCTUS') who was not raised to the Holy See until 1523. We therefore have to assume that the front and the garden side were complete by 1520, while the end was still in a rough state, suggesting that it was intended to continue the building in this direction. The decision to preserve the half-finished building must have been taken some time between 1523 and 1534 (the year Clement VII died). A curious feature is the way the window entablature is continued along the wall, a motif which was adopted on the Palazzo Bartolini, where the panels left between the windows were even hollowed out to form niches. Since this motif, too, comes from Raphael (compare the Palazzo dell'Aquila in Rome), it is reasonable to regard the Palazzo Bartolini as a successor to the Palazzo Pandolfini, and to assume that Raphael's original design for the latter palace also included niches instead of flat panels. – There are some particularly lovely dolphin capitals in the lower storey of the garden loggia.

Palazzo di Parte Guelfa (Piazza di Parte Guelfa)
The office of the Capitani della Parte Guelfa was created in 1267 to administer the confiscated possessions of the rebel party. Around 1420, its directors began a new building, the walls of which were already several metres high when they succeeded in obtaining the services of Brunelleschi. Vasari gives Francesco della Luna, who had already worked on the Ospedale degli Innocenti, as the author of the first plan. The building was not completed.
The principal feature of the building is the main hall which extends over the whole of the upper storey, four windows long and two windows deep, with a beautiful portal and a *Madonna* lunette. It is important as the earliest example in Florence of an articulating order of pilasters. Since the pilasters on the exterior were also presumably intended to cover two storeys (i.e. including the unfinished upper storey with its round windows – or were these round openings to contain terracotta panels?), this would have constituted a kind of colossal order. Cornice and profiles are extremely delicate. In 1557 Vasari built on an addition with a staircase and the small loggia on the north side (Via di Capaccio).

Palazzo Pazzi-Quaratesi (Via del Proconsolo 10, corner of the Borgo degli Albizzi)

*The commission was given to Brunelleschi in 1430, and the palace
may even have been begun after his design, but it was actually
built by Giuliano da Maiano (1462–72) for Jacopo de'Pazzi,
who was killed in 1478 during the notorious and – for the Renaissance – epoch-making Pazzi Conspiracy. In 1843, the building
passed into the hands of the Coburg orphanage; today it houses
a social security insurance company.*

The palace is incomplete; it was to have been continued
along the Borgo degli Albizzi. It belonged to one of the
highest-ranking families in Florence, a family of Roman
origin which had moved down to the city from Fiesole and
had always adhered to the Guelf party. Studying the
façade, the visitor will find that rustication is limited to
the ground floor and even there is used in relatively small
units, with the surface of the blocks left more or less in its
natural state, giving the wall this animated appearance
which is more 'colourful' than 'robust'. The decoration of
the windows of the first storey is particularly beautiful.
The first and top storeys are both plastered and the façade
is terminated by the broad eaves of the sloping roof. The
four large windows on the ground floor were broached at
a later date (Baroque). Iron rings, flag holders and the fine
family coat of arms (apparently by Donatello; it used to
be on the corner outside, but is now on the left in the
passage) remind the visitor of the family that lived here
more than five hundred years ago. The round openings
above the top floor windows are a relatively recent addition. – In the **courtyard** the top floor loggia has been
restored. The capitals in this courtyard are particularly
beautiful. The dolphins are from the Pazzi coat of arms
and the vases with flames licking out of them refer to the
family's ancestral privilege of fetching the Holy Fire from
the high altar of the Cathedral on the Saturday before
Easter, using the 'Carro dei Pazzi'. The privilege was
granted to a Pazzi forebear who had been the first to
climb the wall at the storming of Jerusalem.

Palazzo Pazzi-Ramirez-Montalvo (Borgo degli Albizzi 24)
The design is attributed to Ammannati. An important feature
is the concentrated cartouche, which in its decorative detail
is related to the stucco ornamentation in S. Giovannino
degli Scolopi. – The patron came from Spain at the age of
thirteen as a pageboy to Eleonora of Toledo and later in

life achieved a position of high honour. Characteristic of Ammannati's architectural style were his tendency to produce a dominant central motif, and also his sculptural treatment of window surrounds and portals. – The combination of the window and the cartouche structure in the principal storey is not unlike certain of the portal solutions in the courtyard of the Palazzo Pitti. – Borghini's 'sgraffito' paintings (very much faded today) were criticized by Vasari; in four sections, they depict the virtues and their operation in human life.

Palazzo Pitti and Boboli Gardens

The piazza (in its present form Baroque), flanked by wing-like terrace buildings, slopes up towards the palace. This is one of the most imposing buildings in the whole city. It is more than 200 m long and the central part is more than 37 m high. Today it houses the world-famous picture gallery, the Galleria Palatina, as well as other museums and administrative offices.

The palace takes its name from a wealthy merchant called Luca Pitti, head of one of highest-ranking families in Florence, and the proportions which he gave it testify to his boastful temperament. The original core was erected by Luca Fancelli between 1457 and 1466, that is to say only slightly later than the Medici Palace in the former Via Larga (now the Via Cavour) which it may have been intended to rival. The old theory that Brunelleschi furnished the original design thus belongs to the realm of pure legend.

The first Palazzo Pitti consisted of the front central portion of the present building. On the ground floor, four tall rectangular windows alternated with three portals; both upper storeys contained seven windows each, situated on the axes of the ground floor openings. It may have been possible to walk around on the flat roof.

In 1550 Eleonora of Toledo, wife of Cosimo I, purchased the site. By that time, it had become somewhat neglected. Ten years later Ammannati was commissioned to redesign it. He modified the façade by replacing the side portals with large windows (which later served as the model for other façade windows) and built the courtyard. Giulio Parigi took over as architect in 1592, and in 1620 he extended the

façade by adding three further window bays on to either
side. In 1640, his son Alfonso extended the whole building
to its present proportions. – The decoration of the interior
naturally had to keep pace with the enlargements. In the
last years of the sixteenth century, Poccetti painted first the
loggia on the 'Cortile della Fama' and then the 'Sala di
Bona', depicting the naval achievements of the Grand
Dukes. Later, on the occasion of the marriage of Ferdinando II and Vittoria della Rovere (1637), Giovanni da
San Giovanni, Francesco Furini, Ottavio Vannini and
Cecco Bravo decorated the walls of the first rooms on the
ground floor (now the Argenteria) with allegorical scenes,
while Colonna and Mitelli contributed architectural views.
Volterrano painted the ceiling of the 'Hall of Allegories' on the first floor; Pietro da Cortona painted the
'Sala della Stufa' (assisted by Cirro Ferri) and the ceilings
of the grandducal chambers. It was in these parts of the
palace that the pictures which were later to form the core
of the Galleria Palatina were assembled under Cosimo III.
The eighteenth century brought further extensions to this
already fairly large complex. In 1764, under the Lothringian
grand dukes, Marshal Botta (the governor) commissioned
Ruggieri to design the terrace wings that jut out towards
the west. He began with the one at the south end. In 1766
Pellegrini designed a chapel (never completed). In 1784 the
northern terrace wing was begun; it was not completed,
however, until 1819. The architect was Paoletti, who kept to
the old design. A further addition was the 'Meridiana', a
kind of small summer palace which adjoins to the south-east
with a view out over the Boboli Gardens; this was designed
by Paoletti himself in the Neo-Classical style. It was continued by Poccianti, who also erected the façade. Finally,
in 1896, the staircase on the north side (the visitor can reach
this via the 'Porta del Bacco') was added; this leads up to
what is now the entrance to the Galleria Palatina on the
upper floor (architect: Luigi del Moro).
At the end of the eighteenth century, Giuseppe Maria
Terreni frescoed the 'Sala delle Nicchie' and the brothers
Albertolli decorated the large ball-room (the 'Sala Bianca',
today used as a concert hall) with delicate stucco-work. The
nineteenth century brought about no interruption to the
continuity of the work, but on the contrary was marked by

particularly rich artistic contributions. The Palazzo Pitti
offers the visitor an unusual opportunity of becoming
acquainted with both 'Academic' and 'Romantic' painting,
which were particularly fruitful in Italy. These more recent
fresco painters include – to mention only the most important
names – Luigi Sabatelli, Pietro Benvenuti, Giuseppe Colignon and Cacialli, of whom the last-named, as architect,
was responsible for co-ordinating the work.

The palace, however, is decorated not only with paintings
but with statues as well. Cosimo I himself began collecting
Classical marbles from Rome and also commissioned (as did
his successors) contemporary sculptors such as Giovanni da
Bologna, Bandinelli, Valerio Cioli and Vincenzo de'Rossi.
Corradi's 'Moses', surrounded with figures by Novelli and
Pieratti, dominates the grotto in the courtyard; the delightful putti in the basin are by Giambattista del Tadda. The
large structure above the grotto originally bore Ammannati's
fountain from the Palazzo Vecchio, until it was replaced
by the present many-figured composition by Susini, the so-
called 'Fontana del Carciofo'.

The problem of giving a Baroque 'treatment' to the front
of the palace never ceased to preoccupy artists, and there
are in existence numerous designs for such a project, going
right back to Buontalenti. The construction of the piazza
itself also required a great deal of thought. Buontalenti's
suggestion was to have pavilions at the sides, with curved
flights of stairs and fountains (see the series of drawings in
the Uffizi).

Last but not least, let us recall some of the important dates
in the history of this enormous building. In 1657, Cardinal
Leopoldo founded here the Accademia del Cimento, the
first modern society for scientific research. From 1864 until
1871, while Florence was the capital of Italy, King Victor
Emmanuel II lived here. In 1914, a museum of modern art
(the 'Galleria d'Arte Moderna') was opened on the top
floor, which since the eighteenth century had housed the
Biblioteca Palatina. After 1918 the Argenteria was installed
on the ground floor, assembling in one place the many
scattered collections of gold masterpieces and jewellery (all
originally from the possessions of the Medici). In 1919 both
the Palazzo Pitti and the Boboli Gardens came under the
direction of the Ministry of Education, and since that date

they have both been open to the public.

As the visitor approaches the enormous entrance portal from
the street along the bottom of the piazza, the structure of
the building gradually unfolds before him. It becomes
apparent that each storey is set back some considerable way
from the one below. Standing immediately in front of the
portal and looking up, the visitor can follow the lively
undulating movement of the rusticated blocks. The original
building consisted of only seven bays, and one can see the
joints on either side in the smooth narrow base which
supports the rusticated masonry (the visitor can gain a good
idea of the original appearance of the building if he walks
down the 'Strucciolo' leading into the other side of the
piazza and stops at the point where these seven bays become
visible). – The only regular rhythm in the articulation of the
façade is provided by the tall windows with their slightly
tapering voussoirs against the inner faces of which are
set smooth pillars of dressed stone (compare the use of the
same motif on the Palazzo Rucellai). The arches of the
ground floor were filled with windows following a design
by Ammannati.

The *courtyard* represents one of the most important examples of Mannerist architecture in Florence. Ammannati,
who had already worked in Rome on the Villa di Papa
Giulio without producing any noticeable signs of an individual style, suddenly emerged here for the first time as
the great architect who Vasari, Borghini and Baldinucci had
always recognized him to be. Compared with the freely
picturesque style of the Villa Giulia, this is a more compact
and very much more severe type of architecture. If we were
to attempt to describe this courtyard with one word, it
would be the word 'rational'. The impression it conveys is
one of high tension, so that after a while the visitor feels as
if he is wearing a coat of mail. 'Mannerism' has no relation
to 'caprice': here it is founded on 'system'. The basis is the
traditional order of columns: Doric (or more exactly Tuscan) on the ground floor, Ionic above that and Corinthian
at the top. All three storeys are rusticated. On the ground
floor, the blocks of masonry are set very close together; on
the middle storey they are disposed more loosely, with
larger spaces between them; the blocks on the top storey,
moreover, have a shallower profile. This rustication is

subject to a strict discipline. On the middle storey, the individual blocks are cut at right angles with sharp edges. The effect on the eye is quite different from the quasi-natural form of the exterior façade or the sinister rustication that covers Giulio Romano's Palazzo del Te in Mantua with its rampant bristling growth. – Part of the building's rationality of style lies in the fact that every ambiguity is calculated. The columns are set half-way into the wall, and support an extremely plastic entablature. Superimposed on the wall surface and columns, and blurring the difference between them, is the rustication. 'Column' partakes something of the character of 'wall' and vice versa; on the one hand the wall lies behind the columns, but on the other hand (in so far as one also regards as 'wall' the frontal surface of the rusticated masonry) it projects in front of the columns. In the middle storey, there is a further ambiguity: either one takes the round shape of the shaft and calls the supporting member a column, or one takes the right-angle formed by the layer of rustication and calls it a pilaster. Notice, too, the way the walls are articulated. The grotto side is – apart from the niches – identical to the entrance side. On both sides the entablature proper is interrupted above the surround of the central opening, and on the upper part of the entablature are what appear to be dentils. On closer inspection, however, these turn out to be coffers, set at intervals which relate to the rusticated blocks below and (this is particularly clear on the entrance side) anticipate the spaced-out rustication of the middle storey. This symmetrical construction not only gives the court an extremely compelling form, but also places the visitor in something of a quandary – namely, is the lower zone to be interpreted from the entrance side or from the grotto side? Both appear to be possible. The architectural system is that of the palace, but the details are taken from the grotto (the mossy keystones in the arches!). Looking towards the palace, the visitor has the impression he is standing at ground level; looking towards the grotto, however, one feels one is at basement level – an impression which the single storey of the grotto structure, surmounted by the fountain to which one looks *up*, only serves to heighten. During special festivals, in fact, the ground floor of the court was flooded to form an artificial lake on which mythical battles were staged

between splendidly decorated ships, the spectators watching
from the surrounding first-floor balcony.

The visitor, having thus experienced the ground floor of
the court on the one hand (looking from the entrance side)
as a 'palace' and on the other hand (looking at it from the
opposite wing) as a 'grotto', will be questioning the architect's intention. The phenomena with which we are dealing
here had in fact been introduced into architecture by Michelangelo. It is therefore wrong to attempt to trace this rustication back to the (unfinished) Porta Maggiore in Rome. The
roots of this building lie entirely within the architecture of
the sixteenth century, of the type which tended towards the
theoretical. Serlio wedged pilasters into corners in a similar
way (compare, too, the beautiful busts which are as it were
'clipped' to the window surrounds of the middle storey on
the entrance side), and one is also put in mind of Peruzzi's
fresco of the 'Presentation of the Virgin' in S. Maria della
Pace, Rome, which depicts a building resembling the Palazzo
Pitti (the cornice of the temple in the fresco corresponds
exactly to the second cornice of the Pitti). Ammannati was
making a thorough study of architecture while working on
this palace, and as it happens we have his bookseller's re-
ceipted invoice for the purchase of works by Cattaneo,
Vitruvius, Serlio and Alberti (1564).

There is nothing 'expressive', then, about this art. It is much
more a question of the masterly interweaving and harmonizing of various architectural modes of vision. But if we are
really to appreciate the novelty of this building, a further
brief consideration is necessary. This novelty does not derive
from the invention of new forms, but from the way Ammannati has combined existing forms from the architectural
canon. Ammannati's Mannerism expresses itself here in the
use of relationships which up until then had never been
evolved. In this context, the visitor should direct his attention to the doors and windows surrounding the court. All
the elements – entablature, bracket, volute – are familiar
from Renaissance architecture, yet their original function
has disappeared. The individual members have lost their
interconnection; they have become independent. Their ornamental character is thereby enhanced but their objective
significance has diminished. Alberti could still derive an
Ionic capital from rolled-up matting, but here the artist is

S. Trinita, 'S. Mary Magdalen'
(Desiderio da Settignano and Benedetto da Maiano)

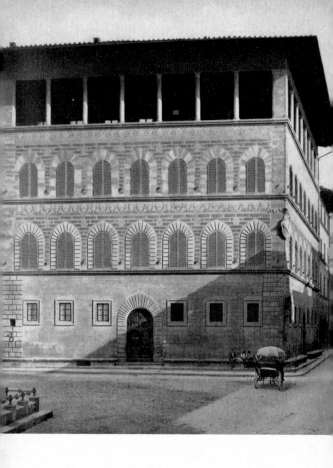

Palazzo Guadagni (Cronaca)

concerned only with pure form. Consistent with this is the differentiated treatment of detail. Each individual part (notice the fluting, particularly) shows the hand of a craftsman. The result is that every member appears to be made of its own particular material. The conception of the homogeneous architectural organism has here given way to a 'composition' of individual parts. One would be correct in asserting that the Renaissance is treated as a 'historical' style.

Looking at the interior of the **grotto**, the visitor is confronted with an elevation which Ammannati hat planned previously for the Uffizi (as an alternative to Vasari's solution); it is the same even down to the detail. For the rest, every available space is filled with ornaments, grotesques and scalloped forms. In the niche in the middle is the porphyry figure of *Moses* which Corradi carved from a Classical torso (completed by Cosimo Salvestrini); the Latin inscription on the socle praising the dispenser of water and the leader of his people refers to Ferdinando I. This is accompanied by four allegorical figures in marble: *Legislation* (A. Novelli), *Zeal* (G. B. Pieratti), *Generosity* and *Power* (D. Pieratti; the last statue obviously depicts Jason; there is an interesting centralized structure beside it).

Outside on the façade of the grotto, in niches, stand *Hercules and Anteus* (left) and a *Hercules* of the Farnese type; both are Classical pieces, but heavily restored. The socles are characteristic of Ammannati; before each one is a fountain basin. On the left (in the passage), just beside the end portal, is Ammannati's touching monument to a faithful mule (Montaigne pointed this out particularly), in the form of a beautiful relief panel. This hard-working animal was employed on the construction of the Pitti courtyard, depicted in the background. – With the permission of the custodian, the visitor can also look at the **chapel** on the south side. The sacristy contains some beautiful works of art including a painting by Cigoli of the *Last Supper* in which the disciples, interestingly enough, are reclining on couches in the Classical manner. The frescoes in the chapel are by L. Ademollo. On the altar is a crucifix by the school of Giovanni da Bologna. – The powerful staircase decorated with statues (most of them Classical, but also the *Genius of the Medici* by Giovanni da Bologna and some further sixteenth century pieces) leads upstairs to the

Galleria d'Arte Moderna

Established about 1860, this collection has grown and grown until today it probably offers the most comprehensive survey to be found on this side of the Alps of nineteenth and twentieth century painting from Tuscany, the rest of Italy and even other parts of Europe. A visit to the gallery is a necessity, though a close study will require some considerable time for there are forty-one rooms. Every picture is labelled.

The Palazzo Pitti, however, is best known for the

Galleria Palatina

The entrance is at the north end of the palace (by the entrance to the Boboli Gardens). The gallery contains a number of masterpieces of the very highest order, hung in a way which still reflects the original character of this princely collection. In fact, the splendour of the arrangement evokes almost as much admiration as the pictures themselves. Throughout the gallery these are hung in several rows one on top of the other, with a view primarily to their decorative effect. The elaborate frames, the furniture and the marvellous decoration of the rooms themselves complete the impression of princely magnificence.

The collection was begun some time before 1620, and the period which followed brought with it considerable augmentations, including those by inheritance (from the Rovere house). In 1799 most of the pictures were carried off to France and not all of them returned in 1815. – In 1833, twenty rooms were opened to the public. The present entrance building was erected in 1895–7.

This museum, the royal chambers ('Appartamenti Reali') and the collection of arts and crafts ('Argenteria') on the ground floor together form a unity. With sixteen pictures by Andrea del Sarto, thirteen by Raphael, twelve by Titian and eight by Tintoretto (as well as a number by Rubens), it is one of the most important galleries in the world.

A modern staircase leads up to the vestibule (with sales stand) in the centre of which is an elaborate fountain basin. This, together with a second upper basin, formed the original base for Verrocchio's 'Putto with a Fish' (now in the first court of the Palazzo Vecchio) and stood in the Villa Careggi, the seat of Ficino's Academy. The Latin inscription, taken in conjunction with the original fountain figure, constituted a Platonic maxim. Around the edge of the 'tazza' are vases and dolphins – a Classical motif which Donatello introduced into Renaissance sculpture; the author of the fountain basin is assumed to have been Francesco Ferrucci. The present figure (*Putto with a Goose*) was added by Tribolo. – Straight ahead, the visitor comes to a smaller room with a large porphyry basin. The pictures on the walls include Luca Giordano's *Triumph of Galatea*, a *Battle* by Salvator Rosa and an *Entombment* by Ludovico Cigoli. The picture gallery proper begins in the **first room** to the south of the vestibule.

This room, actually an enormous hall, was designed by Giuseppe Cacialli; the ceiling was painted by Luigi Sabatelli (scenes from Homer, 1819). In the centre is a *marble group* carved in 1824 by Lorenzo Bartolini, a technically very accomplished sculptor who varied in style between 'Genre' and Classicism. Immediately to the left of the entrance is Raphael's *Gravida*. In fact, the attribution is not entirely certain; an X-ray test would probably give more precise information, because the dark background which, by isolating the face, gives a strongly Ghirlandaio-like impression, is probably a later addition. Andrea del Sarto's *Assumption* of 1526 dominates the centre of the wall; opposite is another equally large work on the same theme which the master left incomplete in 1523. – Further pictures are by Artemisia Gentileschi, Maratta and Sustermans.

The ceiling of the following **Saturn Room** was painted in 1663–5 by Cirro Ferri, probably after a sketch by Pietro da Cortona. The background of Raphael's *Madonna del Granduca* has also been painted over (in good light a portion of landscape can be distinguished on the right beneath the darker overlay). The Madonna's warm and soulful expression is combined with a suggestion of Mantegna-like severity. The *Portrait of Inghirami* is regarded as a good copy of Raphael's original in Boston. One of his most beautiful early works is the *Double Portrait of Agnolo and Maddalena Doni* (1506; on the wall opposite the window), particularly on account of the Umbrian landscape in the background. These delicate pictures were unfortunately somewhat spoiled by bad restoration some time ago. On the back are some (later) chiaroscuro paintings depicting Deucalion and Pyrrha. The small *Ezekiel's Vision* was designed by Raphael but was probably executed in his workshop (Giulio Romano?). The *Madonna del Baldacchino*, however, is at least partly by Raphael's own hand. This composition was begun probably around 1507–8 for the chapel of the Dei family in S. Spirito. Originally, the throne and figures were to have stood in the open air in a landscape. The upper part with the cupola is a Baroque addition (by A. Cassana; it was added when the picture came into the possession of Prince Ferdinando). Raphael himself painted the Madonna and Child, the two angels at her feet and SS. Peter and Bernard on the left; the saints on the right, the two flying angels (which put one in mind of Raphael's angels in S. Maria della Pace, Rome) and the niche (modelled on an architectural type developed by Fra Bartolommeo) may have been painted later by a different hand. The *Madonna della Seggiola* (1514–5), probably Raphael's best known round composition, is painted in deep intense colours. Further pictures here are by Fra Bartolommeo, Andrea del Sarto and Carlo Dolci.

The following **Jupiter Room** takes its name from Pietro da

Cortona's ceiling fresco (painted in 1645 together with Cirro Ferri) with, in the centre, Consani's *Allegory of Victory* (1867). Andrea del Sarto's *St. John* (1523) is full of the sweetness of youth. The *Lamentation* is one of Fra Bartolommeo's finest compositions, with a firm, almost 'constructed' feeling about it. It was commissioned in 1511 for the Certosa di Pavia, and the story of its execution is a complicated one; for example, the composition originally consisted of six figures. The figures of Peter and Paul and the landscape were painted over with dark colours during the sixteenth century and the exemplary composition frequently disregarded. – Raphael's *Fornarina* (Baker's wife) is reputed to depict the artist's mistress. A beautifully painted garment with expressive folds covers an earlier layer from which a palm branch can be made out, suggesting that the figure represents a female martyr.

The next room is dedicated to Mars. The paintings on the ceiling are by Pietro da Cortona and Cirro Ferri (1646). In the painting known as the *Four Philosophers* Rubens depicted himself, his brother Philip, the venerable teacher of Classical philology Justus Lipsius, and Hans van Wouver beneath a niche containing Seneca's portrait and four tulips (two open and two closed: to what hidden allegory do these refer?). Also by Rubens is the *Fruits of War*, painted in 1638 for Ferdinando II. Rubens himself explained this picture in a letter: Mars is extricating himself from the arms of Venus in order to pursue 'Discord'; 'Plague' and 'Famine' are seen flying through the air; behind Venus and before the open temple of Janus, Europa loudly mourns the downfall of the arts, of love and of diligence, seen sinking to the ground on the right.

Pietro da Cortona and Cirro Ferri also painted the ceiling of the following **Apollo Room**, between 1647 and 1660. An *Entombment* by Andrea del Sarto (1523). *Satyr Pursuing a Nymph* by Dosso Dossi. The large *Sacra Conversazione* by Rosso Fiorentino came originally from S. Spirito (a piece has been added all around). *Caritas* by Guido Reni. The most notable picture here, however, is Titian's *S. Mary Magdalen*, painted between 1530 and 1540 for the Duke of Urbino.

Next comes the **Venus Room**, also frescoed by Pietro da Cortona and Cirro Ferri (the stucco ornaments are by Roman artists). Above the door is Sustermans' *Return of the Hunters*. Salvator Rosa was an interesting improvisor, and his landscape style is particularly well represented by two lake views; the colouring is luminous, the accessories are delicate but lack real stability. Matteo Rosselli's *Triumph of David* and Guercino's *Apollo and Marsyas*, with its dark, sinister colouring, both illustrate a particular aspect of seventeenth-century Italian painting. Two landscapes by Rubens are of particular interest. The one on the left, a late work, depicts peasants returning home from work; the other

(obviously with later additions) shows Odysseus with the Phae-
acians and possibly dates from an earlier period. The *Concert*
used to be attributed to Giorgione, but is now thought to be by
the young Titian.
Returning to the second room (that of 'Saturn'), the visitor will
find on the right a further series of smaller rooms. The first of
these is known as the **Odysseus Room** after Martellini's ceiling
painting. – The adjacent **bathroom** was decorated in the Empire
style by Cacialli (the relief on the ceiling depicting the *Rape of
Ganymedes* is by L. Pampaloni, who was also responsible for the
Galatea and *Toilet of Venus* on the walls; in the corner niches
are four Nereids). – The next room is named after Catani's
Education of Jupiter on the ceiling (1819). Notice the small
figure-painting by Callot, Caravaggio's *Sleeping Amor* (an unusual theme which was much copied, e.g. by Caracciolo) and
Allori's *Judith*. – Next comes the **Sala della Stufa** (stove). The
majolica decoration (only partially preserved) depicts the *Triumph
of Bacchus* (by Benedetto Bocchi, 1640); some portions are modern
restorations. The ceiling painting shows *Fame and the Cardinal
Virtues* (Matteo Rosselli, 1622); Pietro da Cortona's *murals*
illustrate the four ages of man.
Continuing the visit on the other side of the 'Odysseus Room',
we come to the **Prometheus Room**. The very mediocre painting
on the ceiling was designed by Colignon (c. 1830). Immediately
to the right of the entrance is *Apollo and the Muses*, a humanistic
theme realized by Peruzzi (the traditional attribution to Giulio
Romano is no longer tenable). Further Florentine paintings from
the fifteenth and sixteenth centuries include Jacopo del Sellaio's
Madonna and Luca Signorelli's *Holy Family*. Works by Botticelli,
Palmezzano and the Sienese artist Beccafumi complete the series
of 'small-format' paintings.
On the left is the **Corridor of the Columns** (Corridoio delle Co-
lonne), so-called after two alabaster columns which stand here.
The corridor features a collection of paintings from the Nether-
lands – works by van Dyck, Teniers, Marten de Vos and Poelen-
burgh, who worked in Florence for a time – representing the nor-
thern influence which affected Florentine art from the beginning
of the Renaissance onwards.
The following **Hall of Justice** (ceiling painting by A. Fedi) is
hung with a number of Venetian works including Tintoretto's
Venus, Vulcan and Amor and the *Saviour* by the young Titian.
A fine male portrait by Moroni and a *Sacra Conversazione* by
Bonifazio Veronese.
Next comes the **Flora Room** (ceiling painting by Antonio Marini,
c. 1830). In the centre is Canova's *Italic Venus*, a gift from
Napoleon for the 'Tribuna' of the Uffizi to replace the 'Medici
Venus' which had been carried off to Paris. It is not unin-
teresting to note the internal differences between this work and the

famous Classical piece which returned to Florence in 1816.
Despite a certain similarity of posture, the differences are none
the less fundamental. Bronzino's beautiful *Portrait of Luca Martini* is an example of the master's mature portraiture. The visitor
should also notice the two paintings by Andrea del Sarto depicting the *Story of Joseph*; the detail of the landscape sections is
reminiscent of Fra Bartolommeo's studies of nature. Puligo
(*Portrait of Pietro Carnesecchi*) stands in immediate line of
succession to Andrea, though with a slight tendency towards the
effeminate.

The following **Putti Room** (ceiling painting by Marini, *c.* 1830)
contains paintings from the Netherlands, including Rubens' early
Graces.

The visitor must now return to the 'Prometheus Room' and turn
left. The small **Poccetti Gallery** also takes its name from the
ceiling decoration. The two particularly beautiful examples of
'heroic' landscape painting by Gaspard Dughet on the right
opposite the window wall reveal the influence of Poussin's style
and must be dated in the late fifties of the seventeenth century.
Further pictures include Rubens' *Duke of Buckingham*, *Hylas and
the Nymphs* in Furini's sultry style, and Ribera's *Martyrdom of
S. Bartholomew.*

Next is the Neo-Classical **Music Room** with its cylindrical furniture. The frescoes (by Ademollo) commemorate the liberation
of Vienna in 1683. A particularly beautiful *female portrait* by
Guido Reni is currently on exhibition here. In the centre of the
room is a remarkable malachite table with a bronze foot by the
Parisian founder Thomire (1819).

The next room was decorated by **Castagnoli**, after whom it is
named. In the centre stands the famous *Apollo Table*, executed
in 1851 in 'pietra dura' work. The bronze foot depicting the
Seasons was modelled by Giovanni Dupré and cast by Clemente
Papi. Notice particularly the banner which Sodoma painted in
1525 for a Brotherhood of S. Sebastian in Siena. It is painted on
both sides: on the front is *S. Sebastian*, a distinctively Leonardo-
esque figure against an enchanting landscape, and on the back a
Madonna and Child, with Saints. The colours have faded
slightly.

From here, the visitor can proceed into the left wing of the court
to the – not always open – **Quartiere del Volterrano**, which takes
its name from Volterrano's **Hall of the Allegories** (all the other
rooms were painted in the nineteenth century). This first room
contains a number of works by Volterrano, together with some
by the probably more gifted Giovanni da San Giovanni. – Then
comes the **Hall of the Arts** (ceiling painting by D. Podestà, after
1815) with works by seventeenth century Florentine artists including Carlo Dolci, Cigoli and Ligozzi. – The ceiling of the
Hercules Room was painted by Benvenuti (1828). The gigantic

vase was a gift from Napoleon to Ferdinando III. It was made
in the factory at Sèvres. The bronze fittings are by Thomire. –
Dawn Room: ceiling painted by Martellini. Paintings include
Vasari's *Vision of Marchese Ugo of Tuscany* and a *Birth of the
Virgin* by Andrea Boscoli. – **Berenice Room**: ceiling painted by
G. Bezzuoli. Notice here particularly the paintings by Salvator
Rosa. – **Psyche Room**: ceiling painted by Colignon. Pictures by
Reni, Sebastiano del Piombo (*Martyrdom of S. Agatha*), C. Dolci
and G. M. Crespi.

Returning to the 'Berenice Room', the visitor may be able to
visit some rooms lying to the north (though they are usually
closed). These are the **Round Cabinet** and the **Bathroom of Maria
Luisa**, the latter decorated tastefully and with unusual lavishness
for Maria Luisa of Bourbon, Queen of Etruria. Also on this side
(entrance from the 'Hercules Room') is a **reliquary chapel** with
a salon-like ante-room.

On several days in the week the visitor can also see round the
Appartamenti Reali

Reigning rulers from the Medici grand dukes to King Victor
Emmanuel III have on many occasions stayed in these pleasantly
comfortable and richly decorated apartments.

We begin in the **Sala delle Nicchie** which served as the dining-
room. This was decorated *c*. 1800 in the Neo-Classical style by Giuseppe Maria Terreni and G. Castagnoli. The walls are hung with
portraits by Sustermans, providing us with one of our most
important sources for the iconography of the Medici. The niches
are occupied by restored Classical statues. There are also some
beautiful Sèvres vases and elaborately carved wooden chandeliers.

The **Green Room** formerly served as the guardroom. The ceiling
painting (inside Castagnoli's chiaroscuro decoration) is by Luca
Giordano; it depicts Jupiter entrusting the Medici coat of arms
to 'Fame' and the 'Virtues' on the conclusion of the feud between
Florence and Fiesole. The walls are hung with excellent French
tapestries from the Gobelins factory, executed by Audran to
designs by de Troys (1737 to 1740). The paintings include (at the
back on the right) an allegorical representation of a picture collection by an artist from the Netherlands.

The throne in the **next room** was used by the kings of Italy when
they took the oath. Some Medici portraits by Sustermans and
Pourbus the Younger. The tapestries belong to the *Esther* series
in the previous room.

Hall of Heaven: more portraits by Sustermans; the tapestries are
Gobelins works designed by Noël Coypel (executed by Jeanse
and Sovet, 1690–1706).

The adjacent small chapel was converted into a salon in the nineteenth century by placing a coping over the altar. Portraits by
Sustermans; a *Madonna and Child* by Domenico Puligo.

Next come the former **Apartments of Queen Margherita**, begin-

ning with the **Parrot Room** so-called because of the pattern on
the walls. Near the window is a *Madonna* by Carlo Dolci in a
splendid 'pietra dura' frame; it was originally in the chapel. –
The adjacent rooms to the south are all closed.

The visitor then reaches the former **Apartments of King Um-
berto I**. The bedroom contains further Medici portraits by Sustermans. The picture of Emperor Franz of Lorraine with Maria
Theresa and their children in Schönbrunn is probably by Martin
van Meytens. – There follow a small study, a salon and an ante-
room with some Florentine tapestries. On the left, *Spring* and
Flora by Giovanni Rost after Bronzino's design (the woman on
horseback is based on Dürer's 'Proserpina' engraving).

The adjacent **Sala di Bona** is decorated with frescoes by Poccetti
which clearly owe a stylistic debt to Bronzino. – A number of
rooms lying to the east and containing some beautiful French
tapestries are all closed, and the visitor comes straight to the
ball-room – architect, G. M. Paoletti; stucco work by the brothers Albertolli from Ticino (1776–80); above the portal, two
allegories of *Fame* by Spinazzi. – Passing through a vestibule, the
visitor comes to a room containing Bandinelli's *Bacchus* and
Francavilla's *Mercury*, with the slain Argus. – The adjacent sculpture gallery, decorated in the late eighteenth century, contains
antiquities; two Florentine tapestries hang on the walls.

Leaving the gallery and descending to the ground floor, the
visitor will find the valuable collection of artefacts known as the
Argenteria

(Open only on days when the 'Appartamenti Reali' are closed.)
– This positively regal collection comprises gold and silver work,
cameos, 'pietra dura' work, vases, ivories, materials and porcelaine assembled from the former possessions of the grand dukes
which at one time were scattered about the town in a number of
collections (mainly in the Uffizi and the Bargello) and from
private collections such as those of A. Conti (porcelaine and
glass) and Vay de Vaya (clocks).

The collection is important not least for the way in which it
testifies to the vigorous blossoming of designed artefacts in the
dukedom of Tuscany. Cellini, Bandinelli, Ammannati and Vasari
all worked for Cosimo I. A tapestry factory was set up in Florence. In 1557 Giovanni Antonio de'Rossi began work on the
famous cameo of the Medici family which he completed in Rome
in 1562. The only serious loss suffered by the collection was the
legacy of Margarethe, daughter of Charles V and at one time
wife of Duke Alessandro; when she married Ottavio Farnese, a
part of the treasure went to Parma and subsequently – with the
Farnese family – to Naples (hence the piece known as the 'Tazza
Farnese', which was once in Florence, is now in the Naples
museum). Ferdinando I added many 'pietra dura' works to the
collection, amongst which was Buontalenti's famous vase. In 1589,

the dowry of Christine of Lorraine, who married Grand Duke Ferdinando I, arrived from France; some of this had previously made the same journey in the opposite direction as part of the dowry of Catherine de'Medici, including the famous crystal vase depicting 'Noah's Ark' and made for Clement VII, known as the 'Tazza di Diane de Poitiers'. – The era of Cosimo II brought with it the valuable relief depicting the duke at prayer (made between 1617 and 1624). It also saw the beginning of the fashion for carved ivories, the best examples of which came from Germany, as did also the amber pieces (the visitor will notice a large tabernacle signed by Georg Schreiber, 1618–9). This museum is unique in Italy, and in the rest of Europe the only collections that can stand comparison with it are those in Vienna, Munich, Dresden and Copenhagen. – Let us look now at the various rooms. The first room was decorated by Agostino Mitelli and Michelangelo Colonna; Jupiter is seen descending from the heavens to bestow the crown and sceptre upon the Medici. Against the left wall is an ebony *prayer stool* with floral decoration in 'pietra dura' and a mosaic *Baptism of Christ*. – Against the wall opposite the windows is an eighteenth century *ebony cupboard* with 'pietra dura' decoration and a statuette of Elector Johann Wilhelm, the German husband of Anna Maria Lodovica. – Set out in the two large glass cases are some very valuable German works from Augsburg (sixteenth and seventeenth centuries) – fifty-four gilded *silver dishes* comprising Biblical scenes as well as depictions of the Virtues, the Months and the Seasons. – Another remarkable piece is the engraved silver *Altar of the Virgin*; sixteen small panels depicting scenes from the Virgin's life surround the central panel depicting the Madonna in a rose arbour. These engraved panels are based on designs by Stradanus, who used certain motifs taken from Dürer (e.g. the hares and flowers in the central panel). They date from *c.* 1580; the present mounting may be assumed to be from a later date. – On the table in the middle of the room is a group of *putti* in the style of Bernini.

The next room, too, was frescoed by Mitelli and Colonna (the story of Alexander and his triumph). In the first case, the visitor will see a *mitre* and two headbands made of pieces of coloured feathers and decorated with holy pictures (on the mitre is the *Crucifixion*); this valuable work of art from Mexico (sixteenth century) is said to have been given to Pope Clement VII by Charles V. – Further exhibits include a five-part *malachite cross* with a heart-shaped centrepiece, a seventeenth century *silver bowl* from Rome depicting the enthroned Amalasunta, a large *silver bowl* by Christian Drentwett Jr. of Augsburg (late eighteenth century), a seventeenth century *gilded silver cross* from Salzburg, a *hexagonal vase* with a Madonna and four saints (1577), probably by Abraham Pfleger, some more gold work from Augsburg and a cylindrical *Arabic perfume box*.

In the middle of the third room (again decorated by Mitelli and
Colonna, this time with allegories of 'Strength', 'Justice' and
'Time') is the famous *German Cupboard* which once stood in the
Uffizi and was probably purchased in Germany by Ferdinando II.
It appears to contain a little world of its own, with numerous
secret drawers, a rotating inner section and a little organ, decorated with mosaics, miniatures, small sculptures and 'pietra
dura' work. – There is also a *small altar* at which Cardinal Leopoldo is believed to have said mass.

Next comes the chapel. The silver cross on the altar was probably made by Andreas Hamburger, who died in 1657. The
two candlesticks bear the coat of arms of the prince-bishops of
Salzburg. The cross on the left is attributed to Giovanni da
Bologna.

The next room, considerably larger than the preceding ones, is
richly decorated. The *frescoes* are by Giovanni da San Giovanni,
Francesco Furini, Ottavio Vannini and Cecco Bravo. The painting
on the ceiling celebrates the marriage of Ferdinando II and
Vittoria della Rovere; those on the walls glorify Lorenzo il Magnifico. It is a characteristic evocation of the history of the early
Medici, giving the grand dukes – and this can be observed in
numerous other cases as well – the requisite historical framework
within which their own glory might shine all the more brilliantly.
Seen in this way, the cycle represents the first 'interpretation'
of the history of the Medici dynasty as conceived by the imagination of the Baroque period. The series begins with the *Destruction
of book of learning by time and the barbarians*. This is followed
by *Mohammed's attempt to exterminate Greek civilization* and
finally *Barbarians invade Parnassus while the Muses flee, pursued
by harpies* (Giovanni da San Giovanni). *Poets and philosophers
make their escape to Florence and Tuscany where they are received by Lorenzo*; *He establishes peace in Italy* (Cecco Bravo).
Between the windows: *Lorenzo among artists and allegories of
Faith and Prudence* (Ottavio Vannini). On the entrance wall:
Lorenzo and the Academy of Careggi and an *Allegory of the
death of Lorenzo* (Francesco Furini). – The cases contain an extensive collection of vases and bowls, most of them quite small,
all made from precious stones and rock crystal. Notice particularly
the *bowl with the seven-headed Hydra* on the lid, surmounted by
a triumphant Hercules in gold (probably the work of Mazzafirri);
also the extremely valuable *goblet* with stem and perforated lid
which – together with many other pieces in this unique collection –
once stood in Catherine de'Medici's cabinet of art treasures in
Paris and came to Florence in 1589 in the dowry of Christine of
Lorraine. A really thorough investigation of this 'French treasure'
by an art historian still remains to be undertaken. – Further pieces
formed part of the legendary wealth of Lorenzo il Magnifico. These
include a number of Classical stone jars, some of them with a

later mounting and with their owner's name engraved on them.
They all came from S. Lorenzo, where they had been donated by
Pope Clement VII. Among the other works, a part of which were
imported from the East, is a magnificent *lapis lazuli urn* with
golden chain by Buontalenti (1583), a more recent example of the
art of stone cutting. The gold work is by Biliverti, the father of
the painter (made for Francesco I). The visitor should equally not
omit the pieces from Augsburg bearing the coat of arms of the
bishops of Salzburg which may be admired in the case on the right
at the rear of the room. They used to be attributed to Cellini,
although they bear no relation at all to his work. – Near the door,
there is a *bronze crucifix* by the school of Giovanni da Bologna.

The next room contains some *Florentine tapestries* depicting scenes
from the lives of Clement VII and Cosimo I. There are also a
number of crystal vessels from the dowry of 1589, including the
crystal ship right at the front on the left (a table decoration; the
turret with cannons dates from a later period). Notice particularly
the *cameos* (some of them Classical) set around the edge of the
ship itself. Of the many pieces which will be of interest to the
connoisseur, we will mention only a few. The *eight statuettes of
Apostles* by Orazio Mocchi were made for a tabernacle in the
Cappella dei Principi in S. Lorenzo. Giovanni Biliverti's *relief* in
'pietra dura' work, gold and diamonds depicting the young
Cosimo II kneeling was made as a gift for S. Carlo Borromeo,
Milan (the design for it is in the Opificio delle Pietre Dure).
Large *cameo* by G. A. de'Rossi depicting Cosimo I, Eleonora of
Toledo and five children (what was in the now empty circular
form?). Large *processional cross* (1751–3), probably by Friedrich
Konrad Mittnacht from Augsburg.

In the next room, together with a large collection of cameos, is
Valerio Belli's famous *casket of rock crystal* decorated with
scenes from the Passion; this was a present from Clement VII to
François I on the occasion of the marriage of Catherine de'Medici
and Henry II in 1533. – The clocks (French and Swiss) exhibited
here are from the Vay de Vaya collection.

Retracing his steps to the third room, the visitor will find a
further series of rooms lying to the south. The first of these, which
is rather dark, contains two tapestries by P. Fevère (one of the
Month of May, the other after Michelangelo's *Entombment*) and
one after a design by Bronzino depicting Apollo and Minerva
holding a shield with the coats of arms of Cosimo I and Eleonora
of Toledo. – Further tapestries and materials in the adjoining
room, and in the next one a number of ivories including a large
crucifix by Balthasar Stockamer (1668), commissioned by Cardinal
Leopoldo and executed from a drawing by Pietro da Cortona.
Another crucifix by Melchior Barthel from Dresden. Also some
curiosities made out of shells and coconuts. – A word about the
ivory vases and the turned work. A total of twenty-seven pieces

are identifiable as being by Markus Heiden and his assistant
Johann Eisenberg from Coburg. Fourteen of the vases are signed
and dated. In 1632, during the Thirty Years' War, Coburg was
plundered by the Imperial army; Prince Matteo de'Medici, who
was with the besieging forces, sent the vases to his brother Grand
Duke Ferdinando II in Florence, where they arrived on 1 April
1633. Many of the vases have verses of a religious or moral nature
(all in Latin) engraved beneath the foot or inside the lid. These
amusing vases thus have a spiritual or mystical 'message' which
in detail still remains to be deciphered. – The collection of ivories
continues in the following room where the visitor will find a
beautiful *Hercules* group by Stockamer (1699), a magnificently
made little *horse* (in the screen) by the Sicilian Filippo Planzone,
as well as pieces by Markus Heiden from Coburg, Franz Eisenberg, the brothers Heifen and Philipp Senger. Some of these pieces
are clearly of a frivolous nature.

Upstairs is the collection of porcelain. The major factories are
represented by some excellent pieces, with some masterly nineteenth-century works deserving special mention.

Behind the palace lie the

Boboli Gardens

This is one of the most beautiful parks in Italy. Well-kept
paths lead the visitor past lawns and shady shrubberies to
artistic waterworks and 'romantic' grottos.

*The park takes its name from the 'Bogoli' or 'Bogolini' family
which is said to have owned part of the land from very early on.
The actual 'Pitti Garden', laid out by Eleonora of Toledo, forms
only a part of this now very extensive site which has been enlarged
over the years by means of fresh acquisitions. The first layout
was by Tribolo; this was subsequently altered by Ammannati who
added the amphitheatre which, optically speaking, counts as part
of the courtyard of the palace. A definite caesura occurs, then,
around the year 1550 (the year of Tribolo's death). One of the
earliest works undertaken was Buontalenti's grotto structure to
the north (near Vasari's corridor leading to the Uffizi), in which
Michelangelo's 'Slaves', which had just come into the possession
of Francesco I, were soon to be exhibited. The figures by Bandinelli and de'Rossi on the front of the grotto as well as Giovanni
da Bologna's 'Venus Fountain' were not placed here until some
time after the grotto was finished.*

*Giovanni da Bologna's 'Oceanus', too, on its tall socle in the
'Isolotto', the fountain in the southern part of the gardens, was
already some years old when it was erected here by Alfonso
Parigi the Younger in 1637. The definitive layout of the whole
park dates from this period. This included shrubbery mazes, a
novel feature which was to be copied later in France (Versailles).
Numerous sculptors – Valerio Cioli, Giambattista Caccini, Pieratti,*

Novelli, Salvetti, Salvestrini – set to work to populate the paths
and intersections with a mass of figures, while the gigantic female
figure (begun by Giovanni da Bologna as a portrait of Giovanna
d'Austria and completed by Salvestrini, a pupil of Tacca, as
'Dovizia') took its place on the highest point on the hill where
it can be seen from far away. Cosimo III added a botanical
garden and Cardinal Leopoldo the little 'del Cavaliere' garden.
Here mulberries and potatoes were planted for the first time in
Italy! A zoo was also added, with a large aquarium and an aviary.
With limitless care and attention, a universe in miniature was
created.
Early in the eighteenth century, Cosimo III had a study built in
the 'del Cavaliere' garden for his son Giangastone. But then, with
the passing of the Medici line, neglect and oblivion invaded the
park. The process of restoration was undertaken by the Lothrin-
gian grand dukes who built the north entrance (Porta del Bacco)
and the 'Coffee House'; Paoletti erected the Egyptian obelisk of
pink granite in the amphitheatre. An attempt by the French to
convert the park into an 'English garden' was reversed when the
grand dukes of Lorraine returned. We can only be grateful that
this unique example of classic Italian landscape gardening was
preserved in Florence.

Entering the park through the Porta del Bacco, the visitor
finds himself in a small piazza. On the left is the grotesque
Bacchus Fountain with the naked figure of Cosimo I's court
dwarf riding on the back of a tortoise (by Valerio Cioli).
Flanking the beginning of the path which ascends diagonally are two Dacian slaves, Roman porphyry statues on
Classical bases.

Turning left, the visitor reaches the **Buontalenti Grotto**.
The construction of this 'grotto grande' continued over
almost forty years from 1556–92. It consists of three rooms
laid out one behind another. In niches to right and left stand
Ceres and *Apollo* (by Bandinelli and de'Rossi respectively).
The entrance arch was designed by Vasari. In the first room
of the grotto is a curious decor of stalactites, shells and
pebbles in the form of a rocky landscape from which a new
race of men is rising after the Flood. Michelangelo's *Slaves*
(plaster casts; the originals are in the Academy museum)
can be seen in the corners twisting themselves out of mud
and stone towards a new life. The explanation of the scenic
effect of this decorative ensemble lies in the fact that it was
modelled on Serlio's description of the 'satirical' stage set;
hence, too, the presence of the satyrs on the fountain basin
of Giovanni da Bologna's *Venus* in the third, rather dark

room. The second room contains Vincenzo de'Rossi's *Paris* and *Helen*. – Poccetti's paintings are in places barely recognizable. The building as a whole is characteristic of Buontalenti's somewhat 'amorphous' style.

The *amphitheatre* constitutes probably the most splendid feature of the whole park. The sarcophagus-like *bowl of granite* came from the Thermae of Caracalla in Rome. The *Egyptian obelisk* (erected in the eighteenth century) was also discovered in Rome. The amphitheatre itself, very firmly defined architecturally, is graduated in tiers. The rows of statues are there to strengthen the impression of a Classical site. From here, the visitor has a view of the two upper storeys of the Pitti courtyard (the lower storey is completely concealed and looks like a kind of dark cellar) and of Susini's richly figured *Fontana del Carciofo* which, according to the long Latin inscription, is intended to be a reminder of the spirits of nature and the animating elements of the 'locus amoenus'.

Descending the hill, the visitor comes to the **Neptune Fountain**. The god, standing on a rocky island, is brandishing a trident from which pours the element over which he presides. This beautiful piece of work was made by Stoldo Lorenzi in 1565. In the **del Cavaliere** garden (only open in summer) is the *Monkey Fountain* with Pietro Tacca's 'Amor'. – From here a wide avenue leads down southwards. The **Isolotto**, a broad, circular space bordered by tall hedges, was designed by Alfonso Parigi in 1618. In the middle of the pond is an artificial island planted with fruit trees, and in the middle of the island rises Giovanni da Bologna's *Oceanus Fountain*. The principal figure is a copy, the original having been removed to the Bargello to protect it from further damage by weathering. The statues at his feet represent the Nile, the Ganges and the Euphrates. – In the little pond are *Andromeda and Perseus* (Ammannati).

For the rest, we prefer to let the visitor discover for himself the many corners containing statues and offering picturesque views which are to be found both to east and west of this extensive park, and to wish him success in his search!

Returning to the Palazzo Pitti, the visitor is recommended to conclude his tour with a visit to the small **Museum of historic coaches** siuated in the south wing ('Rondò') of the forecourt.

Palazzo Ricasoli (Piazza Goldoni 2)
The architect is said to have been Michelozzo, but later alterations
have left little evidence of his work; the façade on the piazza in any
case dates from the early sixteenth century. There are older parts in
the courtyard. The staircase is particularly interesting as being the
earliest tangible example of a free combination with the vestibule,
and as such a precursor of the staircase in the Palazzo Gondi.

Palazzo Rosselli del Turco, formerly Borgherini (Borgo SS. Apostoli 17–19)

This splendid palace, once filled with works by Granacci,
Pontormo and Bacchiacca, was built by Baccio d'Agnolo
and constitutes one of the major works of his early period.
Above the ground floor with its rectangular windows rise
two storeys of more or less equal height with round-arched
windows (some of them filled in); above those of the upper
storey are (possibly later) square mezzanine windows. The
corners are of squared blocks of masonry, edged on each
storey by a small slim column. The capitals of these columns
meet the nicely profiled cornices (compare the corresponding articulation on the Palazzo Guadagni). – The richly elaborated portal is sculpturally extremely animated. – In the
lower vestibule, there are some beautiful composite capitals
and on the right-hand end wall is a sixteenth-century
Madonna (relief) in the style of Benedetto da Maiano.

Palazzo Rucellai (Via della Vigna Nuovo 18)

*Giovanni di Paolo Rucellai was one of those Florentine merchants
who rose from humble beginnings and whose education kept pace
with their increasing wealth. Moreover, by means of some adept
marital politics, he was able to make his family one of the most
prominent in the city. Himself the son-in-law of Palla Strozzi,
he married his eldest son to a Pitti and his youngest to a niece of
Cosimo Medici. At the same time, he planned an enormous palace
– a vast project which, as one can see from the abrupt way in
which the façade breaks off on the right, was to have been even
more extensive than it is. The earliest mention of this building is
in Filarete's treatise on architecture (1464). The period of its
construction can be placed between 1446 and 1451. Vasari quotes
Leon Battista Alberti as the architect. He furnished the plans,
but the greater part of the execution was carried out by Bernardo
Rossellino (who also worked on the courtyard, which remained
unfinished; it was restored in 1931).*
It is to Alberti's genius that we owe the façade (*ill.* facing
p. 385). Completely flat, it is stuck on to the front of the
building like a sheet of paper, continuing only a short way

around the left-hand corner and down the side street. It
differed from anything known until then, and was the first
façade to use an order of pilasters. The portals are rectangular with no arches. The differentiated treatment of
bases and capitals on the individual storeys anticipated the
later 'orders'. Running along the socle is a bench. The
diagonally jointed masonry above the bench betrays a
knowledge of Etruscan and Roman architecture. The portals
(originally three were planned) cut right through the socle;
their surrounds turn at right angles at the bottom – a feature
which goes back to early examples of the type of the
S. Miniato façade (compare too the egg and dart decoration
of the Doric capitals of the ground floor which was modelled on the Baptistery). Square windows dominate the
top of the door surrounds. The storeys diminish in height
towards the top and the pilasters become narrower, so that
their relative proportions remain the same. The architraves
in the arched windows, resting on small columns in the
middle and pilasters at the sides, were another new feature.
The Medici rings can be seen in the spandrels inside the
window arches; the sails were the device of the Rucellai
family. – The façade is in very low relief. The quasi-orna-
mental pattern formed by the joints of the masonry has an
almost graphic quality. Architecture here approaches the
two-dimensionality of painting (something which Alberti
was also able to justify on the theoretical level), and in fact
creates something very like a picture. This, however, did not
mean the rejection of every specifically architectonic
rhythm, as we see from the stress which is laid on the axes
above the portals (where the windows of the upper storeys
are not only slightly wider and higher but are also – on the
middle storey – crowned with a coat of arms), and from the
fact that the storeys become progressively lighter towards
the top – even in colouring, for the upper part of the
façade has a paler appearance than the somewhat dark
lower parts.
On the right, on the broad side of this triangular piazza,
is the **Loggia of the Rucellai**, c. 1460, an example of a
noble family's official hall. It has recently been reopened.

Palazzo Scala-Gherardesca (Borgo Pinti 97)
Giuliano da Sangallo was barely thirty years old when in c. 1473

Palazzo Medici-Riccardi, chapel, detail from
'The Adoration of the Magi' (Benozzo Gozzoli)

Palazzo Rucellai, detail of the façade (L. B. Alberti)

he began this small palace for Bartolommeo della Scala. He completed it in 1477. The building is a rare example of a fifteenth
century ambience for a cultured statesman. It was altered and
enlarged as early as the sixteenth century. Today the building
(which is very well looked after) is the headquarters of the Società
Metallurgica Italiana. – It can be visited only by appointment.

This beautiful building contains a small **chapel** decorated by
Stradanus, a salon on the first floor with the ceiling painted
by Volterrano and an old **courtyard** built in 1475–80. On
each side above the three arches is a curious bronze-coloured
relief. This cycle takes us back into the world of the Italian
fifteenth century. According to Alberti, the three requirements of a private house at that period were that it should
be beautiful, that it should be decorated and that it should
be comfortable. The tunnel vaults of the courtyard arcade
are also reminiscent of Alberti: he used them both in S. Pancrazio and in S. Andrea, Mantua. They are of a Classical
solemnity, with coffers made of precast tiles. The facing of
the pillars on the court side with Tuscan pilasters, the attic
above, which is richly decorated with reliefs, and finally
the presence of a further, originally open storey on top (the
present rectangular windows are modern) all suggest the
composition of a Roman triumphal arch. Not only was the
architect, Giuliano da Sangallo, versed in archeology (he
possessed a collection of antiquities), but Bartolommeo della
Scala himself, a miller's son, was also one of the most cultured men of his time: in 1468 he was Chancellor of the
Florentine Republic, in 1485 Gonfaloniere, and throughout
his life he occupied positions of the highest rank.

The twelve large bronze-coloured stucco *reliefs* (4 m wide
and 1.4 m. high) relate stories from the 'Cento Apologhi'
which the owner of the house had compiled in poetic form.
Based on Classical prototypes, they constitute allegorical
representations of moral maxims not unlike the medallions
by the school of Donatello in the courtyard of the Palazzo
Medici. They were executed by Bertoldo – before 1479, as
we know from a letter to Lorenzo il Magnifico. The frieze
begins on the south side on the left with 'Quies', Orpheus
or Apollo with nine persons, and a grotto with a dragon. –
'Victoria', four figures, a woman on a racing chariot. –
'Tempestas', an old man with a pupil, a group of peasants.
– West side: 'Imperatoria Potestas', Orpheus-Minerva, Emperor and soldiers. – 'Gloria Militaris', chariot with Hercules

and Fortuna. – 'Negligentia', Mercury, group of figures. – North side: 'Ebrietas', centaurs around a boiling pot out of which a pig is climbing. – 'Praelium', cavalry battle. – 'Regnum', a man with animals. – East side: 'Amor', two warriors and a seated old man, Venus with the apple, a naked man chastising Cupid in front of an old woman. – 'Mitas', a naked man, a lion biting an ox. – 'Jurgium', a peasant dance, musicians, a drunkard.
Behind the palace is a large park.

Palazzo Spini (Piazza S. Trinita, on the side towards the Arno)
This colossal building, erected in 1289, is one of the most monumental medieval palaces in Florence. It was restored in 1874. Recently a tower belonging to the palace and a loggia on the ground floor were removed.

Palazzo Strozzi (Piazza Strozzi)
This mature piece of work represents the culmination of Florentine palace architecture. Filippo di Matteo Strozzi, one of the noblest personalities of the Renaissance, began to plan it after he was allowed to return home from exile in 1466. The problem before him was how to provide a new and splendid domicile for his family without re-awakening the jealousy of the leading family as represented in the person of Lorenzo the Magnificent. Pretending at first to have in mind a modest house with smooth walls, he nevertheless allowed his architects to draw up plans of great magnificence. He also announced that shops were to be installed on the ground floor to provide additional income for his children. This, however, Lorenzo would not allow, for such a building – half living quarters and half commercial premises – situated in such a place, ran counter to his ceaseless preoccupation with the embellishment of Florence. He therefore ordered that the new building should at least be decorated with splendid rusticated masonry – and Filippo Strozzi's plans were crowned with success. Lorenzo was to perform a similarly useful service on other occasions as well. – At first, it was intended to make the building completely rectangular (whereas medieval palaces had always followed the direction of the surrounding streets), and the city administration granted permission for the adjacent

street to be corrected. The
first model was furnished
by Sangallo the Elder. The
execution, however, was
placed in the hands of Benedetto da Maiano. Both these
masters stood in the closest
connection with the Medici
family. When finally Filippo
Strozzi entrusted the completion of his palace to Lorenzo il Magnifico in his will,
the consummation of one of
the finest creations of Florentine architecture was contrary to all expectations,
assured. After Benedetto da
Maiano's death (1497), Cronaca became the architect.
Building continued until

Palazzo Strozzi, window

1536. The terminal cornice remained incomplete. – The principal dates known are as follows:

1489 laying of the foundation stone.
1490 the first rusticated block is set in place.
1491 Filippo Strozzi dies. The building has advanced
     approximately to the height of the iron rings set in
     the wall. The portal on the Via degli Strozzi is
     vaulted.
1492 work begins on the ground floor.
1495 completion of the first-storey windows.
1500 completion of the main cornice facing the Piazza
     Strozzi.
1536 cessation of all work.

A wooden model and a number of drawings have been
preserved from the planning stage.

The façade overlooks the Piazza Strozzi. A further piazza
was planned to the north and a garden to the south. On
this side, which is not rusticated, the building is crowned
by a loggia. – The socle, two belt-like storey divisions, the
windows and the cornice provide the articulation. What
lies between, while appearing to be mere 'wall', must be
regarded as a work of art in itself. Every stone, every

edge, in short every part of the visible surface is treated
with such precision and integrated into the structure as a
whole with such refinement that this building has been
described as a 'miracle of the rusticated style'. Each block
of masonry is cut in three directions, so that all the joints
are completely identical and all the 'humps' appear to
bulge out from the uniform mass of the wall in a regular
way. Occasionally, where a longer unit seemed to be
necessary in relation to the whole, two or three blocks
were worked as one. The blocks themselves give the
appearance of bulging muscles and the wall, elastic and
full of energy, seems to soar upwards from bottom to top.
Each block, too, was worked like a piece of sculpture: first
the curvature of the surface was established, and then the
surface itself was roughened with the chisel. The rippling
animation of the wall is restrained slightly in the top three
courses of each storey so as to place more stress on the
tightly profiled cornices and remove any possibility of
disturbance occurring at the junction of the two elements
of wall and frame. Each wall is surrounded by a smooth
strip of masonry which draws the display surface together
like a sort of panel. – Notice the particularly beautiful
rings set in the walls, the torch-holders in the shape of
animals, and the corner lanterns made by the goldsmith
Caparra (from models by Benedetto da Maiano) in the
form of small hexagonal temples with little columns. – The
majestic **courtyard** was designed by Cronaca, who was also
responsible for the cornice on the west and south sides.

Palazzo Strozzino (Piazza Strozzi 6)
This palace belonged to the younger branch of the family, the Palla
Strozzi branch. It was begun some time after 1457 with the participa-
tion of Giuliano da Maiano.

Palazzo Tornabuoni (Via Tornabuoni 16)
The present 'Banca Commerciale', built in 1875, occupies the site of
an old palace which was built by Michelozzo. The stately courtyard has
been preserved; the capitals of its ten columns give a good impression
of Michelozzo's indigenous style.

Palazzi Torrigiani (Piazza de'Mozzi)
Two palaces with the same name stand here side by side (nos. 4 and 5).
The first dates from the seventeenth century; the second was designed
by Baccio d'Agnolo and his son Domenico.

Ponte alla Carraia
The first bridge (wooden, on stone pillars) was built between 1218

and 1220 by 'Lapo' – according to legend the father of Arnolfo di Cambio. The nearby monastery of Ognissanti provided the warden of the bridge. – A new building erected after 1269 is attributed to Fratres Sisto and Ristoro of S. Maria Novella who are thought to have been largely responsible for the development of the Gothic style in Tuscany. In 1304, as crowds of people gathered to watch a religious play directed by Bufalmacco, the bridge collapsed under their weight and dragged numerous victims with it. Heavily damaged, like all the other bridges in the city, in the flood of 1333, it was repaired soon afterwards. Not until 1559 was it properly restored, when Ammannati renewed the two northern arches without, however, changing their shape. In 1867, the bridge was enlarged. It suffered severe damage during the Second World War but has since been completely repaired.
In the sixteenth and seventeenth centuries, many water festivals and re-enactions of mythical naval battles were held on the section of the Arno lying between this bridge and the Ponte S. Trinita.

Ponte S. Trinita
This bridge was built in 1252 by the Frescobaldi family to meet the increased traffic requirements of the western part of the city. It first collapsed in 1269. It was re-erected, and then again destroyed in the terrible flood of 1333. It was not put up again until 1356; the architect on that occasion is said to have been Agnolo Gaddi. In 1566–9, it was rebuilt from scratch by Barto-lommeo Ammannati at the command of Cosimo I. Michelangelo is supposed to have furnished a drawing for it and to have re-commended that the large arches be constructed using the catenary curve. The bridge was almost completely destroyed during the Second World War, but with the cooperation of virtually the entire city, it was possible to reconstruct it from the old material, most of which lay at the bottom of the river, and Florence was able to preserve these marvellously cool and harmonious spans.

The four figures at the corners of the bridge representing the Seasons were executed by Francavilla; the head of *Primavera* (north-east corner) was not found until 1961 after a prolonged search of the river-bed.

Ponte Vecchio
The most famous and – because of the buildings on it – probably most exciting bridge in Florence traces its origins back at least to the Roman period. It formed part of the Via Cassia which at that time was the colony's main communications artery. Accord-ing to tradition there was even an Etruscan bridge here. Originally built of wood, the bridge had to be reconstructed many times completely. The first stone bridge was erected in 1080; this had to be rebuilt after collapsing in 1170 and then again after the

'Great Flood' of 1333, the worst flood Tuscany has ever seen. By 1345, the bridge had again become somewhat fragile and its restoration was taken in hand. Vasari mentions Agnolo Gaddi as having been architect-in-chief. – We know of the existence of shops on the bridge as early as the thirteenth century. At first these 'botteghe' were disposed completely symmetrically and belonged to the state, which derived quite a considerable income from them. They were not sold into private hands until 1495. During the period which followed, picturesque groups of little shops and even tinier stalls began to form, extending vertically as well as outwards on brackets over the water. In the sixteenth century, Vasari's passage from the Uffizi to the Palazzo Pitti was added on the eastern side of the bridge. – In 1593, for the benefit of foreigners, Grand Duke Ferdinando I decreed that only gold-smiths could settle on the old bridge, a decree which is still in force today. Here the visitor will find high-quality examples of what is probably the best known of Florentine crafts. A (modern) bust of Benvenuto Cellini appropriately occupies the open space above the central span. – The south-west wing of the old super-structure was only rediscovered in 1961 beneath a mass of later buildings; the southern end of it has now been exposed.

Porta Romana

Erected in 1326, this most powerful and best-preserved of the city gates of Florence stands proudly at the beginning of the road to Siena. In the arch inside is a *Madonna and Child, with four Saints* by Neri di Bicci, painted over by Franciabigio.

Villa Poggio Imperiale (Viale del Poggio Imperiale)

This enormous complex has seen many changes of ownership. It first came into the possession of the grand dukes in 1565, and then in 1620 under the patronage of Maria Maddalena, the widow of Cosimo II and a member of the house of Habsburg (hence the villa's present name). The building was considerably enlarged by Giulio Parigi, and sub-sequently became the favourite residence of the Medici princesses because of the freshness of the air up here on the hill. The rear façade was erected in the eighteenth century by G. M. Paoletti, the present front façade in the nineteenth century by G. Cacialli. – For the last hundred years and more, it has housed a distinguished boarding-school for girls and is consequently not open to visitors. Some of the rooms are decorated with interesting frescoes and other works of art (Italian and Dutch).

FIESOLE

One of the most pleasant excursions which the visitor can
make from Florence is the day-trip to the charming town of
Fiesole, which lies on the hill to the north of the city. On
the way there, shortly after leaving Florence, one should
stop and pay a quick visit to the church of

S. Domenico
Begun in 1406 and finished in 1435, the church was later enlarged.
The vestibule was added in 1632 by Matteo Nigetti, who also built
the campanile (1611–13).
The church lies directly beside the road. The delightful
interior was largely redecorated in the seventeenth century.
One of the most important works of art here is the first
altar-piece on the left. The figures were painted by Fra
Angelico, who occupied an important position in this
monastery for many years; the architectural background
was added later by Lorenzo di Credi (replacing the original
gold background). The latter also fitted the present frame
(by a pupil of Lorenzo Monaco) around this beautiful
painting. The predella is a rather clumsy copy of the
original one (now in the Louvre). – On the next altar is an
Adoration of the Magi by Antonio Sogliani (completed by
Santi di Tito). – The third altar has an *Annunciation* by
Jacopo da Empoli (1615) and a wooden crucifix attributed
to Andrea Ferrucci.
The visitor then reaches the **Oratory of S. Donatus**, erected
in 1792. The *wooden crucifix* dates from the late thirteenth
century. The **sacristy** (off to the right), built 1595–1606,
contains some beautiful wall cupboards and pews of *c.* 1500,
and Niccolò Guascone's remarkable metal bust of S. Donatus (gilded copper; 1546); in the adjacent small **reliquary
chapel** is a wooden cupboard of 1606.
The whole of the chancel section of the church was built in
1603–15 by Giovanni Caccini; the large *wooden tabernacle*
on the high altar is one of the finest pieces of its type
(Andrea Balatri, 1613). – Of the altars on the right-hand
side of the nave, mention need only be made of the second
one, with Lorenzo di Credi's Verrocchio-like *Baptism of
Christ*, and the first with a *Crucifixion* group by the school
of Botticelli.

Leaving the main road and taking the side road that
branches off to the left, the visitor will come after a few
minutes' walk to the

Badia Fiesolana

*Until 1028, this was the cathedral of Fiesole (consecrated to
S. Peter); it was then given to the Benedictines who renovated
the building and rededicated it to S. Bartholomew. In 1442, the
church passed into the possession of the canons of S. Frediano in
Lucca; beginning in 1459, it was thoroughly renovated in the
style of the Renaissance. At the same time the adjacent monastery
was also enlarged, particularly by the addition of a cloister.*

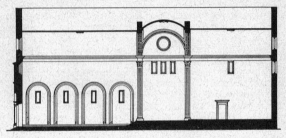

Badia Fiesolana, longitudinal section

Standing before the **façade**, the visitor will see the old
Romanesque façade (thirteenth century) framed by the
mass of unclad masonry. With its white and green marble
decoration, three beautiful arches and narrow windows, it
provides a good illustration of the Tuscan style of incrustation. – To see the **interior** of the church, the visitor
must first obtain permission from the curator. This powerful, magnificently soaring architecture was for a long time
(following Vasari) associated with Brunelleschi. More recent theories, including a suggestion that Alberti was
among the architects responsible, have as yet to be sub-
stantiated. The single-aisled ground plan is in the shape of
a Latin cross. – Built into the wall of the second chapel on
the left is a white marble altar-piece by a certain Magister
Constantinus (1273). – The portals in the transept are
attributed to Francesco di Simone Ferrucci; the high altar,
designed by Pietro Tacca, dates from c. 1600 (some notable

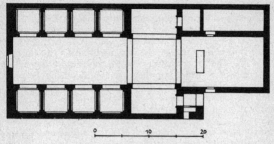

Badia Fiesolana, ground plan

'pietra dura' work).

Back on the main road, which winds in generous curves up the hill to Fiesole, the visitor will see on either side a number of beautiful **villas** including that of Arnold Böcklin. – Entering the little town, we come to the large **Piazza Mino da Fiesole**, named after the sculptor. This was the site of the forum in Classical times. The large building on the west side of the piazza is the **Seminary** (seventeenth century); beside it, with a Baroque façade, is the **Bishop's Palace** (going back to the eleventh century). The greater part of the north side of the piazza is taken up by the

Cathedral

The cathedral is consecrated to S. Romulus. It was begun in 1028, enlarged in 1256 and again in 1348. The simple Romanesque building was thoroughly renovated in 1878–83. The campanile was built in 1213.

The **interior** of this three-aisled basilica is characterized by Classical column shafts, rather unhomogeneous capitals and irregular arches. Above the central portal stands Giovanni della Robbia's terracotta statue of S. Romulus (a bishop of Fiesole) in its garlanded niche (1521). – Against the second pillar on the right is a fifteenth-century pulpit. – The frescoes in the *Salutati chapel* (on the right in the presbytery) were painted by Cosimo Rosselli; on the ceiling are the Evangelists, with SS. Leonard and John the Baptist beside the windows. Two works by Mino da Fiesole adorn the walls: on the right is the *tomb of Bishop Leonardo Salutati*

(1464) and on the left the *altar-piece* in which we see the
Madonna and Child, John the Baptist and SS. Leonard and
Remigio together with a cripple who is begging for alms.
Above is a noteworthy *head of Christ.* – On the high altar
is a triptych devoted to the Virgin by Bicci di Lorenzo
(*c.* 1450). The large frescoes in the round apse depict ten
stories about S. Romulus; they are by Nicodemo Ferrucci.
Under the powerful arch supporting the campanile is the
tomb of bishops Roberto and Guglielmo Folchi (sixteenth
century). – On the left of the chancel the visitor will find a
series of tall dark rooms containing numerous paintings
(mostly from the later sixteenth century) which are in rather
poor condition and difficult to decipher. In the chapel,
there is a beautiful altar by Andrea Ferrucci (1493) with the
figures of SS. Romulus and Matthew. The sacristy has a
fifteenth-century wooden crucifix and a painting of
S. Peter by Passignano. The precious gilded copper *reliquary
bust* of S. Romulus (1584) is also kept here. – The **crypt** is
frescoed inside and outside (fifteenth century); on the right
is a granite baptismal font by Francesco del Tadda (1569).
The beautiful cast-iron *screen* is a Sienese work of 1349.
In the left side aisle is a wooden throne, known as the
Cattedra of S. Andrea Corsini, which possibly formed part
of the inlaid choir stalls built by the Sienese artist, Pietro
Lando (1371). Near the façade wall is a medallion with a
portrait of Francesco Ferrucci, the man who introduced into
Tuscany new methods for the working of hard stones.

The not particularly beautiful **equestrian statue** on the east
side of the piazza commemorates the meeting between
Garibaldi and King Victor Emmanuel II on the Teano
bridge (made in 1906 by Oreste Calzolari). Beyond it and
slightly higher up to the left is the charming **Town Hall**
with its portico, loggia and numerous coats of arms of the
Podestà. Built in the fourteenth century, it was altered in
the fifteenth and enlarged in the sixteenth century. Further
to the right is the pretty church of

S. Maria Primerana
This little oratory, which has its roots far back in history,
was renovated during the Renaissance and has now been
thoroughly restored. In the side walls of the single aisled
interior, one can still see traces of the original columns. On

the right-hand wall before the sanctuary is a self-portrait of
Francesco da Sangallo (1542); continuing eastwards, the
visitor will find some fresco remains in the style of Giotto
and a beautiful fourteenth century marble tabernacle. On
the altar on the left is a particularly noble blue-and-white
terracotta *Crucifixion, with Mary, Saints and Angels* by the
della Robbia workshop. A most noble work of art and one
which the visitor should not miss is the *processional cross*
by Girolamo Spigliati (1560) in the sacristy; the Tuscan
goldsmiths of the later sixteenth century probably produced
few other pieces to match it in beauty.

From the west side of this broad piazza, a path climbs
steeply up the hill. In ancient times Etruscan buildings
stood here; the site was then adopted for votive purposes
by the Romans and it was finally occupied by the
Christians. The visitor comes to a projecting piazza which
offers a remarkable view of the Florentine valley, before
turning right and continuing to the top of the hill (the
nearby basilica of **S. Alessandro** is closed at the time of
writing). Here, on a site which was occupied first by the
Etruscan Acropolis, then by a Roman fortress and lastly
during the Middle Ages by some heavy fortifications
(destroyed by the Florentines in 1125), stands the small
but very impressive **Franciscan monastery**. The church (on
the left) was built in 1330 and is consecrated to

S. Francesco
*The brothers arrived in 1407. They enlarged the existing building,
which was rather modest, and at the same time erected a new
façade. The whole building was extensively renovated in 1905–7.
To the right of the church is a picturesque cloister (not open to
visitors).*
The dark **interior** consists of a single aisle. A monk will
show the visitor the church's art treasures. Immediately on
the right is an early fifteenth-century painting (*Marriage
of S. Catherine*), and on the next altar a *Crucifixion* by Neri
di Bicci. The particularly beautiful *Annunciation* on the
high altar is attributed to Raffaellino del Garbo, while the
terminal arch is thought to be the work of Benedetto da
Maiano. On the second altar on the left is a painting by
Perugino (1502), a *Madonna with SS. Sebastian and Michael*.
The picture of the Virgin on the wall nearby is by Piero di

Cosimo (1480). An *Adoration of the Magi* by an unknown master (c. 1450) adorns the following, first altar. – The **S. Anthony chapel** adjoining the sacristy contains a stucco *Crucifixion* in the style of Donatello.

Lying to the south is a small **monastery garden** where birds are kept in memory of S. Francis' sermon to the birds. From the passage on the north side, a staircase leads steeply down to a series of large rooms containing the extremely interesting **Franciscan Missionary Museum**, with a vast collection of commodities and works of art brought back by members of the Order from the Far East.

Returning to Fiesole itself, the visitor will find behind the Cathedral the small

Bandini Museum

This collection comprises some excellent works of art including Jacopo del Sellaio's panels depicting an allegorical triumphal procession. Each of the rooms has a separate guide which the visitor may consult.

Immediately opposite is the entrance to the

Roman Theatre

Excavations have revealed an instructive site here which gives us a comprehensive insight into the organization of a Roman 'thermae' complex (of which the theatre formed part). At the same time, the remains of an Etruscan temple with a long wall running from east to west were also discovered, which gives the site an even greater importance. For here on this beautiful spot, with a distant view over the hills into the Mugnone valley, the visitor can admire an ancient votive complex in its entirety. The finds from the excavations are exhibited in the nearby museum. – The theatre dates from the first century B.C.; it was embellished under Claudius and again under Septimus Severus. Circular in form, with concentric tiers descending towards the stage building, it was able to seat three thousand spectators. In front of the stage building is a three-tiered structure where the guests of honour sat on marble chairs. The stage itself stood 1.35 m above ground level and measured over 26 m long by c. 6.50 m deep. The visitor will find the entrances and the rear-view of the stage building particularly interesting. – The theatre was discovered as early as 1809, but proper excavations did not begin until 1873. – A little way beyond on the right are the

Thermae

This part of the site was uncovered in 1891–2. The buildings date from the end of the Republican period and were enlarged under Hadrian. – The various sections of the thermae are no longer easily identifiable. Lying exactly on the line of the east wall of the theatre is a rectangular swimming bath. On the right and slightly higher are two smaller basins; these are adjoined to the north by a small loggia, the foundations of which are Etruscan. Due east from here was the entrance to the thermae. The building adjoining to the south has more subdivisions; it housed the heating room, from which lead pipes took the warmed water to the various baths. The rooms were heated by means of warm air passing through shafts in the walls and under the floors; traces of these shafts can still be seen. The small bay in the wall of the room to the south-west constituted a kind of sauna where one could take a cold bath after spending some time in the hot air. – Following the ancient path due west, the visitor comes to a sanctuary with two altars before a raised platform on which stands an Etrusco-Roman

Temple

The first traces of the temple were discovered in 1792. The site was opened up in successive excavations of *c.* 1900, 1910–12 and after 1918. It is a fascinating example of the Romans' capacity for cultural adaptation, showing how they took over an Etruscan temple and turned it into a votive building of their own (first century B. C.). Findings have revealed that the Romans also took over the Etruscan custom of decorating the pediment with terracotta figures. Immediately to the north is the beginning of the Etruscan wall which runs east-west in a straight line. It consists of enormous blocks of stone piled on top of one another without mortar. – Near the entrance to the site is the

Museum

Erected in 1912–14 in the Neo-Classical style, this contains a large quantity of objects discovered during the excavations, including burial steles, portions of a bronze she-wolf (Roman), Etruscan mirrors, urns, statuettes and small artefacts. The rooms were laid out in 1958–9 and are extremely well lit and well arranged.

The parts of Fiesole lying to the east are also well worth seeing. The road passes through very beautiful countryside offering marvellous views of the surrounding landscape.

Appendix

Glossary

Abutment: See Buttress.

Acanthus: Kind of thistle with thick fleshy leaves re-
    produced in carved ornaments of Corinthian capitals
    and other mouldings; first used by the Greeks towards
    the end of the fifth century B. C.; used in a highly styliz-
    ed form by Romanesque architects and revived during
    the Renaissance and Baroque periods.

Acroteria: Plinths for statues or ornaments placed at the
    apex and ends of a pediment; also, more loosely, both
    the plinths and what stands on them.

Aedicule: (Lat. 'aedicula' = little house, little temple).
    The framing of a shrine, door, window, relief (e.g. on a
    burial monument) or other opening with two columns,
    entablature and pediment.

Ambo: A stand raised on two or more steps for the
    reading of the Epistle and Gospel. A feature in medieval
    Italian churches, the ambo was replaced from the thir-
    teenth century onwards by the lectern and the pulpit.

Antependium: A covering for the front of an altar,
    usually of metal or fabric.

Apse: A round-arched recess with a usually semicircular
    ground plan. Adapted from Roman secular architecture,
    it was usually placed at the east or chancel end of a
    basilica and contained the altar, the bishop's throne
    (cathedra) and the thrones of the presbyters. With the
    development of the chancel (through transept and chan-
    cel arm), the function of the apse changed in the early
    Middle Ages, although it remained an essential part of
    Romanesque church architecture. Not until the chancel
    termination was absorbed into the totality of the chancel
    structure during the Gothic period did the apse lose its
    significance. Though not necessarily semicircular in plan
    (polygonal apses were common in the twelfth and
    thirteenth centuries), it was nearly always so.

Arcade: Two or more arches with their supporting
    columns or pillars, taken together and considered as a
    single architectural feature.

Architrave: In Classical, Renaissance and Post-Renais-
    sance architecture, a horizontal stone member supported
    on columns, pillars or pilasters.

Archivolt: The continuous moulding on the face of an arch, following its contour.

Arcosol Tomb: A grave let into a wall and vaulted with an arch (from the 'arcosolium' or niche tomb of the Catacombs).

Aspersorium: Holy water basin.

Astragal: A small moulding, circular in section, often decorated with a bead and reel enrichment.

Atlantes: (From the Greek god Atlas who supported the heavens.) Supports in the form of carved male figures; a Classical feature revived during the Renaissance, though it was not as popular as the Herm. The female equivalents of Atlantes are Caryatids.

Atrium: Forecourt. The Latin word originally meant the main or hearth room; later it was used to refer to the entrance room of a Roman house which had a wide opening in the roof to let in the rain ('impluvium'). The parallel term 'Paradise' appears to derive from a second, eastern root, referring to the forecourt of a temple. In Early Christian and even Early Medieval architecture, the term refers to the forecourt of a basilican church.

Attic Storey: A storey above the main entablature of a building and in strict architectural relationship to it, as in Roman triumphal arches.

Baldacchino: Originally a canopy of costly silk or brocade which was carried over a throne. In architecture, a canopy supported on columns above a tomb or altar (see also 'Ciborium').

Baptistery: A church for baptism. Such churches were first used in the Early Christian period; always attached to an episcopal church, the baptistery was usually a centralized structure with a circular or octagonal ground plan.

Base or Socle: The lowest part or lowest main division of a pillar, column, building, etc.

Basilica: In Roman architecture, an oblong building with double colonnades inside and a semicircular apse or tribune at the end. In Early Christian and medieval architecture, an aisled church with a clerestory.

Bay: Unit of space between the supporting columns or piers of a church or other building; also a vertical unit of a façade.

Blind: Term used to refer to an arch, arcade, window, etc., applied decoratively to the surface of a blank wall.

Bozzetto: A model, usually of clay, for a piece of sculpture.

Buttress or Abutment: Mass of masonry or brickwork abutting a wall inside or outside a building to give additional strength.

Campanile: Bell-tower of a church, standing more or less completely separate from the rest of the building.

Canon: The order of columns established by the architects of the Renaissance and Baroque periods, based on the writings of the Classical architectural theorist Vitruvius (first century B.C.); it assigned the Doric or Tuscan orders to the ground-floor of a building, the Ionic to the middle storey and the Corinthian or Composite to the top storey. This 'canon' applied equally to the use of pilasters.

Capital: (From Lat. 'capitellum' = little head.) The topmost part of a column, pillar or pilaster effecting the transition from support to load. Greek architecture evolved various types of capital (see Orders). The Roman, Romanesque and Gothic periods introduced new forms, but Renaissance and post-Renaissance architects returned to the pure Classical forms.

Cartouche: An ornamental panel in the form of a scroll or sheet of paper with curling edges, usually bearing an inscription and often ornately framed.

Caryatid: see Atlantes.

Cattedra or Cathedra: Bishop's throne (see Apse).

Cenotaph: (From the Greek, literally 'empty tomb'.) A monument, usually in the form of a tomb, to a person buried elsewhere.

Centralized Structure: Building in which all the principal axes are of the same length.

Chancel: The (usually) eastern part of a church comprising the choir and sanctuary.

Chapter-house: The place of assembly for the members of a monastery for the discussion of business or for festivities not directly connected with the life of the Church. The chapter-house was usually a hall-like room situated in the east wing of the cloister.

Chiaroscuro: (Ital.). Light and shade in painting.

Choir: The part of the chancel of a church where divine
    service is sung.

Ciborium: A stone baldacchino supported on columns
    above an altar, much used in early medieval Italian
    churches.

Clausura: (From Lat. 'claudere' = shut in.) The part of
    a convent or monastery reserved to the members of the
    order and to which strangers were as a rule not ad-
    mitted.

Clerestory: That part of the nave of a church which rises
    above the height of the side aisles and contains windows.

Cloister: A quadrangle surrounded by roofed or vaulted
    passages connecting the monastic church with the domes-
    tic parts of the monastery; usually situated south of the
    nave and west of the transept.

Coffer: Sunken square or polygonal ornamental panel
    used to decorate a ceiling or vault.

Colonnade: A series of columns usually supporting a
    horizontal entablature, used either as an independent
    feature or as part of a building; colonnades were very
    popular during the Baroque and Neo-Classical periods.

Colossal Order: Any order whose columns rise from
    the ground through several storeys.

Column: Free-standing upright supporting member with
    circular section.

Composite Order: see Orders.

Corbel or Bracket: Small projecting piece of stone, often
    carved with scrolls or volutes, usually supporting an
    arch, gallery or cornice.

Corinthian: see Orders.

Crossing: The open square formed where a transept
    crosses the nave and chancel.

Crypt: An underground chamber usually below the east
    end of a church; in early medieval times, the crypt was
    used for the burial of martyrs and saints and the worship
    of relics and was sometimes of considerable size. The
    crypt was abolished as an architectural feature by the
    reforming orders of the eleventh and twelfth centuries.

Cupola: A dome, especially a small dome on a circular
    or polygonal base crowning a roof or turret.

Cyma: A double-curved moulding, concave above and
    convex below, or vice versa.

Dentil: A small square block used in series in Ionic, Corinthian, Composite, and more rarely Doric cornices.

Dome: A vault of even curvature erected on a circular or polygonal base. If the original base is square, the transition to a circular base is effected by means of pendentives. A dome is sometimes raised on a cylindrical drum. Very often a circular or polygonal opening at the crown of the dome draws the up into a decorative lantern.

Domical Vault: Kind of dome rising direct on a square or polygonal base, the curved surfaces being separated by groins.

Doric: See Orders.

Dossale: (Ital.). Reredos or altar frontal.

Dosseret: An additional block (impost-block) placed above a capital before the springing of an arch; in Renaissance architecture it often takes the form of a fragment of an entablature.

Drum: A cylindrical structure usually based on pendentives and supporting a dome. The drum often contains windows.

Egg and Dart: Moulding with a pattern based on alternate eggs and arrow-heads, sometimes terminated at top and bottom by a row of pearls; used in the Ionic and Corinthian orders and taken up again in classically-influenced Romanesque and Renaissance architecture.

Engaged Column: Column applied to the surface of a wall or pillar.

Entablature: The upper part of an order, consisting of architrave, frieze and cornice.

Façade: The 'face' on the entrance or display side of a building, usually reflecting the section of the interior but sometimes completely ignoring it. More than one façade is possible on a building (i.e. side or rear façades) but usually one is treated as the main façade.

Fibula: Brooch or clasp.

Fluting: Shallow, concave grooves running vertically on the shaft of a column, pilaster or other surface.

Foil: A lobe or leaf-shaped space within an arch or panel. The number of foils involved is indicated by a prefix, e.g. trefoil, octofoil, etc.

Fresco: From the Italian 'al fresco', i.e. painting applied to fresh plaster. Natural pigments were used which fused with the lime in the plaster during drying, giving them great durability. The opposite, 'al secco', refers to the process of painting on a dry surface, with less durable results.

Gallery: In church architecture, an upper storey over an aisle, opening on to the nave.

Grisaille: Painting in different shades of the same colour (i.e. grey on grey); used in all techniques.

Grotesque: (Ital. 'grottesco'). Ornament of slender foliage into which fantastic human and animal figures, flowers, fruit, trophies and architectural elements are introduced. Grotesques were rediscovered towards the end of the fifteenth century in Classical Roman subterranean buildings and underwent an artistic revival.

Hall: The distinguishing feature of this form of interior is that it comprises two or three (and occasionally even four or five) aisles sharing the same roof. Subsidiary and not essential characteristics are the absence of a transept and the linking of chancel and nave by the continuation of the side aisle around the chancel end. The prototype of the hall-church was the hall-crypt, introduced in the tenth century.

Herm: A pedestal or pilaster tapering towards the base and usually supporting a bust, derived from the Greek god Hermes; herms were used decoratively or as supporting members in Renaissance and post-Renaissance architecture.

Incrustation: The facing of wall surfaces with slabs of marble (sometimes of different colours) or stucco ornaments.

Intarsia: Inlaid work in wood, stone, stucco (see Scagliola) and other materials. Pieces of different colours and (as opposed to mosaic) different sizes are placed together to form a picture or ornamental panel. The technique was perfected during the sixteenth and seventeenth centuries.

Intrados: The inner curve or underside of an arch.

Ionic: See Orders.

Lantern: A small circular or polygonal turret with windows all round, usually crowning a dome.

Lavabo: Basin used by the celebrant at mass for the ritual washing of hands.

Loggia: A passage or hall, usually vaulted, open on one
    or more sides and supported on pillars or columns.

Lunette: A semicircular opening above a door or window
    (see also Tympanum), very often filled with a painted
    or relief decoration. The term can also be applied to any
    flat semicircular surface.

Macigno: Kind of hard grey limestone.

Mannerism: Denotes the style current in Italy from
    Michelangelo to the end of the sixteenth century. It is
    characterized by the use of motifs in deliberate opposi-
    tion to their original significance or context.

Mezzanine: (From Ital. 'mezzo' = half.) A half-storey,
    lower than the normal storey height, recognizable on the
    exterior by its smaller windows. The mezzanine was a
    popular means of articulation in the secular architecture
    of the Renaissance and Baroque periods.

Niello: Black metallic composition for filling in engraved
    designs on silver or other metals.

Nuns' Gallery: An upper storey, usually resting on vaults
    and originally at the west end of convent churches, pro-
    viding a separate place for the nuns to worship in,
    where they could not be seen by other visitors to the
    church. Consequently the nuns' gallery had its own altar,
    choir stalls and devotional pictures.

Obelisk: A tall rectangular tapering stone pillar with a
    pyramidal tip. Much used in Ancient Egypt as a votive
    symbol, the obelisk was popular with the architects and
    craftsmen of the Renaissance as a decorative motif.

Orders: In Classical architecture, a column, pillar or
    pilaster with base, shaft, capital and entablature, de-
    corated and proportioned according to one of the
    accepted modes. The earliest was the 'Doric' order, con-
    sisting of a fluted shaft, a cushion-shaped echinus, a
    square abacus and an entablature decorated with alter-
    nating triglyphs and metopes. The 'Ionic' order was
    distinguished by capitals in the form of two volutes and
    an entablature decorated with a continuous band of relief.
    The 'Corinthian' order featured capitals formed of
    stylized acanthus leaves. The 'Tuscan' order had un-
    fluted shafts and very simple capitals. In the 'Compo-
    site' order the capitals consisted of a combination of
    Ionic volutes and Corinthian acanthus-leaf decoration.

The Doric, Tuscan, Ionic and Corinthian orders were described by Vitruvius, and in 1540 Serlio published a book on the orders which established the minutiae of the proportions and decorations for Renaissance and later architects.

Pavilion: Originally a large rectangular tent; also used to refer to a small, freestanding garden building or projecting subdivision of a larger building, usually decorative and lightly constructed.

Pax, Paces: Tablet bearing a representation of the Crucifixion, kissed by the officiating priests and congregation at Mass.

Pendentive: A spherical triangle employed to effect the transition from the angle between two walls to the base of a circular dome.

Piano Nobile: (Ital.). The main floor of a house or palace, containing the reception rooms. It is usually higher than the other floors, with a basement or ground-floor below and one or more shallower storeys above.

Pietà: Picture or sculpture depicting the Virgin Mary holding the dead body of Christ on her lap.

Pietra Dura: (Ital. = hard stone.) Also known as 'Florentine Mosaic'; a kind of mosaic technique related to incrustation which was used principally for the decoration of table tops and architectural members but also on vases, jewellery, etc. Polished stones of different colours were set contiguously to form a large variety of patterns. The technique was developed to a high point of perfection from the sixteenth century onwards, particularly in Florence.

Pilaster: An engaged pillar projecting from the wall.

Pillar: Freestanding upright supporting member with a square or polygonal section.

Portal: A usually large and splendidly decorated doorway much used in the Romanesque and Gothic church architecture of Western Europe.

Portico: A structure supported on columns or pillars placed against the principal entrance side of a building; much used in post-Renaissance architecture, with the application of an order of columns.

Predella: Painting or sculpture on raised shelf at back of altar or on vertical face of altar-step.

Presbytery: The part of the church which lies east of the choir and where the high altar is placed.

Proto-Renaissance: Term invented by Jacob Burckhardt to cover those areas of the European art of the twelfth century (particularly in Tuscany, but also in Provence) that were strongly influenced by Classical forms.

Putto: (Ital. = child.) Droll, chubby, naked figure of Classical origin much used in the painting and sculpture of sixteenth century Italy.

Refectory: The dining-room of a convent or monastery, usually situated in the south wing of the cloister.

Reliquary: Container for a relic or relics of a saint or for objects sanctified by the memory of a saint, venerated by the faithful and exhibited upon the altar. The form of the reliquary was often determined by the type and shape of the relic it contained. Apart from caskets, boxes and medallions, figurative vessels such as statuettes, busts and vessels in the form of an arm, foot or finger were also used. Occasionally a reliquary assumed an architectural form, the most common of which was the shrine in the shape of a house or basilica which covered a tomb containing relics.

Reredos: See 'Dossale'.

Rib Vault: Vault with a framework of diagonal arched members supporting the segments between them.

Rustication: Masonry cut in massive blocks separated from each other by deep joints, employed to give a rich and bold texture to an exterior wall. The various types include 'cyclopean', with very large rough-hewn blocks straight from the quarry (or artfully carved to look as if they were), 'diamond-pointed', with each stone cut in the form of a low pyramid, and 'smooth', with the blocks neatly finished to present a flat face and chamfered edges to emphasize the joints.

Scagliola: Kind of coloured, polished ornamental stucco work.

Segment: Part of a circle smaller than a semicircle. Also a subdivision of a vault (e.g. as defined by ribs).

Sfumato: (Ital. = smoked.) With indistinct outlines.

Sgraffito: A kind of plaster technique developed by the Renaissance artists of northern Italy. A dark-coloured layer of plaster (usually red, grey or black) was covered with a light-coloured distemper. Before this dried, drawings were scratched in it so that the dark background reappeared.

Spandrel: Space between the shoulder of an arch and the surrounding rectangular moulding or framework, or between the shoulders of adjacent arches.

Springer: The plain or profiled stone at the point at which the curve of an arch or vault leaves the upright support.

Stele: Upright slab or pillar, usually with inscription and sculpture, especially as a gravestone.

Stucco: Mixture of plaster, lime, sand and straw forming a soft mass which sets quickly and consequently has to be worked at great speed. Already known in the Classical period, it was not used to any great extent architecturally until the sixteenth century. For the next two hundred years, it was used to decorate columns, pillars and flat surfaces, sometimes including whole walls.

Tabernacle: 1. An ornamented recess or receptacle to contain the Holy Sacrament. After the Council of Trent, which ended in 1563, the tabernacle became the centrepiece of the high altar, replacing the medieval sacrament cupboard. 2. An ornamental structure (e.g. containing a statue) often supported on columns or pillars.

Terracotta: Fired, unglazed clay; used in the sixteenth and early seventeenth centuries for architectural ornamentation instead of stucco, and as a material for sculpture since the late Middle Ages.

Tondo: Painting, fresco, mosaic or relief in circular form.

Tracery: The ornamental intersecting work in the upper part of a window, screen or panel, or used decoratively in blind arches and vaults.

Transept: The transverse arm (or arms) of a cross-shaped church, usually occurring between nave and chancel; used in church architecture since Early Christian times.

Transom: A horizontal bar of stone or wood across the opening of a window or across a panel.

Transverse Arch: Arch separating one bay vault from the next.

Tribune: 1. The apse of a basilica or basilican church. 2. A raised platform or rostrum.

Tunnel Vault: The simplest form of vault, consisting of

a continuous structure with a semicircular or pointed section.

Tympanum: Usually semicircular arch panel above a door or window.

Veduta: (Ital.). Painted or drawn panorama of a town or landscape, depicted with great accuracy and objectivity.

Volute: Spiral scroll used as a decorative motif in architecture and furniture, originating in the Ionic capital of Greek architecture.

Illustrations

(Numbers Refer to Pages)

INDEX OF ARTISTS

INDEX OF BUILDINGS

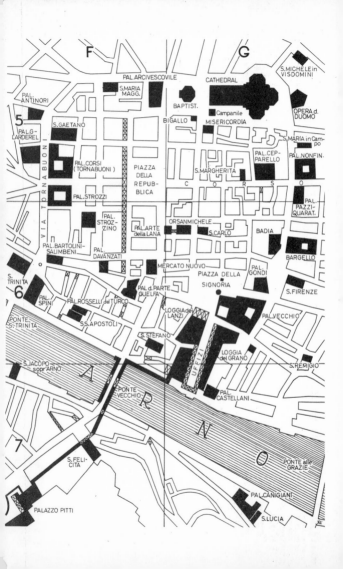

F
G

S.MICHELE in VISDOMINI

PAL.ARCIVESCOVILE
CATHEDRAL

S.MARIA MAGG.

PAL. ANTINORI

BAPTIST.
Campanile

OPERA d. DUOMO

5

BIGALLO
MISERICORDIA

PAL.G-LARDEREL

S.GAETANO

S.MARIA in Campo

PAL.CEP-PARELLO
PAL.NONFIN.

PAL.CORSI (TORNABUONI)

PIAZZA DELLA REPUB-BLICA

S.MARGHERITA

C O R S O

PAL. PAZZI-QUARAT.

PAL.STROZZI

ORSANMICHELE

PAL.ARTE della LANA
S.CARLO
BADIA

PAL.STROZZINO

PAL.BARTOLINI-SALIMBENI

BARGELLO

PAL.DAVANZATI

MERCATO NUOVO

PIAZZA DELLA SIGNORIA

PAL.GONDI

S.TRINITA

PAL d.PARTE GUELFA

PAL.SPINI
PAL.ROSSELLI del TURCO

S.FIRENZE

6

LOGGIA dei LANZI

PONTE S.TRINITA

SS.APOSTOLI

S.STEFANO

PAL.VECCHIO

S.JACOPO sopr'ARNO

U F F I Z I

LOGGIA del GRANO

S.REMIGIO

PONTE VECCHIO

A R N O

PAL.CASTELLANI

7

S.FELICITA

PONTE alle GRAZIE

PALAZZO PITTI

PAL.CANIGIANI

S.LUCIA